KT-457-989

Organization Theory

Modern, Symbolic, and Postmodern Perspectives

THIRD EDITION

Mary Jo Hatch with
Ann L. Cunliffe

OXFORD
UNIVERSITY PRESS

OXFORD
UNIVERSITY PRESS

Great Clarendon Street, Oxford OX2 6DP,
United Kingdom

Oxford University Press is a department of the University of Oxford.
It furthers the University's objective of excellence in research, scholarship,
and education by publishing worldwide. Oxford is a registered trade mark of
Oxford University Press in the UK and in certain other countries

© Mary Jo Hatch 2013

The moral rights of the authors have been asserted

First Edition published 1997
Second Edition published 2006

Impression: 1

All rights reserved. No part of this publication may be reproduced, stored in
a retrieval system, or transmitted, in any form or by any means, without the
prior permission in writing of Oxford University Press, or as expressly permitted
by law, by licence or under terms agreed with the appropriate reprographics
rights organization. Enquiries concerning reproduction outside the scope of the
above should be sent to the Rights Department, Oxford University Press, at the
address above

You must not circulate this work in any other form
and you must impose this same condition on any acquirer

British Library Cataloguing in Publication Data

Data available

ISBN 978-0-19-964037-9

Printed in Great Britain by
Ashford Colour Press Ltd, Gosport, Hampshire

Links to third party websites are provided by Oxford in good faith and
for information only. Oxford disclaims any responsibillty for the materials
contained in any third party website referenced in this work.

SHEFFIELD HALLAM UNIVERSITY
WL
302.35
HA
ADSETTS LEARNING CENTRE

SHEFFIELD HALLAM UNIVERSITY
LEARNING & IT SERVICES
ADSETTS CENTRE CITY CAMPUS
SHEFFIELD S1 1WB

102 087 811 8

SHEFFIELD HALLAM UNIVERSITY
LEARNING CENTRE
WITHDRAWN FROM STOCK

Organization Theory

This book is due for return on or before the last date shown below.

With love, this book is dedicated to my daughter,
Jennifer Cron

About the authors

Mary Jo Hatch is the C. Coleman McGehee Eminent Scholars Research Professor of Banking and Commerce, Emerita, at the McIntire School of Commerce, University of Virginia. She is also an Adjunct Professor at the Copenhagen Business School in Denmark, Visiting Professor at the Gothenburg University School of Business, Economics and Law in Sweden, and an International Research Fellow of the Centre for Corporate Reputation, Oxford University in the UK. An American organization theorist, Hatch has taught management and organization theory, and published research on organizations and organizing, in both the United States and Europe over the past twenty years. Her formal education took place at the University of Colorado, where she studied architecture as an undergraduate; Indiana University, where she studied English literature and creative writing and later earned an MBA in finance; and Stanford University, where she earned her PhD in organizational behavior with an emphasis on organization theory. In addition to her position at the University of Virginia, Hatch held teaching posts at San Diego State University and UCLA in California, the Copenhagen School of Business in Denmark, and Cranfield School of Management in the UK. She is an active participant in the American Academy of Management, where she is a past officer of the Organization and Management Theory Division. You will find her published articles in *Administrative Science Quarterly*, *California Management Review*, *Harvard Business Review*, *Academy of Management Review*, *Ephemera*, *European Journal of Marketing*, *Human Relations*, *International Journal of Cross Cultural Management*, *Journal of Brand Management*, *Journal of Business Ethics*, *Journal of Management Education*, *Journal of Management Inquiry*, *Journal of Psychological Issues in Organizational Culture*, *Marketing Theory*, *Organization*, *Organizational Dynamics*, *Organization Science*, *Organization Studies*, and *Strategic Organization*. Other books by Hatch include: *Organizations: A Very Short Introduction* (2011, Oxford University Press); *Taking Brand Initiative: How Corporations Can Align Strategy, Culture and Identity through Corporate Branding* (with Majken Schultz, 2008, Jossey-Bass); *The Three Faces of Leadership: Manager, Artist, Priest* (with Monika Kostera and Andrzej Kózmiński, 2005, Blackwell); *The Expressive Organization: Linking Identity, Reputation and the Corporate Brand* (with Majken Schultz and Mogens Holten Larsen, 2000, Oxford University Press); and *Organizational Identity: A Reader* (with Majken Schultz, 2004, Oxford University Press). She is the former European Editor of *Journal of Management Inquiry* and holds or has held editorial board positions at *Academy of Management Review*, *Human Relations*, *Organization Studies*, *Organizational Aesthetics*, *Scandinavian Journal of Management*, *Journal of Management Inquiry*, *International Journal of Cross-Cultural Research*, *Corporate Reputation Review*, *Management Learning*, and *Journal of Brand Management*. In 2011 she received the Distinguished Educator Award from the Academy of Management's Organization and Management Theory (OMT) Division.

Ann L. Cunliffe is currently Professor of Organization Studies at the University of Leeds in the UK. She has held positions at the University of New Mexico, California State University, and the University of New Hampshire. She obtained her Master of Philosophy degree and

PhD from Lancaster University Management School. Recent publications in the field of leadership, sensemaking, reflexivity, and qualitative research methods are found in *Human Relations, Organizational Research Methods,* and *Management Learning.* She was awarded the 2002 Breaking the Frame Award from the *Journal of Management Inquiry* for the article that best exemplifies a challenge to existing thought. Ann is currently co-Editor-in-Chief of *Management Learning,* Consulting Editor for the *International Journal of Qualitative Research in Organizations and Management,* and a member of eight international journal editorial boards. She also organizes the biennial conference *Qualitative Research in Organization and Management.*

Preface to first edition

Any narrative depends upon the perspective and location of its author. My perspective is as an American organization theorist, trained and employed in business schools, who has taught management and organization theory, and published research on organizations, in both the US and Europe during the 1980s and 1990s. My formal education took place at the University of Colorado, where I studied architecture as an undergraduate; Indiana University, where I studied English literature and creative writing as an undergraduate, and later earned an MBA in finance; and Stanford University, where I earned my PhD in organizational behavior with an emphasis on organization theory. My learning then continued in the context of my teaching posts—at San Diego State University and UCLA in the US, the Copenhagen Business School in Denmark, and now at the Cranfield School of Management in England—as well as through memberships in professional associations, including the American Academy of Management, the British Academy of Management, the Standing Conference on Organizational Symbolism (SCOS), and the European Group for Organization Studies (EGOS).

These days I live in a rural English village, in a thatched cottage built in the late sixteenth century, with beautiful countryside views. I spend my time doing research, reading, writing, traveling to conferences, giving lectures and seminars at a wide variety of universities, and doing a little oil painting. My research interests involve: organizational culture; identity and image; symbolic understanding in and of organizations; managerial humor as an indicator of organizational paradox, ambiguity, and contradiction; and aesthetic (especially narrative and metaphoric) aspects of organizing. I consider myself to be a symbolic-interpretive researcher whose methodology shifts between interpretive ethnography and discourse analysis. It is upon all of these experiences that I draw in presenting organization theory. Unavoidable biases with regard to organization theory and its history are created by these particular experiences, and thus the book you are holding is influenced in ways that are difficult for me to specify. Other accounts of organization theory are available and will provide other versions of its story.

I came to write this book because, as a symbolic-interpretive researcher teaching organization theory, I was frustrated by the limited choices of textbooks for my classes. There seemed to be only two alternatives: either a modernist exposition on the content of organization theory with an expressly control-centered, rationalistic orientation; or a radical alternative that focused on criticizing the modernist approach and displayed little or no sympathy for the substantial contributions modernist organization theory has made. I wanted a book that paid due respect to the modernist perspective, but that went beyond mere recitation of the findings of modernist research to explore the contributions of ethnographic studies that often challenge modernist notions, and that would give voice not only to the criticisms raised against organization theory as a tool of managerialism, but also to alternatives emerging from interdisciplinary research in the social sciences. I found that if I wanted such a book, I was either going to have to wait for someone else to get around to it, or I was going to have to write it myself. Being impatient, I chose the latter course.

Impatience, however, does not write books. It has taken me ten years to accomplish the task I first imagined in the mid-1980s. The process through which it materialized has been a labor of enthusiasm for the field of organization theory, and of determination to find a way to present material that is commonly believed to be difficult, dry, and boring in the extreme. To translate my vague image into this book required that I delve into my own subjective experience, to draw out the reasons for my enthusiasm and to develop the means of communicating them to others. These tasks I undertook in the classroom, and it is my students who deserve the lion's share of credit for this product—it is they who have been my teachers.

Each chapter of the book was developed through an iterative and interactive process of presenting ideas to my classes, followed by discussions in which I listened and responded to what the students chose to focus on, which generally involved application of the ideas to some aspect of their personal, professional, or anticipated managerial lives. In this way, I was able to observe how students handled the material I presented to them, what they found most interesting in it, and what they thought they might use it for. Along the way I discovered that the best way to present material in anticipation of discussion was to reflect upon what I found interesting in the topic, to press myself to learn something new about it just before going into class (which caused me to be in an active learning mode), and to share through open reflection what I found inspiring and what I was even now learning about it. The students responded well to this approach and appreciated the effort I took, because, as they told me, the enthusiasm I demonstrated for the material was contagious.

As I developed my learning-based style of teaching, I found that the students mimicked me in our discussions. A few would begin to focus on what was pertinent or attractive to them, would have insight based on their own experience in combination with the new material, and their unsuppressed enthusiasm diffused to other students who became engaged with the material until eventually (toward the end of our term of study together), most in the room had had the experience of finding organization theory interesting and useful—at least once in their lives. The effect overall was that, as we spent time together in these endeavors, the students became more and more active in their own education, taking an increasing share of the responsibility for their learning onto their own shoulders. This, of course, was not universally true, as in any classroom there were the perennial plodders, but by and large I was pleased that by focusing on the interesting, by following our collective intuition in the exploration of organization theory, we together carved out what I believe is a fair representation of the knowledge organization theory offers. While it is true that I polished the product through many rounds of review with both students and colleagues (who are experts in the subjects the book develops), on the whole the book was produced in dialogue with my students, and its contents reflect what they have been willing to take on board and use in their efforts to become educated future managers. The book is, in a way, a description of what we did together in the classroom.

A key element in my teaching/learning style is to allow students to explore in the directions their own curiosity takes them. The influence I exercise is then directed at developing their natural curiosity into genuine interest and mature engagement with the subject matter. Getting this process started is half the battle, and I see this book as a collection of stimulations for discussions of various aspects of organizing that have proven of lasting interest to the wide variety of students with whom I have shared the learning experience. This material has been developed over my years of teaching undergraduates, post-graduates (MBA and

PhD), and executives. Because I have not simplified the complex understandings that organization theory offers, but rather have clarified the language in which these ideas were originally (and often subsequently) presented, I find that the material in this book is useful, attractive, and accessible to a wide range of audiences.

There is another aspect to this book that bears mentioning here. At about the time that I concluded my PhD training and took my first job as a faculty member, the push to internationalize business schools reached peak levels in the United States. At the time, I observed that attempts to internationalize the business school curriculum often consisted of simply using examples of companies headquartered or operating in foreign countries. As a culture researcher, I was suspicious of this approach to internationalization because I realized that examples will always be presented using concepts and perspectives that are rooted in the experiences of their author. Thus, if an author has only made brief (or no) visits to other cultures, then her or his analysis is unlikely to invoke anything like an international perspective. My opportunity to live and work in Denmark presented itself at just the moment these ideas were forming and provided me with an alternative. Moving to Denmark (I lived there three and a half years all told) afforded me the chance to internationalize myself, along with the content of my course. My experiences taught me that internationalization goes way beyond the examples and knowledge that you offer; it is about profound changes in the ways you understand that affect your approach to description, analysis, and explanation—in other words, how you theorize.

My internationalization took root at about the same time that I was writing up the first version of this textbook. This coincidence had several important effects on what I was to produce. First, since I was teaching Danes who were fluent in English, but were not native speakers, I found that I had to restrict my vocabulary. While Danish students could easily follow complex and abstract arguments, and were, from my experience as an American, remarkably and delightfully fond of such arguments, they appreciated my keeping the language simple when I explained complex ideas. I obliged them and became intrigued by the puzzle of retaining the complexity of ideas, while reducing the complexity of how the ideas were presented. As I was teaching and writing at the same time, the language I used with my students slipped naturally onto the pages of my textbook. This turned out to be a real blessing, as it improved the means to write a demanding book about a complex subject that is accessible to anyone with a reasonable proficiency in the English language, a proficiency that has become practically essential in the international world of business. When I returned to the US two years later and began using my manuscript as a text in my American MBA classes, I was startled at the strength of the positive response it received. In retrospect, I suppose it is not surprising that accessibility to complex ideas was appreciated by native as well as by non-native English speakers.

A second effect of my time in Denmark was the profound appreciation for multiple perspectives that it provided. I had already been introduced to the idea of multiple perspectives through my research training which involved struggling with debates over whether qualitative or quantitative methods provided a better means of addressing the problems of organizing— a debate that was raging at the time of my PhD training. After moving to Denmark, the idea of accepting multiple perspectives began to take on new meaning. First of all, I became aware of the differences between European academic traditions of social science that focused on ontology and epistemology, and American academic traditions that were far

more concerned with the issues of theory and method. At first I simply substituted my preferred set of terms (theory and method) for theirs (ontology and epistemology), but slowly I
began to discern the differences. Eventually I came to an understanding of just how much
slips between the cracks of translations of any sort, and on this foundation built my concern
to preserve differences even while acknowledging the importance of crossing between different views which highlights their similarities. Out of these experiences, my views about
organization theory as offering a fundamentally multiplicitous approach to understanding
began to take shape. It is this theme that, as my Scandinavian friends would say, provides 'the
red thread' that holds this book together.

The particular perspectives that I identify as crucial to grasping what organization theory
has to offer I label modernist, symbolic (or, to be more accurate, symbolic-interpretive), and
postmodern, after current fashion in the field today. At other times and in other places, these
perspectives have been labeled differently. The modernist perspective has also been known
as the rational perspective, the open systems view, the positivist school, and the quantitative
approach. The symbolic-interpretive perspective has been known as the qualitative approach
and is sometimes equated with the organizational culture school. The postmodern perspective has links to critical organization theory, the labor process school, and radical feminism
as well as to poststructuralist philosophy and literary theory. While these three perspectives
will be distinguished throughout the book, in the end it must be admitted that the contours
of these and other perspectives constantly shift and change so that there can be no final
categorizing of ideas.

Still, there is value in making, for the moment at least, distinctions between several perspectives. For one thing, this practice broadens intellectual horizons and stimulates the
imagination, both of which help to build knowledge and feed creativity. For another, learning
to appreciate and rely upon multiple perspectives increases tolerance for the views of others
and the capacity to make positive uses of the diversity multiple perspectives bring to organization and to life in general. It is my belief that, if we are ever to realize the value of theory
for practice, then we must master the use of multiple perspectives, for it is in bringing a variety of issues and ideas to the intellectual table that we will learn how to be both effective and
innovative in our organizational practices.

Please be aware that I am not attempting integration of the multiple perspectives of organization theory. Each perspective has contributed something of value to my understanding
of organizations and I want to relate that understanding to new students of the subject of
organization theory, whether they are undergraduates, postgraduates, or practicing managers. I have attempted to communicate my enthusiasm for these ideas and to bring them to
life for the reader. The structure I offer, such as it is, is provided by the chronology of the
ideas, which typically progresses from modernist, through symbolic-interpretive to postmodernist. I am not trying to privilege any particular viewpoint, I just want to let students
vicariously experience the ideas in the rough order of their influence on the field (which was
not always their order of appearance in the larger world).

Above all, I want students to feel free to play with ideas, but also to accept the discipline of
focused study. To learn through their own experience that the hard work of studying other
people's ideas can liberate their own thinking. The book is demanding—students who have
used the book say they feel they have to underline *everything* because it all seems important.
They report that they must (and do!) read the chapters multiple times. What is most

important, they start talking about these ideas in class, and by their reports, outside of it as well. The book seems to stimulate interest in organization theory, and that, I think, is its greatest strength.

I do not, however, suffer under the illusion that the book has no faults. I am sure it has plenty. Most of all, it is incomplete—a work in progress as any book on a dynamic field of study must be. I know also that it inspires contradictory opinions—postmodernists complain that it isn't postmodern enough and modernists have said that it goes too far. My view is that organization theory is an open field, filled with controversy and contradiction. I want this book to reflect the many aspects of the discipline and to grow along with the field. In this I rely upon your support and feedback; together we can make this a book that gets better rather than worse with each successive edition. But I get ahead of myself here. First let me thank those who have already provided volumes of feedback and who have shaped the book you have in your hand.

The most important group to thank for inspiring this project, and for providing feedback during its progress, are the many students whose company I have enjoyed in the classroom as well as in private discussions outside of class. The learning experiences we have shared are what made writing this book possible and enjoyable. I have had enormous help from colleagues and friends who, along the way to finishing this version, have offered their expertise as advisors on various chapters. They checked and corrected the content, offered suggestions about the flow and structure of the arguments, and without their sound criticism, guidance, and encouragement, I would not have had the confidence necessary to publish this material. I offer my deep gratitude to Ria Andersen, David Boje, Finn Borum, Frank Dobbin, Eigil Fivelsdahl, Joe Harder, Gerry Johnson, Kristian Kreiner, Livia Markoczy, Bert Overlaet, Susan Schneider, Ellen O'Connor, Jesper Strandgaard Pedersen, Mary Teagarden, Carol Venable, Dvora Yanow, and several anonymous reviewers. I am also indebted to Majken Schultz and Michael Owen Jones with whom I have worked closely in developing related classroom material and on numerous research projects.

In addition to those already mentioned I would like to single out two people whose extraordinary contributions have improved the quality of this book enormously: my husband Doug Conner and OUP editor David Musson. Both of these individuals read every chapter start to finish on multiple occasions and made many helpful suggestions as to both style and substance. Thanks also to Ann Davies of Cranfield University, and to Donald Strachan and Brendan Lambon of OUP for their efforts in bringing this project from manuscript to published work. San Diego State University, the Copenhagen Business School and Cranfield University each supported my work in this project during its various critical stages. The friendship, support, and inspiration of my close friends Kirsten and Jacob Branner helped to sustain me during the long hours that this project has filled. Last, but certainly not least, I would like to thank my daughter, Jennifer Cron, whose consternation at my confusion about her ways of viewing the world initially inspired me to open my mind to the myriad possibilities of exploring multiple interpretations.

M.J.H.
Cranfield
September 1996

Preface to second edition

Much has changed since I wrote the first edition of *Organization Theory: Modern, Symbolic, and Postmodern Perspectives*. The field has expanded considerably, for one, and to tackle its wider reach I happily relate that Ann Cunliffe proved indispensable in producing the second edition. Ann is originally from Manchester, England. She completed an MPhil and PhD at Lancaster University in the United Kingdom, and since 1987 has lived and worked in the United States. She now enjoys life in the high desert, where she teaches and does research at the University of New Mexico.

You can find me in the United States again as well. The University of Virginia became my home institution in 2000 when I was hired by the McIntire School of Commerce. The move meant that I gave up the thatched cottage in England for a cabin in the woods just outside Charlottesville, where I continue to enjoy my life of writing and painting. Apart, that is, from the regular visits of a peliated woodpecker, who seems determined to eat the entire outer layer of my house. Except for him, things are pretty peaceful and extraordinarily beautiful.

As for the second edition of *Organization Theory*, you will find several major changes, though there is also much you will recognize from the first edition. The most important continuity is the presentation of organization theory as a multi-disciplinary field woven from multiple perspectives. The perspectives, naturally, have been elaborated, extended, and challenged by an enormous and ever-growing body of research, and giving these developments their due has been the primary task undertaken by Ann and I in preparing this edition.

One example of a major change to the second edition is the incorporation of more critical theory, which has so deeply infiltrated the field over the last ten years that Ann and I added it in many places in the new edition. Although critical theory was hugely influential in the United Kingdom and some circles elsewhere in Europe even when the first edition was written, it only came into prominence for the rest of the field along with postmodernism sometime in the 1990s, and for a time the differences between these two perspectives were not well articulated. They have, however, become clearer with time so in this edition you will see distinctions being made that were previously ignored. What is perhaps the biggest change in regard to critical theory is the addition of a chapter on organizational power, politics, and conflict to Part II: The Core Concepts of Organization Theory. The placement of this chapter reflects the now established importance of critical theory to the field.

Of course adding power, politics, and conflict to the core concepts covered in Part II meant gutting Part III of the first edition. This made room for other important contributions that Ann and I have grouped into two chapters focused on applications of organization theorizing—one to practice and the other to recent developments. In the new Part III you will find Chapter 9 devoted to a question my students often ask: 'What has all this got to do with the real world?', while Chapter 10 addresses the question most often raised by those who are, or who are studying to become, organization theorists: 'Where do we go from here?'

Other important changes to the first edition have been made. Both symbolic-interpretive and postmodern perspectives receive much more attention in this edition of the book to reflect their growing influence on the field. More examples have been included throughout, along with additional suggestions for ways readers can develop concepts and their capacity to theorize. I have retained as much of the style of the first edition as was possible—no mean feat given the vocabulary of postmodernism!—and I hope that you will find the writing to be as accessible as it was in the first edition.

The new topics covered in the second edition are too numerous to list exhaustively, but include among others: extended discussions of symbolic and postmodern aspects of social structure and technology; the inclusion of narrative, storytelling, discursive and poststructuralist approaches to organizational analysis; and issues relating to gender, hegemony, disciplinary power, and reflexivity. Of course you will encounter many old friends as well. The biggest concession that was made was to leave out the chapter on strategy. The field of strategy has enjoyed almost as much growth over the last ten years as has organization theory and I found it impossible to keep up with both. The bits of strategic thinking that touch most directly on organization theory have, however, been retained, so you will find most of what was covered in the first edition absorbed into various discussions throughout the book.

Beyond her many contributions during revision, Ann has built a website to accompany the second edition. On the website you will find a host of goodies including cases and suggestions for ways to adapt them to the subject matter of the book, downloadable slides, web links to additional material, teaching ideas and resources, and exam questions (for instructors only!!!).

As always the list of people to thank is long. Our students have been our most important partners in the process of revising the book, and we have benefited from the insights of all the people whose works we will tell you about in the pages to follow. In addition, the support and insight provided by Phil Mirvis and my colleagues at the McIntire School is much appreciated. Ann wanted me to thank Mary Ellen Pratt and Michael Clifford for their generous help, which I gladly do. Several anonymous reviewers contributed greatly to refining various chapters, and thanks also to everyone at OUP who helped to get this edition out of our heads and into print!

Finally, to the many friends of the first edition, let me say that I hope you will be pleased by the second. Ann and I have worked hard to make it a useful and enjoyable study tool and we look forward to hearing your comments and suggestions for improving the third edition!

M.J.H.
Charlottesville, Virginia
July 2005

Preface to third edition

To begin, let me thank the many faithful fans of the approach to organization theory this book presents. Without their support and encouragement, along with that of my editor Francesca Griffin at Oxford University Press, the third edition would never have happened. I hope the latest iteration of *Organization Theory: Modern, Symbolic, and Postmodern Perspectives* will continue to serve these old friends while attracting new ones to this rich and useful field of study.

In the years since the second edition appeared, semi-retirement offered a way for me to take painting more seriously while giving me the freedom to visit old and new academic haunts. I have spent time since retiring from the University of Virginia in 2007 as a visiting professor at both Copenhagen Business School, where I am currently involved in a research project focused on Carlsberg Group, and at Gothenburg University's Business and Design Lab, an interdisciplinary partnership between the School of Business, Economics, and Law and the School of Craft and Design. The Università della Svizzera italiana (Swiss University of Lugano) and Singapore Management University offered me additional places to give lectures, teach courses, and work with faculty, while appointment as an International Research Fellow of the Centre for Corporate Reputation at Oxford University allows me to participate in conferences and interact with researchers with whom I share interests in corporate branding and reputation management. The students and faculties of these universities, as well as contact with their business partners, continues to help me better understand the value of organization theory to management practice even as it enriches my life as an itinerant and, I hope, increasingly artistic organization theorist.

A few years ago Oxford University Press invited me to write a volume for their series of Very Short Introductions. In preparing *Organizations: A Very Short Introduction* my thoughts on organization theory clarified, offering me new understanding and appreciation for what this field is becoming. It is this fresh eye that I bring to the third edition. While it is difficult to make this difference explicit, I hope you will find the new edition more readable and better integrated than its predecessors while remaining accessible and inviting to new readers.

The main change made to Part I involves introducing normative interests into the three perspectives framework. This reframing, made explicit in Chapter 1 and applied throughout Parts II and III, is intended to make the links between theory and practice more pronounced. Specifically the modern, symbolic, and postmodern perspectives of organization theory are presented as offering, respectively, explanation, understanding, and critical/aesthetic appreciation of organizations and organizing. Emphasizing the differences explanation, understanding, and appreciation bring to organization theories and their core concepts should help readers grasp what using multiple perspectives contributes to creating useful organizing practices. It is my hope that greater emphasis on the practical side of organization theory will encourage more readers to indulge in theorizing as a means to experience and explore organizations and organizing.

All chapters constituting Part II were refreshed with relevant material published since the second edition appeared, while several new topics are clustered in an updated Part III. In Part

III practice and process theories are linked to ongoing theoretical discussions of organizational design, change, learning, and identity. Two perspectives informing practice and process theorizing—pragmatism and hermeneutics—are introduced as candidates for addition to the modern, symbolic, postmodern perspectives framework. To anticipate other new directions in which organization theory appears to be moving, ideas about distributed phenomena, lines of flight, and hacktivism are discussed in relation to organizational culture, structure, and technology. In general Part III points to ways the field of organization theory has already moved beyond the three perspectives this book relies upon, and should eventually lead to replacement of this framework by another. Such self-deconstruction seems a plausible result of practicing organization theory as presented in these pages and hopefully serves to inspire if not model responsible theorizing.

It has been my ambition from the first edition to share not only the knowledge organization theory continues to produce, but also the excitement of formulating and applying this knowledge. If this edition comes closer to that ideal than did its predecessors it will have served its purpose, but if not, the fault lies with me. This edition is entirely my own doing. Ann's name appears on the cover because she contributed some of what carried over from the second edition; she should not be faulted for its inadequacies.

M.J.H.
Ipswich, Massachusetts
May 2012

New to this edition

This edition has been edited to tighten, refine, and make the presentations of ideas clearer and more compelling.

Chapter 2 has been expanded to include the role normative theory played in the historical evolution of the field. Part III is now built around the theme of 'Looking Back and Looking Forward' to round off the historical overview and anticipate its continuation.

Terminology has been reworked to bring it up to date and to clarify arguments.

The perspectives have been refocused to reveal the motivations of theorists who use them: explanation (modern), understanding (symbolic), and appreciation (postmodern). These motivations have been used throughout the book to explain the differences in approach that each brings to the topics covered.

New concepts and perspectives introduced in this edition include practice and process theories, pragmatism and hermeneutics, distributed phenomena, lines of flight, and hacktivism.

Brief contents

Detailed contents

List of figures

List of tables

Guide to the Online Resource Centre

www.oxfordtextbooks.co.uk/orc/hatch3e/

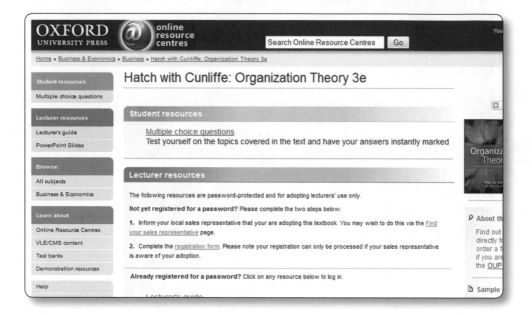

Free resources available to students:

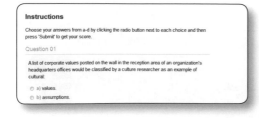

Multiple-choice questions

A selection of multiple-choice questions provides the chance for you to test yourself on various chapters of the textbook and receive immediate feedback.

Resources for registered adopters of the textbook include:

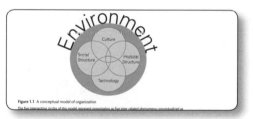

Lecturer's guide

A comprehensive lecturer's guide has been created for each chapter which includes chapter objectives, teaching notes, key points, discussion questions, and suggested class activities.

PowerPoint slides

These PowerPoint slides are completely customizable and can be adapted for use as handouts or incorporated into your lecture notes or slides.

Figures and tables from the book

These have been provided for use in your own presentations or handouts.

Case studies

New to this edition, case studies with teaching notes are offered to accompany chapters in the book where appropriate.

Part 1

What is Organization Theory?

theorist/ˈuɪərɪst/ *n.* a holder or inventor of a theory or theories.

theorize/ˈuɪərɪz/ *v. intr.* (also **-ise**) evolve or indulge in theories.

theory /ˈuɪərɪ/ *n.* (*pl.* **-ies**) **1** a supposition or system of ideas explaining something, esp. one based on general principles independent of the particular things to be explained (opp. HYPOTHESIS) (*atomic theory; theory of evolution*). **2** a speculative (esp. fanciful) view (*one of my pet theories*). **3** the sphere of abstract knowledge or speculative thought (*this is all very well in theory, but how will it work in practice?*). **4** the exposition of the principles of a science etc. (*the theory of music*). **5** *Math.* a collection of propositions to illustrate the principles of a subject (*probability theory; theory of equations*). [LL *theoria* f. Gk *theoria* f. *theoros* spectator f. *theoreo* look at]

Oxford Encyclopedic English Dictionary

Why study organization theory?

Before you answer 'Why indeed?' and walk away, consider this: people have discovered many different reasons to study organization theory and one or more of these might apply to you. Some people are motivated by curiosity. They wonder what it would be like to think like an organization, to get inside organizing processes, or to understand the patterns that structure organizations. Others are attracted by the opportunity to stretch their minds in new ways. Organization theory draws on the sciences, the humanities, and the arts, and so promises the intellectual challenge of interdisciplinary thinking stretched across the full array of human knowledge.

Need a more practical reason? Kurt Lewin, a founder of social psychology, once said, 'there is nothing so practical as a good theory.' Practical people find that embracing organization theory improves their chances of becoming successful executives in business, government, or non-profit organizations. To fire up your imagination for its practical benefits, Table 1.1 describes how organization theory applies to an array of different management specialties.

Let me be honest with you. There is another reason some people study organization theory: they are forced to do it. That was my story. My doctoral program required me to study this subject. To say that I did not appreciate organization theory when I first encountered it would be a gross understatement. It seemed abstract, dry and, well, far too theoretical! In a way, my initial reactions inspired this book. When I started teaching, my search for ways to bring this subject to life for my students taught me how interesting and useful organization theory can be. The contrast between my early feelings and my later experiences transformed me from a reluctant student of organization theory into an enthusiastic theorizer. From there it was a short step to writing this book.

If you are like me, it will take some time to build the body of concepts and skills required to appreciate organization theory and start to theorize. But, if you work hard and hang in there, I promise to introduce you to intriguing ideas and help you discover how to be creative in applying them to organizations and your own organizing and theorizing practices.

What is theory?

The *Oxford English Dictionary* defines 'theory' as 'the sphere of abstract knowledge.' Such a definition makes it all sound pretty intimidating. Therefore you might be surprised to learn that you already use theory, and probably use it every day. As an example, take any old adage

Table 1.1 Some practical applications of organization theory

Strategy/Finance	Those who want to increase the value of a company need to know how to organize to achieve strategic goals; those who want to monitor and control performance must understand how to structure activities and design organizational processes that make sense within the context of the organization's culture and allow for needed human growth and creativity.
Marketing	Marketers know that to create successful brands the organization must stand for and deliver the brand promise; a thorough understanding of what organization is and how organizations behave will make their efforts to align an organization with its brand strategy and identity more trustworthy and productive.
Information technology (IT)	The way information flows through the organization affects work processes and outcomes, so knowing organization theory can help IT specialists identify, understand, and serve the organization's informational needs as they design and promote the use of their information systems.
Operations	Value chain management requires that managers interconnect their organizing processes with those of suppliers, distributors, and customers; organization theory not only supports the technical aspects of supply chain and business systems integration, but explains their political, social, and cultural aspects as well.
Human resources (HR)	All HR activities from recruiting to compensation have organizational implications and hence benefit from knowledge provided by organization theory; organizational development and change are particularly important elements of HR that demand deep knowledge of organizations and organizing, and organization theory provides content for executive training programs.
Communication	To design communication systems, corporate communication specialists must be sensitive to the interpretive processes of employees and other stakeholders. Organization theory helps them understand how people interact with each other and the environment so that information and knowledge can be shared.

you learned as a child. 'You can lead a horse to water, but you can't make it drink' is an apt example drawn from many my mother taught me. A familiar saying like this one presents a theory about how the world works.

Through application a theory offers practical guidance. To apply the 'leading-a-horse-to-water' theory, consider yourself the horse, organization theory the water, and my job to lead you to it. This adage reminds me of your right to decide if and how you will 'drink.' Does it make you realize that much of the burden of learning organization theory and developing theorizing skill rests on your shoulders?

Whenever you start examining yourself or reality you form ideas about things, feelings, experiences, values, or expectations that can inspire you to theorize. Without effort and training, most people won't take their theorizing any further than repeating the common sense contained in old adages. But with training your everyday theorizing skills can be refined into extraordinary appreciation, understanding, and explanation of whatever interests you. The basic difference between everyday and advanced theorizing is the added care experts take to specify and reflect on their practice, correct its errors, and connect their theories to those of others, thereby contributing to the accumulated body of knowledge.

Defining theory, phenomena, concepts, and abstraction

Put most simply, a **theory** is a set of concepts whose proposed relationships offer explanation, understanding, or appreciation of a **phenomenon of interest**. Consider Albert Einstein's theory concerning how matter relates to energy. E (for energy) was Einstein's phenomenon of interest, which he explained using the concepts of mass (m) and the speed of light (c, for constant, because Einstein assumed that the speed of light does not vary). Squaring the product of m multiplied by c explains how the concepts of mass and light speed are related to energy, namely $E=mc^2$.

The formula $E=mc^2$ illustrates how a set of concepts and the relationships between them can produce a theory about the phenomenon of interest. It is not always this straightforward, however. When theorists confront social behavior or aim to enhance understanding or appreciation of organizations and organizing, then theory does not lend itself so easily to formulaic statements like $E=mc^2$. Nonetheless, this basic definition of what a theory is provides an entry point to discuss theory. The basic building blocks of theory are concepts, such as energy and mass.

Concepts provide mental categories into which you can sort, organize, and store ideas in memory. They are formed by **abstraction**, a process that involves mentally separating an idea about something from particular instances of it. Once the idea is distilled from its instances you can assign a label and talk about the concept in a general way. Take a concept most of us hold in common—'dog.' Your 'dog' concept, like mine, can be applied to all dogs and we use it when we talk about them, as we do now. But each of us built our concept upon personal encounters with particular animals, so our concepts may not be identical. Yours has been built on exemplars such as dogs you owned or met, or that bit you, but also with non-dogs like cats or goats. Concepts build upon both positive and negative instances and these are not identical for all the users of a concept, even though, through abstraction, we may have all arrived at the same set of features and similar understandings.

As you can see, although concepts are associated with specific examples, they are not an aggregation of all the information you acquire about them. They are more compact than this. As you form a concept you start ignoring what is unique about specific examples and focus on only what is common to all of them. Thus, the concept 'dog' is associated with four legs, a tail, a cold wet nose when it is healthy, and two ears, but not black spots, big paws, or a habit of barking or jumping on strangers, which are features of particular dogs, but not all dogs.

Removing the unique details of particular examples produces an abstraction. Through the abstraction process you distill the common aspects from a set of examples and give them a place in the knowledge structure of your memory. Such an effort produces a single abstract idea that can be related to all your examples but also to other examples of a similar kind you encounter in the future.

You may be wondering why you should drop the details out of your experience in order to build concepts. Shortening the time it takes to process information is one benefit. When you encounter a new example of a well-developed concept, you can instantly apply your prior knowledge to it. For example, recognizing that an animal is a dog will make you instantly aware of the possibility that it will growl and then bite if it feels threatened. In addition to speeding up your information processing, abstract conceptualization also makes it possible for you to communicate your knowledge. Your knowledge about dogs will not only prevent you offering your hand to a growling dog, you can also teach your children what a dog is and then pass on your knowledge.

Chunking and generalizability

In addition to rapid processing and communication of knowledge, abstraction allows you to pack large quantities of knowledge into a single concept and thereby to process what you already know efficiently. You can see the importance of efficient processing in terms of a cognitive phenomenon known as chunking. Cognitive psychologists tell us that humans have the capacity to think about, roughly, seven (plus or minus two) chunks of information at one time.[2]

Chunking means that you can think about seven different dogs and nothing else, or, through forming bigger chunks using abstract conceptualization, you can think about all the dogs in the universe and six other kinds of animal as well. You can even think about the entire animal kingdom and have room to think about six more things besides. Chunking allows you to manipulate large blocks of knowledge distilled by abstraction into concepts, a handy capacity to have when your daily activity demands that you understand and stay abreast of developments within a complex phenomenon such as an organization that is embedded in the even more complex phenomenon of its environment.

Chunking makes a significant contribution to theorizing—it permits you to relate immense bodies of knowledge to each other and manipulate them to generate new knowledge. Remember, a theory is rooted in the relationships between a set of concepts. When the concepts upon which a theory is built are defined at the highest levels of abstraction, the theory may achieve **generalizability**, which means that it applies across many situations with few limiting conditions, as $E=mc^2$ does.

As with most things in life, generalizability has drawbacks as well as benefits. For example, if you assume your knowledge is more generalizable than it is, you may apply it to the wrong situations or be more likely to impose your beliefs on others when it is inappropriate or misleading to do so. The main benefit is that, the more general the theory, the more cases to which it can be applied. But because you sacrifice specificity to achieve generalizability, the more general the theory, the less obvious or direct its application will be. My mother would have said the devil is in the details, and you meet this conundrum in abstraction.

Abstract concepts give you the ability to think rapidly and efficiently about numerous instances, but you lose the rich detail that those instances contain. Without considering the specifics of the organization to which you want to apply your theory, you will miss some of the nuances required for successful application. When you want to apply an abstract concept or theory, you have to reverse the abstraction process and add crucial details back into the picture. In other words, you need to customize applications of concepts and theories to fit the organization with which you are dealing. Theory application demands creativity!

The challenges of theorizing

The Oxford English Dictionary defines a 'theorizer' as one who evolves or indulges in theory. Whether for you theorizing is a matter of indulgence or evolution, change is required, and change can be hard on some people. So, if at first organization theory seems dry and boring, consider this: the concepts you are building as you study organization theory will most likely be introduced to you before you have had time to discover their richness. If when you encounter a new concept it seems empty and meaningless, it probably *is* empty and meaningless—*for you*! But it doesn't have to stay that way.

You can get to work enriching unfamiliar concepts by trying to relate them to personal experiences in the same way you did when you built your 'dog' concept. Start right away exploring your world looking for instances that might fit new concepts and trying ideas out to see which ones bring insight about yourself and the organizations you know or meet. This should be fun and rewarding; if it isn't you need to work harder! Read about organizations that interest you and apply organization theory to these examples.

While I will offer examples to get you started down the path to conceptualization and theorizing, your own examples count the most. For that reason I won't just hand you my examples, I will present them in ways designed to trigger associations with *your* experiences. Think of it as me leading you to water and hoping you will drink. Reading this actively may be more work than you are used to with other textbooks, but more work brings more rewards!

Your ability to handle concepts and theories will expand as you continue to read this book. You can check your progress by answering a few reflexive questions at different points on your journey:

What previously hidden or overlooked aspects of your experience have you discovered?
What surprises or insights have you had that changed your thinking, attitudes and/or
    behavior?
How would you at this moment define 'organization'?

Changes in how you answer these questions now and at various points in the future will show you how much progress you have made and give you confidence that you are learning organization theory even if and when you feel it is all just a frustrating and confusing mess.

Your capacity to handle the material this book covers will grow with exposure and practice. So, if the content you are reading leaves you feeling overwhelmed, try coming back to read it again later. If you find you need to read some of the material more than once, rest assured you are not alone. And remember, the highlighted terms in this book are much more than jargon; they are the basic vocabulary of organization theory and the concepts from which its theories are formed. You have to master a sufficient number of them before you can begin to theorize, which is why you may feel overwhelmed at times during your study of this field.

Bear in mind that abstraction does not happen in one move, nor is the process of conceptualization ever really finished. You will find as you work through the book that the concepts you form become increasingly richer. A person who trains dogs learns more about them all the time, and your knowledge of organizations and organization theory is going to grow. Building a steadily expanding body of theories about how concepts are related will eventually make you an expert, but it also means your work is never done.

For any and all of the reasons presented, most people become frustrated by organization theory from time to time, including me. I can all but guarantee that the messiness in the middle of translating other people's abstract concepts, theories, and perspectives into your own will confuse and frustrate you, particularly as the concepts and theories start to multiply. But as your conceptualizing and theorizing skills strengthen you should experience moments of clarity and insight. Then you will taste the thrill of organization theory. After that it gets, not easier exactly, but much more rewarding.

I have often heard people complain that theory isn't good for anything because it does not give immediate answers to their problems. Theory alone cannot solve your specific problems, only applications of theory can do that. It is wrongheaded to reject theory as having little practical value simply because you have not yet learned how to use it.

In the end, learning to theorize is probably more important than learning theories, but learning theories is essential to learning to theorize. An ancient, most likely Chinese, proverb states: 'Give a man a fish and he will eat for a day. Teach a man to fish he will eat for a lifetime.' Organization theory may be full of fish, but its gift is to teach you how to fish for ideas to improve organizations and organizing. Organization theorists constantly find new ways to appreciate, understand, and explain organizations. This book will introduce you to what they have learned so far, but be aware that what you are studying now will change, just as you will.

What about those perspectives?

Defining relationships between concepts builds theory, but related theories form even bigger chunks: **theoretical perspectives**. Theoretical perspectives evolve from similarities in the way phenomena are defined, theorized, and studied and this book draws mainly upon three that have come to dominate organization theory over the past 50 or so years—modern, symbolic, and postmodern.[3] All three followed on the heels of a prehistory that grew out of practical demands for normative knowledge concerning how to achieve success through organization and organizing. The normative urge is interwoven with the three perspectives since its demands to relate theory and practice never go away. Its concerns are so pervasive it could even be considered a perspective in its own right.

Taking a **normative perspective** means defining a theory by its practical applications. Being normative implies assessing a phenomenon on the basis of an ideal, a standard, or a model of how things *should* be. Advising organizations on the best technology and social structure for their purposes, or the most effective factory or office layouts, are popular normative pursuits. Today the normative perspective is exemplified by **best practices** and

benchmarking. Normative theories of best practice and benchmarking propose that emulating the methods or techniques of the most successful organizations will lead to similar success. Their danger lies in assuming that one organization's success can be transferred to another. Calling for **evidence-based practice** is one way to improve the transferability of normative solutions, but providing evidence means grounding normative advice in theory drawn from one of the other perspectives.

The **modern perspective** focuses attention on causal **explanation**, which requires defining the antecedents and consequences of the phenomenon of interest.[4] Its methods often rely upon mathematical reasoning. However, although advocates of the modern perspective strive for the mathematical precision of theoretical physics, the data they use are often too messy to realize this aim. The wider variability of organizational behavior compared to the behavior of matter or energy often means resorting to statistical probabilities and relying on correlations to suggest the presence of causal relationships. For example, those who use the modern perspective make inferences addressing questions like: 'How does the technology of an organization affect the relationship between its structure and performance?' A grave danger of this approach involves confusing correlation with causality. Modern organization theorists devote a great deal of their time and energy to developing, testing, and applying mathematical methods for confirming causal inferences based on quantitative data analysis.

The **symbolic perspective** moves outside the limits imposed by the ways of knowing favored by modernists to study phenomena embedded in subjectivity. For example, culture, the use of symbols, narrative, and meaning-making are among the phenomena symbolic researchers brought to prominence in organization theory. Taking a keen interest in subjective experience and interpretation processes produces **understanding**, which is the contribution to knowledge provided by the symbolic perspective. Getting into the symbolic perspective means putting yourself into situations framed by those you want to understand and studying how they define, interact with, and interpret phenomena that interest them. The qualitative methods of description, ethnography being the most popular, are favored over those of causal explanation both because they are better able to communicate subjective experience and because it is so difficult to objectively represent subjective experience. The danger here is that the researcher over-generalizes, for example, assuming the interpretations of a phenomenon they have studied in one group apply to people they did not study, or mistaking their own subjective experience for someone else's.

Rather than seeking either explanation or understanding, the **postmodern perspective** offers critique and other forms of **appreciation**. The primary phenomena that interest postmodernists are modern management practices. Methods preferred by postmodernists involve reframing the concepts and theories of modernism by adopting a critical or aesthetic stance toward them. For example, postmodernists are fond of pointing out that modernist organization theorists too often uncritically (i.e., without awareness or reflection) adopt the perspective and interests of managers to the detriment of lower level employees, society, or the environment. Postmodernists offer appreciation, both as an alternative to explanation and understanding, and to provoke reflexivity and greater awareness of the moral and ethical implications of managing, organizing, and theorizing from any perspective. By promoting appreciation of power and its uses and abuses they hope to inspire emancipation from the domination of modernist organizing practices like hierarchy. Their work builds upon emotional empathy and aesthetic appreciation to increase resistance to any and all restrictions to human freedom.

Table 1.2 presents two dimensions for comparing the perspectives that frame this book. Inside the boxes you will find ways to think about the types of theorizing that each supports. Be attentive to the two-by-two matrix used here. This is an analytical tool borrowed by organization theory from sociology that you will meet again.

The two-by-two presented in Table 1.2 relies upon two dimensions extracted from the similarities and differences between the perspectives—what disciplines inspired theorizing and how theorizing is shaped by the role the theorist adopts. You can make these two dimensions work even harder by exploring these differences. Digging deeper into ideas is something theorists do to develop their theories.

The first dimension embedded in the framework (look at the columns shown in Table 1.2) identifies that which inspires theorists working within different perspectives. Theories inspired by the sciences, such as those of the modern and normative perspectives, stand in sharp contrast to those of the symbolic and postmodern perspectives inspired by the arts and humanities. This distinction sharpens by recognizing that the sciences prosper from their ability to predict and control outcomes, as do modern theories and the normative advice extracted from them, whereas the arts and humanities thrive on creativity, self-insight, and liberation, the central concerns and contributions of symbolic and postmodern theories.

A second way you can differentiate the perspectives (now look at the rows of Table 1.2) stems from examining the role the theorist adopts in each perspective. While in their normative applications all theories influence decisions and actions, theorists who take different perspectives are not equally comfortable influencing their phenomena while they are investigating them. Modern and symbolic theorists emphasize the importance of observing their phenomena without any unnecessary interference from the researcher, whereas getting others to change is the whole point of doing research for normative and postmodern theorists. The main difference between those comfortable in the role of influencer is that those advocating the normative perspective are more likely to base influence attempts on their beliefs about what governs success, while those adopting the postmodern perspective typically base their change efforts on ethical, moral, or aesthetic considerations.

I will limit myself in Part II to presenting concepts and theories drawn from the modern, symbolic, and postmodern perspectives, with occasional reference to their normative implications. Once you have achieved a level of comfort switching between these perspectives, others competing to become part of organization theory will be introduced, including recent efforts to reposition normative theory using pragmatic philosophy, but I will save that discussion for Part III.

Table 1.2 Theories, theorists, and theorizing practices in perspective

	Theories Inspired by the Sciences	Theories Inspired by the Arts and Humanities
Theorist as Observer	Modern Perspective: Theory as causal explanation	Symbolic Perspective: Theory as deep understanding
Theorist as Influencer	Normative Perspective: Theory as practice	Postmodern Perspective: Theory as critical appreciation

The philosophy of perspectives: Ontology and epistemology

In addition to their contributions to explanation, understanding, appreciation, and practical guidance, differences between perspectives can be stated in terms of their ontology and epistemology. **Ontology** is a branch of philosophy that studies assumptions about existence and definitions of reality. **Epistemology**, another branch, studies how we know and what counts as knowledge. The two are interrelated because our epistemological assumptions define the kind of knowledge that will be used to address what our ontological assumptions define as real.

With or without awareness, you make assumptions about what exists, for example, whenever you think about or discuss reality. Ontology is important to organization theory because different perspectives holding different ontological assumptions bring different phenomena of interest (aspects of reality) into focus. You similarly make assumptions about how knowledge is formed whenever you conceptualize or theorize, and these assumptions vary with the perspective taken.

Because different criteria for evaluating truth are adopted by different perspectives, what one considers true, another may deny, leading to disagreements and misunderstandings. For example, by privileging objective ontology, interpretive epistemology, or the use of language to constitute reality, you lay claim to one or another theoretical perspective and thereby undercut the others. The ontological and epistemological differences between the modern and symbolic perspectives were the first to come to light in organization theory. Some time later, adopting the linguistic turn in philosophy, postmodern organization theorists formulated its opposition to the modern perspective.

Ontology as objectivism versus subjectivism

Modernists embrace **objective ontology**, which means they believe in an unshakable reality existing outside human influence. For them, things (objects) exist exclusive of our knowledge about them and therefore knowledge can be verified through independent observation. Notice the assumption modernists make that knowledge is always knowledge *about things*. Treating all phenomena as if they are objects, by objectifying them if they are not literally objects, is a hallmark of the modernist perspective.

Independent observation implies that different people, all having the same relationship to an object, can make similar (reliable) observations about it. Their observations should not be biased by their subjective feelings about phenomena, or by preconceived notions or expectations of them. For hardcore objectivists, subjective understanding equates to personal bias that needs to be shed to establish valid knowledge about what exists. Thus, within the modern perspective, knowledge is produced by testing theories against objective observations of and in a real world.

Those who adopt **subjective ontology** believe that many phenomena would be unknowable using objective ontology. For example, culture would be unobservable if not for our capacity to experience and communicate what can only be approached subjectively. In contrast to objectivist worries about bias, subjectivists deliberately focus on what is revealed in private thoughts, feelings, and by allowing oneself to be influenced by context. Thus the phenomena that interest subjectivists require use of the very observational biases objectivists dismiss as making research findings unreliable.

Given their positions on ontology (what is regarded as real) and epistemology (how you can know reality), it is no wonder the advocates of modern and symbolic perspectives find it so challenging to see eye to eye. But there is more to their story. Because the phenomena that interest subjectivists are difficult if not impossible to perceive using the five senses alone, knowing them requires empathy and intuition as well as reason. This raises epistemological concerns.

Epistemology as positivism versus interpretivism

Because one would not expect two subjective experiences of a phenomenon to be the same, the question of how to treat interpretation arises. While those holding to a positivist epistemology discount interpretation because of the subjective bias it introduces, for interpretivists it is the only way of knowing and communicating subjective experience.

Positivist epistemology assumes you can discover the truth about phenomena through application of the scientific method. Acceptable knowledge is generated by developing hypotheses and propositions on the basis of theory, and then testing these by gathering and analyzing data that allow you to compare the implications of your theory to external reality.

Interpretivist epistemology assumes that knowledge can only be created and understood from within the contexts that give meaning to experience. That is, each of us makes sense of what is happening based on the situation we face at the time, and any memories and expectations we bring to that situation. This assumption implies that there may be many different understandings and interpretations of reality co-existing at one place and time depending upon who is involved.

Because interpretivists believe that all knowledge is filtered through subjectivity, many believe that objective ontology is insupportable. Therefore interpretivists reject the traditional scientific method and turn instead to interpretive methods developed within the arts and humanities. Methodological choices specify how to conduct oneself as a researcher, what counts as data, and how to go about collecting them. For example, organization theorists who adopt positivism prefer 'hard' data, such as numbers gleaned from financial records or by surveying large samples of the population studied. Interpretivists prefer 'soft' data, such as those produced by unstructured interviews or through participant observation in the contexts in which the researchers' informants live and work.

Some objectivists admit that it is impossible to remove all bias from observation, thus they accept part of the subjectivist argument: we cannot know anything separate from interpretations of it. They then use this revised objectivist ontology to deny the need for interpretive epistemology: 'We have managed thus far in spite of the constant intercession of interpretation, so why change?' Instead of ceding any philosophical territory to the symbolic perspective, they claim that the symbolic perspective makes no distinctive contribution to knowledge.

Observing all this maneuvering leads postmodernists to claim that the modernists' revision of objectivism appropriates rather than accepts subjectivism's ontological position thereby revealing its hegemonic intentions. They accuse modernists of weakening their position merely to maintain dominance. To see how postmodernism justifies its position you need to know about the linguistic turn the arts and humanities took and how this sensibility moved into organization theory.

The postmodern (linguistic) turn

Postmodernism starts by denying that words represent things. Instead they believe that language constitutes reality; what is spoken is real (at least until it is overturned by another instance of speech). As German philosopher Martin Heidegger put it: 'In the saying it comes to pass that the world is made to appear.' In making the case for defining reality linguistically—the **linguistic turn**—Heidegger accused Plato of leading his followers astray by focusing attention on things and their properties instead of attending to what grants these entities existence.

Heidegger wanted to know how being appears as substantial—as things—and concluded that language and the discourses created by speaking, writing, and reading give the state of being a substantial appearance. Recognizing, thanks to Heidegger, that existence is insubstantial provided postmodernism its point of departure: the claim that the world is made by, rather than mirrored in, language. Postmodernists claim that, when modernists treat language as a mirror reflecting nature, they ignore the effects of language. Postmodernism reveals the errors modernism hides and attempts to correct them.

To experience the linguistic turn, consider the subject position 'I' in a sentence beginning 'I am' and assume that using this statement constitutes your existence, just as anyone's saying this or that 'is' constitutes reality. Adopting the postmodern perspective implies there can be no identity or reality apart from that created in and by language because language grants us, and the things that appear around us, whatever substance it has.

Within the context of language, things exist as texts written or spoken within a discourse that speech and writing constitutes. Discourses provide contexts that enable and constrain how language is used such that texts and discourses are mutually constituted in and by language use. For the postmodernist, everything is a text located in one or more discourses so there is no escaping the effects of language (adopting this assumption performs the linguistic turn). Epistemologically, postmodernists believe you cannot truly know anything. This belief does not necessarily deny epistemology, as some postmodernists assert, rather it can be regarded as an epistemological assumption in its own right. Similarly, the postmodern denial of the existence of reality outside language defines an ontological position, though for some it seems a nihilistic one.

Many postmodernists share several beliefs stemming from the linguistic turn. First, the discourses in which we engage shape our reality by influencing how we use language and what we talk about (e.g., things or processes; organizations or organizing). Second, speaker, spoken, and speech are all constituted in and through language. And finally, meaning cannot be fixed, nor can reality—these remain in flux as they move within and between discourses, potentially changing with each new utterance. There is no independent reality against which to test knowledge, as assumed by modernists, all is text read or performed in the moment of their continual becoming. Therefore postmodernism is not so much an anti-philosophy as it is a philosophy whose foundation floats adrift in perpetual change.

Power and communication are central phenomena within postmodernism because anyone who controls discourse can make something exist, or disappear. For example, maladies such as multiple sclerosis (MS) or attention-deficit hyperactivity disorder (ADHD) were not considered treatable until they were given existence by being defined within the discourse of medical practice by influential doctors. After its linguistic invention, the diagnosis of ADHD permitted treatment with powerful mind-altering drugs. The power of words transfers to those who have better access to or influence on mainstream discourse, for example, experts, journalists, and celebrities. Power gives rise to communicative distortions when imbalances of power supported by ignorance of what produces reality allow some to define the reality in which others must live, creating the potential for exploitation and abuse.

Emancipation from linguistically induced exploitation can be gained only through awareness of how language embedded in discourse produces reality. Since our language writes and rewrites us into discourses constructed through language, it also suggests an escape route. Postmodernists offer us the option of joining forces through participation in discourse. Doing so reflexively, that is, with awareness of the effects of language, permits desired change. If we find organizing processes to be degrading or exploitative, it is up to us to voice our concerns and thereby change the discursive reality that sustains what we oppose.

For example, criticizing organizations or governments is an important step toward emancipation from injustice. Just think about the Facebook moment in which participants in the Arab Spring movements of 2011 realized they were not alone in their criticism of government and went out into the streets to create a new discourse that changed reality in Tunisia and Egypt. Occupy protestors similarly seek to change the terms of a dominant discourse they believe serves only the wealthy. There is a strong flavor of democracy running through postmodernism, which helps it to define an ethical/moral position that combines with its anti-foundational ontological and epistemological assumptions.

Table 1.3 summarizes the key philosophical differences constituting the modern, symbolic, and postmodern perspectives and their implications for organization theory. For now I have left the normative perspective out of view as its assumptions depend on what theory, if any, it relies upon. Ideas about the role of normative theory will come up again in Part III when discussing possible futures of the field.

One last thing, if you find you did not fully grasp any of the material presented in this chapter, I hope you will return to it later. And even if you feel you 'get' it now, returning to read it again after grappling with Part II will bring deeper insight and greatly benefit your learning.

A conceptual framework and tips for using this book

To this point I have said almost nothing about organizations or organizing. The reason is that this entire book addresses the question: What is organization? This devil will be found in the details presented as the six big chunks shown in Figure 1.1, each of which will be treated to its own chapter in Part II.

Please don't mistake the diagram in Figure 1.1 for a theory. It is only a framework dividing up the territory organization theory covers. The highly abstract concepts indicated in the figure—environment, technology, social and physical structure, culture, and power—each embrace a whole range of other concepts and theories, and each will reveal something different about organization, types of organizations, or organizing practices. There will be points of contact between all of these different ways of thinking, shown as overlapping areas connecting the circles of Figure 1.1, and their implications will be discussed as we distinguish one concept from the others.

Table 1.3 The modern, symbolic, and postmodern perspectives of organization theory

Modern Perspective	Symbolic Perspective	Postmodern Perspective
Ontology	**Ontology**	**Ontology**
Objectivism—belief in an external reality whose existence is independent of knowledge of it; the world exists as an independent object waiting to be discovered	Subjectivism—the belief that you cannot know an external or objective reality apart from your subjective awareness of it; what we agree exists, exists for us, of and in our intersubjective awareness	Postmodernism—belief that nothing exists separate from renderings of it in speech, writing, or other forms of expression; the world is made to appear in language, discourse and artwork without referents because there is nothing to which to refer
Epistemology	**Epistemology**	**Epistemology**
Positivism—belief that truth is discovered through valid conceptualization and reliable measurement, which allows the testing of knowledge against the objective world; knowledge accumulates, allowing humans to progress and evolve	Interpretivism—belief that truth is relative to the knower and can only be understood from the point of view of individuals who are directly involved; truth is socially constructed via multiple interpretations by the subjects of knowledge, thereby they and their truth are co-constructed and change over time	Postmodernism—belief that because there is no independent reality, there can be no truth about it, truth is an empty concept; there are no facts, only renderings and interpretations, therefore every claim to knowledge is only a power play
Organizations are	**Organizations are**	**Organizations are**
Objectively real entities operating in a real world; when well-designed and managed they are systems of decision and action driven by norms of rationality, efficiency, and effectiveness directed toward stated objectives	Contexts continually constructed and reconstructed by their members through symbolically mediated interaction (e.g., organizational dramas); socially constructed realities where webs of meaning create bonds of emotion and symbolic connection between members	Sites for enacting power relations, giving rise to oppression, irrationality, and falsehoods but also humor and playful irony; as they are texts or dramas, we can rewrite organizations so as to emancipate ourselves from human folly and degradation
Focus of Organization Theory	**Focus of Organization Theory**	**Focus of Organization Theory**
Discovering the universal principles and laws that govern organizations, defining the theories that explain them and/or their performance, and developing methods to test theory and its implications; emphasizes structure, rules, standardization, and routine	Describing how life unfolds within the organizational context in rituals and other meaningful activities in order to produce understanding of how organizing happens; favors interpreting symbols to reveal organizational culture through its assumptions, values, artifacts, and practices	Appreciating and/or deconstructing organizational texts so as to reveal managerial ideologies and destabilize modernist modes of organizing and theorizing; favors marginalized and oppressed viewpoints; encourages reflexive and inclusive forms of theorizing and organizing

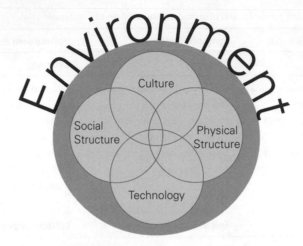

Figure 1.1 A conceptual model of organization

The five intersecting circles of this model represent organization as five inter-related phenomena conceptualized as shown. Power, a sixth, is indicated with the grey tint infusing the other circles. These six concepts will be examined in depth in Part II of the book.

A popular assignment for students of organization theory involves using Figure 1.1 to guide analysis of a particular organization. It will help you to do this if you focus on a real problem the organization faces, or imagine one for it. For example, an organization may need to rethink its competitive strategy, implement a new technology, or deal with cultural change. In the context of the stated problem, any of the concepts and theories presented in this book has the potential to provide insight and suggest desirable courses of action. But you won't know until you try them out which concepts and theories are best suited to addressing the problem.

Don't just guess at which concepts and theories might apply. My advice is to keep looking at your organization and its problems using as many concepts and theories as you can until your struggle to explain, understand, and appreciate starts to pay off with insights and surprises. The five circles model of Figure 1.1 can serve as a checklist to make sure you do not leave out something important—Did I remember power? Did I skip over physical structure?—but you cannot derive much insight from these umbrella notions without applying them one concept or theory at a time.

Applying concepts and theories to your own experiences and examples will give you practice and provide depth to your knowledge of organization theory. At the same time it will help you learn to relate the different parts of Figure 1.1 to each other. As you find your way to selecting appropriate concepts, theories, and perspectives from the range organization theory makes available and applying them to concrete examples, you will find yourself theorizing about organization. You know you are starting to theorize when you are able to draw surprising conclusions about an organization or an organizing experience that call forth explanation, understanding, and/or appreciation. Organization theory will seem more useful, the organizations you study richer, and your observations and reflections more valuable, as a consequence of your efforts.

Summary

This book presents organization theory, which is really a bunch of theories rather than just one. A theory is built from a set of concepts whose relationships offer appreciation, description, or explanation for the phenomenon of interest chosen as the focus of theorizing. The primary phenomenon of interest to organization theorists is broadly defined as organization, which includes different kinds of organizations as well as organizing activities and processes.

I believe that the best theories are those that match your own experience of organization and organizing. In this book you will learn about concepts and theories that others have developed and how and why they created them. This will give you a foundation for theorizing as well as introducing you to the knowledge and discipline organization theory offers.

As a student of organization theory, you will want to learn to use concepts, abstraction, and theorizing because they permit you to process information rapidly and efficiently and to appreciate, understand, explain, and communicate ideas. But you should also remember that theorizing through abstract conceptual reasoning alone will not provide all that you need to analyze and solve problems or take advantage of opportunities in a specific organization. Applying theory demands that you be able to add important details back into abstract formulations. Developing your concepts and theorizing skills with a broad base of personal experience will help you to translate abstractions for the specific application of concepts and theory to unique situations.

Finally, you have your own reasons for studying organization theory. Mine are that organization theory broadens my appreciation of organizations and the world in general and opens my mind to new ideas and possibilities. I am constantly renewed by my work in this field and find that my continuing study of its offerings generates new concepts and nurtures my skill in applying them to creatively solve problems and generate other innovations. Although it may hold other meanings and possibilities for you, I hope that my enthusiasm and example will inspire you to explore and learn to use organization theory to enhance your knowledge, creativity, and career.

Key terms

theory

phenomenon of interest

concepts

abstraction

chunking

theoretical perspective

   normative

   modern

   symbolic

   postmodern

explanation

understanding

appreciation

ontology

   objectivist

   subjectivist

epistemology

   positivist

   interpretivist

the linguistic turn

Endnotes

1. Lewin (1951: 169).
2. Miller (1956).
3. Thomas Kuhn's 1970 book *The Structure of Scientific Revolutions* combined with Graham Allison's (1971), *The Essence of Decision*, an analysis of the Cuban Missile Crisis from different theoretical perspectives, inspired many organization theorists to adopt multiple perspectives. Gibson Burrell and Gareth Morgan (1979) provided the earliest comprehensive survey of organization theory framed by the perspectives of functionalism, interpretivism, radical humanism, and radical structuralism. John Hassard and his colleagues (1991; Hassard and Pym, 1990; Hassard and Cox, 2012) have since been active in promoting and extending Burrell and Morgan's framework. Others to frame organization theory with multiple perspectives were W. Richard Scott (1981/1992, rational, natural, and open systems) and Joanne Martin (1992, integration, differentiation, and fragmentation).
4. Whetten (1989).

References

Allison, Graham (1971) *The Essence of Decision: Explaining the Cuban Missile Crisis.* Boston: Little, Brown.

Burrell, Gibson, and Morgan, Gareth (1979) *Sociological Paradigms and Organizational Analysis.* London: Heinemann.

Hassard, John (1991) Multiple paradigms and organizational analysis: A case study. *Organization Studies*, 12/2: 275–99.

——and Cox, Julie W. (2012) Organizational analysis: Paradigmatic possibilities for post-paradigms times. Academy of Management Annual Meeting. Boston, MA.

——and Pym, Denis (1990) (eds.) *The Theory and Philosophy of Organizations: Critical Issues and New Perspectives.* London: Routledge.

Kuhn, T. S. (1970) *The Structure of Scientific Revolutions.* Chicago: University of Chicago Press.

Lewin, Kurt (1951) *Field Theory in Social Science: Selected Theoretical Papers* (Dorwin Cartwright edn.). Oxford: Harpers.

Martin, Joanne (1992) *Cultures in Organizations: Three Perspectives.* Oxford: Oxford University Press.

Miller, George A. (1956) The magical number seven, plus or minus two: Some limits on our capacity for processing information. *Psychological Review*, 63/2: 81–97.

Scott, W. Richard (1992) *Organizations: Rational, Natural, and Open Systems* (3rd edn., first edition published 1981). Englewood Cliffs, NJ: Prentice-Hall.

Whetten, D. A. (1989) What constitutes a theoretical contribution? *Academy of Management Review*, 14: 490–95.

Further reading

Corley K. G. and Gioia, D. A. (2011) Building theory about theory building: What constitutes a theoretical contribution. *Academy of Management Review*, 38/1: 12–32.

Sutton, R. I. and Staw, B. M. (1995) What theory is *not. Administrative Science Quarterly*, 40, 371–84.

Weick, K. E. (1989) Theory construction as disciplined imagination. *Academy of Management Review*, 14: 516–31.

A brief history of organization theory

One of the enticements to study organization theory lies in the multi-disciplinary ideas upon which it draws. My way to indicate the broad range of founding ideas and the considerable span of time across which they entered organization theory is shown as a diagram in Figure 2.1. This historical overview indicates when different perspectives first became established within organization theory and the contributing disciplines and thinkers who helped develop them.

The timeline of Figure 2.1 is incomplete, indicating that more perspectives may yet take root in organization theory. You will meet some of the most promising contenders in Part III, while Part II focuses on concepts and theories developed within the modern, symbolic, and postmodern perspectives. However, since these perspectives can all be traced to seeds planted before organization theory was born, this history begins with theorists whose ideas predated its birth.

The prehistory of organization theory

There was precious little written about organizations and organizing as the industrial age took hold in the late eighteenth and early nineteenth centuries in Europe and the US, but there was growing demand for knowledge coming predominantly from two sources. Normative interests expressed by executives and consultants to industry focused research attention on how best to design and manage organizations to enhance their productivity, while academic interests expressed by economists and sociologists focused attention on the changing shapes and roles of organizations within industrializing societies. Soon interest in the practical problems of industrial business management would extend to government bureaus and other public sector organizations as theorists made the conceptual leap from organizing to achieving efficiency in industry, to bureaucratic rationalization.

The executives and consultants who helped found organization theory offered solutions to common organizational problems and advice to those responsible for implementing them. Because their primary audience was business managers and administrators of government and other public sector organizations, they came to be known as classical management or administrative theorists. Their work was offered mainly in the form of normative

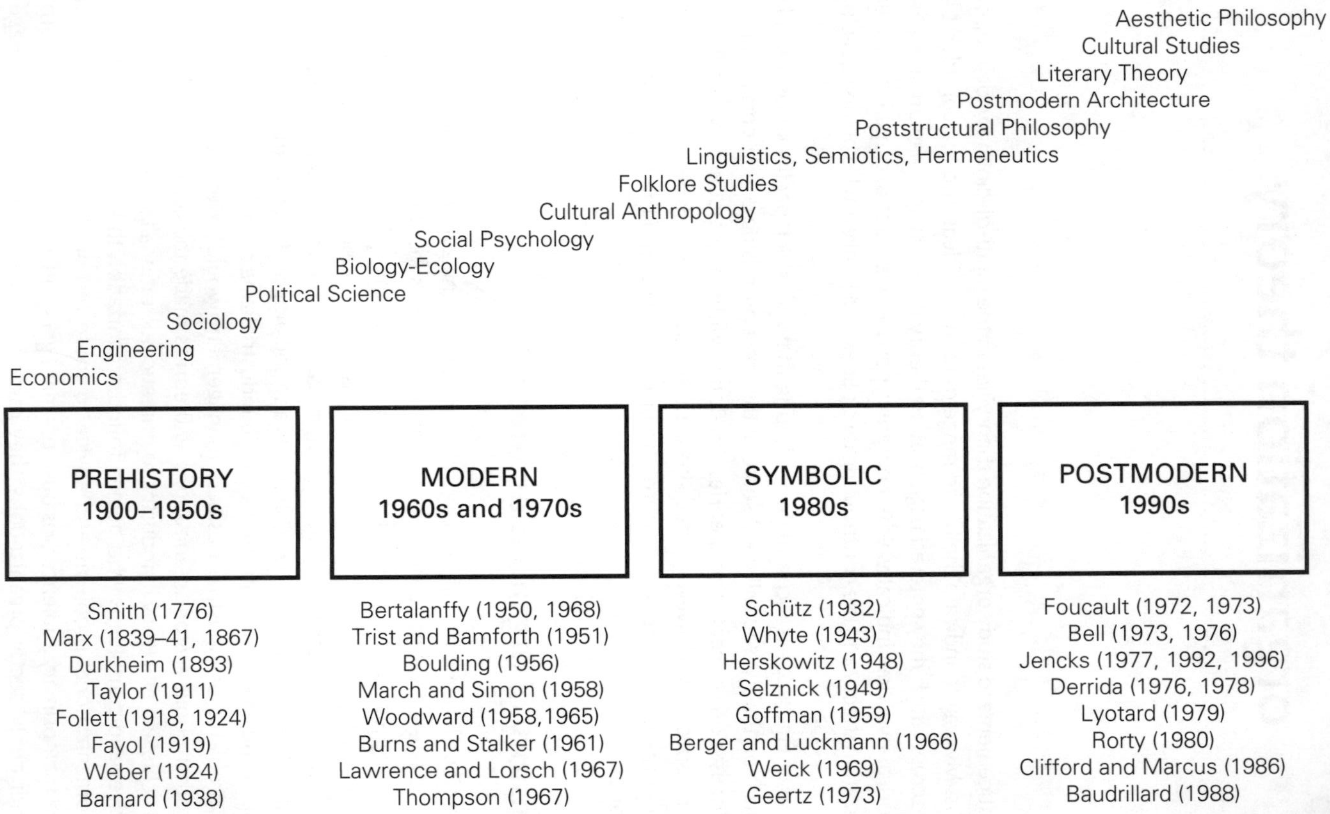

Aesthetic Philosophy
Cultural Studies
Literary Theory
Postmodern Architecture
Poststructural Philosophy
Linguistics, Semiotics, Hermeneutics
Folklore Studies
Cultural Anthropology
Social Psychology
Biology-Ecology
Political Science
Sociology
Engineering
Economics

PREHISTORY 1900–1950s	MODERN 1960s and 1970s	SYMBOLIC 1980s	POSTMODERN 1990s

PREHISTORY 1900–1950s

Smith (1776)
Marx (1839–41, 1867)
Durkheim (1893)
Taylor (1911)
Follett (1918, 1924)
Fayol (1919)
Weber (1924)
Barnard (1938)

MODERN 1960s and 1970s

Bertalanffy (1950, 1968)
Trist and Bamforth (1951)
Boulding (1956)
March and Simon (1958)
Woodward (1958, 1965)
Burns and Stalker (1961)
Lawrence and Lorsch (1967)
Thompson (1967)

SYMBOLIC 1980s

Schütz (1932)
Whyte (1943)
Herskowitz (1948)
Selznick (1949)
Goffman (1959)
Berger and Luckmann (1966)
Weick (1969)
Geertz (1973)

POSTMODERN 1990s

Foucault (1972, 1973)
Bell (1973, 1976)
Jencks (1977, 1992, 1996)
Derrida (1976, 1978)
Lyotard (1979)
Rorty (1980)
Clifford and Marcus (1986)
Baudrillard (1988)

Figure 2.1 Sources of inspiration for the perspectives of organization theory

The boxes in the center of this figure are ordered along a timeline showing when the modern, symbolic, and postmodern perspectives became established within organization theory. The disciplines from which these perspectives are borrowed appear above the timeline in the rough order of their initial influence, while the contributing theorists are listed below, alongside publication dates for the works you will find referenced at the end of the chapter.

principles, but can be seen to have followed along lines laid out by political-economists and organizational sociologists who were hard at work studying how the industrial age was changing economic and social life. Together these diverse interests established organization theory as a field of study.

The diverse normative and academic interests present at its founding created a tension between practice and theory present throughout the history of this field.[1] Even if the label organization *theory* makes it seem like practice takes on less importance, practical application of theory has always been of concern to this applied discipline. But bear in mind that the challenges of applying theory, particularly in using abstractions to inform concrete situations, are never resolved. At their best, the interests of theory and practice produce creative tension; at their worst they form politicized factions.

Below you will meet in quick succession authors of classical management and administrative theories, political-economists, and sociologists whose ideas conjoined as organization theory emerged from both practice and theory.

Adam Smith, Scottish political-economist (1723–1790)

Although organizing and management were much in evidence in the pyramids of ancient Egypt and no doubt occurred even further back in human history, our formal knowledge does not extend to those times.[2] What we do know is that Adam Smith was the first on record to publish a theory of organization. In 1776, Smith's *An Inquiry into the Nature and Causes of the Wealth of Nations* explained how the **division of labor** creates economic efficiency. Be sure to notice Smith acknowledging his debt to practice as he explains how his theory applies to the efficiency of making pins:

> To take an example . . . in which the division of labour has been very often taken notice of, the trade of the pin-maker; a workman not educated to this business (which the division of labour has rendered a distinct trade), nor acquainted with the use of the machinery employed in it (to the invention of which the same division of labour has probably given occasion), could scarce, perhaps, with his utmost industry, make one pin in a day, and certainly could not make twenty. But in the way in which this business is now carried on, not only the whole work is a peculiar trade, but it is divided into a number of branches, of which the greater part are likewise peculiar trades. One man draws out the wire, another straights it, a third cuts it, a fourth points it, a fifth grinds it at the top for receiving the head; to make the head requires two or three distinct operations; to put it on, is a peculiar business, to whiten the pins is another; it is even a trade by itself to put them into the paper; and the important business of making a pin is, in this manner, divided into about eighteen distinct operations, which, in some manufactories, are all performed by distinct hands, though in others the same man will sometimes perform two or three of them . . . I have seen a small manufactory of this kind where ten men only were employed, and where some of them consequently performed two or three distinct operations. But though they were very poor, and therefore but indifferently accommodated with the necessary machinery, they could, when they exerted themselves, make among them about twelve pounds of pins in a day. There are in a pound upwards of four thousand pins of a middling size. Those ten persons, therefore, could make among them upwards of forty-eight thousand pins in a day. Each person, therefore, making a tenth part of forty-eight thousand pins, might be considered as making four thousand eight hundred pins in a day. But if they had all wrought separately and independently, and without

any of them having been educated to this peculiar business, they certainly could not each of them have made twenty, perhaps not one pin in a day; that is, certainly, not the two hundred and fortieth, perhaps not the four thousand eight hundredth part of what they are at present capable of performing, in consequence of a proper division and combination of their different operations.

In every other art and manufacture, the effects of the division of labour are similar to what they are in this very trifling one; though, in many of them, the labour can neither be so much subdivided, nor reduced to so great a simplicity of operation. The division of labour, however, so far as it can be introduced, occasions, in every art, a proportionable increase of the productive powers of labour.[3]

Smith's theory of the effects of the division of labor on economic outcomes described important industrial management practices that would lead to widespread use of management techniques like production simplification and time and motion studies. The division of labor, including the **differentiation** of work tasks and the **specialization** of laborers, is central to the concept of **social structure**, one of the core concepts of organization theory. However, while Smith assumed that industrialization would lead to economic success and social progress, others saw reason to be skeptical about this assumption, starting with Karl Marx.

✗ Karl Marx, German philosopher-economist and revolutionary (1818–1883)

Marx's **theory of capital** begins with the human need to survive, and the will to thrive once survival needs are met. According to Marx, survival needs create economic order when, in trying to cope with danger and feed, cloth, and house themselves, people discover the economic efficiencies of collective labor and the social structures that support it. Economic **efficiency** eventually creates resource surpluses of raw material and time that can be invested in cultural enhancement to fulfill desires for human self-expression and advancement.[4]

This is all well and good, but for the problem of power. In Marx's theory, the economic base on which people build their cultures is subject to the relations of power worked out between the interests of capital and those of labor. The relations of power pit the capitalists who own the means of production, including tools, equipment, and factories, against the laborers who produce the output of the production process. Their antagonism lies at the heart of capitalism.

Contention between the interests of capital and those of labor arises over how to divide the excess profits generated when products or services are exchanged on a market at a price that is higher than their costs. Since profit is generated by a combination of labor and capital, Marx explained, each side can reasonably claim this surplus. Laborers base their claim on having performed the profitable work, while capitalists claim that without their investment labor would have no work from which to profit.

The **social conflict** between labor and capital, Marx went on, intensifies with demands for **profitability**. Without profit, the survival of the individual firm and the entire capitalist economy would be in jeopardy because capital would cease to be invested and work would disappear. Profitability depends upon the organization of work activity subject to the laws of competition.

Competition from other firms puts downward pressure on the prices of products and services, which in turn causes firms to want to reduce their production costs in order to maintain profit for their capitalists. Since the biggest production cost is typically labor, capitalists pressure laborers to work more efficiently (or at least more cheaply), which is achieved by continuously imposing new forms of managerial control on work processes that put an even bigger squeeze on labor's claim to a share of the profit.

The story of labor under capitalism becomes gloomier still, Marx noted, when, in the drive for efficiency, capitalists define **labor** as a cost of production. Such thinking equates labor with any other commodity bought and sold on a market and gives humans a purely instrumental relationship with one another based on the economic value of their potential to do work. When this **commodification** of labor is deemed acceptable, labor can be treated like any other raw material that is exploited for its economic value.

By focusing on the economics of work rather than on the welfare of workers or society, the commodification of labor leads to the **exploitation** of labor by capitalists and to the **alienation** of laborers from their own work. Alienation occurs when workers, who see their labor as a commodity that they willingly sell, engage in self-exploitation by accepting terms of employment that favor the interests of capital. Unless workers organize resistance to **managerial control**, for example by forming labor unions, exploitation and alienation of workers under capitalism is inevitable.

Marx predicted that the dynamics of capitalist economies would sustain a society only until a culture willing to overthrow capitalism develops from its economic base. This has been the most controversial prediction Marx drew from his theory, and many people interpreted the collapse of communism in the Soviet Union as proof that Marx was wrong. However, recent social upheavals initiated by the Arab Spring, Los Indignados, and the Occupy Wall Street Movement suggest Marx's theory may yet prove insightful in explaining why new subcultures that question the distribution of the wealth produced under capitalism are forming and predicting the rise of some new means of organizing production and the material resources it consumes and controls.

Marx's ideas about labor and capitalism inspired critical theory thereby providing a foundation upon which to critique management as a profession. His focus on social conflict and the dynamics of change within politically influenced capitalist economies offered a point of stark difference with the more harmonious visions set forth by Durkheim and Weber.

Émile Durkheim, French sociologist (1858–1917)

Published in 1893, Durkheim's *The Division of Labor in Society* explained the structural shift from agricultural to industrial societies in terms of the effects of the increased specialization of labor that industrialization brought about. Durkheim's theory echoed Adam Smith's, but added **hierarchy** and the **interdependence** of work roles and tasks to the division of labor. These ideas, known collectively as **social structure**, became core concepts for those adopting the modern perspective in organization theory, as were the **quantitative research methods** of statistical description and analysis that Durkheim promoted in two other books, *The Rules of Sociological Method* and *Suicide*.

In addition to defining the social structure of formal organization, Durkheim proposed the concept of **informal organization**. This idea emphasized workers' social needs in contrast to the **formal organization** embedded in the division of labor, hierarchy, and task interdependence. Studies revealing the effects of informal organization helped to establish the fields of organizational behavior and industrial and organizational psychology, and paved the way for organizational culture to make its debut in organization theory. Furthermore Durkheim's distinction between formal and informal organization exposed a tension in organization theory between (hard) economic and (soft) humanistic aspects of organizing that rivals the challenge of bringing theory and practice together under one disciplinary roof.[5]

Karl Emil Maximillian (Max) Weber, German sociologist (1864–1920)

Like Marx and Durkheim, Weber wanted to understand how industrialization affects society. What interested him particularly was a new kind of **authority structure** that industrial organization brought with it. According to Weber, before industrialization, societies organized themselves using either traditional or charismatic authority, but with industrialization came rational-legal authority.

Traditional authority rests upon inherited status as defined and maintained by such things as bloodlines and the ownership of property. For example, aristocratic societies transfer property and status from parent to child. While tradition stabilizes the social order in a traditional society, the heirs to status and power may not be fit or willing to lead. Succession issues also challenge societies organized by **charismatic authority** in which the attractiveness of certain individuals justifies and legitimates their influence over others. In ancient times Jesus Christ and Muhammad exuded charisma while more recent examples are found in Gandhi, John Fitzgerald Kennedy, and Martin Luther King, Jr., each of whose deaths disoriented the societies they served.

Weber predicted that **rational-legal authority** would replace the nepotism of traditional authority and the personality cults of charismatic authority, with merit-based selection driven by rationally formulated rules and laws. Societies based on rational-legal authority would, in principle, ensure the appropriate behavior of those in charge by binding them to the same laws and rules that define their right to lead. What is more, they would draw on a bigger and better pool of leaders because almost anyone can lead by following the rules and laws of a society based upon rational-legal authority.

Weber was aware that the promise of rational-legal authority might never be realized in practice. He described the risks in 1924 in his *The Theory of Social and Economic Organization*. In this book Weber proposed that **bureaucracy** could extend the technical efficiency of industrial organizations to all of society by rationalizing the social order. His insight depended on an analogy between the way in which technology rationalizes the economic order of business organizations and how bureaucracy might similarly improve the efficiency of organizations such as government bureaus. Weber's analogy led modernist organization theorists of the 1950s and 1960s to believe the converse of Weber's point, namely that bureaucratic rationalization would produce technical efficiency.

Weber was the first to acknowledge that the outcomes of bureaucratic rationalization depend upon human values. In this regard Weber distinguished between formal and substantive rationality. **Formal rationality** involves techniques of calculation, such as those developed by engineers to measure technical efficiency, or by managers to track and elimi-nate costs. **Substantive rationality** refers to the desired ends of action that direct the uses of the calculative or 'hard' techniques of formal rationality implying that the ends of manage-ment need to be questioned. Weber believed both were needed.

Adopting formal rationality without considering substantive rationality leads, Weber warned, to an **iron cage** capable of making every human a 'cog in an ever-moving mecha-nism.'[6] Critical postmodernists echo this warning as they strive to free humankind from the restrictive practices of management driven, they believe, almost exclusively by formal rationality. At the same time Weber's interest in how cultural values, beliefs, customs, and morality influence social behavior contributes to the symbolic perspective of organization theory.[7]

Frederick Winslow Taylor, American engineer, manager, and founder of scientific management (1856-1915)

At the tender age of 28 Taylor was named chief engineer at the Midvale Steel Company where his first efforts to manage combined persuasion with force, the accepted practice of that time. Taylor became disaffected with this approach when he realized that, to manage workers effectively, he needed to know about the technical aspects of their work and workers' psychological motivations. Based on his belief that applications of scientific research methods would improve management practice, Taylor conducted scientific experiments at the Bethlehem Steel Company and several other places. His experiments focused on the handling of raw material, the use of tools and machines, and worker motivation.

His experiments inspired Taylor to develop the idea of **scientific management**, from which he derived many management principles. His principles included the use of work standards to provide a target rate of performance (to be set higher than the average rate at which laborers ordinarily worked), and uniform work methods to guarantee that workers could achieve the targets, including instruction cards, order-of-work sequences, materials specifications, and inventory control systems. Taylor also recommended skill-based job placement, supervision methods, and incentive schemes.

Taylor believed that the standards and principles he based on scientific research and experimentation would allow managers to pay high wages while lowering production costs. He believed this would maximize the benefits of factories to society and achieve high levels of cooperation between management and labor. Scientific management prac-tices, according to Taylor, would maximize capitalist profits by motivating workers to perform at or above the standards set for them, and that paying workers fairly in accord-ance with their productivity would avoid the social conflict Marx predicted would topple capitalism.

Taylor's work inspired an international efficiency movement. Among the early adopters of his ideas were time and motion studies experts like Frank and Lillian Gilbreth, a married couple who devoted their lives to enhancing worker productivity. For example, Frank Gil-breth invented a method of bricklaying that reduced the number of movements required to lay one interior brick from 18 to 2, thus increasing the bricklaying rate of a single individual from 120 to 350 bricks per hour.

Such impressive productivity gains led many heads of state and business leaders including Lenin, Stalin, and Henry Ford to adopt scientific management, which many also referred to as **Taylorism**. Today quantifying workers' inputs and outputs for the purpose of evaluation and control can be observed in businesses around the world. When applied to assembly line production some call Tayloristic management practices **Fordism** in homage to Henry Ford's more or less wholesale adoption of scientific management techniques.[8]

At the time Taylor's scientific management appeared, many workers and even business owners considered it dangerous and subversive. They believed it would ruin trust and coop-eration between management and workers, threatening capitalism in the ways Marx had predicted. In this milieu, attempts to introduce Taylor's principles into a government organi-zation led to union opposition and a strike, which precipitated an American Congressional investigation of scientific management. Fears were soon replaced, however, by the threat of communism that led to the disenfranchisement of Marx's theories in the US. Meanwhile in the United Kingdom, France, Sweden, and Denmark, where worker rights were better defended along with Marx's theories, scientific management was resisted for a longer time. Today it appears that these societies, too, have succumbed to Taylorism as devotion to tech-nical efficiency and formal rationality spreads throughout the globalizing economy.

Taylor's belief in the powers of objective measurement and the discovery of laws governing worker efficiency carried over into the modern perspective where scientific management tech-niques justify all manner of **rationalization** schemes. Critical postmodernists, on the other hand, regard Taylorism, not as a way to make organizations more rational through efficiency, but as a rationale to justify the unprecedented power capitalists and managers enjoy today.

Mary Parker Follett, American scholar, social reformer, government and management consultant (1868–1933)

Based on consulting work with community centers, government, and business organizations, Follett formed her theory that the principles that make social communities strong can be applied to creating successful government and other organizations. In 1924 Follett presented a management theory based on the principle of self-government, which she claimed would facilitate 'the growth of individuals and of the groups to which they belonged.' She argued that 'by directly interacting with one another to achieve their common goals, the members of a group fulfilled themselves through the process of the group's development.' Her ideas anticipated by many decades the current interest in **workplace democracy** and **nonhierarchical networks**.

Follett promoted the view that organizations within a democratic society should embrace democratic ideals, and that power should be power *with* not power *over* people. As she put it:

> You cannot coordinate purpose without developing purpose, it is part of the same process. Some people want to give the workmen a share in carrying out the purpose of the plant and do not see that that involves a share in creating the purpose of the plant.[9]

Thus, in opposition to Marx, Follett proposed the idea that power is a source of creative energy. She saw the process of creating joint power over a conflict situation as an alternative to viewing power as a competitive force based in domination.

Follett considered domination to be only one of three possible approaches to conflict resolution. Compromise, the second, is just as negative as domination, in that none of the parties' interests are served completely. Of the three, only integration respects everyone's interests by realizing all in a creative redefinition of the problem. To illustrate integration Follett used the example of two people reading in a library. One wants to open a window; the other prefers to keep it shut. While a dominant person might exercise their will at the expense of the other's interests, an integrative approach would be to open a window in an adjoining room. Follett arrived at the integrative solution by recognizing that the person who wants the window open really only desires fresh air (opening the window being only one means of achieving this goal), while the person who wants it closed merely does not want the wind to blow directly upon them. This solution is not a compromise because both parties get what they want (fresh air, no wind).

Although Follett's work is currently experiencing something of a revival, many are surprised by how often historical surveys of organization theory ignore her. By contrast her work has long been recognized in Japan where the Mary Parker Follett Association dedicated to the dissemination of her ideas has existed since the 1950s. Some feminists attribute the slow uptake of Follett's ideas in Europe and the US to her gender, an interesting comment on the influence of power conceptualized as domination. Even so, Follett's work on organizations as communities contributed to theories of organizations as communities of knowledge, practice, and learning and her democratic principles of organization apply wherever workplace democracy is invoked as an ideal.

Henri Fayol, French engineer, CEO, and administrative theorist (1841–1925)

Fayol, an engineer and manager in the mining industry, earned great admiration as a CEO for his successful turnaround of a failing French mining company. Upon retirement he established a center for the study of administration to codify and pass on the **administrative principles** he had followed during his career. In 1919 his book *General and Industrial Management* presented universal principles applicable to the rational administration of organizational activities.

Among Fayol's rational principles, **span of control** defined the optimal number of subordinates to be overseen by one manager. That subordinates should handle **routine** matters using standardized operating procedures was his principle of **delegation** designed to leave managers free to handle exceptions as they arose. The principle of **departmentalization** involves grouping similar activities within units (or departments), each of which takes responsibility for a portion of the overall activity of the organization. The **unity of command** principle states that each subordinate should report to only one boss.

Fayol also addressed **esprit de corps**, which he defined as the unity of sentiment and harmony existing among employees in smoothly functioning organizations. This idea would later reappear in the concept of strong culture popular amongst those adopting the modern perspective in organization theory.

Luther H. Gulick, American administrative theorist (1892–1992)

In 1937 Luther Gulick, Professor of Municipal Science and Administration at Columbia University, co-edited with Lyndall Urwick a collection of articles by various authors known as *Papers on the Science of Administration*. In his own chapter entitled 'Notes on the Theory of

Organization' Gulick wrote that organizational efficiency in government could be increased by dividing work into small, specialized segments, allotting the work to those skilled in that specific segment, and coordinating the work through supervision, clear task definition, instruction, and direction.

Gulick thought that a science of administration could be a means of rationalizing and professionalizing management and public administration and he proposed seven functions for realizing this ambition that were based on Fayol's list of five (planning, organizing, commanding, coordination, and control). Gulick's list, captured by his famous mnemonic **POSDCoRB** includes planning, organizing, staffing, directing, coordinating, reporting, and budgeting.

Chester Barnard, American executive and management theorist (1886–1961)

In Barnard's 1938 book *The Functions of the Executive*, this former president of the New Jersey Bell Telephone Company suggested that managing the informal organization identified by Durkheim was a key function of successful executives. Barnard presented normative advice for developing organizations into **cooperative social systems** by focusing on the **integration** of work efforts through the communication of **goals** and attention to worker **motivation**, ideas that echoed Mary Parker Follett as well as Frederick Taylor.

Postmodernists sometimes blame the significance Barnard attached to the cooperative aspects of organizations for having blinded early organization theorists, especially in the US, to the importance of conflict that Marx suggested was a fundamental aspect of all organizations. Nonetheless, the consideration Barnard gave to issues of value and sentiment in the workplace identified themes that reappear in symbolic research on organizational culture, meaning, and symbolism.

As you should be able to see by now, economic and sociological theories about how industrial management practices affect society blended together with early management and administrative scholarship focused on how best to organize and control workers. The confluence of these ideas cleared the ground on which organization theory would build. The first edifices constructed there took shape within frameworks defined by the modern perspective.

Modern organization theory

The story of modernism, from which the modern perspective derives its name, reaches back to the Enlightenment of eighteenth-century Europe. Also known as the Age of Reason, this historical period was filled with the hope of human progress held dear by those emerging from the Dark Ages. Celebrated Enlightenment thinkers such as René Descartes (France), John Locke (England), and Immanuel Kant (Germany) sought to free humankind from slavery and superstition with the help of reason. They believed that an accumulation of rational knowledge would propel humankind ever forward, an idea that considerably preceded the Enlightenment.

In 1159 John of Salisbury attributed the progressive idea that 'we stand on the shoulders of giants' to twelfth-century French philosopher Bernard of Chartres:

> We frequently know more, not because we have moved ahead by our own natural ability, but because we are supported by the mental strength of others, and possess riches that we have inherited from our forefathers. Bernard of Chartres used to compare us to puny dwarfs perched on the shoulders of giants. He pointed out that we see more and farther than our predecessors, not because we have keener vision or greater height, but because we are lifted up and borne aloft on their gigantic stature.[10]

Kant's ideal of a human race unified by justice and individual freedom provided another source for modernism. Unfortunately, according to postmodern critics, these ideals turned into ideology. This ideology, used in the twentieth century to justify colonialism on the grounds that it would lead to universal improvement of the human condition, led to the ruination of indigenous cultures around the world. To help cultures repel the injustices of modern ambition, some reformulate Kant's modernism as **modernization**—belief in the value of copying Western scientific progress in order to gain its material advantages while resisting its ideology.

Adopting the modern perspective today most often means seeking ways to diagnose and solve organizational problems so as to create competitive advantage and profitability. This perspective recommends that organizations balance internal and external pressures, develop core competencies, and adapt to change, all while optimizing to achieve efficiency in order to minimize the use of scarce resources. Three ideas will offer you a taste of the appeal the modern perspective holds: general systems theory, socio-technical systems, and contingency.

General systems theory

In the 1950s, Austrian born biologist Ludwig von Bertalanffy examined the possibility of theoretical unity among all the sciences. Called **general systems theory**, his ideas were based on the observation that societies contain groups, groups contain individuals, individuals are comprised of organs, organs of cells, cells of molecules, molecules of atoms, and so on. Von Bertalanffy considered each of these phenomena, which have their own dedicated science, to be a **system**, and he sought the laws and principles generic to all of them. One of his followers, American economist Kenneth Boulding, articulated the **hierarchy of systems** you see in Table 2.1, in which he included a transcendental level rising above the social.[11]

Boulding's framework posed a question that has vexed modernist organization theorists ever since: what is the proper **level of analysis** for studying organizations? To find the level at which you should analyze any phenomenon of interest, you define your phenomenon as the focal system, then treat the level above it as the supersystem, and the interacting entities that constitute the level below as its subsystems. To study an organization as a whole, the organization would be your level of analysis, its units or departments become subsystems, and the environment plays the role of supersystem. If you define a department as your focal system, then groups and/or individual members of the department form its subsystems, and the organization becomes the supersystem.

In theory, systems analysis permits you to isolate what is unique about the level where your system resides, which provides the terms of comparison with other systems occupying the

Table 2.1 Boulding's hierarchy of systems

Level	Characteristics	Examples
1. Framework	• labels and terminology • classification systems	anatomies, geographies lists, indexes, catalogs
2. Clockwork	• cyclical events • simple with regular (or regulated) motions • equilibria or states of balance	solar system simple machines (clock or pulley) equilibrium system of economics
3. Control	• self-control • feedback • transmission of information	thermostat homeostasis auto pilot
4. Open (living)	• self-maintenance • throughput of material • energy input • reproduction	cell river flame
5. Genetic	• division of labor (cells) • differentiated and mutually dependent parts • growth follows 'blue-print'	plant
6. Animal	• mobility • self-awareness • specialized sensory receptors • highly developed nervous system • knowledge structures (images)	dog cat elephant whale or dolphin
7. Human	• self-consciousness • capacity to produce, absorb, and interpret symbols • sense of passing time	you me
8. Social organization	• value system • meaning	businesses governments
9. Transcendental	• 'inescapable unknowables'	metaphysics aesthetics

Source: Based on Boulding (1956).

same level. But be wary of the confusion you will create if you shift your focus from one level to another in the middle of an analysis. To see the importance of confronting systems at their own level, consider an automobile. No matter how much you know about each automotive subsystem (e.g., electrical wiring, fuel pump, engine), unless you understand how all the parts relate to each other, it will be difficult to assemble a car in a workable way, or fix one that breaks down.

Systems theory implies that you cannot define a system solely by explaining its subsystems as expressed in the cliché 'the whole is greater than the sum of its parts.' But neither can you ignore the supersystem—the terrain on which an automobile will be driven or local laws governing how it may be driven, for example—even though knowing its context will not tell you what makes a particular automobile unique. Economists and sociologists, for example, both have a tendency to make a black box out of organizations by their attempts to predict organizational outcomes on the basis of a supersystem of historical or societal patterns and trends alone. From their societal level vantage point they cannot see the subsystems that operate inside a particular organization or appreciate its uniqueness relative to other organizations, thus their ability to inform the managers of one organization is limited to knowledge that applies equally to their competitors.

Be aware, too, that explaining social organization implies transcending the limits of human understanding. To address organizations at the level of social organization demands learning to think like an organization. This is something the modern perspective on organization theory promises to deliver, but that its critics regard as impossible. Thus one startling implication of systems theory is that humans will never be smart enough to find solutions to problems that stretch so far over their heads! Meanwhile, the alternative of addressing global problems piecemeal from lower levels of analysis will always fail by being incomplete. So far these critical readings of systems theory have not dissuaded modernists from trying to solve problems defined at levels above the human.

Socio-technical systems theory

In the 1960s, concern for the interaction between two organizational subsystems—social structure and technology—led to the development of socio-technical systems theory. The Tavistock Institute of Human Relations in the UK theorized that any change in technology affects social relationships, attitudes, and feelings about work, which in turn affect the use and use of the technology. Consequently, Tavistock researchers surprisingly recommended finding the best combination of technical and social systems to serve a particular goal, even if it means compromising the optimality of one or both subsystems.

Socio-technical systems theory evolved from the work of Tavistock researchers Eric Trist and Ken Bamforth, who examined the impact of technology on worker productivity, motivation, morale, and stress in a British coalmine in the early 1950s.[12] In the then dominant long-wall method of coal mining, all miners worked independently at stations situated along a conveyor belt that ran the length of the coal face. Miners working in this dangerous and monotonous environment had little influence over their work or the work of others because there was minimal personal contact. Trist and Bamforth noted a number of shortcomings with this method including high stress, absenteeism, labor turnover, low productivity, and constantly laying blame for poor performance on other workers, particularly those working different shifts.

One Durham mine had adopted a short-wall method in which multi-skilled work groups were responsible for the whole cycle of coal mining on their shift. Work groups controlled their own task assignments and managed their productivity. Trist and Bamforth found that although the methods developed by these **autonomous work groups** were technically not as efficient as those designed by engineers, more work was accomplished and workers were much more satisfied with their jobs. In other words, the suboptimization of the technical and social systems they observed paradoxically optimized the performance of the two systems combined, and they believed that this result would generalize to other work settings.

Fred Emery, another Tavistock researcher, mapped the impact of the technical and social systems on the psychological needs of individuals to suggest that production systems be redesigned to allow for teamwork, multi-skilling, and self-management.[13] He stated that organizational performance depends upon each subsystem (or group) being able to adapt to problems and integrate with every other subsystem, and with the whole. Many of Emery's ideas feed the theory of self-organizing systems and complexity theory.

The work of the Tavistock researchers focused attention on a number of humanistic issues: organizations as social systems, the social and psychological consequences of work design, the importance of the work group compared to the individual, and the need for a division of labor that considers increasing rather than decreasing the variety of work skills and tasks. They also suggested that self-managed teams should be the building blocks of organizational design, and that this could reduce the need for hierarchical forms of organizing.

As you can see, the proposals of socio-technical theory were contrary to many of the principles of scientific management, but like Taylor, their proponents intended to offer the means to overcome the disempowering, socially conflicted tendencies Marx identified with capitalism. Tavistock researchers took their work into many organizations around the world including calico mills in India, shipbuilding and fertilizer plants in Norway, an American mining company, and oil refining plants in the UK and Canada. Socio-technical systems theory also underpins newer forms of organization such as matrix structures and networks, and lends support to Follett's ideas about workplace democracy and Durkheim's about informal organization.

Contingency theory

Until around the 1960s normative interests urged organization theorists to use science to discover the best way to organize for optimal performance. But the science was not working, and ambiguous answers regarding the one best way to design an organization caused some to realize that what works best is contingent upon factors like the environment, goals, technology, and people involved. Their approach came to be known as **contingency theory**, which extended the work of both general systems and socio-technical systems theorists.[14] For contingency theorists, effective organizations are those in which multiple subsystems are aligned to maximize performance in a particular situation.

Contingency theorists identify the key contingencies in each situation and try to determine the best fit between them. You can usually identify a contingency approach by the general phrase 'If this situation exists . . . then that should be done.' For example, if a manufacturing organization exists in a highly competitive environment and has to produce a dependable number of widgets each day to precise quality standards—then the production process should be highly standardized, there should be clear output goals, formalized standards and operating procedures, and close supervisory control.

Today contingency theory holds a dominant position in the modern perspective, although the complexity introduced by the specification of more and more contingencies makes it increasingly unwieldy. One reason contingency theories have remained so popular over the years is because they seductively offer recipes for success. But note that contingency theory is typically assessed on criteria of technical rationality and efficiency, which implies a constrained way of thinking compared with those encouraged by other perspectives.

Enter the symbolic perspective

In spite of the fact that the founders of the field held more encompassing perspectives, by the time the modern perspective was established as mainstream within organization theory, most had forgotten that this was not the only way to think about organizations and organizing. But while organization theorists were hard at work exploring the modern perspective and developing its applications, other fields—particularly interpretive sociology, social psychology, and cultural anthropology—began developing an alternative based in subjectivity and interpretation.

In 1928, American sociologist William Isaac Thomas offered an idea that would prove inspirational for the new approach: 'If men define situations as real, they are real in their consequences.'[15] Similarly, the symbolic perspective suggests that, if subjective beliefs affect behavior just as objective reality does, then 'social facts' are just as real, ontologically speaking, as objective facts. American poet Wallace Stevens vividly illustrated the difference between modern and symbolic perspectives with these lines from his 1937 poem *The Man with the Blue Guitar*:

> They said, 'You have a blue guitar,
> You do not play things as they are.'
>
> The man replied, 'Things as they are
> Are changed upon the blue guitar.'[16]

From the symbolic perspective, interpretation, like the blue guitar in the poem, changes reality. This view of reality appealed to organization theorists who had become dissatisfied with the objective boundaries set around notions of organization and organizing. They felt that interpretively nuanced understanding complemented positivistic explanation by bringing different aspects of organization and organizing into view, particularly phenomena involving symbols and meaning that are fraught with interpretation. Social construction, enactment, institutionalization, and culture were among the phenomena they pursued using methods involving ethnographic thick description, narrative, and reflexive theorizing.

Social construction theory

In a small 1966 book entitled *The Social Construction of Reality*, German sociologists Peter Berger and Thomas Luckmann presented the big idea that the social world is negotiated, organized, and constructed by our interpretations of objects, words, actions, and events, all of which are communicated through symbols. The authors claimed that within **socially constructed reality** symbolism—not structure—creates and maintains social order.

Berger and Luckmann proposed that interpretations are based on implicit understandings formed intersubjectively. **Intersubjectivity** is that realm of subjective experience occurring between people that produces a sense of shared history and culture. Locating the process of social construction in intersubjectivity makes this theory of reality a *social* theory; which contrasts with modernist definitions of objective reality as independent of human experience.

According to Berger and Luckmann, social construction operates through three mechanisms: externalization, objectification, and internalization. Learning to use **symbols**—meaning-laden objects, actions, and words—allows humans to externalize meanings. **Externalization** occurs when meaning is carried by and communicated through symbols because in this way meaning travels outside the strictly private realm of one's personal self. Such intersubjectively produced understandings appear to be objectively real but instead are objectifications. **Objectification** involves treating as an object that which is nonobjective. In **internalization** one unquestioningly accepts the intersubjectively externalized and objectified understandings of a social group as reality. Over time, ongoing externalization, objectification, and internalization processes sustain shared social constructions of reality and transfer them to succeeding generations.

You will become aware of social construction processes whenever you are socialized into a new organization. In the first days of **socialization** you are likely to come home exhausted even though you have done nothing that you would normally consider tiring. This is evidence of the intersubjective work you do to internalize the externalized and objectified socially constructed reality of others. Eventually you will find your place, as established ways of doing things in the organization become second nature to you. Ironically, even if you resist being socialized, your identity as a misfit will depend on your acceptance of the socially constructed ways of defining inclusion and exclusion within this particular group.

As you might imagine, socially constructed reality can be complicated to study. It is a local phenomenon that goes on in all directions starting from everywhere and extending both backward and forward in time. This implies that your participation only grants access to a portion of any given socially constructed reality. What you perceive through objectification and externalization appears as reality, but socially constructed reality only exists in interaction with the others with whom you engage. Thus the processes that socially construct reality are distributed amongst its enactors who all the while undergo continuous change.

Change in socially constructed reality occurs when something new is externalized (e.g., by borrowing a symbol from another group or inventing one), objectified through acknowledgment and use, *and* internalized. All of this occurs within the same ongoing social construction processes that produce stability. Stability and change intertwine over time as new symbols become linked to old meanings, and old symbols take on new meanings.

Enactment theory

Following cognitive psychology in defining reality as the product of mental representation, American social psychologist Karl Weick was among the first to treat organization as a cognitive process. He claimed that organizations exist only in the minds of organization members where they appear as cognitive maps of socially constructed reality.[17] Weick used the metaphor of cartography to suggest that humans create mental maps to help them find their way around what they presume exists. He called organizations 'convenient fictions' talked into existence by their members, and argued that organizing should replace organization as the phenomenon of interest to organization theorists. Verbs, not nouns, inspire his theorizing.

Weick combined Berger and Luckmann's externalization and objectification into the cognitive process of **reification** (meaning to make something real). He claimed that by mistaking a cognitive map for the territory, humans reify organization and order their interactions accordingly. Of course human interaction implies a certain amount of cooperation in the mapping process and one of the most compelling implications of Weick's theory is that organizations are products of a collective search for meaning by which experience is ordered. This ordering occurs through the **enactment** of beliefs about what is real. Thus **sensemaking** is not about discovering the truth, but creating it by organizing experience in ways that produce (make) understanding (sense). All of this leaves behind a cognitive perception that can be reified as an organization.

Weick stated in *The Social Psychology of Organizing* that he carefully selected the term 'enactment to emphasize that managers construct, rearrange, single out, and demolish many "objective" features of their surroundings . . . When people act they unrandomize variables, insert vestiges of orderliness, and literally create their own constraints.'[18] Weick and others used enactment theory to understand phenomena like the bandwagon effect in stock trading, years before the global financial crisis of 2008 provided convincing evidence of the power of enactment to transform environments.

According to Weick, a rumor that a trader has a good record for finding hot stocks leads others to mimic the trader's buying behavior. This in turn increases exchange activity around certain stocks, which often raises their value (i.e., making them hot), thus supporting the trader's reputation. Confirmation of belief in the trader encourages further mimicry, attracting more buyers and further enhancing certain stock prices, at least for a time. As Weick stated: 'The fact that a bandwagon effect drove up share prices, and not the quality of the stock, suggests a powerful pathway for enactment in the investment community.'[19] It also shows how enactment, sensemaking, and social construction combine to explain behavior that is inexplicable from the purely objective and rational perspective of modern organization theory.

Institutions and institutionalization

In 1949 American sociologist Philip Selznick wrote about the Tennessee Valley Authority (TVA). The US government funded the TVA to build dams to produce electricity and control flooding in the Tennessee River Valley, an important agricultural region. Additionally the project promised to protect forests, develop recreational areas, and aid local farmers.

Selznick's *TVA and the Grass Roots: A Study in the Sociology of Formal Organization* described how the TVA, promoted as a grass roots project conducted to benefit society, had been co-opted by various interests including land grant colleges, county extension agents, politicians, and business leaders. He claimed that **co-optation** had transformed the organization from an efficient distributor of resources and coordinator of tasks into a distinctive American institution. In becoming institutionalized, however, it had ceased serving the purposes for which it had been created.

In his 1957 *Leadership in Administration* Selznick explained the paradox of institutional legitimacy he had witnessed at the TVA by distinguishing organization and institution on the basis of their values. For Selznick, an organization is a rational tool for achieving economic efficiency, such that, if another organization offers greater efficiency, it will replace the first one. Organizations therefore should be dispensable. What then explains the perpetuity of non-rational organizations like the TVA? Selznick offered the concept of institutionalization as his answer, claiming that institutions make themselves appear indispensable by asserting their value to society, something the TVA did in the US by linking itself to the idea of grass-roots democracy, in spite of the fact that its behavior diverged significantly from the expectations set by this claim to legitimacy.

As American sociologists John Meyer and Brian Rowan later explained, **institutionalization** presents a myth that hides an organization's behavior from public view and allows co-optation of resources to go undetected for long periods of time. Some regard the claim by big banks of being 'too big to fail' as the most recent example of the power of an institutional myth to protect inefficient or even malfeasant organizational behavior.

The idea of invoking myths and values to create institutional legitimacy created interest in the role culture plays in organizations.[20] After all, myths and values are the stuff of culture. But most organizational theorists who were inspired by the symbolic aspects of Selznick's institutionalism were less interested in institutionalization as the co-optation of societal values than they were in phenomena like organizational cultures. Thus some turned from Selznick to cultural anthropology for their inspiration.

Culture

The American cultural anthropologist Clifford Geertz defined **culture** by invoking none other than Max Weber, the German sociologist many modernists turned to for their own legitimacy. In the opening pages of his 1973 book *The Interpretation of Culture* Geertz famously aligned himself with Weber:

> Believing, with Max Weber, that man is an animal suspended in webs of significance he himself has spun, I take culture to be those webs, and the analysis of it to be therefore not an experimental science in search of law but an interpretive one in search of meaning.[21]

Having co-opted Weber, Geertz firmly staked his claims within the symbolic perspective and his approach to culture attracted a host of young organizational scholars looking for alternatives to the modern perspective. Geertz's method of thick description introduced them to ethnography, or at least to his symbolic variant of it.

Thick description exposes symbolic meaning lurking beneath the surface of everyday events to show how culture works. A passage from one of Geertz's ethnographies will give you a feel for his method. Listen as Geertz explains how he and his wife, recently arrived in Bali to conduct ethnographic research, gained acceptance by the normally aloof Balinese, who typically treat strangers as invisible. The Geertz's were no exception, until:

> ten days or so after our arrival, a large cockfight was held in the public square to raise money for a new school. . . . Of course, like drinking during Prohibition or, today, smoking marihuana, cockfights, being a part of 'The Balinese Way of Life,' nonetheless go on happening, and wit

extraordinary frequency. And, as with Prohibition or marihuana, from time to time the police (who, in 1958 at least, were almost all not Balinese but Javanese) feel called upon to make a raid, confiscate the cocks and spurs, fine a few people, and even now and then expose some of them in the tropical sun for a day as object lessons which never, somehow, get learned, even though occasionally, quite occasionally, the object dies.

As a result, the fights are usually held in a secluded corner of a village in semisecrecy, a fact which tends to slow the action a little—not very much, but the Balinese do not care to have it slowed at all. In this case, however, perhaps because they were raising money for a school that the government was unable to give them, perhaps because raids had been few recently, perhaps, as I gathered from subsequent discussion, there was a notion that the necessary bribes had been paid, they thought they could take a chance on the central square and draw a larger and more enthusiastic crowd without attracting the attention of the law.

They were wrong. In the midst of the third match, with hundreds of people, including, still transparent, myself and my wife, fused into a single body around the ring, a superorganism in the literal sense, a truck full of policemen armed with machine guns roared up. Amid great screeching cries of 'pulisi! pulisi!' from the crowd, the policemen jumped out, and springing into the center of the ring, began to swing their guns around like gangsters in a motion picture, though not going so far as actually to fire them. The superorganism came instantly apart as its components scattered in all directions. People raced down the road, disappeared headfirst over walls, scrambled under platforms, folded themselves behind wicker screens, scuttled up coconut trees. Cocks armed with steel spurs sharp enough to cut off a finger or run a hole through a foot were running wildly around. Everything was dust and panic.

On the established anthropological principle, 'When in Rome', my wife and I decided, only slightly less instantaneously than everyone else, that the thing to do was run too. We ran down the main village street, northward, away from where we were living, for we were on that side of the ring. About halfway down another fugitive ducked suddenly into a compound—his own, it turned out—and we, seeing nothing ahead of us but rice fields, open country, and a very high volcano, followed him. As the three of us came tumbling into the courtyard, his wife, who had apparently been through this sort of thing before, whipped out a table, a tablecloth, three chairs, and three cups of tea, and we all, without any explicit communication whatsoever, sat down, commenced to sip tea, and sought to compose ourselves.

A few moments later, one of the policemen marched importantly into the yard, looking for the village chief. (The chief had not only been at the fight, he had arranged it. When the truck drove up he ran to the river, stripped off his sarong, and plunged in so he could say, when at length they found him sitting there pouring water over his head, that he had been away bathing when the whole affair had occurred and was ignorant of it. They did not believe him and fined him three hundred rupiah, which the village raised collectively.) Seeing me and my wife, 'White Men', there in the yard, the policeman performed a classic double take. When he found his voice again he asked, approximately, what in the devil did we think we were doing there. Our host of five minutes leaped instantly to our defense, producing an impassioned description of who and what we were, so detailed and so accurate that it was my turn, having barely communicated with a living human being save my landlord and the village chief for more than a week, to be astonished. We had a perfect right to be there, he said, looking the Javanese upstart in the eye. We were American professors; the government had cleared us; we were there to study culture; we were going to write a book to tell Americans about Bali. And we had been there drinking tea and talking about cultural matters all afternoon and did not know anything about any cockfight. Moreover, we had not seen the village chief all day; he must have gone to town. The policemen retreated in rather total disarray. And, after a decent interval, bewildered but relieved to have survived and stayed out of jail, so did we.

The next morning the village was a completely different world for us. Not only were we no longer invisible, we were suddenly the center of all attention, the object of a great outpouring of warmth, interest, and most especially, amusement. Everyone in the village knew we had fled like everyone else. They asked us about it again and again (I must have told the story, small detail by small detail, fifty times by the end of the day), gently, affectionately, but quite insistently teasing us: 'Why didn't you just stand there and tell the police who you were?' 'Why didn't you just say you were only watching and not betting?' 'Were you really afraid of those little guns?' As always, kinesthetically minded and even when fleeing for their lives (or, as happened eight years later, surrendering them), the world's most poised people, they gleefully mimicked, also over and over again, our graceless style of running and what they claimed were our panic-stricken facial expressions. But above all, everyone was extremely pleased and even more surprised that we had not simply 'pulled out our papers' (they knew about those too) and asserted our Distinguished Visitor status, but had instead demonstrated our solidarity with what were now our covillagers. (What we had actually demonstrated was our cowardice, but there is fellowship in that too.) Even the Brahmana priest, an old, grave, halfway-to-heaven type who because of its associations with the underworld would never be involved, even distantly, in a cockfight, and was difficult to approach even to other Balinese, had us called into his courtyard to ask us about what had happened, chuckling happily at the sheer extraordinariness of it all.

In Bali, to be teased is to be accepted. It was the turning point so far as our relationship to the community was concerned, and we were quite literally 'in'. The whole village opened up to us, probably more than it ever would have otherwise (I might actually never have gotten to that priest, and our accidental host became one of my best informants), and certainly very much faster. Getting caught, or almost caught, in a vice raid is perhaps not a very generalizable recipe for achieving that mysterious necessity of anthropological field work, rapport, but for me it worked very well.[22]

Geertz's text illustrates the basics of thick description: contextualizing, descriptive detail, documentation of how unexpected events and other surprises made him feel, sources quoted verbatim, presenting the interpretations provided by cultural members, and exposing the contrasts between outsiders' assumptions and beliefs and those of cultural members. But in addition to exemplifying his method and providing legitimacy to the symbolic perspective, Geertz also showed social scientists how much *fun* **storytelling** could be.

Narrative and reflexivity

Geertz's facility with language and his personal touch, one of the hallmarks of his use of subjective epistemology, attracted attention to **narrative** in writing by offering a sharp contrast between the lively style of his prose and the drier one that the objectivism of the modern perspective mandates. The contrast called attention to the ways researchers write, and one of the first to write about writing in organization theory was American sociologist John Van Maanen. In his 1988 Book *Tales of the Field* Van Maanen suggested that all social science writing is storytelling. According to him storytelling comes in realist, confessional, and impressionist styles.

Realist tales, typical of those who adopt the modern perspective, are written as objective reports of social facts that claim to know what really goes on in organizations. Calling them 'realist' encourages us to see how modernist researchers rhetorically construct subjective experience as objective fact, while hiding their identity as researcher/narrator by never mentioning themselves. Realist tales stand in stark contrast to **confessional tales**, in which the author is very much present as she or he confesses prejudices and mistakes made along the way. **Impressionist tales** offer an even more extreme departure from realist tales. These highly personal accounts put readers in the context of the events being related, thereby allowing them to vicariously appreciate the teller's experiences, as Geertz did with his Balinese cockfight story that contains confessional elements as well.

American anthropologists James Clifford and George Marcus moved the discussion of writing closer to postmodernism in their 1986 book *Writing Culture: The Poetics and Politics of Ethnography*. They claimed that all research accounts are partial fictions because they are products of the situated perspectives of their authors. **Situated perspective** means that the interpretive community in which a researcher claims membership has particular interests and ways of talking that influence what they describe and how they interpret phenomena. For example, you may study an organization using ideas found in this book, but organizational members may not share your theories or use your vocabulary.

So who is right? Whenever someone imposes their worldview on others, which postmodern critics accuse modernists of doing, you have the conditions for hegemony and totalitarianism. **Reflexivity** comes to the rescue; being reflexive in a research context means asking questions such as: What assumptions underlie my choices of what to study and my research methodology? How do these assumptions influence how I define phenomena and carry out my research? What impact does this have on the knowledge claims I make and on those I study? A reflexive researcher or manager recognizes that socially constructed realities are incomplete and negotiated accounts open to multiple interpretations and meanings.

Using ideas grounded in reflexive appreciation for the tenuous state of 'reality' the postmodern perspective took flight.

Postmodern influences

After legitimating themselves for decades with modernist claims of bringing progress to primitive peoples, colonial governments around the world faced growing demands from the colonized for self-determination. Anthropologists, whose government grants had allowed them to study the colonies, found themselves in the line of fire. They stood accused of serving their benefactors rather than the colonized. In the early 1980s, when colonialism collapsed, it nearly took cultural anthropology down with it.

Anthropology's **crisis of representation** provoked by the collapse of colonialism centered on the contested belief that anthropological methods accurately represent culture.[23] The most vocal critics insisted that the 'native' view had been misrepresented and they wanted to know by what right anthropologists could claim greater authority than that of the natives themselves.[24] A famous photograph illustrates the controversy; it shows a group of natives lined up outside a tent. Inside, Malinowski, one of cultural anthropology's founders, sits at a small table intently typing his field notes. Absorbed by the task of recording his observations, he fails to observe his subjects observing him! The photograph ironically subverts the modernist view of anthropology by reversing the relationship between observer and observed.

Although difficult to find points of agreement among postmodernists, they all in various ways like to subvert modernist definitions of reality like Malinowski's photograph does. This explains why many people experience postmodernism as critical, though as the photo shows, it can also be playful and creative in the artistry and imagination it licenses. Overturning the foundational assumptions of modernism often leads to charges of nihilism, though the intent most often claimed is to emancipate humankind from totalizing mindsets and hegemonic practices. Ironically postmodernism displays its own brand of hegemony when it invents new rules for conduct that superimpose postmodern morality on its modern targets.

Those who adopt the postmodernist perspective, like those who favor the symbolic, do not believe in objectively definable reality. Epistemologically speaking, for them knowing is at best a tenuous affair, undergoing incessant revision. At worst it is impossible, a chimera, or an outright con. Based on ideas borrowed from poststructural philosophy and literary theory, postmodernists believe that, since language cannot fix meaning, which is always and everywhere adrift, we should stop searching for truth and be suspicious of all knowledge claims. These ideas converged with those promoted by the Frankfurt School critical philosophers Theodor Adorno, Max Horkheimer, and Herbert Marcuse in post-World War II Germany. Ideas from these quite divergent strands were loosely woven into the postmodern perspective of organization theory. Some of them are outlined here, beginning with the most critical.

The Enlightenment Project, the Progress Myth, and Grand Narrative

Postmodernists ironically refer to modernist ambitions to replace superstition with reason as the **Enlightenment Project**. Their irony points to the use of Enlightenment values and ideals to legitimize the imposition of Western ideology on the rest of the world (its project). Following the lead of vocal critics of these practices, the idea of progress became a popular target.

By 1932 English physician Montague David Eder had already demonstrated his resistance to modern faith in continuous human improvement by referring to progress as a myth.[25] According to postmodernists, who refer to his idea as the **Progress Myth**, belief in progress justifies abuses of power, such as those that took place under colonial rule. Calling progress a myth is meant to reveal its character as dogma sustained by propaganda, rather than the product of scientific truth validated by objective evidence, as modernists claim. Postmodern methods deny the possibility of neutrality asserted by modernists to be the hallmark of objective explanation. Instead they call on all who make knowledge claims to reflect on the context of their knowledge-making efforts and on the role played in unleashing and directing the power that knowledge conveys.

Taking the critical view further, in *The Postmodern Condition* French philosopher and literary theorist Jean Francoise Lyotard accused the Enlightenment Project and the Progress Myth of supporting a **Grand Narrative**, one that is intellectually and politically totalitarian because it provides the storyline modernists use to justify devotion to reason on the grounds that it brings progress, creates wealth, makes us free, and reveals Truth. Be sure to take note of the capital letters postmodernists employ to emphasize the self-asserted power of the modernist ideas they point to.

In Lyotard's view, knowledge and society are closely linked because institutions such as education, business, and government are created on the basis of expert knowledge, which in turn legitimates particular ways of thinking and acting. For example, universities expound particular forms of knowledge (notably scientific), and businesses embrace prevailing norms of management (most often to do with maximizing profit), to which students and employees are expected to conform. Thus the Grand Narrative of modernism masks the ambition to create knowledge and institutions that promote the interests of some over those of unsuspecting others.

Language and language games

The modernist view of language, in evidence still today, contends that language mirrors reality; words carry their particular meanings because of some essential link between words, meanings, and things. Swiss linguist Ferdinand de Saussure overturned this view with his revolutionary theory of language.[26]

In Saussure's theory, there is no natural or necessary connection between words (as **signifiers**) and the concepts of the things to which they refer (that which is **signified**), their relationship is arbitrary. For example, consider the many words in use that signify a feathered flying creature. English uses *bird*, Danish offers *fugl*, French *oiseau*, and so on. According to Saussure, the meaning of a word is given by its position relative to other words within the structure of language. This assumption implies that a word's meaning will shift whenever it meets a new word.

Coupling the arbitrariness of language with the ever-shifting meaning of words, implies that the structure supporting language is unstable, an idea that requires moving one's orientation from the pole of stability to that of change. This idea affected other disciplines than linguistics and literary theory due to structuralism in the social sciences having emerged in part from the idea that social structures follow the same laws that govern language. Saussure's theory raised mind-altering questions: Can there be a structure of language, or of anything else for that matter, in light of the instability of language? Denying structure has the power to stabilize society ushered poststructuralism into literary theory and combined Saussure's theory with ideas brewing in postmodernism.

Saussure's idea that the structure of language (langue, in French) varies with the flow of relationships between words in use (parole), inspired German philosopher Ludwig Wittgenstein's metaphor of **language games**.[27] Just as soccer and chess have rules of play that guide behavior, the rules of language vary by the communities that employ them. The way you use language and how you respond to the statements of others differs depending on the language game you engage. For example, adopting the modern, symbolic, or postmodern perspective in organization theory places you in a different language game that promotes different ideas and ways of theorizing organizations, not to mention determines the journals in which you will find various ideas being discussed and the universities that employ their proponents. Adhering to one language game can make it difficult to communicate with those from another community, and unreflectively switching between language games can create considerable confusion.

In important respects, one opportunity you face in studying organization theory is to learn several different language games at once. Learning how language games work and how to move comfortably between them will serve you well when working in cross-functional teams; or across boundaries created by other communities you join or encounter. But you should be aware of the politics that arise among different communities and the effects of power implicit in them.

Truth claims, power/knowledge, and giving voice

Following Wittgenstein's notion of language games, Lyotard reinterpreted scientific facts as agreements within communities of scientists to regard certain claims as true. He concluded that there can be no truth, only **truth claims**. Those given the right to decide which truth claims will be honored have the ability to dominate a community and its language game. However, Lyotard suggested that truth claims collapse when other, more widely accepted claims arise, or when a different community is engaged. In this view, no truth can last for long. If the current distribution of power in a community determines the body of knowledge it holds as truth, when the distribution of power changes, truth shifts.[28] Seen in this light, resistance to change by the currently powerful can be understood in terms of desire to maintain the truth value of one's own claims.

Once you accept the proposition that power is involved in knowledge creation, you can easily understand Lyotard's concern about the uses of power to silence or eliminate someone from a community. He regarded the silencing of opposition as an act of totalitarianism pointing out that this also occurs whenever a community has no procedures for presenting or engaging with whatever is different. He claimed that if different views and ideas are silenced, there can be no new ways for a community to think or act; therefore, **giving voice to silence** is an antidote to totalitarianism.

The belief that free speech repels totalitarianism is one reason why so many critical theorists and some postmodernists support democracy and advocate for pluralism.[29] Yet many postmodernists argue that, in forming a shared ambition to overturn totalitarian tendencies, you are in danger of creating an alternative Grand Narrative that only privileges a different group rather than overthrowing privilege itself. Consequently they call for the creation of multiple texts and toleration of all differing interpretations of them as a path to liberation.

Discourse and discursive practices

Lyotard's notions about silencing opposition echo through the work of French philosopher and social theorist Michel Foucault who examined the effects of power exercised through **normativity**. Foucault argued that approved knowledge is a primary tool for the exercise of power because deciding who can speak and what can be said determines what is regarded as normal behavior.[30] Those who do not conform are considered abnormal, deviant troublemakers who must be excluded, disciplined, or institutionalized.

Foucault studied the history of psychiatric hospitals and prisons to investigate how psychiatry and social work established conceptual categories of insanity and delinquency into which people were sorted for institutional treatment. He claimed that by making insanity and delinquency into problems that society needed to address, psychiatrists and social workers established their own powerful social positions from which they could incarcerate or otherwise control certain people in order to protect society from them. Foucault went on to similarly interrogate the histories of literary criticism, psychology, psychoanalysis, sociology, anthropology, criminology, political science, and economics. He concluded from these studies that modern Western societies have delegated to the human sciences the authority to determine social norms.[31]

In the process of raising and answering questions about what is normal, Foucault argued, the human sciences forged a link between power and knowledge. Because the knowledge academic disciplines produce is used to categorize, control, and in some cases incarcerate the least powerful members of society, knowledge and power are really the same; we should not think of them as two things, but as one.

Power/knowledge is exercised through practices that arise in discourse to regulate what will be perceived as normal. According to Foucault, **discursive practices** derive from language such as that found in academic jargon or in the technical terminology used in industry or the many branches of government. They are closely related to Wittgenstein's language games, though they imply a stronger normative position because, as Foucault and others point out, without knowledge of discursive practices, the powerless cannot defend themselves.

The concept of **discourse** emerged from poststructuralist linguistics. It is a mindset, a cultural worldview, and/or an institutionalized logic that provides the, always partial, perspective of a particular group.[32] For Foucault discourses were constructed historically according to the relationships of power existing within a society at a particular point in time. Those who exercised power allowed some things to be said, written, and thought, but not others and these controlled practices gave rise to the discourse that guides meaning making within its boundaries.

One implication of discourse theory is that, when people engage a discourse, their identity adapts to its discursive formations. In other words, your identity is an effect of your community's use of language. To illustrate, you make self-references when you speak ('I did this or that'), and these, coupled with what others say about you ('you are lazy') and about others ('she is brilliant'), give you the idea that you exist by forging your identity, even though the impressions these practices leave on you and others are only referential effects of language.

By this reasoning Foucault arrived at his contentious idea that individuality only appeared in modern times by our becoming self-reflexive, and will disappear again 'like a face drawn in the sand' if ever we stop talking about ourselves.[33] Thus Foucault presented a highly personalized corollary to German philosopher Martin Heidegger's proposition: 'It is in the saying it comes to pass that the world is made to appear.' According to Foucault, by not referring to ourselves, 'man' will disappear from the discourses defining reality, just as suddenly as he appeared in an earlier time.

To give you an organizational sense of the **disappearance of man**, consider the importance attached to the customer within the mainstream management discourse.[34] Where once employees were encouraged to attend to the wishes of their managers, a new corporate discourse encourages them to attend to customers, thereby repositioning or **decentering** the manager within their linguistically and discursively forged reality. Could this linguistic move account for recent delayering of management with the legions of managerial redundancies it brought about in corporations?

Similarly, in the field of public administration, citizens have recently taken center stage away from administrators who traditionally avoided responding to citizen needs by using bureaucratic rules and processes as reasons why something could not be done. In theory at least, moving citizens to the discursive center renders concerns over administrative procedures less powerful and allows the discussion to shift from why something cannot be done to how to do it. According to this post-bureaucratic perspective, the once dominant identity of administrator will soon disappear from governance conversations, and administrative power will be effectively decentered.[35]

Focusing on the repressed or hidden elements of a discourse changes existing discursive practices and thereby alters the construction and maintenance of established mindsets. For example, modern discursive practices in the field of history dismiss the use of novels, myths, and diaries as filled with fiction, superstition, and subjective bias. New historians, however, believe that because they are embedded in the times in which they were written, fiction, myth, and autobiography give important historical evidence.[36] The work of the new historians alters the discursive practices of history when it forges links between its discourse and that of literature thereby altering the power relations between these two fields and shifting their trajectories.

Deconstruction, différance

Algerian born, French poststructuralist philosopher Jacques Derrida became fascinated by the poststructuralist idea that language has no fixed meaning.[37] As Saussure demonstrated, the meaning of a particular set of words depends upon the context of other words to which it is related in a particular discourse. On this basis Derrida claimed that, if contexts are interchangeable, then no context can claim to be more appropriate than another; therefore one meaning cannot possibly be correct, and you need only wait for a new context to form in order for another meaning to appear. An important implication of Derrida's theory is that, by changing the context surrounding a text (a set of symbols) you can change its meaning. This idea underlies Derrida's practice of deconstruction.

Deconstruction is a way of reading and then rereading texts in the contexts of different discourses in order to expose their potential for multiple interpretations and thereby destabilize and undermine their authority to indicate or make particular meanings. Derrida concluded from deconstruction that meaning forever eludes us because texts are always situated within ever changing historical, cultural, political, and institutional contexts. Most consequentially for postmodernism, Derrida argued that truth and knowledge are as unstable as any other linguistic and discursive constructions. The purpose of deconstructing a text lies not in finding ultimate or essential meaning, but is to reveal a text's assumptions, contradictions, and exclusions in order to show that no text can mean what it says, a profoundly reorienting assertion that captures the non-essentialism of the postmodern perspective.

Deconstruction makes the central features of constructed reality visible and thereby liberates us from their influence on our ways of thinking and acting. Saussure suggested that language is structured by the use of words, which is ever shifting. Derrida elaborated this idea by claiming that binary or dichotomous thinking is a structural underpinning of the way modernists use language. This allowed him to deconstruct the central concepts of modernist discourse (e.g., monarch/subject, master/slave, boss/subordinate) to show how modernists linguistically and discursively construct centers and peripheries within societies and organizations by privileging one set of terms (monarch, master, boss) over others (subject, slave, subordinate). Thus our use of language creates categories, names centers, draws boundaries, expresses social power, and reproduces or changes reality.

Racism (white at the center, non-white on the periphery), for example, has been shown to lead to disparities in income, housing, health care, and education, with whites systematically enjoying more of these benefits than non-whites. Deconstructive analysis provides an explanation of these and other effects of racism by pointing out that whiteness has been made a focal center within discourse, but that its centrality depends upon maintaining the difference between white and non-white. Thus the meaning of whiteness provided by contrasts with non-whiteness determines the value of all other races by their proximity to the white center that, in turn, justifies racial inequality within any discursive community that employs this terminology.[38]

While developing deconstruction, Derrida invoked the term **différance**—a play on the French verb *differer* that means both to differ and to defer.[39] Derrida argued that a word derives its meaning from differences with its opposite (e.g., truth/falsehood, good/bad, male/female), thus even when you use only one term in a binary, you invoke its opposite. The absent opposite defers to its present partner. So, for example, when modernist organization theorists talk about organization they implicitly draw meaning from the difference between organization and disorganization or chaos. This analysis reveals that at least part of the value modernists place on organizations and organizing derives from the ability of such meaning-laden concepts to keep disorganization at bay. You can see how such thinking would serve to justify modernist organization theory from within the discourse this perspective supports, and why modernists are so resistant to travelling outside their discourse.

In regard to *différance* Derrida further proposed that the meaning of any word points to other meanings because, as you try to explain the meaning of one word, you replace it with other words that defer to still other words, and so on. By speaking or writing, you move further and further away from the original concept you are addressing because the processes of differing and deferring continue. Thus the concept of *différance* shows how meaning becomes ever more diffuse and distant from its starting point as it travels across time and space. It also shows why postmodernists regard meaning as fluid.

Simulacra and hyperreality

In the Wachowski brothers' film *The Matrix* we see a world taken over by artificial intelligence, where machines breed and keep humans in pods as power sources for the computer that controls human thought and thereby produces images of realities that no longer exist. The humans think they live normal lives, but instead a computer program, The Matrix, simulates the world of the late twentieth century, a world that is now a nuclear wasteland.

The film's central character, symbolically named Neo, takes a pill that allows him to awaken from this computer-simulated dream. In order to survive and rescue others from the treachery of the machines, he has to move between the post-nuclear reality, where he and a small band of other awakened humans do battle with the machines, and the pre-nuclear simulation. In the simulation, Neo fights computer-enhanced images of superhuman bureaucrats using powers derived from his knowledge that the world is simulated; denying the power of the simulation to persuade him of its existence gives Neo the freedom and strength to resist the simulated bureaucrats and destroy the computer program behind it all.

The confusion of the real and the simulated portrayed in *The Matrix* is a central theme of French social philosopher Jean Baudrillard, an early advocate of postmodernism. In *Simulacra and Simulation*, Baudrillard argued that the image has passed through a progression of successive phases that make it increasingly impossible to talk about what is real. These stages, according to Baudrillard, began with images that reflect reality, which turned into images that mask reality, then images that mask the absence of reality, ending in images bearing no relation to reality whatsoever. In Baudrillard's terms the image in postmodern times ceased even being a simulation of reality and became a **simulacrum**, that is, a totally imagined reality.[40]

According to Baudrillard, in pre-modern times a simulation was assumed to represent reality, just as a map was assumed to represent the physical geography it described. However, the distinction between reality and the image began breaking down in modern times when mass production led to the proliferation of copies of originals ranging from reproductions of artwork to designer fashion knock-offs. People discovered that it was possible for images to mask reality or even to hide the absence of reality, and so the great con began. For example, in a bow to conceptual art, British painter David Hockney made artworks directly on a photocopy machine; his images looked like copies of original artworks but there were no originals, only copies!

The postmodern age is marked by endless simulations and contortions of meaning such as Hockney's 'original copies.' So-called reality TV similarly produces fabrications that have no relation to any reality but the show's own pretensions. Disneyland provides another instance where, as Baudrillard pointed out, real actors portray cartoon characters and guests take real riverboat rides down a fake Mississippi. In simulacra there is no deep meaning or underlying structure hidden beneath the surface on which such images play. Simulacra show that concepts like meaning and structure, reality and fabrication, copy and original, can be overthrown by postmodern thinking.

Baudrillard claimed that in postmodernism opposing poles, such as reality/image, fact/fantasy, subject/object, public/private, and so on, implode to create **hyperreality** where 'illusion is no longer possible, because the real is no longer possible.'[41] In the hyperreal we immerse in simulation, nostalgically trying to reproduce what we thought was real, but which was never anything but images. According to Baudrillard, simulacra, like reality TV, form the plural contexts of our lives.

Baudrillard claimed that Disneyland is the ideal simulacrum because it creates the architecture, community, and traditional family values of a Main Street America that never existed.[42] Although we may think Disneyland is imaginary (just a performance) and the rest of the world is real, it is the rest of the world that is an ongoing performance through which we strive to live up to the images fed to us by Disneyland, the media, government, businesses, and other modern institutions. Just as *The Matrix* portrayed a simulation within which humans live, we create our lives using images to define ourselves to ourselves.

While Baudrillard's ideas might at first seem unrelated to organization theory, you get a sense of hyperreality when you consider how images floating around us every day are produced by the organizations they serve. For example, most consumer-oriented businesses count on our willingness to buy products based on images they project through seductive brands and advertising. Or consider how, for a time at least, Enron managed to hide billions of dollars in debt and operating losses by creating fake partnerships (with names inspired by the film *Star Wars*), misleadingly complex accounting schemes, and nonexistent departments. When Wall Street analysts visited Enron in 1998 to assess its credit rating, 75 people relocated to an empty floor and a fake trading room where they pretended to buy and sell energy contracts. This simulacrum was staged with ringing phones and family photos on desks—a performance used unethically to support Enron's falsely inflated stock price.[43] Although such sting operations have occurred throughout history, the difference now is that they are becoming the rule rather than the exception and this has the potential to push humanity across a new threshold.

Summary

Academic contributors to the prehistory of the field came from different disciplines, primarily political science, economics, and sociology, while other contributors were engineers, executives, or consultants to the new industrial organizations appearing at the time organization theory was founded and each of its perspectives introduced. Their ideas combined to forge a starting point and they continue to serve by echoing through the perspectives of organization theory, presented here as a brief history.

The normative ambitions of organization theory were present in its infancy and remain strong today in concerns to find practical applications of theory from all perspectives, though each perspective encourages different normative responses. The modern perspective provides explanations that afford the analytical frameworks, predictive models, and principles for organizing that managers use to diagnose problems and design organizations. Those who adopt the symbolic perspective prefer to study how we construct organizational realities via processes of interpretation, the applications of which lead managers to imagine their main responsibility as the management of symbols and meaning. Taking a postmodern perspective means giving up the structures and social constructions favored by modern explanation and symbolic understanding, to focus instead on flux and change as modeled by the structures of language in use, which reveal the power relations from which humans should seek liberation.

Several contrasts between the main concerns and mindsets offered by modern, symbolic, and postmodern perspectives are presented in Table 2.2.

The ideas you encountered as this brief history unfolded provide a basic vocabulary for tackling Part II of this book. You may want to come back to this material from time to time as you flesh out your knowledge with the ideas presented in the following chapters. Returning to these framing ideas will continue to challenge and develop your understanding of concepts, theories, and theoretical perspectives and thereby help you to remake organization theory to serve your own purposes, which I hope will in turn be challenged and developed by organization theory.

Table 2.2 Comparison of the three perspectives

	Modern	Symbolic	Postmodern
Reality is a	Pre-existing unity	Socially constructed diversity	Constantly shifting and fluid plurality
Reality is recognized via	Convergence	Coherence	Incoherence Fragmentation
Knowledge is	Universal	Particular	Provisional
Knowledge is developed through	Facts Information	Meaning Interpretation	Denial Deconstruction
Model for human relationships	Hierarchy	Community	Self-determination
Overarching goal	Prediction Control	Understanding Tolerance	Appreciation Liberation

Key terms

division of labor

differentiation

specialization

social structure

theory of capital

efficiency

social conflict

profitability

labor

commodification

exploitation

alienation

managerial control

hierarchy

interdependence

social structure

quantitative research methods

informal organization

formal organization

authority structure

    traditional authority

    charismatic authority

    rational-legal authority

bureaucracy

rationality

    formal

    substantive

iron cage

scientific management

    Taylorism

    Fordism

rationalization

workplace democracy

nonhierarchical networks

administrative principles

    span of control

    routine

    delegation

    unity of command

esprit de corps

POSDCoRB

cooperative social systems

integration

goals

motivation

The modern perspective

modernization

general systems theory

   system

   subsystem

   supersystem

hierarchy of systems

level of analysis

socio-technical systems theory

contingency theory

The symbolic perspective

socially constructed reality

intersubjectivity

externalization

objectification

internalization

socialization

reification

enactment

sensemaking

co-optation

institutionalization

culture

thick description

storytelling

narrative tales

   realist tales

   confessional tales

   impressionist tales

   situated perspective

   reflexivity

The postmodern perspective

crisis of representation

critical postmodernism

   Enlightenment Project

   Progress Myth

   Grand Narrative

poststructuralism

   signifier and signified

   language games

   truth claims

   giving voice to silence

   normativity

   power/knowledge

   discursive practices

   discourse

   disappearance of man

   decentering

   deconstruction

   différance

   simulacrum

   Hyperreality

Endnotes

1. For discussions of organization theory as the product of the tension between sociological theory and management practice, see Perrow (1973) and Barley and Kunda (1992).
2. C. S. George, Jr. (1968) observed that the division of labor and other managerial practices were in use from the time of the Egyptians. He speculates that they were probably a feature of prehistoric life as well.
3. From A. Smith, *An Inquiry into the Nature and Causes of the Wealth of Nations*, Vol. 1, ed. R. H. Campbell and A. S. Skinner, W. B. Todd (textual edn.) (Oxford: Clarendon Press, 1976), 14–16.
4. For a review of Marx's influence on organization theory, see Adler (2009).

5. The tension between economic and humanistic interests in organization theory has been discussed by Wren (1987); Bernard (1988); Boje and Winsor (1993); Steingard (1993); O'Connor (1996).

6. Weber (1946: 228).

7. For a thorough discussion of Weber's contributions to the symbolic perspective, see Schroeder (1992).

8. It is uncertain where the term originated, but Aglietta used 'Fordism' in 1979 in *A Theory of Capitalist Regulation* (London: Verso).

9. Cited in Graham (1995: 56).

10. Cited in Calinescu (1987: 15). The phrase 'on the shoulders of giants' was used as the title of an influential text by American sociologist Robert Merton (1965) that presented the case for integrating theory and practice.

11. Boulding (1956).

12. Trist and Bamforth (1951). See also Emery and Trist (1981).

13. For example, see Emery (1969).

14. See Donaldson (1985) for a review and defense of contingency theory.

15. Thomas and Thomas (1928: 572).

16. Stevens (1937), http://writing.upenn.edu/~afilreis/88v/blueguitar.html

17. Weick (1995); Weick and Bougon (1986).

18. Weick (1979 [1969]: 243; 1995: 30–31).

19. Weick (2003); see also Mitch Abolafia and Martin Kilduff (1988), who described attempts to corner the silver market in the 1980s using enactment theory.

20. Gagliardi (2005).

21. Geertz (1973: 5).

22. Geertz (1973: 413–16). Used with permission of the author.

23. See Clifford and Marcus (1986).

24. Stocking (1983).

25. Eder, Montague David (1932) The myth of progress. *The British Journal of Medical Psychology*, Vol. XII: 1.

26. Saussure (1959).

27. Wittgenstein (1965).

28. Lyotard (1983).

29. For example, see Calas and Smircich (1991).

30. Foucault (1977).

31. Foucault (1973).

32. Moran (2002: 14).

33. Foucault (1970: xxiii), cited in Moran (2002: 135–36).

34. For examples, see articles about relationship marketing in business periodicals such as the *Harvard Business Review*.

35. King, Feltey, and Susel (1998).

36. Moran (2002: 136–37).

37. Derrida (1976).

38. See Dwyer and Jones (2002); Linstead (1993) and Kilduff (1993) on deconstructing organizations.

39. Derrida (1978).

40. Baudrillard (1994: 6).

41. Baudrillard (1994: 19).

42. Baudrillard (1994: 7).

43. *Wall Street Journal*, February 20, 2002. For videotaped insider accounts and related material, view the 2005 documentary, *Enron: The Smartest Guys in the Room*. The film was based on a book by *Fortune* reporters Bethany McLean and Peter Elkind, entitled *The Smartest Guys in the Room: The Amazing Rise and Scandalous Fall of Enron* (2003, New York: Penguin Group).

References

Abolafia, Mitchell Y., and Kilduff, Martin (1988) Enacting market crisis: The social construction of a speculative bubble. *Administrative Science Quarterly*, 33: 177–93.

Adler, Paul S. (2011) Marxist philosophy and organization studies: Marxist contributions to the understanding of some important organizational forms. In H. Tsoukas and R. Chia (eds.), *Philosophy and Organization Theory (Research in the Sociology of Organizations)*, Vol. 32, pp. 123–54. Bingley: Emerald Group.

Barley, Stephen and Kunda, Gideon (1992) Design and devotion: Surges of rational and normative ideologies of control in managerial discourse. *Administrative Science Quarterly*, 37: 363–99.

Barnard, Chester (1938) *The Functions of the Executive*. Cambridge, MA: Harvard University Press.

Baudrillard, Jean (1988) *Selected Writings* (ed. M. Poster). Palo Alto, CA: Stanford University Press.

—— (1994) *Simulacra and Simulations* (trans. S. F. Glaser). Ann Arbor: University of Michigan Press.

Bell, Daniel (1973) *The Coming of Post-industrial Society*. New York: Basic Books.

—— (1976) *The Cultural Contradictions of Capitalism*. New York: Basic Books.

Berger, Peter L. and Luckmann, Thomas (1966) *The Social Construction of Reality: A Treatise in the Sociology of Knowledge*. Garden City, NY: Doubleday.

Bernard, Doray (1988) *From Taylorism to Fordism: A Rational Madness*. London: Free Association Books.

Bertalanffy, Ludwig von (1950) The theory of open systems in physics and biology. *Science*, 111: 23–8.

—— (1968) *General Systems Theory: Foundations, Development, Applications* (revised edn.). New York: George Braziller.

Boje, David M. and Winsor, R. D. (1993) The resurrection of Taylorism: Total quality management's hidden agenda. *Journal of Organizational Change Management*, 6/4: 58–71.

Boulding, Kenneth E. (1956) General systems theory—The skeleton of science. *Management Science*, 2: 197–208.

Burns, Tom and Stalker, G.M. (1961/1995) *The Management of Innovation*. Oxford: Oxford University Press.

Calas, Marta and Smircich, Linda (1991) Voicing seduction to silence leadership. *Organization Studies*, 12: 567–602.

Calinescu, Matei (1987) *The Five Faces of Modernity*. Durham, NC: Duke University Press (first published in 1977 by Indiana University Press).

Clifford, James and Marcus, George E. (1986) (eds.) *Writing Culture: The Poetics and Politics of Ethnography*. Berkeley: University of California Press.

Derrida, Jacques (1976) *Of Grammatology*. Baltimore, MD: Johns Hopkins University Press.

—— (1978) *Writing and Difference* (trans. Alan Bass). London: Routledge and Kegan Paul.

Donaldson, Lex (1985) *In Defence of Organisation Theory*. Cambridge: Cambridge University Press.

Durkheim, Émile (1966) *Suicide: A Study in Sociology* (trans. John Spaulding and George Simpson). New York: Free Press (first published in 1897).

—— (1982) *The Rules of Sociological Method* (trans. W. D. Halls). New York: Free Press (first published in 1895).

—— (1984) *The Division of Labour in Society* (trans. W. D. Halls). New York: Free Press (first published in 1893).

Dwyer, O. and Jones III, J. P. (2002) White socio-spatial epistemology. *Social and Cultural Geography*, 1: 209–22.

Emery, Fred E. (1969) *Systems Thinking*. Harmondsworth: Penguin.

—— and E. Trist (1981) The evolution of socio-technical systems. Occasional paper No. 2, Ontario Ministry of Labor Quality of Working Life Centre. http://www.sociotech.net/wiki/images/9/94/Evolution_of_socio_technical_systems.pdf

Fayol, Henri (1949) *General and Industrial Management*. London: Pitman (first published in 1919).

Follett, Mary Parker (1923) *The New State: Group Organization and the Solution of Popular Government*. New York: Longmans, Green and Co. (originally published 1918).

—— (1924) *Creative Experience*. New York: Longmans, Green and Co.

Foucault, Michel (1972) *The Archeology of Knowledge and the Discourse on Language* (trans. A. M. Sheridan Smith). London: Tavistock Publications.

—— (1973) *The Order of Things: An Archaeology of the Human Sciences* (trans. Alan Sheridan-Smith). New York: Vintage Books.

—— (1977) *Power/knowledge*, (ed.) Colin Gordon. New York: Pantheon.

Gagliardi, Pasquale (2005) The revenge of gratuitousness on utilitarianism. *Journal of Management Inquiry*, 14: 309–15.

Geertz, Clifford (1973) *The Interpretation of Cultures*. New York: Basic Books.

George, Claude S., Jr. (1968) *The History of Management Thought*. Englewood Cliffs, NJ: Prentice-Hall.

Goffman, Erving (1959) *The Presentation of Self in Everyday Life*. Garden City, NY: Doubleday Anchor.

Graham, P. (1995) (ed.) *Mary Parker Follett: Prophet of Management*. Boston, MA: Harvard Business School Press.

Gulick, Luther and Urwick, Lyndall (1937) (eds.) *Papers on the Science of Administration*. New York: Institute of Public Administration, Columbia University.

Herskowitz, Melville J. (1948) *Man and His Works: The Science of Cultural Anthropology*. New York: Alfred A. Knopf.

Jencks, Charles (1977) *The Language of Post-modern Architecture*. London: Academy.

—— (1992) (ed.) *The Post-modern Reader*. London: St. Martin's Press.

—— (1996) *What Is Post-modernism?* (4th edn.). New York: John Wiley & Sons Inc.

Kilduff, Martin (1993) Deconstructing organizations. *Academy of Management Review*, 18: 13–31.

King, C. S., Feltey, K. M., and O'Neill, Susel B. (1998) The question of participation: Toward authentic public participation in public administration. *Public Administration Review*, 58/4: 317–26.

Lawrence, P. R. and Lorsch, J. W. (1967) Differentiation and integration in complex organizations. *Administrative Science Quarterly*, 12: 1–47.

Linstead, Steve (1993) Deconstruction in the study of organizations. In John Hassard and Martin Parker (eds.), *Postmodernism and Organizations*. London: Sage, 49–70.

Lyotard, Jean-François (1979). *The Postmodern Condition: A Report on Knowledge* (trans. G. Bennington and B. Massumi). Minneapolis: University of Minnesota Press.

—— (1983) *The Differend: Phrases in Dispute* (trans. G. Van den Abeele). Minneapolis: Minnesota University Press.

March, James G. and Simon, Herbert (1958) *Organizations*. New York: John Wiley & Sons Inc.

Marx, Karl (1973). *Grundrisse: Foundations of the Critique of Political Economy*. Harmondsworth: Penguin (first published in 1839–41).

—— (1974) *Capital*, Vol. 1. London: Lawrence and Wishart (first published in 1867).

—— (1975) *Early Writings* (trans. R. Livingstone and G. Benton). Harmondsworth: Penguin (first published as *Economic and Philosophical Manuscripts*, 1844).

Merton, Robert (1965/1993) *On the Shoulders of Giants*. Chicago, IL: Chicago University Press.

Moran, Joe (2002) *Interdisciplinarity*. London: Blackwell.

O'Connor, Ellen S. (1996) Lines of authority: Readings of foundational texts on the profession of management. *Journal of Management History*, 2/3: 26–49.

Perrow, Charles (1973) The short and glorious history of organizational theory. *Organizational Dynamics*, Summer: 2–15.

Rorty, Richard (1980) *Philosophy and the Mirror of Nature*. Princeton, NJ: Princeton University Press.

Saussure, Ferdinand de (1959) *Course in General Linguistics* (trans. Wade Baskin). New York: McGraw-Hill.

Schroeder, Ralph (1992) *Max Weber and the Sociology of Culture*. London: Sage.

Schütz, Alfred (1967) *The Phenomenology of the Social World* (trans. G. Walsh and F. Lehnert). Evanston, IL: Northwestern University Press (first published in 1932).

Selznick, Philip (1949) *TVA and the Grass Roots*. Berkeley: University of California Press.

—— (1957) *Leadership in Administration*. Berkeley: University of California Press.

Smith, Adam (1776/1937) *An Inquiry into the Nature and Causes of the Wealth of Nations*. New York: Modern Library.

Steingard, D. S. (1993) A postmodern deconstruction of total quality management (TQM). *Journal of Organizational Change Management*, 6/4: 72–87.

Stocking, G. W., Jr. (1983) (ed.) *Observer Observed: Essays on Ethnographic Fieldwork, a History of Anthropology*, Vol. 1. Madison: University of Wisconsin Press.

Taylor, Frederick W. (1911) *The Principles of Scientific Management*. New York: Harper.

Thomas, William I. and Thomas, D. S. (1928) *The Child in America*. New York: A.A. Knopf (free online at http://www.archive.org/details/childinamerica00thom).

Thompson, James (1967) *Organizations in Action*. New York: McGraw-Hill.

Trist, Eric L. and Bamforth, K. W. (1951) Some social and psychological consequences of the long wall method of coal getting. *Human Relations*, 4: 3–38.

Van Maanen, John (1988) *Tales of the Field: On Writing Ethnography*. Chicago, IL: University of Chicago Press.

Weber, Max (1906–24/1946 trans.) From Gerth, Hans H. and Mills, C. Wright (eds.), *Max Weber: Essays in Sociology*, New York: Oxford University Press.

——(1947) From A.H. Henderson and Talcott Parsons (eds.) *The Theory of Social and Economic Organization*. Glencoe, IL: Free Press (first published in 1924).

Weick, Karl E. (1969 [1979]) *The Social Psychology of Organizing*. Reading, MA: Addison-Wesley.

——(1995) *Sensemaking in Organizations*. Thousand Oaks, CA: Sage.

——(2003) Enacting an environment: The infrastructure of organizing. In R. I. Westwook and S. Clegg (eds.), *Debating Organization: Point-counterpoint in Organization Studies*. London: Blackwell, 184–94.

——and Bougon, Michel (1986) Organizations as cognitive maps: Charting ways to success and failure. In Sims, Jr. H. P. and Gioia, D. A. (eds.) *The Thinking Organization*, 102–35. San Francisco: Jossey-Bass.

Whyte, William F. (1943) *Street Corner Society*. Chicago, IL: University of Chicago Press.

Wittgenstein, Ludwig (1965) *Philosophical Investigations*. New York: Macmillan.

Woodward, Joan (1958) *Management and Technology*. London: Her Majesty's Stationery Office.

——(1965) *Industrial Organization: Theory and Practice*. London: Oxford University Press.

Wren, D. (1987) *The Evolution of Management Thought* (3rd edn.). New York: John Wiley & Sons Inc.

Further reading

Clegg, Stewart (1990) *Modern Organizations: Organization Studies in the Postmodern World*. London: Sage.

Harvey, David (1990) *The Condition of Postmodernity*. Cambridge, MA: Blackwell.

Hassard, John and Parker, Martin (1993) (eds.) *Postmodernism and Organizations*. London: Sage, 49–70.

Knudsen, C. and Tsoukas, H. (2003) (eds.) *The Oxford Handbook of Organization Theory: Meta-theoretical Perspectives*. Oxford: Oxford University Press.

Kumar, Krishan (1995) *From Post-industrial to Post-modern Society: New Theories of the Contemporary World*. Oxford: Blackwell.

Lash, Scott and Urry, John (1987) *The End of Organized Capitalism*. Cambridge: Polity Press.

Piore, Michael and Sabel, Charles (1984) *The Second Industrial Divide*. New York: Basic Books.

Rosenau, Pauline Marie (1992) *Post-modernism and the Social Sciences: Insights, Inroads, and Intrusions*. Princeton, NJ: Princeton University Press.

Rousseau, Denise (1985) Issues of level in organizational research: Multi-level and cross-level perspectives. In L. Cummings and B. M. Staw (eds.), *Research in Organizational Behavior*, Vol. VII: 1–37. Greenwich, CT: JAI Press.

Simon, Herbert (1957) *Administrative Behavior* (2nd edn.). New York: Macmillan (first published in 1945).

Part 2

Core Concepts and Theories

In the chapters that make up this part of the book you will become familiar with six core concepts that organization theorists rely upon to construct their theories—environment, social structure, technology, culture, physical structure, and power/control. As you move through Part II, you will be challenged to build these concepts and then use them to create theories, gradually increasing the complexity of your theorizing along the way. In keeping with our theme of multiple perspectives, each core concept will be addressed from within the modern, symbolic, and postmodern perspectives, though, as you will soon see, some ideas are better suited to one or another of these ways of thinking.

Organization–environment relations

When general systems theory introduced the notion of levels of analysis in the 1950s, organization theorists began to define **organizational environment** as the supersystem of which organizational systems are a part. This idea seemed revolutionary to management theorists inclined until then to treat organizations as if their internal operations were the sole source of management concern, apart from the economics of competition, of course. All of that was to change with the appearance of concepts like external forces, organizational fields, and populations, all of which eventually coalesced into the study of how organizations relate to their environments.

Until recently, most theorizing about organization–environment relations was conducted from within the modern perspective. However, after the symbolic perspective established itself, theories involving institutionalized and enacted environments began to appear. Since then postmodern critiques of organization theory have introduced different concerns into discussions of organization–environment relations, such as stakeholder rights, sustainability, and corporate social responsibility.

This chapter begins at the beginning, historically speaking, with early modernist definitions of the organizational environment still in wide use today. Four theories of organization–environment relations will be reviewed—contingency theory, resource dependence theory, population ecology, and institutional theory—the last of which brought symbolic thinking to the study of organizational environments. I will present the postmodern perspective in terms of a brief summary of post-industrial history, moving from there into stakeholder theory, and concluding with a postmodern deconstruction of modern concepts of environment.

Defining and analyzing organizational environments: The modern perspective

In the modern perspective the environment appears as an objective entity lying outside an organization's boundary (see Figure 3.1). From the environment's point of view, organizations are instruments for producing products and/or services in demand within the environment. From the organization's viewpoint, the environment provides the raw materials and other

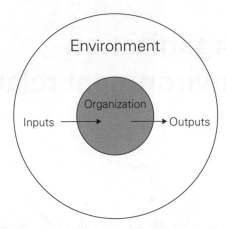

Figure 3.1 The organization in its environment

A simple distinction showing the organization as an entity (system) embedded within a larger system (supersystem) that supplies its resource inputs and absorbs its outputs (goods and services). Notice the modernist presumption of a discernible boundary separating the organization from its environment.

inputs it needs to produce output, and then absorbs that output, thereby supplying the means to acquire more inputs, and so on.

Defining an environment as what lies outside an **organizational boundary** involves making decisions about inclusion and exclusion. Deciding what lies inside and what remains outside can get tricky. Think of a university. Are students members of the university? Customers? Raw material? Products? What about the membership status of visiting professors or non-tenured faculty, guest lecturers, alumni, and benefactors? There is no simple solution to drawing an organizational boundary; the best approaches will be informed by the purpose of your analysis.

In the university's case, if you are analyzing the environment because the university wants to know the likely effects of imposing a tuition increase, then it will be useful to consider students as customers and, thus, members of the environment rather than of the organization. If the university is making an application for outside research funds, then defining students as members of the organization will give you reason to describe how they will benefit from the proposed research activities, which might support the application. If, however, you are interested in discovering how the environment is responding to a university's new education programs, then viewing students as products of the organization is likely to provide useful input to your analysis.

Another challenge you face in defining the environment of an organization comes from the different levels of analysis you can choose your focus. Modern organization theorists define and analyze organization–environment relations at the levels of:

a. stakeholders and the inter-organizational networks they form,

b. the conditions and trends within environmental sectors, and

c. the global environment emerging from interactions among the organizational and environmental subsystems of which it is comprised.

Figure 3.2 Organizations operate within environments comprised of stakeholders and competitors

Defining relevant actors in your organization's environment using this model will help you to recognize the influence of key stakeholders and address their needs, interests, and activities.

You need to be vigilant as you study organization–environment relations using these schemes; it is easy to get confused as you move between levels of analysis and confront the many interrelationships among their constituents.

Inter-organizational networks, stakeholders, and the supply chains

Every organization interacts with other actors (i.e., individuals, groups, other organizations) within its environment.[1] These interactions allow organizations to do all sorts of things such as acquire raw materials, hire employees, secure capital, sell products and services, obtain knowledge, and build, lease, or buy facilities and equipment, as well as participate in, regulate, and oversee exchanges with other actors.

The actors interacting to form an organization's immediate environment are often described as **stakeholders**. Typically these include investors, competitors, suppliers, distributors, partners, advertising and consulting agencies, trade associations, consumer groups, local communities and the general public, unions, government regulators such as tax authorities and licensing agencies, financial analysts, and the media. In its narrow sense, the term stakeholder refers to any actor vital to an organization's survival or success. Those who take stakeholders' interests into account offer a more inclusive definition arguing that every actor affected by the organization's activities should be given consideration in organizational decision making.[2] The categories of stakeholders shown in Figure 3.2 appear in most environmental analyses.

Together the relationships established among an organization's set of stakeholders form its **inter-organizational network** (see Figure 3.3). Nodes of the network represent actors while links between nodes represent channels through which resources, information, opportunities, and influence flow. Network analysis promotes sensitivity to a variety of measurable variables whose analysis reveals characteristics of the network and its members.

At the organizational level, for example, network analysis can reveal an organization's **centrality** within the network, shown in Figure 3.3 by the size of the nodes used to represent each actor. You can measure centrality by counting the number of links to a node, called 'ties,' and weight each link by its importance to some relevant outcome. At the level of the network, the concentration of links across the entire network reveals **network density**, while the absence of links in an area of the network pinpoints a **structural hole**. Measuring an organization's centrality, a network's density, and identifying structural holes allows you to compare inter-organizational networks and assess their benefits, say for the performance of their members or to identify differences in innovativeness of some networks relative to others so as to try to theorize why such differences occur.[3]

A popular application of the inter-organizational network concept with which you may be familiar is the **supply chain**. This concept focuses attention on the flow of raw material that forms a more or less linear chain of connections originating with the supply of the most basic raw materials (e.g., petroleum by oil companies) and subsequently flowing through intermediary organizations (e.g., oil refineries, petroleum distributors, and gasoline stations) to reach end users (e.g., drivers of gasoline-powered vehicles). In the case of services the focus turns to value-added activities that form a value-chain, but is much the same idea as the supply chain. You can visualize a supply chain or a value chain by cutting a slice through an inter-organizational network that includes all suppliers, partners, distributors, and end users of a given production process or service delivery system. Supply and value chain thinking helps organizations manage all the relationships of a production process or service practice as if

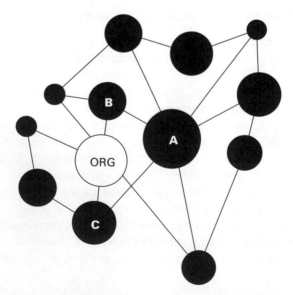

Figure 3.3 The inter-organizational network

This model depicts an inter-organizational network in which organization A, a competitor of the focal organization (ORG), is most central, B is a supplier of both ORG and A, while C is a customer to both.

they were organized as one entity without the necessity of their being integrated into a single firm. This management practice promotes efficiency insofar as dividing the required tasks among supply chain partners brings the advantages of division of labor without the costs of adding layers of management or bureaucracy to monitor and control their collective performance.

Conditions and trends in the environment of an organization

In addition to specific actors and their relationships in the inter-organizational network, a host of environmental forces impinge on participants in the environment. These external forces will have effects throughout the network, yet analysis of the network itself is unlikely to reveal them. Thus, to fully appreciate organization–environment relations you need to track conditions and trends in the environment in addition to doing an inter-organizational network analysis. This analysis typically begins by subdividing the environment into the **sectors** shown in Figure 3.4.

The **social sector** of an environment is associated with class structure, demographics, mobility patterns, lifestyles, social movements, and traditional social institutions including educational systems, religious practices, trades, and professions. In the United States and Western Europe, aging populations, increasing workforce diversity, and professionalization of many types of work, including management, are all examples of recent trends affecting organizations operating in those parts of the world. Recent migrations of people from Central and Eastern Europe and North Africa into the wealthier nations of Western Europe are examples of social mobility patterns in the environment of organizations operating in these areas. Recycling illustrates a social movement present in many countries around the world.

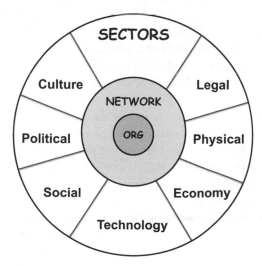

Figure 3.4 Sectors of the environment

Be sure to track all environmental conditions and trends that might influence the survival and success of your organization. Typically this is made easier by carving the environment into sectors and then monitoring their influences on each other, on the network, and on the organization of interest.

Concern with the **cultural sector** revolves around issues such as history, tradition, normative expectations for behavior, beliefs, and values. Examples of conditions in the cultural sector for Western firms include emphasis on leadership, technical rationality, and material wealth, while cultural sector trends in these parts of the world show decreasing value for hierarchical authority and increasing value for ethical business practices, human rights, and protection of the physical environment. Be sure to notice how social and cultural trends intersect. For instance, the increasing diversity found in many workforces shows up as a change in values for the contributions that differences of gender, race, and cultural background bring to organizations. These value shifts, in turn, influence the legal and political sectors.

The **legal sector** is defined by the constitutions, laws, and legal practices of nations in which an organization conducts its business. It involves such matters as corporate, anti-trust (anti-monopoly), tax, and foreign investment law. Examples of trends in the legal sector are often difficult to separate from trends in the political and economic sectors. For instance, trends involving both the regulation and deregulation of industries are of major concern for affected organizations. The legal sector has close links to social and cultural trends because cultural values and social institutions create pressures to legalize various behaviors, or to declare them illegal. For example, heightened concern over unethical behavior by US businesses led to the passage of the Sarbanes-Oxley Act in 2002. This piece of legislation created mechanisms to expose and punish acts of corporate corruption, promote greater accountability by financial auditors, and protect small investors and pension holders. You can easily see how Sarbanes-Oxley arose from activities within both the political and economic sectors.

The **political sector** is usually described in terms of the distribution and concentration of power and the nature of political systems (e.g., democratic vs. autocratic) in those areas of the world in which the organization operates. The renunciation of communist rule across Eastern Europe in 1989 is an example of significant change in the political (and economic) sector of organizations doing or seeking to do business in this region of the world. The political sector has close ties with the legal sector and both are influenced by trends in other sectors. For example, in the US women and minorities have become more politically active since their entry into the workforce (social sector), and their increased political participation (political sector) has resulted in affirmative action, anti-discrimination, and anti-harassment legislation (legal sector).

Sometimes the political and economic sectors are so intertwined that it does not make sense to try to analyze their influences separately. For example, many governments (political sector), under pressure from businesses (economic sector), have relaxed trade barriers via trade agreements with other countries that reduce national autonomy, as has happened in relation to free trade zones. Economically driven political alliances such as the EU, ASEAN, MEROCUR, and NAFTA further erode national autonomy in favor of supporting the free flow of trade in various regions of the world. Similarly, privatization has made businesses out of organizations that were formerly run by governments including prisons, hospitals, airlines, schools, and universities. These and other transfers of power from political to business leaders bring political and economic sectors closer.

The **economic sector** is comprised of labor and financial markets, and markets for goods and services. The extent to which private versus public ownership prevails, whether or not centralized economic planning is attempted, fiscal policies, consumption patterns, patterns of capital investment, and the banking system all contribute to shaping the economic sector. Examples of economic conditions commonly found in this sector include: the balance of payments, hard currency issues, economic alliances with other countries, trade agreements, price controls, access to raw materials markets, interest and inflation rates, price indexes, unemployment rates, excess production capacity, and investment risk. Economic sector trends have implications for the other sectors of the environment. For instance, the shift from a communist planned economy to democratic capitalism in Poland (a political-economic sector change) had implications for every other sector in the environment of organizations operating in Poland.

The **technology sector** provides knowledge and information in the form of scientific developments and applications that organizations can acquire and use to produce outputs (goods and services). In a sense, the environment possesses the knowledge to produce desired outputs and contributes this knowledge to various organizations that then carry out production processes for the benefit of at least some other part of the environment. Such knowledge takes the form of educated employees, equipment and software, and services provided by consultants and other professionals. A significant recent trend in the technological sector of many organizations has been the availability of computer-based technologies such as personal computers, robots, video-recording equipment, computer-aided design and manufacturing (CAD-CAM), and social media. Applications of these technologies are creating enormous changes in organizations around the world, such as organizations doing an increasing proportion of their business online. Trends indicate many new technological advances forthcoming from the fields of genetics, subatomic physics, and fiber optics.

There are endless examples of ways in which the technological sector intertwines with other sectors of the environment. Software pirating, reverse engineering, and theft of copyrighted material become easier with digitalization, a trend that began in the technological sector and has spread to the legal and economic sectors in the form of threats to intellectual property rights. Satellite communication replaces some travel and connects previously remote places in Africa, Latin America, Asia, and elsewhere to the global economy. Computer technology inspires shifts in organizational forms and practices such as virtual organization and outsourcing. Businesses now operate 24/7, partly as a result of advances in global communication technology that have affected cultural expectations for access and responsiveness. Changes in the technological sector affect the social and economic sectors as technology creates further socio-economic divisions between those who have electricity and can read, and those who do not read or have no access to electrical power.

The **physical sector** includes natural resources and the effects of nature. Some organizations have direct and immediate concerns with physical sector elements ranging from coal and oil reserves (e.g., firms operating in the oil industry), accessible harbors (e.g., firms in import/export trades or those operating shipping companies), viable transportation routes (e.g., trucking companies), and pollution levels (e.g., manufacturing concerns), to severe weather conditions (e.g., firms in the air transportation, shipping, construction, and tourism industries). Examples of general conditions and trends worth watching in the physical sector include changing weather patterns (e.g., global warming), the disappearance of rainforests, and disasters such as drought, earthquake, flood, famine, and volcanic activity.

Except for the case of dwindling natural resources, changes in the physical sector are extremely difficult to predict. Nonetheless, firms that depend on this sector for resources or favorable working conditions will obviously be economically affected by events and changes that occur here. Disasters such as earthquakes can have more than economic impact. For example, changes in attitudes and values about safety issues following earthquakes (cultural sector) often initiate changes in building codes (legal sector) that stimulate the development of new building techniques (technical sector). Of course other sectors influence the physical sector as well, such as when population growth or migration (social sector) taxes the physical resources of regions where settlement occurs.

Many more examples of sectors could be given, of course, and thinking of others will help you develop these concepts in your own terms. Don't forget that the usefulness of this, or any other organization theory you read about in this book, will depend upon your elaborating it with specific information based on your knowledge and experience. Also bear in mind that although you can separate the environment into sectors as we have done here, the sectors do not evolve independently. Their interdependence will always give rise to additional considerations as conditions change or trends develop.

The model of environmental sectors presented in Figure 3.4 is only meant as a stimulus to your analysis, not a rigid solution. After you become familiar with its categories and notice their independence, you may find that you prefer to use only five or six sectors for a particular analysis. For instance, collapsing the social and cultural, or political and legal categories may make sense, or you may want to expand the model to include new sectors. You should feel free to treat this and all other theoretical models as templates that can be changed to suit the purposes of analysis, but do not alter them just to avoid facing a tough problem, such as not having the data to do a full analysis readily at hand! When a theory indicates you are missing information, take note of the absence and raise it as a question for further study.

Internationalization, regionalization, and globalization

As soon as organizations start interacting across national borders their **internationalization** generates new levels of environmental complexity with consequences for the organizational level. For example, as organizations in regions such as the Pacific Rim or Central and Eastern Europe (CEE) broaden their scope of activity to embrace the entire region, regional markets form, often attracting business from even further afield, resulting in increased competition for all but also greater availability and variety of products and services, and often lower prices to the end user, to name a few of the effects internationalization brings with it.

Regionalization occurs alongside internationalization when governments sponsor programs and legislation, such as the North American Free Trade Agreement (NAFTA). Regionalization has organizational level effects, which can be seen for example in the growth of Mexican maquiladoras. Maquiladoras are plants where parts imported from foreign markets are assembled into products that are then shipped back to the original markets. Often operating just inside Mexico's border with the US, the locations of these organizations inside a designated zone grants them special tariff status that reduces their costs and makes them highly competitive.

As changes within regions and internationalizing organizations take hold they create knock-on effects around the world as regions and their organizations interact to produce economic globalization. But globalization moves well beyond the economic sector because conditions and trends from other sectors converge on international organizations operating within various regions. This globalization affects all areas of life with consequences for people and organizations everywhere. Table 3.1 shows some of these influences categorized by sectors.

Globalization typically refers to the exchanges and relationships established between organizations and their networks that render existing borders and boundaries between them (such as those dividing nation-states or economic partnerships) permeable or irrelevant.[4] Globalization means recognizing the new level of complexity and interdependence depicted in Figure 3.5.

Table 3.1 Contributions of environmental sectors to global complexity and change

Sector	Contribution to global change
Technology	Personal computers
	The Internet and WIFI
	Digital cameras and HDTV
	Smartphones and social media
	Communication satellites
	Rapid transit trains, supertankers
	Space exploration
Economic	Global capital markets
	Technology exchanges
	Worldwide trade
	Transnational corporations
	International economic institutions (e.g., IMF, World Bank, WTO)
	Regional trading systems and global retailing
Political/Legal	Breakdown of the authority of the nation-state
	Erosion of territorial borders
	Global governance institutions (e.g., UN, WHO, World Court)
Social/Cultural	Global media coverage
	Popular culture (e.g., slang, fashion, brands, TV, music, tourism)
	English as global language of science, politics, and business
	Materialism and consumerism
	Multi-racialism, multi-culturalism, multi-lingualism
	Social media (e.g., chatrooms, Facebook, Twitter)
Physical	Population growth
	Loss of biodiversity
	Hazardous waste and industrial accidents
	Global warming and climate change
	Pollution
	Disease and food insecurity
	Genetically modified (GM) foods

Source: Based on Steger (2003).

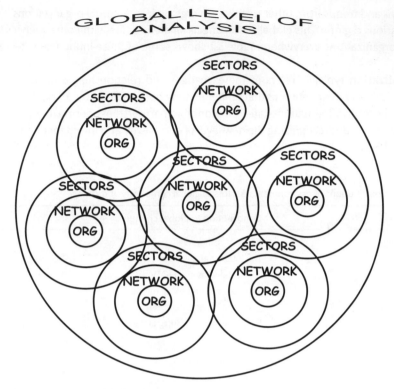

Figure 3.5 One way to picture globalization

This figure maps the growing interdependence among organizations, their networks, and environmental conditions and trends leading to globalization. Notice this model depicts four levels of analysis, the organization (ORG), its inter-organizational network (NETWORK), conditions and trends in sectors affecting all members of an environment (SECTORS), with the global level emerging from the multiple interacting lower level systems.

To see how complex and interrelated globally convergent trends can be, consider the example of cultural homogenization. Examples of this widely recognized phenomenon include English as the accepted language of business, science, and the Internet, easy access to fast food, and the wearing of blue jeans, T-shirts, and training shoes. As homogenization signals the loss of local customs and traditions, those who desire to maintain the old ways respond by asserting communal affiliations, such as supporting other trends, for example religious fundamentalism. Thus cultural homogenization contributes to both appreciation and fear of cultural diversity with multiple effects; in some quarters diversity encourages appeals for democratically inspired self-determination and individual freedom, while in others it inspires religious warfare and ethnic cleansing. And this represents a brief analysis of only one segment of the globalizing environment.

As globalization unfolds amidst all these interacting forces, organizations created explicitly to operate on the global stage appear and push global interdependence further along. These include the United Nations (UN), the World Trade Organization (WTO), the World Health Organization (WHO), the International Monetary Fund (IMF), and the World Bank, not to mention numerous NGOs (nongovernmental organizations) such as the International Red Cross, Doctors Without Borders, and Greenpeace. You may be surprised to hear that some of these organizations are quite old, for example the Red Cross was founded in 1863. Of course the path to globalization dates back at least to the Silk Road that opened between Europe and Asia sometime around the second century BCE.

The complexity of the level of analysis on which the concept of globalization rests can boggle the mind. Don't get too carried away by being able to model this complexity in abstract terms. While analysis using abstract models like the one in Figure 3.5 will increase your awareness of the many important influences an organization faces, you will probably never be able to identify and track them all or put the whole complex puzzle together in a meaningful way. There are too many moving parts to keep up with all their changes even if you could get your head around so many concepts at once.

At its best, analysis using abstract models will make you aware of the risks of not understanding everything that affects an organization, and encourage you to keep observing and learning. Use multiple levels of analysis to imagine what interactions among parts of the complex environment surrounding an organization will reveal *in relation to the purpose of your analysis*.

Modern theories of organization–environment relations

By the late 1970s most modernist organization theorists and managers had taken the importance of the environment to heart, and interest shifted to explaining how environmental influence operates; thus the first theories of organization-environment relations came into being. Three of the most influential of these came out of the modern perspective: environmental contingency theory, resource dependence theory, and population ecology. A fourth—institutional theory— will be presented in the section on institutional theories of organization-environment relations to honor its contribution to the symbolic perspective.

Environmental contingency theory

British sociologists Tom Burns and George Stalker, along with American organization theorists Paul Lawrence and Jay Lorsch, were among the first to argue that the environment dictates the best form of organization to use. To explain this relationship between environment and organization, Burns and Stalker theorized that in stable environments the **mechanistic** form of organization works best because of the efficiencies it can generate using standard procedures to perform routine activities.[5] Under stable environmental conditions organizations can learn to optimize their activities and use of resources so as to minimize costs and maximize profit.

When environments are rapidly changing, however, the advantages of mechanistic organization are lost. The profitability routinization brings soon disappears when the organization must constantly alter its activities in order to adapt. The flexibility of **organic** forms of organization is better adapted to a changing environment because it supports needed innovation and adaptation. Burns and Stalker's explanation of when to use mechanistic versus organic forms of organization is an early example of contingency theory, the contingency being, in their case, the set of environmental factors the organization in question faces.

Early contingency theorists presented **environmental uncertainty** as the key variable explaining why particular forms of organization were successful, and uncertainty in the environment was defined as the interaction between complexity and rate of change (see Figure 3.6). **Complexity** refers to the number and diversity of the elements of environment, while **rate of change** refers to how rapidly the environment including all of its elements is changing.

The problem with early environmental uncertainty theory was that it assumed that conditions in the environment were objectively real. Studies showed, however, that everyone does not experience an environment in the same way; the same environment might be perceived as certain by one set of managers but be described as uncertain by another. Researchers concluded that **perceptual uncertainty** predicted decisions about the form of organization adopted better than did objective measures of environmental uncertainty.[6]

In modern organization theory this evidence of the importance of perceptions as a moderating factor in understanding how environments affect organizations developed into an information theory.[7] The **information theory of uncertainty** argues that managers experience uncertainty in the environment when they lack the information they feel they need to make sound organizational decisions. Figure 3.7 specifies the links between perceived environmental conditions and information that explain different levels of perceived uncertainty.

In Figure 3.7 managers see environments as stable and as having minimum complexity when the information they need is both known and available; when this occurs they perceive and report low levels of environmental uncertainty. Managers recognize environments to have either high complexity or to be rapidly changing when they confront either too much information or constantly changing information, in which case moderate levels of uncertainty are experienced. Managers perceive a highly complex and changing environment when they face an overwhelming amount of information that is constantly changing; under

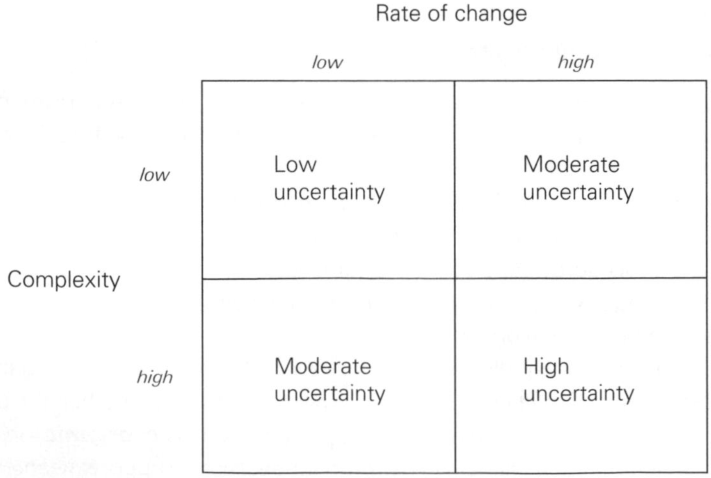

Figure 3.6 Environmental uncertainty is defined by the complexity in and the rate of change of the organization's environment

Source: Based on Duncan (1972).

these conditions their uncertainty is greatest. This is because when managers don't know what information they need and are confronted with an overabundance of information, uncertainty reaches its highest levels. Think about the rate at which YouTube video is produced. Current estimates are that 60 hours of video are uploaded to this website every minute, and the rate is increasing. If you needed to analyze the content of all this video to make a decision about how to organize your company, and you perceived these facts about YouTube as negatively affecting your ability to perform your analysis, you would likely find yourself in a state of high uncertainty.

Another early effort to explain how organizations respond to uncertainty relied on the concepts of requisite variety and isomorphism. The **law of requisite variety**, borrowed from general systems theory, states that for one system to deal effectively with another it must be of the same or greater complexity. In organizational terms this means that successful organizations map perceived environmental complexity with their internal structures and management systems. The mapping results in **isomorphism**: if the environment is simple, the organization takes a simple form; complex environments favor complex organizations. When environments are changing, of course, the concepts of isomorphism and requisite variety suggest that organizations will change as well.

American organization theorists Paul Lawrence and Jay Lorsch discussed the implications of isomorphism in their 1967 book *Organization and Environment*. They suggested that organizations confront many different conditions and elements in their environments, which creates pressure for differentiation inside the organization. Differentiation allows different units of the organization to specialize in handling different demands from the environment. These specialized functions produce internal complexity in organizational structures that allows them to map complex environments. But it also produces pressure to integrate across the differentiated tasks and this adds structural complexity in the form of higher-level managers to coordinate the expanding units and responsibilities within the organization.

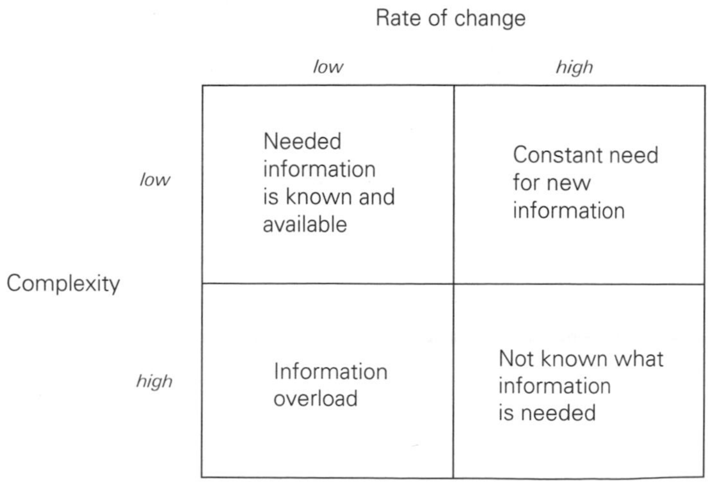

	Rate of change	
	low	*high*
low	Needed information is known and available	Constant need for new information
high	Information overload	Not known what information is needed

Complexity (row label)

Figure 3.7 Links between conditions in the perceived environment and information that contribute to uncertainty in organizational decision making

Resource dependence theory

Resource dependence theory was most fully developed by American organization theorists Jeffrey Pfeffer and Gerald Salancik who published their ideas in 1978. Their book was provocatively titled *The External Control of Organizations* to emphasize their theory that the configuration of the environment is a powerful influence on management strategy and organizational structure.

The basic argument of resource dependence theory is that an analysis of the inter-organizational network can help an organization's managers understand the **power/dependence** relationships that exist between their organization and other network actors. Such knowledge allows managers to anticipate likely sources of influence from the environment and suggests ways in which the organization can offset some of this influence by creating countervailing dependence for others.

An organization's dependence on its environment is the result of its need for resources such as raw materials, labor, capital, equipment, knowledge, and outlets for its products and services—resources that are controlled by the environment. The environment derives power over the organization from this dependence, which it uses to make demands on the organization for such things as competitive prices, desirable products and services, and efficient organizational structures and processes. However, the dependence of the organization on its environment is neither singular nor undifferentiated. A complex set of dependencies arise between an organization and the specific elements of its inter-organizational network as shown in Figure 3.8.

Resource dependence analysis begins by identifying the resource inputs and outputs of the organization. Next trace the resource flows to where they begin and follow the outputs to their end users. For example, firms that provide raw materials and equipment will be found among the organization's suppliers, while tracing the organization's outputs will identify specific customers in the network. Tracing suppliers of labor, capital, and knowledge will identify still other network actors such as employment agencies, universities, financial

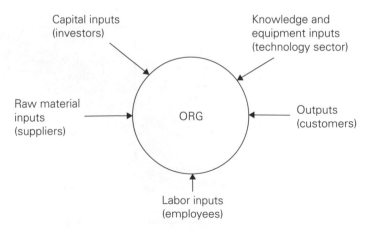

Figure 3.8 Applying resource dependence theory

Trace your organization's resources to their sources using this extended model of the inter-organizational network.

intermediaries, and think tanks. Competition over raw materials, customers, and employees can be other sources of potential resource dependence, so be sure to bring key competitors into your analysis. Any government agencies or lawmakers whose policies or practices regulate your organization's exchanges with the environment should be included (e.g., labor law, consumer protection agencies, trade regulators). And don't forget special interests, people or groups that attempt to influence the activities of the organization via political, economic, and/or social pressure. Examples of special interests include unions and nongovernmental organizations (NGOs).

In practice it will be impossible to consider every source of dependence an organization faces or every potential competitive, special interest, or regulatory move, so after specifying sources and destinations of resource inputs and outputs among the actors of the organization's inter-organizational network, resource dependence analysis moves to prioritizing responses to these dependencies. Prioritization involves assessing the criticality and scarcity of the resources involved. Assessing resource **criticality** provides a measure of the relative importance of a particular resource. For instance, beef is a critical resource for McDonalds, whereas drinking straws are not. Assessing **scarcity** provides an indicator of the risk of not being able to procure a critical resource. Gold, platinum, and uranium are scarce, as is water in a growing number of regions. Resources that are both scarce and critical are prioritized and a plan of action for tracking and managing these dependencies is developed.

Managing resource dependence calls for imagination with respect to balancing the power of others by developing countervailing power within your own organization. Pfeffer and Salancik described numerous ways organizations do this. Establishing multiple sources of supply helps manage dependence by reducing the power of any one supplier. Where there are benefits to using a limited number of suppliers, such as with supply chain management, contracting is a common strategy for managing dependency. Creating joint ventures with customers or suppliers or acquiring or merging with them (called vertical integration), or forming alliances or merging with competitors to concentrate negotiating power over suppliers and customers (called horizontal integration) are additional strategies. All aspects of marketing—sales, advertising, distribution, branding—can help an organization to manage dependencies on consumer purchases. Corporate image campaigns will help counteract negative public opinion or critical reports in the media.

Labor and knowledge dependencies can be managed with recruitment strategies for attracting talented personnel. A common strategy for managing regulatory dependencies is to send lobbyists to influence legislators to vote for advantageous trade agreements, favorable corporate tax laws, or government funding of research and development. Trade association membership can prove beneficial too, as it enables members to share the costs of monitoring conditions and trends in the environment and pools their influence, not just in hiring lobbyists, but also through category marketing. Of course trade associations are open to criticism and even legal action if they are not careful to guard themselves against price fixing and other unfair or illegal business practices. In societies in which price fixing is not outlawed, price agreements and cartels such as OPEC are common means of managing environmental dependence between competitors.

If other strategies fail, the organization can release itself from unwanted dependency by changing its environment, as when an organization enters or exits a line of business or alters its product/service mix through diversification or retrenchment, joint ventures, spin-offs, mergers, and acquisitions. Population ecology theory also sometimes leads to a recommendation to flee a non-supportive environment, though it pitches its theorizing at a different level of analysis.

Population ecology

Both resource dependence theory and population ecology assume that dependency gives the environment considerable power over the organization. However, whereas resource dependence theory is rooted in the organizational level of analysis, population ecology focuses the bulk of its attention on the environment. What interests population ecologists is not how one particular organization procures its own survival via competition for scarce and critical resources (as in resource dependence theory), but the patterns of success and failure among all the organizations that compete within a given resource pool, called an **ecological niche**.[8]

Population ecology as it applies to organization theory derives from the influential British naturalist Charles Darwin's principles of evolution—variation, selection, and retention—and his theory that these processes explain the dynamics of natural selection within a species of animal observed over time. Among those who applied these ideas to organizations were American organization sociologists Michael Hannan, John Freeman, Howard Aldrich, and Glen Carroll.[9] Their theories explain how competitive ecological processes result in the variety of organizational forms we see around us today, thus for them economic competition is a form of natural selection.

In population ecology theory the environment of an organization selects from a group of competitors those organizations that best serve its needs. As in Darwin's theory, variation, selection, and retention explain the dynamics of natural selection within a **population** of organizations. **Variation** occurs primarily through entrepreneurial innovation that results in new organizations and through the adaptation of established organizations as they respond to new threats or opportunities in their environments. Variation processes provide diversity to the selection process.

Selection occurs as organizations that best fit the needs and demands of their ecological niche are supported with resources, while those that do not meet the criterion of fitness starve. Non-selection does not always necessitate organizational decline and death. It can also lead to flight from an existing environment and/or finding a different resource niche to inhabit (e.g., exiting a business that does not have long-term profit growth potential, entry into new businesses). Flight feeds back into variation by producing organizational adaptations such as downsizing, spin-offs, mergers, acquisitions, and new business development.

Retention means that resources are continuously fed to the organization; thus achieving and maintaining fitness equals organizational survival in the short run. However, change in environments demands continual adaptation so that retained organizations need to take part in further variation, which explains the intense interest of many long-lived organizations in innovation, merger and acquisition strategies, and new business development.

Studies of population ecology have focused, for example, on competition in populations of restaurants, newspapers, small electronics firms, day care centers, breweries, and labor unions and reveal the birth and death rates among organizations operating within these populations.[10] They also identify the forms and strategies that the most successful organizations within the population studied adopted (e.g., being generalists with many lines of business serving multiple markets, or specialists devoting attention to one line of business or to serving a single market).

Some find population ecology theory difficult to apply to management because its level of analysis lies outside the organization's boundary and thus largely outside its control. Nonetheless, the viewpoint offered by this theory is often useful when communicating with members of government or regulatory agents whose perspective is normally defined by the environmental level of analysis due to the large numbers of organizations their policies affect. If you belong to these types of organization, you will likely feel more comfortable with the recommendations of population ecology than with those of resource dependence theory.

There are other issues to consider in applying population ecology theory. First, as with Darwin's theory, the definition of fitness is a problem—survival is explained by fitness, but fitness is defined as survival—this central tautology means you cannot predict survival on the basis of an independent assessment of fit; you can only recognize it once it has occurred. Second, the theory applies most readily to populations that are highly competitive and not all populations conform to this requirement. Populations dominated by a few large organizations, or facing significant barriers to entry or exit such as high start-up costs (e.g., automobile manufacturing) or complex legal regulation (e.g., pharmaceuticals) do not make ideal candidates for the application of population ecology theory. In these circumstances the institutional view often proves more useful.

Symbolic environmental analysis

Those adopting the symbolic perspective view the environment as a social construction arising from and in enactment, cognitive mapping, and sensemaking processes. Interpretation is a factor in all social construction processes, as are the symbols that invoke and carry meaning within them. Environments emerge from intersubjectively shared symbolism and beliefs about the environment; and by expectations set in motion by these symbols and beliefs. Just as for modernists, environments constituted by social construction have material consequences for those adopting the symbolic perspective. These consequences arise from organizational members' cognitions and feelings about the features of the environment they attend to and to which they respond. Different organizations construct their environments differently, and the same organization will change its behavior in response to its environment when its constructions change.

For institutionalists, actors are often unwitting dupes of environment level systems that form institutional fields. Institutional fields organize actions and activities within an environment, whereas for enactment theorists environments are constructed through the social interactions and relationships arising between individual actors and from their actions. Different levels of analysis give these two views their quite different positions within symbolic organization theory, just as different levels of analysis differentiate resource dependence and population ecology theory within the modernist perspective. Structuration theory occupies a position that does not privilege one analytical level over the other, nor does it choose between the modern or symbolic perspective, but I will wait to present this theory until we develop the concept of organizational social structure.

Institutional theories of organization–environment relations

Institutional theory argues that, not only do organizations require raw materials, capital, labor, knowledge, and equipment, they also depend upon the acceptance of the societies in which they operate. This idea inspired modernist organization theorists to add social legitimacy to the list of inputs depicted in the open systems model of organization, as shown in Figure 3.9. This addition granted the symbolic perspective an inroad into organization theory by virtue of its acknowledgment of the importance of human values.

Elaborating on Selznick's idea that organizations adapt to and express the values of their society, American sociologists Paul DiMaggio and Woody Powell argued that 'organizations compete not just for resources and customers, but for political power and institutional legitimacy, for social as well as economic fitness.'[11] In other words, environments place demands on organizations in two distinguishable ways: (1) they may make technical, economic, and physical demands that require organizations to produce and exchange their goods and services in a market or a quasi-market, and (2) they may make social, cultural, legal, or political demands that require organizations to play particular roles in society and to establish and maintain certain outward appearances. Environments dominated by technical, economic, and/or physical demands reward organizations for efficiently and effectively supplying the environment with goods and services, while environments dominated by social, cultural, legal, and/or political demands reward organizations for at least outwardly conforming to the values, norms, rules, and beliefs upheld by social institutions, such as government, the law, religion, and education. The reward for conformity to institutional influence is social legitimacy, and social legitimacy can be as much a boon to survival as any other input to the organization's transformation process.

Recognizing the socio-cultural and politico-legal bases of environmental influence on organizations raises the question: Who or what directs this influence? According to American institutional sociologist W. Richard Scott, aspects of the organizational environment through which institutional influences operate include: regulatory structures, government agencies, laws and courts, professions, interest groups, and mobilized public opinion.[12] But how do institutional agents such as these do their work?

Neo-institutionalists ('neo' because they no longer strictly follow Selznick) move well beyond mere recognition of legitimizing institutional foundations to describe the processes

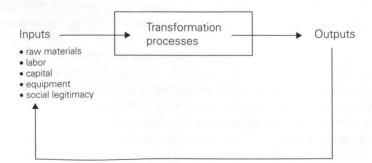

Figure 3.9 Social legitimacy as an organizational resource

Institutional theory suggests that social legitimacy be considered an input to the organizational transformation process along with raw materials and other resources upon which this process depends.

by which organizations and their repeated activities become institutionalized. For instance, Scott defined institutionalization as 'the process by which actions are repeated and given similar meaning by self and others.'[13] Thus, not only can government, religion, and education be conceptualized as institutions, but so can actions such as voting, bowing to show respect, or shaking hands, or in organizations such things as recognizing authority, following routine, or adopting the latest management fad.

The idea of institutions as repeated actions and not just shared meanings or conceptions of reality, gives social construction explanatory power (notice that this formulation amounts to a concession to the modernist perspective). When shared meaning becomes crystalized in repeated actions, such as when expectations of repeated actions are transformed into rules or laws, then institutions such as governments and courts can be regarded as agents; they are transfigured into institutional actors, just like any other organized entity.

Different institutional mechanisms support repeated action. Powell and DiMaggio identified three: coercive, normative, and mimetic.[14] When the pressure to conform to expectations comes from governmental regulations or laws, then **coercive** institutional pressures are at work. When conformity pressure comes from cultural expectations, for instance via the education or religious beliefs of organizational members, then **normative** institutional pressures are at work. Conformity in service to gaining legitimacy by looking like a successful organization rather than being one (e.g., Selznick's interpretation of the TVA) is a response to **mimetic** institutional pressures. These days mimesis has become the normative activity of **best practice**, which involves copying the structures and practices of successful organizations. This strategy often emerges among organizational decision makers when uncertainty about how to succeed is high.

The most important implication of institutional theory for organizations is that conforming to institutionalized expectations wins social support and ensures **legitimacy**, which enhances the prospects for an organization's survival. Legitimacy is not granted because an organization makes more money or produces better products or services, but because it goes along with accepted conventions.[15]

Often certain structural characteristics, such as bureaucracy in government, or matrix structures in the defense industry, become institutionalized standards by which organizations are judged as appropriate and thus granted social legitimacy regardless of their performance. This is one way to explain how extant beliefs like the 'too big to fail' argument invoked on behalf of big banks during the 2008 financial crisis, were never objectively tested. Because everyone accepts such beliefs as 'true,' there is no reason to question them; they have become the stuff of **institutional myth**.

Once an organization has learned how to look good (e.g., to look like a rational organization), it need do only face work to attract the other resources it needs to survive (including technical support and financial backing), which allowed institutionalized organizations like the TVA, or big banks in the financial crisis, to appear legitimate while behaving in ways that were decidedly not. The lack of any objective criteria by which to judge an organization's performance means that institutionalized organizations are not accountable to society except in a very superficial sense.

Obviously there are limits to what institutionalization permits. Public outcry against unethical business practices not only threatens an institution's survival, it can kill the institution outright. For example, in the late 1990s Enron (US), Arthur Anderson (US), and Parmalat

(Italy) all failed as the result of public scandals, and at the start of this century AIB and Lehman Brothers fell when they were perceived as having violated corporate ethics. Freddie Mae and Freddie Mac, the US government sponsored enterprises that provide a secondary market for trading mortgages, though not destroyed, were seriously threatened and have yet to recover from their severe losses of legitimacy when they were implicated in the 2008 financial crisis. Human and animal rights activists as well as environmental protection groups offer other examples of environmental forces able to de-legitimize organizations and sometimes entire industries (e.g., the fur trade) through mobilization of public opinion and direct action such as boycotts, demonstrations, letter writing, and e-mail, blog, Facebook, or Twitter campaigns.[16] These examples reveal the importance of social legitimacy by showing what can happen if it is threatened or withheld.

In applying institutional theory to an analysis of a particular organization you should consider how the organization adapts to its institutional context. For instance, analyze the sources (e.g., regulatory agencies, laws, social and cultural expectations) and types of institutional pressure (e.g., coercive, normative, mimetic) exerted by the environment on the organization. Also consider how decision-making processes are being shaped by institutional myths that may hide institutional forces behind a mask of technical rationality. Finally, try to imagine how the organization might gain greater legitimacy within its institutional context and what risks accompany such efforts.

The enacted environment

According to enactment theory, while organizational members may assume the environment is objectively reflected in the data they use for its analysis, analysis itself creates the environment to which their organization responds. Enactment theory reaches beyond the modernist information theory of perceived uncertainty. Instead of arguing that complexity and change challenge organizational decision makers with an increased need for information, enactment theory maintains that when decision makers respond to their perceptions, they enact the environment they imagine and anticipate.[17]

Along the lines of the information theory of uncertainty, cognitive organization theorist Karl Weick started from the assumption that, regardless of belief in the existence (or not) of an objectively real environment, conditions in the environment cannot be separated from perceptions of those conditions. But Weick blended this idea with social construction theory to suggest that if organizational decision makers assume the environment is real, they will gather and analyze information in order to create accurate forecasts and make rational decisions. If decision makers perceive the environment as complex and unanalyzable, then more data, and approaches to managing the environment based upon them, will be used.

Acting on constructed complexity enacts a complex environment as databases grow making analysis of an ever-growing database more and more uncertain. In this enacted world, people interpret uncertainty as a lack of information that they attribute to environmental complexity and change, but complexity and uncertainty arise from their efforts to monitor and control the environment. This paradoxical situation offers opportunities to organizations as well as challenges to decision makers. For example, Steve Jobs of Apple Computer interpreted the perceived complexity and rapidly changing context of computer technology applications in a unique way that can be interpreted as an enactment of a world in which smartphones and tablets have become part of everyday life everywhere.

It is important to understand how enactment can accommodate material reality, as this constitutes the main difference between the symbolic and modern perspectives. This may be easiest to explain in reference to the cult film classic *The Gods Must Be Crazy*. The story begins when someone flying in an airplane passes over a remote village inhabited by a primitive tribe. When a Coke bottle from the plane is inadvertently dropped into their midst, tribe members, having no idea what it is, nonetheless find many uses for it (e.g., rolling pin, hammer, ant collector). They eventually find this 'new technology' so indispensable they start fighting over it. Their chief, demonstrating great wisdom, throws the bottle away and soon the tribe resumes its former peaceful existence.

Just so, according to enactment theory, we generate complexity with alluring material such as that which technology offers. Consider, for example, how smartphones carrying Facebook apps revolutionized social action during the Arab Awakening. The flash mob movement of the West that preceded these and other recent political actions may have seemed innocuous at the time they arose, but they helped enact a technologically supported trend for grass roots political action that emerged a world away, and that will have more consequences as the lessons learned by those engaging in these movements enable a sharing of knowledge and ideas enacting further developments.

A corollary to Weick's enactment theory can be found in his concept of **equivocality**. According to Weick, humans equivocate when they multiply perceived possibilities that they then use to enact contradictory realities, which in turn promote further equivocation. Equivocality leads to experiences of uncertainty and to the closely related concept of **ambiguity**. To explore how ambiguity not only challenges but can also benefit organizations, particularly in terms of enabling adaptation to changing environments, political scientists James March (American) and Johan Olsen (Norwegian) argued for defining organizational ambiguity as: 'a strategy for suspending rational imperatives toward consistency [to help organizations] explore alternative ideas of possible purposes.'[18]

Eric Eisenberg, an American communication theorist, expanded on March's ideas about ambiguity by pointing out that people sometimes purposely omit contextual cues and thereby introduce ambiguity into communication that encourages multiple interpretations.[19] Eisenberg claimed that by strategically encouraging multiple interpretations of goals and vision, managers can produce **unified diversity**, an idea that challenges notions of unity such as Gulick's concept of the unity of command, or Fayol's harmonizing notion of esprit de corps, without going as far as the postmodern desertion of all modern management principles.

American organization theorist Deborah Meyerson provided an example of unified diversity in her study of the ambiguities confronted by hospital social workers.[20] She found that social workers in the hospitals she studied shared a common orientation and purpose as well as performing similar tasks, but the ambiguity of their experience of doing social work in the tense and uncertain environment of the hospital resulted in their using different techniques to arrive at widely varied solutions to what would seem to be objectively similar problems. Intriguingly, she found that when a hospital's culture accommodated and supported the multiple and often conflicted meanings social workers associated with their practice, they experienced less burnout.

Scenario analysis, an approach to environmental analysis pioneered at Royal Dutch Shell, provides another illustration of purposeful ambiguity creation. Instead of carrying out a rational analysis of objective environmental conditions and trends, scenario analysis asks organizational decision makers to create narratives about different ways the future might unfold and then assess the likelihoods and risks of each. This may all seem pretty rational in a modern perspective, but consider that, as each scenario is produced, either via mental rehearsal or through play acting, decision makers are anticipating the organization's future.[21] This anticipation begins the process of making the environment real to its enactors, albeit ambiguously in the sense of defining multiple anticipations. Then again, sharing such an ambiguous future no doubt fraught with uncertainty, could produce enough discomfort to unify those involved behind belief in a single strategy for confronting the environment.

Postmodernism and organization–environment relations

One implication of enactment theory not normally taken up within the symbolic perspective is that, once we recognize our role as social constructors of reality, we can free ourselves from situations we do not like by deconstructing distasteful social constructions. Using this sort of thinking postmodernists push for radical change that begins with linguistic deconstruction of discourses and texts supporting an existing social construction, but which can end in material change. For example, some believe that postmodern ways of thinking led to the physical destruction of the Berlin Wall, as well as to all that this deconstruction symbolically represents today. Others see these ideas at work behind changes such as the Arab Awakening that has already brought down governments and rallied hopes for democracy, or in the Occupy movement.

The postmodern perspective often strikes an ethical chord, reminding us that the organizations and other socially constructed realities we inhabit ultimately reflect our values and choices. It politicizes the concept of legitimacy from institutional theory and borrows the agency of enactment theory, to move into entirely new philosophical territory that challenges both the symbolic, but most particularly the modern perspective.

Some postmodern organization theorists take as their departure point the history of industrialization from which organization theory emerged. They reason that, just as the modern period of industrialization forever changed the world, so too will postmodernism, so named to indicate what lies beyond the modern.[22] Following along the trajectory that originates in industrialization shows how postmodern organization aligns in many revealing respects with the post-industrial organizing practices that are redefining the contours of life today.

Three phases of industrialization

Tom Burns defined the trajectory of Western industrial development in terms of three distinguishable phases.[23] The first phase, which ushered in the factory system, grew out of the use of machines to extend and enlarge the productivity of work. The factory system offered an alternative to subcontracting, which was the way labor was organized in the craft-based economies that existed before factories appeared.

In subcontracting, groups of individuals, typically working under a master craftsman, contracted out for specific jobs. In factories, the subcontractor's role was replaced by that of the foreman who worked at the discretion of the factory owner, often directed by a general manager hired to protect the owner's interests. And even though the social status of both remained roughly the same, a foreman's responsibilities and freedoms were considerably less than those of a subcontractor. For example, while subcontractors were responsible for hiring and firing, assigning work tasks, and defining the pace of work, in a factory these responsibilities belonged to owners and their executives.

Industrialization's first phase got started in the British textile industry where collections of machines tended by feeders and by maintenance and repair workers were all located in a single place—the factory. The machines in these early factories were typically all of a single type and usually performed only one task in a simple, repetitive process. More complex tasks were still carried out using the older system of subcontracting among craft workers. While the maintenance workers and supervisors in the early factories were nearly always men, most of the machine operators were women who were, in turn, assisted by children. Thus in phase one of industrialization in Britain, gender relations in factories generally reflected gender relations in society. Typically, men had higher status and greater opportunity than women, while both men and women had greater status and opportunity than children, forming what most considered a natural hierarchy.

During the second phase of industrial development, which began roughly in the 1850s and 1860s, the factory system diffused into clothing and food manufacturing, engineering, and chemical, iron, and steel processing, all of which depended upon more complex production processes than those of the textile industry. According to Burns, the increased technical complexity of manufacturing operations demanded parallel growth in systems of social organization and bureaucracy with emphasis on control, routine, and specialization. These changes were reflected in substantial increases in the ranks of managers and administrative staff (e.g., professional and clerical personnel) and were accompanied by improvements in transportation and communication, freer trade, and growing public interest in the consumable products of industrial manufacturing. An armaments revolution also followed the development of machine tools and improvements in steel and chemical technology made possible by industrialization such that developments similar to those in industry were seen in the growth of national armies and governmental administrations.

It was the changes introduced in the second phase of industrialization that, according to Burns, attracted the attention of the sociologists whose ideas founded organization theory. For instance, Weber and Marx both predicted that industrialization would create a new middle class of managers, clerical workers, and professionals who would be employed in large, hierarchical organizations. These theorists also anticipated some of the problems the third phase of industrialization would bring, including gloomy projections concerning the iron cage of bureaucracy, and the greedy exploitation of resources and humankind that capitalism would unleash on the world.

Burns claimed that in the third phase of industrial development production would catch up with and overtake spontaneous domestic demand. Under these conditions, capitalism's dependence on economic growth leads to (1) enhanced sensitivity to the consumer and to new techniques for stimulating consumption (e.g., product development, design, consumer and market research, professionalized sales forces, advertising, branding), (2) the internationalization of firms in search of new markets, and (3) new technological developments that increasingly occur within industrial firms via research and development activities. Burns believed that the convergence of these changes within organizations would lead to greater flexibility, a strong customer-orientation, international activity and hence internationalized identities, and constantly increasing technological sophistication. Similar ideas occurred to other observers of these changes.

According to American futurist Alvin Toffler in his 1970 book *Future Shock*, a good way to envision the significance of social transformation initiated by computer and telecommunications technology is to compare it to the transformation of agricultural into industrial societies brought about by industrialization. American sociologist Daniel Bell gave these new developments the name **post-industrialism** in his 1973 book *The Coming of Post-industrial Society*, where he argued that, whereas industrial societies are organized around controlling labor for the production of goods, post-industrial society is organized around the creation of knowledge and the uses of information. Emphasis on information led Bell, among others, to predict the rise of the service sector and the decline of manufacturing, with knowledge workers (technical specialists and other professionals) joining capitalists as the most powerful members of society. Globalization, in this view, was an expression of the newfound ability to instantaneously share information and knowledge around the world.

Another correlate of post-industrialization, initially remarked by American futurist John Naisbitt in his book *Megatrends*, is the abandonment of hierarchies in favor of communication networks with a consequent shift from vertically to horizontally structured organizations. Discussions of post-industrial organizations, or post-bureaucratic where public organizations were in focus, typically involved comparisons of the forms of work and organization favored during phase two of industrialization with those anticipated with the coming information age. Much energy has been devoted to describing what, in particular, was changing and Table 3.2 presents some of these contrasts in relation to the environment, technology, social structure, culture, and physical structure, and their consequences for work and organizations. Be sure to read the post-industrial column of Table 3.2 with the sector changes listed in Table 3.1 in mind—I am sure you can find many more ideas to add to these lists to honor the constant change of postmodern/post-industrial life.

The idea of post-industrialization was originally developed using the assumption that the changes referred to are objectively real. But postmodernism brought with it a critique of this modern perspective. Many who adopt the postmodern perspective think that the most influential changes associated with the computer will not be found in the objective world so much as in the ways that computer use recursively turns back on our selves. In other words it is we who have been altered by using the computer, multi-media, and various forms of rapid transportation and instant communication.

Stakeholder theory

The prototypical post-industrial organizational form is the network, but other forms associated with post-industrialism include joint ventures, strategic alliances, and virtual organizations as well as the democratically inspired labor-managed firm and the post-bureaucratic organization. One distinguishing feature of post-industrial organizations is **boundarylessness**. Their boundaries with the environment are either transparent or

Table 3.2 Comparison of organizational implications of industrialism and post-industrialism

	Industrial period	Post-industrial period
Environment	Nation-states regulate national economies Mass marketing standardization The Welfare State	Global competition De-concentration of capital with respect to nation-state Fragmentation of markets and international decentralization of production Rise of consumer choice, demand for customized goods Rise of social movements and single-issue politics (e.g., recycling, Occupy) Service class Pluralism, diversity, location
Technology	Mass production along Taylorist/Fordist lines Routine Manufacturing output	Flexible manufacturing, automation Use of computer for design, production, and stock control Just-in-time systems (JIT) Emphasis on speed and innovation Service-information emerging as most important organizational outputs (a.k.a., value-added activities)
Social structure	Bureaucratic Hierarchical with vertical communication emphasized Specialization Vertical and horizontal integration Focused on control	New organizational forms (e.g., networks, strategic alliances, virtual organization, supply/value chain) Flatter hierarchies with horizontal communication and devolved managerial responsibility Outsourcing Informal mechanisms of influence (participation, culture, communication) Vertical and horizontal disintegration Loose boundaries between functions, units, organizations
Culture	Celebrates stability, tradition, custom Organizational values: growth, efficiency, standardization, control	Celebrates uncertainty, paradox, fashion Organizational values: quality, customer service, diversity, innovation
Physical structure	Concentration of people in industrial towns and cities Local or nationalistic worldview predominant Time experienced as linear	De-concentration of urban areas Reduction in transportation time links distant spaces and encourages international orientation and globalization or 'glocalization' Compression of time (e.g., the shortening of product lifecycles)

(continued...)

Table 3.2 (*continued*)

	Industrial period	Post-industrial period
Nature of work	Routine	Frenetic, changing unpredictably
	Deskilled labor	Knowledge-based skills required
	Functional specialization of tasks and jobs	Cross-functional teamwork
		Emphasis on continuous learning
		Outsourcing, subcontracting, self-employment, teleworking prevail

Source: Based on Clegg (1990); Harvey (1990); Heydebrand (1977); Kumar (1995); Lash and Urry (1987, 1994); Piore and Sabel (1984).

permeable. Boundaries between internal groups also disappear as distinctions cease to be made between departments, hierarchical positions, and even jobs. Instead employees collaborate with an ever-changing mix of others in temporary cross-functional and cross-organizational teams that emphasize learning in order to keep up with the rapid and never-ending change to which these organizations are well suited and which they help to create. Post-industrial organizational life is thus characterized by uncertainty, contradiction, and paradox; states that contrast sharply with the industrial organization's stability, routine, and rationality. Such views take Burns and Stalker's organic form of organizing well beyond its initial conceptualization.

The boundarylessness of organic organizations extends to the organization's stakeholders whose interests meld with those of the organization as the result of mutual influence. Although different interests are represented by the environment, it becomes impossible to set these off against one another or to privilege one set of interests, an argument that has been examined in depth by American ethics professor R. Edward Freeman.[24]

According to Freeman, corporations operate via a social contract with society that guarantees certain rights to those who have an interest (a stake) in the organization's activities and/or outcomes. The theory is that organizations that attend to the demands of all stakeholders will outperform organizations that ignore some of their stakeholders while privileging others. Notice that stakeholder theory expands the concept of a contract from its narrow political–legal meaning to include social legitimacy. For example, consider the issue of corporate governance to which Freeman applied stakeholder theory. Legal interpretations of corporate responsibility are often restricted to the protection and enhancement of shareholder wealth. Freeman argued that although this is part of corporate responsibility, it is not to be achieved at the expense of respecting ethical considerations such as the potential of organizational activities to do harm (e.g., pollute local air or water supplies, damage a local economy with a plant closing, cause a species of animal to become extinct). In its adoption of social legitimacy as a criterion for governance, stakeholder theory appears to be an application of institutional theory. Furthermore, insofar as stakeholder theory offers justification for reining in the self-interested actions of a privileged stakeholder group (i.e., owners and executives), it resonates with key aspects of critical theory and postmodernism.

One important implication of stakeholder theory is that ethics obligates organizations to consider their impact on the wider social and physical environments from which they take their resources. Environmental sustainability and corporate social responsibility are two movements in which some companies participate in acknowledgment of these obligations. For example, Interface, the US-based floor cover manufacturing company, a self-professed former 'plunderer of the Earth,' underwent enormous change when it opened itself to the influence of environmental activists and became the standard bearer for environmental protection through environmentally sustainable manufacturing.[25] Danish pharmaceutical company Novo Nordisk provides another example. This company was one of the first to use triple bottom line accounting practices to voluntarily report the company's annual performance in terms of environmental and social responsibility alongside the measures of economic performance demanded by law.

The moral of postmodern theory—avoid hegemony

Most postmodernists oppose replacing modern theories of organization with a bunch more theories, therefore the term postmodern theory is a bit of an oxymoron. Distaste for theorizing is based on the belief that all abstractions are value laden and hence disguise hegemonic intentions (e.g., using the logic of efficiency to conceal Western exploitation of resources around the world). In Marxist theory, from which critical postmodernism draws much support, **hegemony** is a form of domination in which the interests of the ruling class become the status quo through unquestioning acceptance. This is why postmodernists deconstruct the Grand Narratives of modern organization theory; deconstruction reveals the complicity of these narratives in the capitalist hegemonic order and undermines its hold on us.

But for other postmodernists, deconstruction is only an emancipatory first move toward freedom from modernist habits of thought (e.g., belief that their applications of rationality are universally beneficial). These postmodernists imagine organizational reconstructions based on non-modernist conceptions. For this purpose the assumptions and values of the indigenous peoples whose voices have been silenced by modernist hegemony can prove useful. For example, many American Indian cultures believe that responsibility for protecting the environment (Mother Earth) lies in their hands. Contrast their point of view with the modern belief that exploitative practices, such as strip mining, traditional logging, hunting species to extinction, overgrazing prairies, and destroying the rainforests, are the right of those possessing legal claim to those resources. In this context, postmodern critics ask how modern societies manage to silence such voices as those of indigenous peoples and with what consequences?

A key to applying the postmodern perspective lies in noticing how language is used to construct reality and define identity, and then challenging and changing the terms used in a given discourse. For instance, notice that the distinction between the First and Third Worlds implies a hierarchy of dominance and submission that seems natural to those who accept these identifying labels. Postmodernism supports the efforts of marginalized people to define their own identities by choosing empowering labels and insisting that those in positions of dominance use them (e.g., 'developing world' versus 'Third World').

Recognition of the legitimacy of self-chosen identifying labels within a given discourse community symbolically equalizes all the participants in that linguistic community whose old ways of thinking are opened to change by new ways of speaking. While linguistic strategies such as this cannot perform miracles overnight, there is much reason to believe they unleash transformative powers in society. Take the cases of women and African-Americans in the US, whose powers of self-determination greatly increased along with choosing their own identity labels—woman instead of girl or lady; Black or African instead of Negro or colored.

According to some postmodernists, there is a great need to challenge dominant conceptualizations of the environment and some acknowledge that application of postmodern strategies could help. Organization theorist Paul Shrivastava, for example, turned postmodern deconstruction on organization theory by arguing that conceptions of the environment, such as those provided by the categories and language of modernist organization theory marginalize sustainability. He claimed that by giving so much voice to capitalistic concerns about markets, competitors, industry, and regulation, the natural environment has been denatured, that is, modernist discourse discursively reduces the environment to 'a bundle of resources to be used by organizations.'[26] He warns that the modernist rhetoric of economic necessity has silenced concern for environmental sustainability and justified possibly irreversible abuses to our environment. Deconstructions like this open minds to new possibilities such as Shrivastava's call to place the protection of nature at the center of organizational discourse and to replace the value for wealth with a value for health.

Summary

In conducting environmental analysis from a modernist perspective first define the organization whose environment you are interested in analyzing, then identify the links between this organization and others with which it interacts, or that can influence it through competition, regulation, or social pressure. Using the stakeholder model given in Figure 3.2 will help you make sure you have not left out any important elements of the inter-organizational network. Next consider conditions and trends in the sectors of the environment and assess how the network and its members are likely to be affected by the conditions and trends you have identified. In this effort you are likely to find resource dependence theory and population ecology theories quite helpful.

Remind yourself that distinct levels of analysis are offered by the theories of resource dependence (organizational level) and population ecology (level of the environment), and that the symbolic perspective is invoked when you describe the environment using institutional or enactment theory. These theories derive from differing assumptions about whether the organization is more or less at the mercy of its environment (population ecology and institutional theory), or whether it reciprocally influences the environment (resource dependence and enactment theory).

Institutional theory derives from the environmental level of analysis and tells us that environments vary in the degree to which they are institutionalized and thereby enabled to impose conformity pressures, regardless of whether these take the form of coercion, formal rules and socio-cultural norms, or mimesis. Enactment theory assumes that all sectors of the environment are socially constructed at the organizational level and thus focuses attention on explaining how and why certain types of environmental analysis hold sway at a particular point in time. Ambiguity theory differs in that it often assumes the individual level of analysis as it focuses on the conflicting and contradictory ways individuals cognitively construct organizational contexts, but it feeds the more organizationally focused enactment theory.

Sectors of the environment help differentiate population ecology, which explains the influences generated by the technical, physical, and economic sectors of the environment; and institutional theory, which focuses on the influences of social, cultural, political, and legal sectors. While population ecology and institutional theory are both formulated at the level of the environment, population ecologists attempt to explain the diversity of organizational forms, while institutional theorists try to explain why so many organizations look alike. In spite of their differences, population ecology and institutional theory are similar in that both depict organizations as relatively passive elements of an environment that shapes them and determines their outcomes. Resource dependence and enactment theory, on the other hand, represent organizations as having an active role through counteraction or outright creation of the environment.

It is important to consider all environment-organization theories—population ecology, institutional, resource dependence, and enactment theory. Even though one may seem to fit an organization better than the others, it is good practice to look at the situation through the different lenses provided by these different reference points for describing and analyzing organization-environment relations. Only after trying them all will you be in a position to evaluate their usefulness for the purposes of your analysis. Look for surprises that the juxtaposition of different perspectives and levels of analysis offer you.

Keep in mind as you go through this book that the theoretical categories on offer are not cast in stone, they are ways to think—different categories stimulate different ideas. Postmodernists encourage openness to multiple points of view and try to soften any rigidity in categories and identifying labels. As you apply what you are learning about organization theory to examples you draw from your experience, you will probably find your examples will fit into many categories, and that your examples will want to shift you from one category to another as you consider how they illustrate various theories. This will likely bring you both confusion and insight and may make you uncomfortable. If your discomfort comes from not being able to pin everything down and find the 'right' answer, try to relax. Remind yourself that everything cannot be pinned down where organizations are concerned, partly because, as systems theory suggests, they are always and everywhere more complex than we are. Or, as suggested by social construction theory suggests, they are ongoing works of enactment and sensemaking. As postmodern organization theory suggests, adopt a healthy skepticism about all static structures like categories and participate in deconstructing them.

No matter the approach you take to organization-environment relations, always ask yourself what assumptions lie behind the categories you are using and whose voices are silenced by this particular construction of reality. Try to imagine what biases you bring to your analysis and seek to counteract them. My plea is not to stop categorizing or making distinctions altogether—these are necessary for thought. The message I encourage you to take from postmodernism is to think, talk, and act in full consciousness or, in other words, be self-reflexive.

Key terms

organizational environment	isomorphism
organizational boundary	resource dependence theory
stakeholders	*power/dependence*
inter-organizational network	*criticality*
centrality	*scarcity*
network density	population ecology theory
structural hole	*ecological niche*
supply chain	*population*
sectors of the environment	*variation, selection, retention*
social, cultural, legal, political, economic, technological, and physical	institutional theory
internationalization	*coercive, normative and mimetic conformity pressures*
regionalization	*best practice*
globalization	*social legitimacy*
organizational forms	*institutional myth*
mechanistic	enacted environment
organic	*equivocality*
environmental uncertainty	*ambiguity*
complexity	three phases of industrialization and post-industrialism
rate of change	stakeholder theory
perceptual uncertainty	boundarylessness
information theory of uncertainty	hegemony
law of requisite variety	

Endnotes

1. This formulation can be traced to Dill (1958), Evan (1966), and Thompson (1967). What is here called the inter-organizational network they referred to as the task environment of the organization.
2. Freeman and Reed (1983); Freeman (1984).
3. Granovetter (1985); Burt (1992).
4. Steger (2003).
5. Burns and Stalker (1961).
6. Duncan (1972).
7. Galbraith (1973); Aldrich and Mindlin (1978).
8. Aldrich and Pfeffer (1976).
9. Hawley (1950) is often cited by these population ecologists as a source of inspiration. See Aldrich and Pfeffer (1976) and Aldrich (1979) for reviews. Weick (1979 [1969]) offers a symbolic interpretation of the ideas of variation, selection, and retention for organizational theory.

10. Hannan and Freeman (1977); Carroll (1984); Singh (1990); Carroll and Swaminathan (2000).

11. Selznick (1957); DiMaggio and Powell (1983: 150).

12. Scott (1987).

13. Scott (1992: 117).

14. DiMaggio and Powell (1983); Powell and DiMaggio (1991).

15. Meyer and Rowan (1977).

16. Baron (2003).

17. Weick (1979).

18. March and Olsen (1976: 77); March (1978).

19. Eisenberg (1984: 230).

20. Meyerson (1991).

21. Schwartz (1991).

22. Bell (1973); Lyotard (1979); Harvey (1990).

23. Burns (1962).

24. Freeman and Reed (1983); Freeman (1984).

25. Amodeo (2005).

26. Shrivastava (1995: 125); see also Boje and Dennehy (1993).

References

Aldrich, Howard E. (1979) *Organizations and Environments*. Englewood Cliffs, NJ: Prentice-Hall.

—— and Mindlin, Sergio (1978) Uncertainty and dependence: Two perspectives on environment. In Lucien Karpik (ed.), *Organization and Environment: Theory, Issues and Reality*. London: Sage, 149–70.

—— and Pfeffer, Jeffrey (1976) Environments of organizations. In A. Inkeles, J. Coleman, and N. Smelser (eds.), *Annual Review of Sociology*, Vol. 2. Palo Alto, CA: Annual Reviews, 79–105.

Amodeo, Romona Ann (2005) 'Becoming sustainable': Identity dynamics within transformational culture change at Interface. Doctoral Dissertation, Benedictine.

Baron, David (2003) Face-off. *Stanford Business*, August.

Bell, Daniel (1973). *The Coming of Post-industrial Society*. New York: Basic Books.

Boje, David and Dennehy, Robert (1993) Managing in the postmodern world: America's revolution against exploitation. Dubugue, IA: Kendall Hunt.

Burns, Tom (1962) The sociology of industry. In A. T. Walford, M. Argyle, D. V. Glass, and J. J. Morris (eds.), *Society: Problems and Methods of Study*. London: Routledge, Kegan and Paul.

—— and Stalker, George M. (1961) *The Management of Innovation*. London: Tavistock.

Burt, Ron (1992) *Structural Holes: The Social Structure of Competition*. Cambridge, MA: Harvard University Press.

Carroll, Glenn R. (1984) Organizational ecology. *Annual Review of Sociology*, 10: 71–93.

—— and Swaminathan, Anand (2000) Why the microbrewery movement? Organizational dynamics of resource partitioning in the U.S. brewing industry. *The American Journal of Sociology*, 106/3: 715–62.

Clegg, Stewart (1990) *Modern Organizations: Organization Studies in the Postmodern World*. London: Sage.

Dill, William R. (1958) Environments as an influence on managerial autonomy. *Administrative Science Quarterly*, 2: 409–43.

DiMaggio, Paul J. and Powell, W. W. (1983) The iron cage revisited: Institutional isomorphism and collective rationality in organizational fields. *American Sociological Review*, 48: 147–60.

Duncan, Robert B. (1972) Characteristics of organizational environments and perceived environmental uncertainty. *Administrative Science Quarterly*, 17: 313–27.

Eisenberg, Eric (1984) Ambiguity as strategy in organizational communication. *Communication Monograph*, 51: 237–42.

Evan, William (1966) The organization set: Toward a theory of interorganizational relations. In D. Thompson (ed.), *Approaches to Organizational Design*. Pittsburgh, PA: University of Pittsburgh Press, 175–90.

Freeman, R. Edward (1984) *Strategic Management: A Stakeholder Approach*. Boston, MA: Pittman.

—— and Reed, D. (1983) Stockholders and stakeholders: A new perspective on corporate governance. *California Management Review*, 25/3: 88–106.

Galbraith, Jay (1973) *Designing Complex Organizations*. Reading, MA: Addison-Wesley.

Granovetter, Mark (1985) Economic action and social structure: The problem of embeddedness. *American Journal of Sociology*, 91: 481–510.

Hannan, Michael T. and Freeman, John H. (1977) The population ecology of organizations. *American Journal of Sociology*, 82: 929–64.

Harvey, David (1990) *The Condition of Postmodernity*. Cambridge, MA: Blackwell.

Hawley, Amos (1950) *Human Ecology*. New York: Ronald Press.

Heydebrand, Wolf (1977) Organizational contradictions in public bureaucracies: Toward a Marxian theory of organizations. *Sociological Quarterly*, 18/Winter: 83–107.

Kumar, Krishan (1995) *From Post-industrial to Post-modern Society: New Theories of the Contemporary World*. Oxford: Blackwell.

Lash, Scott and Urry, John (1987) *The End of Organized Capitalism*. Cambridge: Polity Press.

——— (1994) *Economies of Signs and Space*. London: Sage.

Lyotard, Jean-François (1979) *The Postmodern Condition: A Report on Knowledge*. Minneapolis: University of Minnesota Press.

March, James G. (1978) Bounded rationality, ambiguity, and the engineering of choice. *Bell Journal of Economics*, 9: 587–608.

—— and Olsen, Johan P. (1976) *Ambiguity and Choice in Organizations*. Bergen: Universitetsforlaget.

Meyer, John W. and Rowan, Brian (1977) Institutionalized organizations: Formal structure as myth and ceremony. *American Journal of Sociology*, 83: 340–63.

Meyerson, Debra (1991) 'Normal' ambiguity? In P. Frost et al. (eds.), *Reframing organizational culture*, 131–44. Newbury Park, CA: Sage.

Pfeffer, Jeffrey and Salancik, Gerald R. (1978) *The External Control of Organizations: A Resource Dependence Perspective*. New York: Harper & Row.

Piore, Michael and Sabel, Charles (1984) *The Second Industrial Divide*. New York: Basic Books.

Powell, Walter W. and DiMaggio, Paul J. (1991) (eds.) *The New Institutionalism in Organizational Analysis*. Chicago, IL: University of Chicago Press.

Schwartz, Peter (1991) *The Art of the Long View*. New York: Currency Doubleday.

Scott, W. Richard (1987) The adolescence of institutional theory. *Administrative Science Quarterly*, 32: 493–511.

—— (1992) *Organizations: Rational, Natural, and Open Systems* (3rd edn.). Englewood Cliffs, NJ: Prentice-Hall.

Selznick, Philip (1957) *Leadership in Administration*. New York: Harper & Row.

Shrivastava, Paul (1995) Ecocentric management for a risk society. *Academy of Management Review*, 20: 118–37.

Singh, Jitendra V. (1990) (ed.) *Organizational Evolution: New Directions*. Beverly Hills, CA: Sage.

Steger, Manfred B. (2003) *Globalization: A Very Short Introduction*. Oxford: Oxford University Press.

Thompson, James D. (1967) *Organizations in Action*. New York: McGraw-Hill.

Weick, Karl E. (1969 [1979]) *The Social Psychology of Organizing*. Reading, MA: Addison-Wesley.

Further reading

Donaldson, T. and Preston, L. E. (1995) The stakeholder theory of the corporation: Concepts, evidence, and implications. *Academy of Management Review*, 20/1: 65–91.

Hannan, Michael T. and Freeman, John H. (1989) *Organizational Ecology*. Cambridge, MA: Harvard University Press.

Karpik, Lucien (1978) (ed.) *Organization and Environment: Theory, Issues and Reality*. London: Sage.

Lawrence, Paul R. and Lorsch, Jay W. (1967) *Organization and Environment: Managing Differentiation and Integration*. Cambridge, MA: Harvard University Press.

Meyer, John W. and Scott, W. Richard (1992) *Organizational Environments: Ritual and Rationality.* Beverly Hills, CA: Sage.

Oliver, Christine (1991) Strategic responses to institutional processes. *Academy of Management Review*, 16: 145–79.

Zucker, Lynne G. (1987) Institutional theories of organization. In W. R. Scott (ed.), *Annual Review of Sociology*, Palo Alto, CA: Annual Reviews Inc., 13: 443–64.

—— (1988) (ed.) *Institutional Patterns and Organizations: Culture and Environment.* Cambridge, MA: Ballinger.

4 Organizational social structure

Organization theorists often claim that organization arises when people learn what they can accomplish if they pool their efforts, resources, knowledge, and/or identities. That groups can outperform individuals in terms of the efficiency of labor has already been discussed in terms of pin manufacturing, while NASA illustrates the superior effectiveness of groups in making it possible to do things that no individual acting alone could accomplish. NASA's achievements in space exploration, for example, required the organized efforts of scientists, engineers, and astronauts, but also technicians, production workers, maintenance workers, clerical employees, and managers, not to mention equally important organized efforts within the scientific community, the defense industry, and the United States government. NASA also illustrates how failures of organizing can destroy lives and careers and threaten an organization's survival, all of which happened when NASA lost two space shuttle crews in horrific explosions.

Of all the theoretical concepts organization theory has produced, social structure has probably been around the longest. The term **structure** refers to the more or less stable relationships among parts of any system or entity. For example, the relationships between the foundation, frame, roof, and walls of a building give it the structure it needs to stand and provide shelter to its occupants, just as relationships between bones, organs, blood, and tissue structure a human body and enable its many life supporting functions – mobility, digestion, respiration, circulation, and so on.

Organization theorists are particularly interested in two types of structure: physical and social. Physical structure refers to the spatio-temporal relationships between material elements of an organization such as its buildings, their geographical locations, and the heritage and other symbolic meanings they embody. Social structure meanwhile refers to relationships among the people and the roles and responsibilities they assume within the organization, such as the groups or units to which they belong (e.g., functional departments, divisions). Of course the physical and social structures of organizations are not completely separate; they overlap in the same sense that people have both physical bodies and social identities. This chapter will cover the social structure of organizations and organizing while physical structure, which is the most recent concept to develop in the core of organization theory, will be taken up in Chapter 7.

The elements and dimensions of organizational social structure (sometimes simply called organizational structure), introduced during the prehistory of organization theory, will provide a starting point for discussing this concept as the modern perspective represents it. Even today one of the assumptions most modern organization theorists make is that social structure is objective, an entity with identifiable and measurable characteristics. Most often an organization's social structure is assumed to be stable unless or until management decrees a change, which is where normative interests intersect with those of modernist explanation. If a change in structure means a change in the organization, then as the environment changes so too must the organization in order to fit into its changing context. Thus it was that social structure came to be viewed as a pragmatic tool for controlling employee behavior and achieving desired organizational outcomes.

As organization theory developed, the assumptions underpinning the modern perspective in organizations were challenged and new understandings and appreciation for the benefits of loosening the grip of formal authority and other modernist structural mechanisms were added. The chapter more or less follows the historical progression of the social structure concept, one step at a time, beginning with its pre-modern origins and ending with new appreciations of organizational social structure made available by those who adopt the symbolic and postmodern perspectives.

Origins of the social structure concept

Early organization theorists were keenly interested in finding the most effective and efficient way of achieving an organization's stated purpose or goal through the structural arrangement of people, positions, and work units. The trouble was that there was no agreement over which dimensions of organizational structure revealed the one best way to organize. The debate traces back to Max Weber's definition of organizational social structure, part of his theory of bureaucracy.

Weber's ideal bureaucracy

Max Weber published his theory of organization in the early 1900s, though his work was not translated from German into English until the mid-1940s, coinciding with the birth of organization theory in its modern form. In numerous essays, Weber offered an ideal model of organization as a **bureaucracy**, whose main characteristics are:[1]

- A fixed division of labor.
- A clearly defined hierarchy of offices, each with its own sphere of competence.
- Candidates for offices are selected on the basis of technical qualifications and are appointed rather than elected.
- Officials are remunerated by fixed salaries paid in money.
- The office is the primary occupation of the office holder and constitutes a career.
- Promotion is granted according to seniority or achievement and is dependent upon the judgment of superiors.
- Official work is to be separated from ownership of the means of administration.

- A set of general rules governing the performance of offices; strict discipline and control in the conduct of the office is expected. (*Source*: Parsons (1947); Scott (1992).)

Weber's use of the term ideal might not be what you expect; he used it in the sense of a pure idea—something that can only be known through the imagination—rather than a perfect or desirable entity or existential state. In his original discussion of ideal types, he made reference to similar notions in other academic disciplines, such as ideal gases in physics, or ideal competition in economics. Ideals in Weber's usage do not indicate goodness or virtue; instead their abstract nature makes them a useful basis for theorizing, even if we cannot expect them to exist in the world around us.

The ideal bureaucracy that Weber imagined offered a model for turning employees with no more than average abilities into rational decision makers serving the clients and constituencies of a bureaucracy with impartiality and efficiency. Conceptualized in this way, the bureaucratic form promised reliable decision making, merit-based selection and promotion, and the impersonal, and therefore fair, application of rules. Modernist organization theorists based their definition of three core components of organizational social structure on Weber's theory: division of labor, hierarchy of authority, and formalized rules and procedures.

Division of labor

The **division of labor** refers to splitting the work of the organization among employees, each of whom performs a piece of the whole output-generating process. It distributes responsibilities and assigns work tasks. When labor is properly divided the combination of work tasks produces the desired output of the organization with efficiency and effectiveness. Smith's description of the division of labor in a pin-manufacturing firm provided a simple example of how the division of labor organizes work (one draws out the pin, while another attaches the head), but you can easily think of other examples such as the assembly line of an automobile manufacturing plant, or the processes involved in providing banking, education, or health care services.

The ways in which tasks are grouped into jobs and jobs into organizational units is also part of the division of labor. Grouping similar or closely related activities together into organizational subunits produces departments (e.g., purchasing, production, marketing) and/or divisions (e.g., consumer products, international sales) from which combinations of organizational structures are built. Because administrators or managers typically oversee the subunits created by this **departmentalization**, the division of labor is closely related to hierarchy of authority, the second of Weber's components of organizational social structure.

Hierarchy of authority

Hierarchy refers to the distribution of authority in an organization. Some people believe that hierarchy is a fundamental aspect of life; they find evidence to support their belief in things like the pecking order observed among chickens and the way wolves and dogs demonstrate domination and submission in their relationships to each other and to humans. Organizational hierarchies, they believe, are the human form of these animalistic tendencies.

Regardless of whether or not you agree that hierarchy is natural, you will probably recognize it as a feature common to most if not all organizations. According to Weber, a top position in the hierarchy confers legal authority—the rights to make decisions, give direction, and reward and punish others. One's authority is strictly a matter of position, so when an individual retires or moves to a new position or different organization, the authority of their former position remains behind to be assumed by their successor.

The hierarchy defines formal reporting relationships such that it maps the organization's vertical communication channels—downward (directing subordinates) and upward (reporting to management). When each position in an organization is subordinate to only one other position, a phenomenon Fayol called the scalar principle, authority and vertical communication combine to permit the most highly placed individuals to gather information from, and to direct and control the performance of, all individuals throughout the organization in an efficient manner.

In the past, many managers believed that every member of an organization should report to only one person so that each member has one clear path through the hierarchy stretching from themselves to their boss, to their boss's boss, all the way to the pinnacle of the organization. But dual reporting relationships are increasingly common, as are nonhierarchical lateral connections used to integrate an organization's diverse activities and promote flexibility of response to environmental pressures. Weber's third component of social structure sometimes serves as a substitute for hierarchical authority as it replaces some of the control lost to flattened hierarchical authority structures or when work is distributed across large distances in global organizations.

Formalized rules and procedures

Formalization involves the extent to which explicit rules, regulations, policies, and procedures govern organizational activities. Indicators of formalization in an organization include: written policies, handbooks, job descriptions, operations manuals, organization charts, management systems such as Management by Objectives (MBO), and technical systems such as PERT (program evaluation review techniques) or supply chain management systems. Formal rules, procedures, position descriptions, and job classifications specify how decisions should be made and work performed.

Government organizations are often associated with both bureaucracy and high levels of formalization. For example, in 2003 the State of California had 4,500 formal job classifications (groupings of jobs defined by similar responsibilities and training) defining the work of 230,228 employees.[2] These job classifications defined the division of labor, specified the type of position appropriate to each level in the hierarchy, and provided the basis for making hiring decisions, determining pay levels, and coordinating work throughout the state.

Along with strict observance of positional authority, formalization contributes to the feeling of impersonality often associated with bureaucratic organizations. It reduces the amount of discretion employees have in performing their work tasks while increasing the control managers maintain over their employees. Studies have shown that formalization tends to discourage innovation and suppress communication.[3] By contrast the lack of formalization, sometimes referred to as informality, denotes the flexibility and spontaneity of non-bureaucratic organizations. However, to really appreciate the concept of bureaucracy it is important to recognize the difference between Weber's ideal bureaucracy and the organizational reality with which you are probably familiar.

For Weber, bureaucracy is not the ponderous frustrating bastion of mediocre service many people associate with this way of organizing. At least in its ideal form, bureaucracy provides a rationalized moral alternative to the common practice of nepotism and other abuses of power rampant in the feudal pre-industrial world from which modern bureaucratic and industrial organizations emerged. Since Weber's time we have learned much about the negative face of bureaucracy, particularly its tendency to over-rationalize decision making to the point of turning people into unfeeling, unthinking automatons, an inclination satirized in Joseph Heller's novel *Catch 22* and Terry Gilliam's film *Brazil*, both of which emphasized the nonsense created by overreliance on bureaucratic formalities. Weber himself recognized the potential for trouble, warning that bureaucracy could easily become an iron cage imprisoning all who wandered into its clutches.

In spite of the drawbacks, when organizations are large and operate routine technologies in fairly stable environments, bureaucracy offers benefits enough for many societies to continue to create and maintain numerous bureaucratic organizations in spite of distaste for the working conditions they foster and disappointment in the level of service they provide, all of which lie far from Weber's ideal. Today you will find bureaucracy in most governments, nearly every university, the Catholic Church, and large organizations such as McDonald's, Telefónica, and Royal Dutch Shell.

Measuring organizational social structure

In their search for general laws that would reveal the best way to organize employees to perform work, classical management scholars used their considerable practical experience as executives and consultants to empirically examine Weber's idealized concepts of division of labor, hierarchy of authority, and formal rules and procedures. Their efforts to refine and extend Weber's theory resulted in specification of numerous dimensions, some of which appear in Table 4.1.

Measures such as those listed in Table 4.2 render the dimensions of social structure amenable to statistical analysis and comparison. The modern perspective in organization theory got its initial boost from studies correlating measures of organizational social structure with measures of performance defined at the individual, group, and organizational levels of analysis. Explanations of statistically significant correlations produced the first distinctly modern theories of organization.

Some of the earliest theories rested on comparisons made between the effectiveness or efficiency of different organizational forms defined by combinations of structural dimensions. For example, differences of social structure were revealed when combining measures of hierarchy and division of labor such as those shown in Figure 4.1. Figure 4.1a shows an organization with a flat structure spread out over many departments (a high degree of horizontal differentiation) with few hierarchical levels (low vertical differentiation). Figure 4.1b, by contrast, shows a tall organizational structure having fewer departments (low horizontal differentiation) but many more hierarchical levels (high vertical differentiation). The data meant to determine which of these and other combinations of structural features produced

Table 4.1 Commonly used dimensions of organizational social structure

Dimension	Measure
Size	*Number of employees in the organization*
Administrative component	Percentage of total number of employees that have administrative responsibilities, often broken into *line functions* (departments involved directly in the production of organizational outputs) and *staff functions* (departments that advise and support line functions with strategic planning, finance, accounting, recruitment, training, and so on).
Differentiation	*Vertical* differentiation, shown in the number of levels in the hierarchy, or *horizontal* reflecting the extent of the division of labor as shown in the number of departments or divisions spanning the entire organization and sometimes reflected in the average span of control of managers.
Integration	The coordination of activities through accountability, rules and procedures, liaison roles, cross-functional teams, or direct contact.
Centralization	Extent to which authority to make decisions concentrates at the top levels of the organization; in *decentralization* decision making is spread across all levels in the hierarchy.
Standardization	The extent to which standard procedures govern the organization's operations and activities rather than using individual judgment and initiative to respond to events as they arise.
Formalization	Extent to which an organization uses written (i.e., formal) job descriptions, rules, procedures, and communications, as opposed to communication and relationships based on informal, face-to-face interaction.
Specialization	Extent to which the work of the organization is divided into narrowly defined tasks assigned to specific employees and work units.

the greatest likelihood of success, proved inconclusive. In some studies one configuration would prevail, while in another something different emerged as the victor.

Over time the empirical approach modernists hoped would reveal the best way to organize led them to define more and more dimensions of social structure, as Table 4.1 attests. Yet what the body of research ultimately demonstrated is that no one structural configuration can be deemed universally superior to the others. Instead many modernist organization theorists came to believe that the best structural choices were contingent upon other variables.

Modernist theories of organizational social structure

Contingency theorists claim that the dimensions of organizational structure relate to each other and to performance differently depending upon the environment the organization faces, and on its size as well as the technology and strategy it employs. Contingency theorists

(a) A flat organization structure

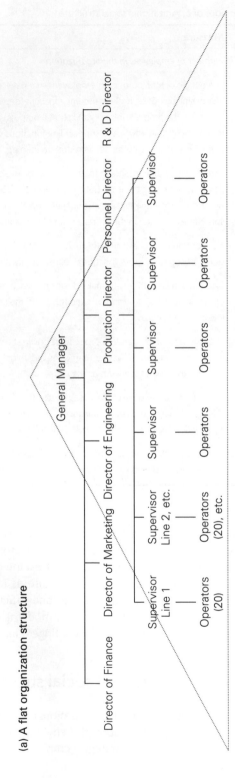

Figure 4.1 A comparison of flat (a) and tall (b) organization structures

These organization charts provide a quick impression of what is meant by steep or tall hierarchies as opposed to flat, less hierarchical organizations.

(b) A tall organization structure

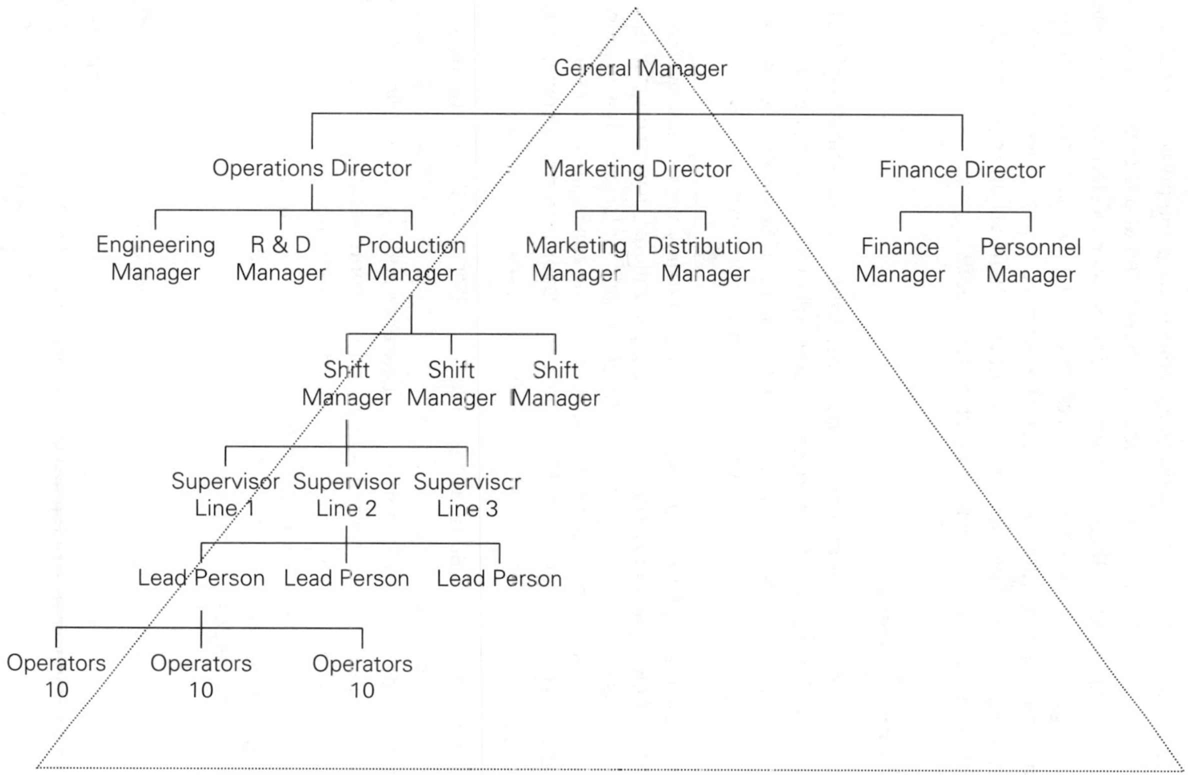

Figure 4.1 (continued)

today still believe that by analyzing structural dimensions in relationship to other variables describing organization, they can offer recipes for successful organizing to practitioners drawn to their way of thinking.

Contingency theory produced several structural typologies and taxonomies that identify particular constellations of structural dimensions found in practice. These constellations allow theorists to group multiple characteristics in order to map the organizational forms they find in practice. This approach only provides static representations of structure, however, and empirical data based on these theoretical frameworks collected over time reveal that structures change. This finding led to models of structural growth and change that promote active engagement in structuring processes. The dynamic approach would eventually open modernist researchers to the symbolic perspective, in part via an important theory lying midway between the two perspectives: structuration theory.

Structural contingency theory

Contingency theorists focus on discovering what constellations of organizational factors contribute to organizational survival and success. Many organizational contingencies have been proposed and validated by empirical study such that, in his 1996 review of contingency theory, Australian organization theorist Lex Donaldson could claim that:

> There are several contingency factors: strategy, size, task uncertainty and technology. These are characteristics of the organization. However, these organizational characteristics in turn reflect the influence of the environment in which the organization is located. Thus, in order to be effective, the organization needs to fit its structure to the contingency factors of the organization and thus to the environment. Hence the organization is seen as adapting to its environment.[4]

British organization theorists Tom Burns and George M. Stalker were the first to suggest in 1961 that effective organizational design is based on fitting the internal organizational structure to the demands of the environment. Paul Lawrence and Jay Lorsch followed close on their heels with their 1967 empirical study of how contingencies created by the environment influenced an organization's patterns of differentiation and integration. At roughly the same time, a group of researchers from Aston University in the UK conducted research showing that an organization's social structure is contingent on its size. These empirical studies collectively shaped contingency theory.

Mechanistic and organic organizations, centralization, and leadership styles

Burns and Stalker's contingency theory not only contributed to theorizing environmental uncertainty, but also produced one of the first studies of how the form an organization takes influences its chances of success. Recall that the studies these researchers conducted in the electronics industry and in research and development (R&D) firms showed mechanistic organizations outperforming organic organizations in stable environments, while in unstable environments organic organizations were more successful.

The theory Burns and Stalker offered in explanation of their findings employed **innovation** as an intervening variable because their studies had shown that innovation tended to be limited in mechanistic forms of organization. They theorized that high levels of hierarchical control, clearly defined roles and tasks, and centralized decision making all impede flexibility and creativity. Likewise formalization interferes with innovation because change requires rewriting policies and rules and disseminating the revisions to supervisors who must then implement the new rules and ensure that others comply with them. They concluded that, whenever innovation is needed for adaptation or responsiveness to changes in the environment, mechanistic structures hinder performance.

In contrast to mechanistic forms, Burns and Stalker reasoned, organic forms are more likely to be innovative and to grant greater discretion to employees performing tasks since they are not bound by the formality of rules and procedures, and decentralized decision making pushes authority and responsibility to lower levels of the hierarchy. This means that employees hired for their knowledge and expertise have the discretion to use their skills and training, and the flexibility to experiment and solve problems as they arise. In organic forms, so the theory goes, systems and people are more proactive and adaptable to changing circumstances. In rapidly changing environments, where organizations need to innovate to survive, teams of knowledgeable employees working together to anticipate and respond quickly to shifting environmental demands are needed.

You can discover the difference between mechanistic and organic forms of organizing for yourself by comparing some common organizations; most college libraries, post offices, and government agencies have the characteristics of mechanistic organizations, while hospital emergency rooms, research laboratories, and outings with your friends tend to be organic. Of course, all organizations combine these two forms of organizing, which is revealed when you drop to lower levels of analysis.

At the level of university departments for example, most administrative work is done in a mechanistic way, while the best faculty research and teaching gives evidence of organic organization. At the level of tasks, however, all jobs have both mechanistic and organic elements. Take university teaching as an example. Teaching is partly mechanistic (e.g., testing knowledge, reporting grades) and partly organic (e.g., designing curricula, facilitating group learning experiences, answering student questions). At the even lower level of subtasks lie even more mechanistic and organic components, and on it goes.

The mechanistic–organic distinction is useful as a way to characterize the central tendencies of different forms of organizing at any level of analysis. The chief differences between them are summarized in Table 4.2.

One of these dimensions, centralization–decentralization, figures prominently in most theories involving organizational social structure and is often invoked when choosing an appropriate leadership style. In a centralized organization, control is maintained by making decisions almost exclusively at the top of the hierarchy, and by expecting employees to accept their executives' decrees without question. However, because centralization minimizes participation among lower-level employees, it often leaves those lower in the hierarchy feeling uninvolved in the organization and can impede their understanding and dampen their enthusiasm for achieving its goals.

By contrast, decentralized organizations rely on the participation of many members of the organization in decision-making processes and so encourage a sense of involvement and feelings of responsibility for outcomes. However, because decentralized organizations are more difficult to control, their executives have to be willing to accept a certain amount of

Table 4.2 Comparison of the characteristics of mechanistic and organic organization

Mechanistic structures *(predictability, accountability)*	Organic structures *(flexibility, adaptability, innovation)*
High horizontal and vertical *differentiation*—a hierarchical structure of authority and control.	High/complex horizontal and vertical *integration*—a network of authority and control based on knowledge of the task.
High formalization—the definition of roles, responsibilities, instructions, and job methods is stable.	Low formalization—tasks and responsibilities are redefined depending on the situation.
Centralization—decisions made at the top of the hierarchy.	Decentralization—decisions made by those closest to and most knowledgeable about the situation, and/or by those with responsibility for implementation.
Standardization through written rules, procedures, SOPs.	Mutual adjustment and redefinition of tasks and methods through joint problem solving and interaction.
Close supervision with authority and prestige based on position.	Personal expertise and creativity without supervision. Prestige attached to expertise.
Vertical (superior–subordinate) communication in the form of instructions.	Frequent lateral communication, often in the form of consultation between people from different departments.

control loss to effectively lead them, which changes the leadership role from one of directing and controlling organizational activities, to inspiring, supporting, and facilitating them.

Differentiation and integration

Like Burns and Stalker, Lawrence and Lorsch believed that effective organizational performance is determined by the fit between an organization's social structure and its environment. In particular, the most successful organizations are those wherein the degree of differentiation and the means of integration match the demands of the environment. In their initial study of six organizations in the plastics industry (at that time a complex and unstable environment), they found that organizational subunits were confronted with different degrees of uncertainty that caused each department (sales, production, applied research, and fundamental research) to vary in terms of its degree of differentiation. Using four dimensions of differentiation—degree of formality, relative amount of attention given to task performance and relationship building, orientation to time, and goal orientation—their data revealed that:

- Departments operating in the most stable environments (production) were more formalized, hierarchical, and carried out more frequent performance reviews than those facing environmental uncertainty (R&D); sales and applied research departments fell in between these two extremes.

- Departments with greater task uncertainty (sales) were more relationship-oriented than departments facing less task uncertainty (production), which were more task-oriented.

- Sales and production departments held short-term orientations and required rapid feedback on results, while R&D departments had long-term orientations (of at least several years out, depending on the length of their projects).

- The goal orientations of sales departments were concerned with customer issues, while production had a goal orientation defined by cost and process efficiency.

In the businesses Lawrence and Lorsch studied, differentiation occurred as sales departments focused on customer satisfaction and building customer relationships, for instance by meeting individual customer requests for customized products, or reducing response times. Meanwhile the production departments in their study were more task-oriented, focusing on daily and weekly output goals, and the efficient use of people and equipment by producing large amounts of a standardized product and minimizing the time required to retool equipment and change work processes for individual orders. You can see how these different orientations might lead to conflict between these departments, especially when performance measures are tied to substantial rewards.

According to Lawrence and Lorsch's theory, the more complex the organization, both in terms of horizontal and vertical differentiation, the greater the need for integration and communication.[5] These researchers defined **integration** as the collaboration required to achieve unity of effort (i.e., getting everyone to pull in the same direction). The most common organizational integration mechanism is hierarchy—creating formal reporting relationships that allow managers to coordinate activities and resolve problems by exercising their authority. Formal rules, procedures, and scheduling are other common integration mechanisms, as are liaison roles, committees, task forces, cross-functional teams, and direct communication between departments. For example, an organization might have a technical sales engineer in a liaison role to talk with the customer, coordinate with purchasing, production planning, production, quality control, finance, and the legal department to ensure a contract is satisfactorily completed on time. A hospital might have a cross-functional team of medical, nursing, therapy, finance, and social services staff to manage an individual patient's health care program.

Differentiation and integration bear an interesting co-dependent relationship; adding hierarchical levels in an organization creates greater vertical differentiation that, in turn, requires more integration. Although the hierarchy of authority makes a substantial contribution to overall coordination, hierarchy alone cannot keep up with a growing organization's endless and ever-increasing demands for integration. At some point, the mechanistic organization gives way to the organic one. In response to this dilemma, numerous additional integrating mechanisms have been devised to complement if not replace the hierarchy of authority.

In a follow-up study, Lawrence and Lorsch scrutinized the relationship between environmental stability and internal structure.[6] They selected two organizations from the packaged foods industry, an industry at the time confronting an unstable environment with many diverse elements, and two from the container industry, where a stable environment prevailed. They concluded that high performing organizations had the appropriate degree of differentiation for their environments and used forms of integration consistent with the coordination demands of their differentiated activities. In particular they found that:

- Unstable environments required a higher degree of differentiation than stable environments in order to meet varying and complex demands.

- Both stable and unstable environments required a high degree of integration, but the means of integration differed: in stable environments, hierarchy and centralized coordination were favored, in unstable environments there is a need to push decision making to lower hierarchical levels so that problems can be dealt with through direct communication with those possessing relevant knowledge.

Lawrence and Lorsch concluded that appropriate levels of differentiation and methods of integration vary depending on the particular organization or department in question and the relevant environment. Their data showed that goodness of fit correlated with higher levels of organizational performance in the sample of businesses and departments they studied.

Organizational size

Researchers from the UK's Aston University developed quantitative measures of six variables defining organizational social structure: the degree of specialization, standardization, formalization, centralization, configuration, and flexibility.[7] They gathered comparative data from 52 organizations on each of these variables. For example, to measure degree of centralization, the researchers assessed the level at which 37 common decisions were made in the organizations surveyed by asking which level in the hierarchy had the authority to make each decision. They averaged the data for all 37 decisions to create an overall centralization score for each organization.

Breaking down the centralization measure, however, revealed that while an organization may be highly decentralized with respect to work-related decisions, it can at the same time be highly centralized with respect to strategic decisions.[8] Different decisions call for different level decision makers. In universities, for instance, decisions about course offerings, new faculty hires, and the distribution of travel funds are typically made in the academic departments, and so you would consider them to be decentralized. Decisions about university fundraising campaigns or charting new directions for university growth are made by the university president and their board of trustees and so are centralized. Once again dropping down one level of analysis presented organization theorists with a more comprehensive but also a more complicated picture.

The Aston studies revealed that **size** interacts with other dimensions of social structure in unexpected ways. Subsequent research showed that when centralized organizations are large, decision bottlenecks can undermine organizational performance by slowing organizational responses to environmental pressure. This explains why most studies of large organizations indicate a negative relationship between formalization and centralization, that is, these organizations often trade off centralization for formalization because formal rules and procedures direct subordinates to make the same decisions their managers would make. Thus large decentralized organizations, particularly bureaucracies are more likely to be formalized than are large centralized organizations.[9]

This finding solves what was once a puzzle for organization theory. Like these early organization theorists you, too, may think that mechanistic and bureaucratic are two words for the same thing. Experience with bureaucracies often creates this belief because the image of an unfeeling machine fits with the red tape associated with bureaucracy. Notice, however, that there is one feature of bureaucracies that distinguishes them from mechanistic organizations—the bureaucracy is decentralized whereas the mechanistic organization is centralized.

The trick to resolving the decentralization puzzle is to understand what it means to say that a bureaucracy is simultaneously highly formalized and decentralized. In a bureaucracy, many routine decisions are pushed to low levels of the organization, but there are strict rules and procedures that govern how those decisions are made. Thus street-level bureaucrats (police, social workers, teachers, clerks, etc.) often have discretion, but can only exercise it within strict limits. Like mechanistic organizations, the bureaucracy remains highly controlled, but it does so by being decentralized in such a way that allows lower-level bureaucrats to make all the programmed decisions, while freeing higher-level bureaucrats to form policy and make unprogrammed decisions.

Contingency theory today

In his historical review of contingency theory, Donaldson insisted that contingency is the essence of organization theory. Although others argue that its endless discovery of yet more contingencies erects practical barriers to finding an answer to the question of how best to organize, it clearly lives on in the logic of modernist organization theory in that almost all modernists try to find predictive relationships between variables representing the organization, its environment, and its performance. Contingency theory demonstrates that all organization theories have boundary conditions, each theory only applies to a subset of all organizations. Thus the primary contribution of contingency theory has been to make us aware that there are many different ways to organize successfully. The enumeration of organizing possibilities and consequences remains the task of the contingency theorist today.

Examples of the boundary conditions specified by contingency theorists include showing when mechanistic forms of organizing are inappropriate. Small organizations do not need formalization, since direct supervision through daily contact with the boss is cheaper and more satisfying for members of the organization than are formal rules and procedures. Similarly, non-routine technologies and unstable environments undermine the effectiveness of mechanistic organizations, but for different reasons. Under these conditions formal rules and procedures cannot cover all the possibilities and problems that arise in the course of doing business.

Large organizations that exist in stable environments and provide standardized services or products operate most efficiently when they use mechanistic forms, but as environments change, organizations need to change also. Most people are familiar with McDonald's—the hamburger organization that operates under the sign of the Golden Arches. As of 2012 McDonald's has 33,000 restaurants in 119 countries, 1.7 million employees, and serves in excess of 68 million people every day. Their goal is to be their customers' favorite place and way to eat.[10]

Ten years ago, McDonald's was widely respected for its size, use of mechanistic structure, and its high degree of formalization, which includes an operations manual over 400 pages long. Uniformity of product offer and retail design meant you could instantly recognize McDonald's anywhere in the world and know exactly what you would buy there. Since then, increasing competition and changes in nutritional habits have led McDonald's to move in the direction of taking a more flexible, organic approach. Already in 2005 the McDonald's website described structural changes underway in these terms:

> Decentralization is fundamental to our business model—and to our corporate responsibility efforts. At the corporate level, we provide a global framework of common goals, policies, and guidelines rooted in our core values. Within this framework, individual geographic business units have the freedom to develop programs and performance measures appropriate to local conditions.[11]

Types and taxonomies

Inspired by Weber's definition of bureaucracy, and Burns and Stalker's distinction between mechanistic and organic organizational forms, several modernist organization theorists created their own typologies of organizational forms. The best known is probably Canadian organization theorist Henry Mintzberg's five types of organizational structure shown in Table 4.3.[12]

Typologies like Mintzberg's encourage prescriptive theories of organizational structure, sometimes collectively referred to as the **organizational design** school, according to which different organizational forms are recommended depending upon the internal and external needs of the organization. Such theories assume managers can adopt appropriate organizational forms by design, hence the design school label.

A taxonomical approach to addressing the variety of organizational forms was offered by modernist organization theorist William McKelvey who proposed that, just as biological organisms are categorized and compared by taxonomists to map their genetic structure, so an organizational taxonomy might account for different species of organizations.[13] McKelvey's application of genetic theory from the field of biology to the higher-level system of social organization is reflected in calls to study **organizational DNA**, a metaphoric reference to a code or structure capable of explaining organizational forms and predicting their behavior.

Models of structural change

In spite of its inclusion of organic organizational forms as responses to changing environmental conditions, contingency theory itself presents a fairly static approach to organizational structure in that the contingencies determining organizational success are assessed at specific moments in time. By contrast other modernist models focused on how organizational social structure changes.

Models describing how organizational social structures change typically take one of two forms. Evolutionary models explain how organizations develop over time through a progression of more or less static states or stages. The other type of structural change model focuses on the dynamics of change as these occur in the contexts of everyday organizational life. In these dynamic theories the seeming stability of social structure is undermined by discovering that numerous interactions shape and transform social structure on a more or less continuous basis. Evolutionary or stage models stay within the boundaries of the modernist approach, while models of the dynamics of everyday interaction move toward the symbolic perspective.

Table 4.3 Mintzberg's structure in fives

	Description	Appropriate for
Simple structure	Most basic structure. Power centralized in top management, with few middle managers employed. Usually small companies use this form and control is exercised personally by managers who are able to know all their workers and talk to them directly on a daily basis.	Entrepreneurial companies, companies with simple or single products. Examples: most start-ups.
Machine bureaucracy	Highly efficient but not flexible, these organizations emphasize standardization of production processes. Most employees perform highly specialized tasks that require few skills. The organization needs detailed planning and so requires administrative management.	Companies involved in mass production, or that produce simple products in stable environments. Examples: McDonald's, UPS.
Professional bureaucracy	Relies on standardized skills, rather than standardized processes. Use of professionals permits organization to give its employees discretion in performing tasks for which they have been professionally trained. Have less hierarchy than machine bureaucracies although professionals are supported by more mechanistically organized staff.	Best suited to companies operating in complex, stable environments. Examples: universities, hospitals, large consulting houses such as McKinsey and KPMG.
Divisionalized form	Relatively autonomous divisions run their own businesses, each producing specialized products for particular markets. Divisions overseen by corporate staff who set divisional goals, control behavior by regulating resources, and monitor performance using standardized financial measures (e.g., sales targets, rates of return, brand equity).	Best in complex, somewhat unstable environments because divisions can shut down or be spun off and new businesses started up more easily than with bureaucratic forms. Examples: General Electric, General Motors.
Adhocracy	A structure of interacting project teams whose task is to innovate solutions to constantly changing problems. Employs many experts who produce non-standardized products to their customers' or clients' specifications. Decision making is highly decentralized and strategy emerges from actions taken throughout the company.	Best in turbulent environments when an organization needs constant innovation. Examples: small consulting houses such as advertising agencies, biotechnology firms, think tanks.

Source: Based on Mintzberg (1981, 1983).

Two theories portray different ways to think about the stages of development that organization structures typically go through. Larry Greiner's lifecycle theory depicts organizational growth as a sequence of evolutionary periods punctuated by revolutionary events, while Katz and Kahn's open systems model describes a social structure as it emerges from organizational responses to both technical and environmental pressures. Anthony Giddens's structuration theory and his conception of the duality of structure and agency will describe the dynamic play of elements that constitute organizational structure.

The organizational lifecycle

Just as a child passes through infancy and childhood to adolescence and maturity, so, according to American organization theorist Greiner, an organization passes through entrepreneurial, collectivity, delegation, formalization, and collaboration stages (see Figure 4.2).[14] Greiner theorized that, in each stage of its lifecycle an organization is dominated by a different focus and each stage ends with a crisis that threatens its survival—bringing about a revolutionary change through which the organization passes into the next developmental stage.

In the **entrepreneurial stage**, an organization is focused on creating and selling its product. This phase usually takes place in a small setting in which every member of the organization is familiar with what the other members are doing. The entrepreneur can easily control most activities personally and this personal contact makes it easy for other employees to sense what is expected of them and to receive direct feedback and close supervision. If successful (and remember, the majority of organizations fail at this early stage), the entrepreneurial organization will find itself in need of professional management. Entrepreneurs are usually idea people or technical experts rather than organizers, and further organizational development often necessitates bringing management skills in from outside the organization, although sometimes professional management develops from within. In rare cases the entrepreneur evolves along with the needs of the organization (e.g., Bill Gates at Microsoft, Michael Dell from Dell Computers, Steve Jobs at Apple).

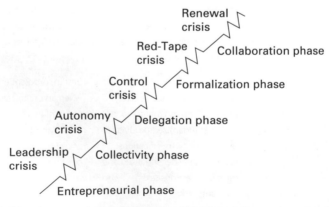

Figure 4.2 Greiner's model of organizational lifecycles

Source: Adapted and reprinted by permission of *Harvard Business Review*. From 'Evolution and revolution as organizations grow' by Larry Greiner, 50 (July–August) 1972. Copyright 1972 by the President and Fellows of Harvard College, all rights reserved.

It often takes a crisis to convince the entrepreneur that professional management is required, since the early successes that allowed the organization to survive and prosper will also give the entrepreneur the impression that things are fine the way they are. However, growth brings differentiation and sooner or later the organization becomes too complex for a single individual to monitor everything that is going on. This condition can be compounded by an entrepreneur's distaste for management activities. According to Greiner, the result of this early differentiation, coupled with inadequate attention to integration due to lack of managerial oversight, throws the organization into a **leadership crisis**. Successful resolution of the leadership crisis moves the organization into the collectivity stage.

The introduction of the organization's first professional management usually brings the organization through the leadership crisis and provides it with centralized decision making and a renewed focus on its purpose. The primary concern of the new management is to provide a sense of direction and to integrate the differentiated groups operating within the organization. In this **collectivity stage**, concern for clear goals and routines takes over the production and marketing focus of the entrepreneurial stage. In this stage the organization's complexity grows through differentiation until, once again, the organization becomes too much for the existing social structure and its management to handle. This time crisis arises from an overloaded decision-making process, the result of too much centralization.

During the collectivity stage centralization gives the organization its sense of a clear direction because decisions are coordinated by a set of well-integrated decision makers (i.e., the new professional management). However, at some point even the most effective managers of a centralized social structure cannot keep pace with the decisions required by an ever more differentiated organization. Thus, sooner or later, centralized decision making becomes a bottleneck for action, and decisions must be pushed down the hierarchy if the organization is to continue functioning. Greiner called this the crisis of autonomy. The reason this situation produces a crisis is that most managers find it difficult to relinquish control over formerly centralized decisions. It is typical for management to wait overlong in initiating decentralization and their hesitation is what provokes the **autonomy crisis**.

The solution to the autonomy crisis is delegation, and the next stage of the organizational lifecycle is described as the **delegation stage**. However, once delegation is initiated, usually via decentralization of decision making, the need for further integration arises. This need grows steadily until a **crisis of control** occurs. The response to loss of control is usually to create formal rules and procedures to ensure that decisions are made in the way that management would make them if they could do so themselves. This is the point at which bureaucracy appears; Greiner labeled it the formalization stage.

During the **formalization stage**, the organization continues to grow and differentiate, adding more and more formal control mechanisms in an attempt to integrate an increasingly diverse set of activities through planning, accounting and information systems, and formal review procedures. The tendency to control through bureaucratic means eventually leads to the **crisis of red tape**. The red-tape crisis is what has given bureaucracy a bad name. It is not, however, that bureaucracy is the villain, but rather that, in this situation, management overindulges and ends up with too much of a good thing. Attempts to apply formal rules and procedures in a universal and impersonal manner create an organizational environment that becomes not only ineffective, but increasingly distasteful to workers. Things will generally worsen when management's first response to the breakdown of bureaucratic controls is to implement even more bureaucracy. The problem reaches crisis proportions when employees either cannot figure out how to make the system of rules and procedures work, or when they rebel against it.

If the organization is to emerge from the red-tape crisis, it will generally proceed to the **collaboration stage**. During this stage the organization uses teamwork as a means of re-personalizing the organization by distributing the now over-differentiated tasks into more recognizable chunks and assigning shared responsibility for them to groups of individuals in ways that render work once again comprehensible. What was too complex or dynamic for rules to regulate can be reorganized into smaller units managed from within by teams that are granted decentralized decision-making authority. A greater focus on trust and collaboration is often required in these circumstances.

The collaboration stage of organizational development requires a qualitative change in organizational form as well as in the integration skills and leadership styles demanded of managers. Instead of the former emphasis on controlling the organization, top management must shift its concern to constantly regenerating motivation and staying focused on organizational goals and purposes. However, if at some point management fails to provide regeneration, the organization will undergo a **crisis of renewal** marked by what in humans would be described as lethargy. The primary symptom of this crisis is employees and managers who suffer from burnout and other forms of psychological fatigue due to the strains associated with temporary assignments, dual authority, and continuous experimentation. According to Greiner, the crisis of renewal will either lead to a new form of organization or to organizational decline and eventual death.

Greiner used his theory to emphasize the point that every stage of an organization's development contains the seeds of its next crisis. This is because the organizational arrangements and management strategies that are adaptive for one stage in the lifecycle will be seen as maladaptive when the organization grows more complex. Therefore, old structural arrangements and leadership styles must be constantly replaced throughout the life of the organization. Greiner's model has been extremely popular, but did little to illuminate *how* the social structure of an organization develops. Daniel Katz and Robert Kahn's theory made up for this deficiency.

An open systems model of the development of organizational structures

According to Katz and Kahn's open systems model, structure first develops out of technical needs and later from internal integration pressures in combination with shifting demands from the environment.[15] At first, a primitive organization emerges from cooperation between individuals who wish to pool their efforts to achieve a common goal, such as bringing a new product to market. This primitive organization is not actually structured in the usual sense of the term because the cooperative effort is more the result of individual motivation than it is an organizational achievement. However, if the primitive organization is going to survive beyond its initial project, it will begin to develop a social structure. The development from primitive to fully elaborated organizational structure will occur in several stages, each of which involves differentiation and integration. Katz and Kahn's model describes these stages.

In the first stage, activities such as purchasing and marketing are structurally differentiated from core production tasks. This initial differentiation is a natural extension of the primitive production process that also required procurement and disposal processes, but on such a restricted scale as to be easily accomplished by members of the production core who take time away from production to purchase raw materials or distribute output to customers. This stage of differentiation provides the organization with buffering capacity in the sense that it permits employees working to produce organizational output to focus all their attention and energy on transforming raw materials into products. Meanwhile, other individuals specialize in the tasks of purchasing raw materials to feed the transformation process and transferring the organization's products to its environment so that new inputs can be acquired and production can proceed uninterrupted (see Figure 4.3). Katz and Kahn called these **support activities**.

Once the initial differentiation of activities is underway, pressures to integrate begin to appear. In elaborating itself to ensure continuous input of raw material, and production and sale of output, the organization produces three different pockets of activity that can lose track of one another. The three functions of purchasing, production, and sales must be aligned, so that the correct levels of raw materials are brought into the organization and so that production output balances with sales. This requires integration that is usually provided by a general manager who oversees purchasing orders and production schedules while taking sales projections into account.

At this point in the development of its social structure, the organization has usually survived long enough to require maintenance—employees quit and others must be recruited and trained, bookkeeping tasks expand to include corporate tax considerations and financial planning, physical facilities require regular upkeep and modification, and the community may begin making inquiries about the organization and demands regarding its community

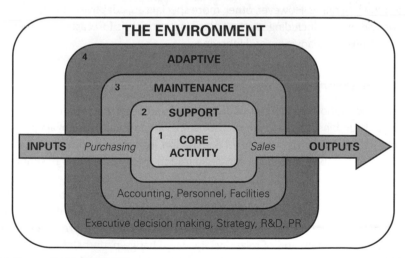

Figure 4.3 Katz and Kahn describe the development of social structure in relation to the needs of the technical core and demands of the environment

According to this theory, a primitive technical core is first elaborated with support structures, then maintenance structures appear, and finally adaptive structures are added.

Source: Based on Katz and Kahn (1966).

involvement. It now becomes necessary to supplement core production and support activities with accounting, personnel, facilities management, and public relations. Katz and Kahn grouped all of these into the category of maintenance activities.

Maintenance activities help to preserve the organization in a steady state of readiness to perform, while the production core does the performing. Because the activities of the maintenance group are not highly interdependent with those of purchasing, production, and sales, the maintenance function can be carried out with considerable independence of the production core. This represents further differentiation of the organizational social structure, which, in turn, demands more integration. The addition of managers to achieve this integration is typical, but now, with multiple managers, a new level of management emerges in the form of an executive to oversee the other managers. Thus integration designed to overcome the problems introduced by differentiation breeds further differentiation by creating hierarchy.

If the organization survives the early stages of development described above, it will probably exist long enough to encounter some change in the environment that affects demand for the organization's product. Such changes create problems for the organization, such as predicting what amount of output will be sold and, thus, what level of raw material needs to be ordered and how much product should be produced. Mistakes in scheduling production runs will be acutely felt as both over- or undersupply of customers' demand can threaten the firm's cash flow position as well as its reputation. If demand for the company's product is waning, new products may need to be developed to keep the organization in business. In order to face these problems, another elaboration of social structure occurs. This one introduces adaptive activities into the social structure.

Adaptive activities are responsible for attending to changes in the environment and for interpreting the meaning of the changes for the rest of the organization. The earliest manifestation of the adaptive function is executive decision making, which in one form or another exists from the beginning. However, other, more specialized, adaptive activities emerge over a longer period of time, including strategic planning, economic forecasting, market research, R&D, tax planning, legal advising, and lobbying.

Structuration theory

The term structuration occupies middle ground between the modern and symbolic perspectives. It combines the static concept structure with the active idea of agency associated with structur*ing* and highlights processes of domination, legitimation, and signification, thereby not only bringing symbolic sensibility into organization theory but critical postmodernism as well.

One of the great debates in sociology has centered on whether structure or human agency has the greater significance in explaining society. In organization theory institutional theorists typically advocate for structure, arguing that institutions are relatively durable social structures (e.g., networks of relationships or exchange patterns) that shape and constrain the behavior of actors operating within a given social system. Other versions of institutional theory focus, as did Selznick's work, on symbolic structures, such as the cultural values in play at the founding of the TVA. Those advocating for agency want to know where structures come from, what sustains them, and how structural change can be explained. They argue that regularities in individual actions and interactions produce the patterns of relationship that, when viewed at the organizational or societal level of analysis, appear as social structure.

In structuration theory, as developed by British social theorist Anthony Giddens, structure and agency interact—social structures enable and constrain action that constitutes social structure—neither concept supersedes the other in theoretical importance.[16] This idea reminds me of M. C. Echer's famous etching showing two hands drawing each other. Giddens called his idea the **duality of structure and agency**, wherein agents are both enabled and constrained by structures comprised of resources, routines, and expectations. Agents are enabled to the extent that structures of signification, domination, and legitimation support their activity, and constrained whenever they do not. But of course the activities shaped by these structures fuel the next round of structuration, and so on (see Figure 4.4).

Everyone confronts the duality of structure and agency on a daily basis. For example, we construct systems to manage ourselves (e.g., legal systems, bureaucracies) and then tell ourselves we cannot do something because the system will not allow it. Our failure to recognize our complicity in constructing the system prevents us from realizing that it can be changed using the same creative forces that produced it in the first place. We imprison ourselves in our habits, routines, and expectations, all of which are supported by those in power who use their influence to maintain the status quo that keeps them powerful. All the while, minute changes within the ever-present dynamics that produce and reproduce social structure, keep structures from ever attaining more than the appearance of solidity. Accordingly even the most stable social structures are defined by the fragile cooperative movements of their agents.

Giddens explained social system dynamics in terms of three mutually supportive dualities of structure and agency: signification-communication, domination–power, and legitimation-sanction. According to Giddens, these dualities are mediated by different types of rules and resources actors use to construct their structural contexts: interpretive schemes for defining what symbols mean (e.g., language games, discourses, and speech genres), relationships within which the exercise of power occurs (e.g., hierarchy, division of labor), and norms (e.g., found in

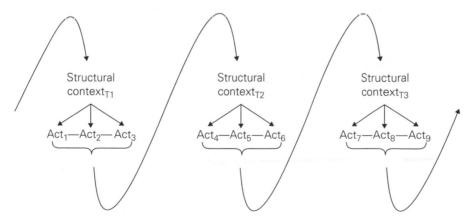

Figure 4.4 The duality of structure and agency

The mutual construction of structure and agency as portrayed in Giddens's structuration theory.

Source: Based on Barley and Tolbert (1997).

the exercise of conformity pressure via socialization and culture). Table 4.4 shows structures, forms of agency, and rules and resources that mediate between them as a matrix of material and symbolic social practices that, through mutual influence, produce the social context and outcomes (both structures and actions) of social systems.

While Giddens was criticized for overemphasizing the agency side of the structure–agency reconciliation, French social theorist Pierre Bourdieu presented two concepts that emphasize the structure side: field and habitus.[17] According to Bourdieu, a **field** is a structure with an internal logic that establishes hierarchical relationships on the basis of the distribution of capital. Bourdieu defined capital as resources used by the powerful and influential to distinguish themselves from those without power or influence. He then claimed that capital takes various forms, one for each field. For example, the cultural field is structured by cultural capital (celebrity status, prestige), the academic field by academic capital (academic reputation and honors), and the economic field by economic capital (wealth).

According to Bourdieu's version of structuration theory, a field is constituted through the signifying practices of its agents whose actions, therefore, are capable of transforming it. Bourdieu used the field of literature as an example. In literature, a subsystem of the cultural field, including authors, critics, publishers, and readers, produces and consumes literary works wherein actors' responses, interpretations, and texts legitimize social differences. The structure of these social differences, in turn, determines which individuals get to have enough power and influence to change the field, which of course they are then unlikely to do unless they are certain it will not affect their standing within it.

Permeating any given field, the **habitus** gives individuals a feel for the game that allows them to know how they and others should behave depending upon their hierarchical position, which, in turn, is determined by the amount of field-relevant capital they control. Because the internal logic of a field can be kept hidden, the habitus can be well protected from outsiders and may operate as tacit knowledge among insiders who thus reproduce the field and its hierarchies without awareness of their involvement. Through the habitus members of a field tap into the rules and resources that Giddens described as the tissue connecting agency and structure.

American sociologists Mustafa Emirbayer and Ann Mische presented a third version of structuration theory that is more temporally sensitive than either Giddens's or Bourdieu's approach, though, like Giddens, these social theorists emphasized agency.[18] Emirbayer and Mische claimed that the key processes by which agents produce structure are: iteration (repetition of past behavior), practical evaluation (as the basis for taking action in the present), and projection (into the future). In the iterative process, agents reactivate their prior patterns of behavior as routines that reproduce existing structures. Practical evaluation allows agents to

Table 4.4 How rules and resources mediate agency and structure

Structures of:	Signification	Domination	Legitimation
Rules and resources mediating structure and agency:	Interpretive schemes	Relationships within which power is exercised	Normative influence
Forms of Agency:	**Communication**	**Power**	**Sanction**

make informed judgments relevant to their ever-changing circumstances and these judgments influence their behavior in ways that either reproduce or change existing structures. Finally, through projection, the possibilities of the future signal creative options that allow for the intentional or even planned reconfiguration of existing structure. Taken together, these three processes help to set structuration in motion by permitting agents to reach both backward and forward in time to structure their present activities.

One thing structuration theory brings home to me is the endless refinement that modernist theorizing begets. I am reminded of the story by the Argentinean writer Jorge Luis Borges about the mapmaker who kept refining his map, making it ever more detailed, until one day his map completely covered the territory he was mapping because only in this way could he make the perfect map. The trouble is, too many refinements to a theory reduce its practical value for summarizing and encapsulating knowledge in useable chunks. Once the map becomes as complex as the territory, who needs the map? Nonetheless, in its attempt to cross the boundary between individual and organizational levels of analysis, and modern and symbolic perspectives, structuration theory makes a bold theoretical move that sets the stage for thinking about organization structure from outside the modern perspective.

Symbolic approaches: Social practices, institutional logics, and community

Imagine the buildings of an organization containing only desks, machines, computers, raw materials, and documents, but empty of people. Does the organization have a social structure? Modernist organizational theorists, drawing from objectivist ontology, would say that organizations are social structural objects consisting of elements such as hierarchy, lines of authority, and accountability, along with various integrating mechanisms. From this perspective you need only analyze such things as organization charts, policies, rules, and coordination mechanisms to confirm the existence of an organization's social structure and draw conclusions about it. Those who take the symbolic perspective disagree, arguing from their subjectivist ontology that an organization's social structure does not exist independently of human consciousness and social interaction. They claim that organizational realities emerge as people work and interact with each other and with the material resources surrounding them. From this perspective the study of organizational structure looks remarkably different from explanations provided by the modernist perspective.

The difference between modernist and symbolic-interpretive perspectives can be summarized in this way: modernist organization theorists see structures as things, entities, objects, and elements, while symbolic theorists see structures as human creations, they are dynamic works-in-progress that emerge from social interaction and collective meaning making. Thus, as Weick argued, there are no organiza*tions*, there is only organiz*ing*.

Along with Giddens's theory of structuration, Weick's insight turns our attention away from understanding social structures as systems for designing and controlling interaction and social relationships, and toward interest in how the everyday practices of organizational members construct the patterns of organizing that guide their actions. In the section on social practices I will introduce you to two practices that figure strongly in theorizing the dynamics of social structure from the symbolic perspective: routine and improvisation.

These practices will show how an organization's activities can be constructed, maintained, and changed through the interactions of their members.

Social practices: Routine and improvisation

In the first years of its alliance with Renault, Nissan senior assembly-line workers and engineers wrote standard operating procedures (SOPs) to help transfer knowledge about effective work practices to their alliance partner. For example, Nissan gave Renault's dashboard assembly-line workers directions that included hand-drawn sketches showing the exact order in which dashboard wires were to be connected, what tools to use, and how to reach the wires.[19] Routines like this have long been regarded an integral part of organizational life that helps to build a stable organizational social structure.[20]

Routines are found everywhere in organizations, from techniques associated with the use of production tools and factory equipment, to the hiring and firing of employees, strategic planning cycles, annual performance evaluations, quarterly reporting, and budget reviews. These and many other routines preserve organizational knowledge and transfer capabilities so that work can be successfully accomplished and coordinated in an uninterrupted stream through time.[21]

Modernist organization theorists have likened routines like Nissan's dashboard wiring process to organizational habits, programs, or genetic codes.[22] However, as American organization theorist Martha Feldman argued, routines contain the seeds of change as well as offering stability. Feldman defined routines as flows of connected ideas, actions, and outcomes and suggested that they emerge as organizational members try to understand what to do in particular contexts when facing specific situations.[23] Routines are endlessly recreated because people do not reproduce actions and behaviors in exactly the same way every time they engage in a routine. For example, a police officer or social worker dealing with an incident of domestic violence knows the expected routine for dealing with the situation because they have been trained in policing procedures and have developed particular ways of dealing with these situations from their own experience. However, such routines can be combined in a variety of ways to deal with the specific circumstances of domestic violence confronted on a given occasion. Differences in the enactment of routines introduce change that subsequently affects the routine itself as variance spreads within the organization or even across organizations (e.g., via institutional mimesis). Alternatively routines may die out through lack of use.

The idea of changing a routine comes close to the concept of organizational **improvisation**.[24] Karl Weick, who has written extensively about this subject as it applies to organizations, proposed viewing organizational structure as an emergent and unfolding process of interacting routines and improvisations with routines operating more like recipes than blueprints.[25] In performing routine activities, organizational members reinforce existing interaction patterns and thereby reproduce organizational social structures to give them a degree of stability. However, incorporating improvisation into routines, organizational members will, at times, interact outside established pathways and perform in the gaps that exist in the current version of a social structure. In doing so they behave like jazz musicians who refuse to play what has been played before and thus deliberately step into new territory. Organizational improvisations may help the organization to react to a threat or take advantage of an opportunity.[26] Improvisations will disappear once they have served their immediate purpose, or they will either be incorporated into old interaction patterns or used to establish new ones. Once institutionalized through repetition and widespread acceptance, an improvisation becomes routine (which is why jazz musicians do not consider riffs and other repetitions to be 'real' contributions to jazz).

In an article that examined how the structuring of jazz performance applies to organizations, I argued that social structures always have coordination gaps due to the impossibility of structurally interrelating all organizational activities.[27] In order to minimize the problems created by these structural gaps, organizational members might want to adopt some of the techniques jazz musicians use for the purpose of improvising on their structures. For example, jazz tunes are performed in successive waves of improvisation that begin with the playing of the head of a selected tune in a recognizable and often routine way (e.g., think of the first chorus of 'I've Got Rhythm'). The head provides the musicians with a basic structure of melody, harmony, and rhythm to use as a departure point for their playing. As the performance of the tune unfolds, each soloing musician in turn attempts to lead the band away from the originating structure by playing in the empty spaces within that structure (beats not played and the spaces between beats are two rhythmic examples). Different musicians, taking turns soloing, will improvise differently and each successive musician can build on ideas introduced by the others until, collectively, a unique playing of the tune is achieved that nonetheless retains a relationship to its origin in the head. This relationship between old and new is demonstrated at the conclusion of the tune when the musicians replay the head, embellishing it with some of the best ideas their improvising produced. In this way a structure and its empty spaces are combined to create a performance, whether it is of a jazz tune or an organizational process.

The article offered jazz as a metaphor that organizations can use to talk about the ever-present limits of structuring faced by all organizations. It also suggested literally using the same practices jazz musicians use to bring structural stability and flexibility into direct connection. Doing the organizational equivalent of playing jazz could continually renew the social structure by offering new options for organizing even while maintaining some existing routines and practices.

Social structures as institutionalized logics

Institutional theorists interested in the processes by which institutions emerge in the wake of new social practices have compared the dynamics of institutionalization to the formation of social movements. For example, within their study of the history of the recycling movement in the US, American sociologists Michael Lounsbury, Marc Ventresca, and Paul Hirsch explained the emergence of recycling as an institution around which a new industry developed.[28]

Another group of institutional theorists believe that social structures are embedded in and contextualized by **institutional logics** that manifest in the mindsets, cognitive frames of reference, and mental models that configure thought, compel argument, and organize systems within society. As contexts for organizational action, institutional logics make objective behavior dependent upon shared (symbolic) meaning. According to organization theorists Robert Drazin, Mary Ann Glynn, and Robert Kazanjian: 'Structures can become invested with socially shared meanings, and thus, in addition to their "objective" functions, can serve to communicate information about the organization to both internal and external audiences.'[29]

Notice how these institutional theorists mixed together aspects of both modern and symbolic perspectives. For instance, Drazin and his co-authors used objective ontology in assuming that structures are objects to be invested with meaning, as opposed to being momentarily constructed social realities; yet they also employed interpretive epistemological assumptions such as that organizational meaning is shaped by its institutional context and all knowledge of it must therefore be context-specific. Lounsbury and his co-authors showed similar sensitivity to context by using historical methods in their study of the recycling movement.

Social structure as community

Whereas modernist scholars tend to view a community in objective terms, such as by studying the occupational statuses it confers, those adopting the symbolic perspective focus on how understandings of reality are socially constructed and maintained or changed for a community of people through their recurring interactions and use of shared symbols.

Introduced by educational theorists Etienne Wenger and Jean Lave, the concept of **communities of practice** initially offered an answer to the question of how learning occurs through social interaction.[30] These theorists defined a community of practice as a group of people, informally bound together by common interests in learning and the development of knowledge, who share repertoires (e.g., routines and vocabularies). A community of practice, described as self-designing and self-managing, forms when a group of people collectively develop ideas, knowledge, and practices as they learn together.

Because humans belong to many different communities of practice, each having their own ways of talking that produce a context for local meaning making and identity construction, an organization's social structure can embrace multiple communities of practice, each emerging spontaneously in response to particular interests, needs, desires, or problems. Communities of practice can cross boundaries drawn between business units and project teams, hierarchies, or any other dimension of social structure. Individuals can move between different communities, sharing and brokering knowledge as they do so. Like networks, communities of practice are characterized by connections rather than hierarchical or formalized relationships, making the manager's role one of enabling organizational learning and innovation.[31]

Sometimes organizations attempt to institutionalize communities of practice as IBM Global Services did by defining over 60 internal teams as communities of practice. Created to address issues such as e-business, industry sectors (e.g., distribution, health care), and applications development, they were meant to encourage the formation of emergent networks connecting individuals and groups.[32]

An interesting question IBM's effort raises is whether attempting to institutionalize communities of practice undermined their effectiveness. Did IBM appropriate a concept from the symbolic perspective without understanding fully the differences to modernist ways of managing? The symbolic perspective encourages managers to understand how communities of practice emerge from the problems and interests that employees take responsibility for, rather than proposing issues around which they would like to see communities of practice form and then setting expectations for their formation.

A concept that seems a close cousin of communities of practice, **language community**, is based on Wittgenstein's concept of language games and Foucault's concept of discourse. Organization theorists apply this concept to the ways organizational members talk about their organization in order to see if they can identify distinct discourses or language games within or between organizations, and to find out what individual speech acts reveal about how organizational members coordinate their actions.[33]

A language community dictates what can be said; it structures work through the way it allows words and their associated ideas to be used. By developing shared vocabularies, rhetorical styles, root metaphors, and other distinctive forms of expression, organizational members will come to share particular ways of talking about their organizational experience that will create and maintain features of their organization's social structure, just as enactment theory claims they do in constructing their environment. All this happens within everyday conversations without anyone needing to be aware it is going on, and all the while it influences the activities taking place as these are coordinated through conversations and interactions.

You can see language communities at work by considering the word preferences of organizational theorists who adopt different perspectives. When organization theorists adopt the modern perspective they talk about cause and effect, structures and outcomes, and discovery and explanation, whereas the language of those adopting the symbolic perspective is inflected with terms such as meaning, interpretation processes, and understanding. Contrast these expressions with the terms fragmentation, deconstruction, and discourse employed by postmodernists.

The words you use to express knowledge can give you a sense of objectivity because they appear to stabilize (i.e., enable and constrain) particular features of your reality. While this stability promotes ease of communication and coordinated interaction, according to the theory of language communities this objectivity is only an illusion, a product of intersubjectively constructed interpretation shaped by language use. Hence language communities are filled with potential for change and thus, paradoxically, embody both stability and instability.[34] Their properties of instability and illusion link them to the postmodern concept of discourse.

Postmodern social structure: De-differentiation, feminist organizations, and anti-administration

Many postmodernists believe reality is formless and fragmented, an illusion, a simulacra perpetrated on us by the ways in which we use language; there is no hidden stable order as intimated by the concept of structure, surface is everything and so superficiality prevails. As you might expect, postmodernists are extremely skeptical of modernist organizing principles expressed in terms like hierarchy, centralization, control, and integration. They insist that no structure defines existence; only words can legitimize concepts and these most often help those in power maintain their dominance over unsuspecting others. Therefore, they deconstruct concepts, structures, and management practices to reveal how they presuppose order, rationality, or the need for managerial control, thereby showing the ways in which concepts and theories always privilege some while exploiting and/or marginalizing others.

Bureaucracy particularly draws the ire of postmodernists. Recall that even Weber saw its dark side in the drive for rationality, calculation, and control that increases technical efficiency at the cost of exercising free will. Critical postmodern theorists have applied Weber's metaphor of the iron cage to examinations of how social life is colonized and freedom subverted by rationalistic ideologies and the structures and control mechanisms they depict as necessary.

In an influential series of articles, British organization theorists Robert Cooper and Gibson Burrell depicted modernist organization theory as concerned entirely with formal organization, an expression of their drive to create order out of disorder. They associated the term formal with words like unity, distance, routine, and rational, claiming that these associations define a moral code built upon suppressing disorder. Acceptance of this moral code is predicated on the fear that arises when the villainized term disorganization (associated with the chaos of the informal, local, spontaneous, and irrational) is presented in relation to the privileged term organization.[35] The modern desire to suppress disorganization hides any phenomena and people associated with it behind a wall of silence and repression.

Many deconstructionists do not specify alternative constructions to those they attack—they believe doing this would only impose different Grand Narratives. Nonetheless, some suggest that by deconstructing taken-for-granted ideologies and practices, a space for new organizing possibilities opens. Into this space alternatives inspired by postmodernism find room to grow, including the concepts of de-differentiation and feminist organization, and anti-administration theory.

De-differentiation

Recall that Lawrence and Lorsch defined differentiation as the division of the organization into different hierarchical levels and specialized departments. Their theory suggests that differentiation produces a need for integration, which creates more differentiation, and so on, thus locking organizations into continuous developmental trajectories such as were described by Greiner, and Katz and Kahn. In opposition to these modernist theories, postmodernists offer the concept of de-differentiation.

British sociologist Scott Lash claimed de-differentiation marks the defining moment of postmodernism in that it reverses the modernist progression of ever greater specialization and separation, for example of rich and poor, weak and powerful, right and wrong. Borrowing Lash's idea, Australian organization theorist Stewart Clegg accused today's over-differentiated organizations of causing their members to experience them as incoherent, thereby creating dependence on elite members of the hierarchy who then gain the power necessary to define organizational reality.

An antidote to such organizational malevolence, Clegg claimed, can be found in de-differentiation, which is not the same thing as integration.[36] Whereas integration implies the coordination of differentiated activities, de-differentiation reverses the very conditions of differentiation that created the need for integration in the first place. In de-differentiation, organizations integrate activities, not through hierarchical or structural elaboration, but by allowing people to self-manage and coordinate their own activities. De-differentiation satisfies the emancipatory interests of critical postmodernists by undermining the controlling mindset they believe dominates modern thinking, even as it aligns with symbolic ideas like communities of practice.

The self-organizing or semi-autonomous team concept from socio-technical systems theory likewise offers an example of de-differentiation from the modernist perspective. Workgroups organized as semi-autonomous teams are given responsibility for a broadly defined set of tasks; they schedule their own time and monitor, assess, and correct their performance, including quality. For example, in Volvo's Kalmar Plant in Sweden, entire automobiles were assembled start to finish by teams of self-managing workers. Examples like Kalmar's suggest that integration can be achieved independently of hierarchy. Thus de-differentiation makes it easier to imagine democratic organizations in which integration and coordination are the responsibility of everyone and not just management's concern. This is the idea behind labor-managed firms such as United Airlines or the John Lewis Partnership that operates department stores in the United Kingdom, both of which are owned and operated by employees. However, some postmodernists warn that these types of organization will turn out to be just another servant of managerial interests, one that projects an image of democracy, autonomy, and self-management, but that merely disguises the power struggle by dressing it in new clothes.

Feminist organizations

You may remember from Chapter 2 that the notion of *différance* challenges the modernist focus on presence (things we take to be entities and objects) suggesting instead that meaning resides in the continuous movement between what is present and what is absent in our language. This means that we can use oppositional logic to deconstruct the assumptions and practices associated with modernist ideas of structure as presence, thereby exposing its absences for further examination.

For example, feminist scholars have deconstructed bureaucracy to show it as a male-gendered and typically white male-dominated form of organization.[37] They propose that bureaucracies privilege and justify hierarchy by claiming that power and position are based on the objectively rational criteria of technical competence, yet these organizations define the terms objective, rational, and competence from a white male-centered viewpoint that results in the domination of women, people of color, and minorities. These gender- and race-based structures, reinforced through unspoken assumptions and taken-for-granted objectifications, exist within and are supported by modernist organizational discourses. In modernist discourse, individual performance is generally evaluated against formal criteria such as decisiveness and the possession of leadership qualities. Feminists claim that criteria like these are defined in ways that favor the male gender. In contrast, feminist organizations (e.g., women's health centers, domestic violence shelters) evidence more equitable and flexible structures, participatory decision making, cooperative action, and communal ideals. In feminist organizations men and women, people of different ethnicities, young and old experience greater equality than do members of traditional (modernist) bureaucracies.

One hybrid form based on postmodern and feminist theories is Karen Lee Ashcraft's idea of feminist bureaucracy.[38] Critics have challenged both bureaucratic and feminist forms, in particular the dominating tendencies of the former, and the sustainability of the latter when faced with growth and demands for formalization by funding organizations. Ashcraft's hybrid keeps the seemingly incompatible elements of bureaucratic and feminist characteristics in simultaneous play as organizational members do their work. For example, tasks will be formal and informal, specialized and general, and hierarchy and centralization will exist but constantly be challenged by egalitarian and decentralized practices. Ashcraft's research in a non-profit organization concerned with domestic violence studied the interplay of bureaucratic elements and necessities (a hierarchical organization chart) with feminist ideals of ethical communication (the right to express views and emotions and to be heard). This hybrid employed the tensions between its contradictory elements to help it cope with paradoxical pressures (e.g., bureaucratic conditions associated with getting external funding and the need to stay small, flexible, and responsive to individual clients) to achieve its goal to serve abused women.

Anti-administration theory

David Farmer, an American philosopher and economist, suggested that we can counteract the logic of bureaucratic administration by confronting it with anti-administration, much as matter and anti-matter annihilate one another.[39] Government bureaucracies serve their political masters and enforce justice by privileging hierarchy, efficiency, and technical expertise. Anti-administration theorists deconstruct this view and surface its oppositions. Farmer did not advocate anarchy, instead he argued that anti-administration is part of the administrative act, a part that involves radical skepticism toward its ends, means, and hierarchical rationality. By engaging in anti-administration, administrators reflect on presence and absence in their policies, procedures, and actions to deepen their understanding of the implications of their administrative actions. Bureaucratic justice is normally equated with the rationality and efficiency of actions—what happens if we juxtapose these values with moral justice? Instead of imposing justice based on rationality, administrators might be persuaded to concentrate on removing injustice.

Summary

Every organization consists of social elements including people, their positions within the organization, and the groups or units to which they belong. Three types of relationship among people, positions, and units used by modernist organization theorists define social structure as hierarchy, division of labor, and coordination mechanisms. The division of labor indicates who does what in terms of task assignments. Task assignments in turn create expectations about who is dependent upon whom. The hierarchy of authority defines formal reporting relationships, but these only account for some of the interactions necessary to support an organization. Coordination mechanisms, ranging from formal rules and procedures to spontaneous hallway conversations, further define and support the social structure of the organization. Classical dimensions of social structure that continue to interest modernist organization scholars include complexity, centralization, and formalization. These dimensions offer a means of distinguishing between mechanistic, organic, and bureaucratic organizations.

Contingency theory offers a way to combine empirical findings about multiple dimensions of social structure. For example, contingency theory has demonstrated that small organizations operating in stable environments are best organized as simple structures with minimal hierarchy and highly centralized decision making. However, as organizations grow in size (number of employees), they differentiate thereby increasing the number of hierarchical levels and departments, which causes them to add integrative mechanisms such as rules, liaison roles, and/or cross-functional teams. Formalization will come along with the increased routineness of work tasks that is likely to accompany the specialization introduced by the greater division of labor in large organizations. Unstable environments and internal differentiation mean that organizational structures will require decentralization so that decisions do not overburden the hierarchy and can be made at the point of knowledge. And on it goes. As new contingencies are discovered, new webs of relationships can be spun out from the findings of contingency research.

Symbolic-interpretivists see social structure as emerging from relationships that form through human interaction. Individuals interact and over time these interactions stabilize into recognizable relationships that define the social structure and contribute to the ways that work is accomplished. These relationships link the formal hierarchical positions into groups and the groups into departments and divisions. However, although structure serves to direct and constrain deviations from expected patterns of behavior, structuration theory reminds us that these constraints are nothing more than our willingness to do things in routine ways. Structuration theory stresses that social structure both influences and is influenced by the everyday interactions of the members of the organization.

Postmodernism and network organizations challenge many modernist ways of looking at social structure, focusing research attention instead on processes and relationships. Symbolic-interpretive and postmodern perspectives remind us that organizations have other resources beyond the social structure to aid in the integration of differentiated activities, as you will see in Chapters 5, 6, 7, and 8 on technology, organizational culture, physical structure, and power.

Key terms

structure

bureaucracy

division of labor

departmentalization

hierarchy

formalization

specialization

organizational forms

   mechanistic

   organic

centralization

innovation

differentiation

horizontal

vertical

integration

size

organizational design

   simple structure

   machine bureaucracy

   professional bureaucracy

   divisionalized form

   adhocracy

organizational DNA

organizational lifecycle

   entrepreneurial stage

leadership crisis	*adaptive activities*
collectivity stage	structuration theory
autonomy crisis	*duality of structure and agency*
delegation stage	*field*
crisis of control	*habitus*
formalization stage	routines
crisis of red tape	improvisation
collaboration stage	institutional logics
crisis of renewal	communities of practice
decline and death	language community
open systems model	de-differentiation
support activities	feminist organizations
maintenance activities	anti-administration theory

Endnotes

1. See Weber (1946, 1947).
2. http://www.sco.ca.gov/ppsd/empinfo/demo/index.shtml (accessed October 23, 2003).
3. Hage (1974); Rousseau (1978).
4. Donaldson (1996: 57).
5. The link to communication was established later by Galbraith (1973).
6. Lawrence and Lorsch (1967).
7. Pugh et al. (1968); Pugh and Hickson (1979).
8. Grinyer and Yasai-Ardekani (1980).
9. Pugh et al. (1968, 1969); Blau and Schoenherr (1971); Mansfield (1973).
10. McDonald's website http://www.aboutmcdonalds.com/mcd/our_company.html (accessed February 2012).
11. McDonald's website http://www.mcdonalds.com/corp/values/socialrespons/sr_report.html (accessed April 2005).
12. Mintzberg (1983).
13. McKelvey (1982), the idea of genetic material was first introduced to organization theory by Nelson and Winter (1982).
14. Greiner (1972).
15. Katz and Kahn (1966).
16. Giddens (1979, 1984); see also Ranson, Hinings, and Greenwood (1980); Riley (1983); Barley and Tolbert (1997).
17. Bourdieu (1980/1990).
18. Emirbayer and Mische (1998).
19. Yoshino and Fagan (2003: 9).
20. See, for example, Stene (1940) and Cyert and March (1963).
21. March (1991); Argote (1999).
22. Huber (1991); Stene (1940) used the metaphor of habits; March and Simon (1958) suggested the metaphor of programs; the metaphor of genetic material was introduced by Nelson and Winter (1982), see also McKelvey (1982).
23. Feldman (2000); Feldman and Pentland (2003).

24. See Kamoche, Cunha, and da Cunha (2002) for a recent selection of influential articles on organizational improvisation.

25. Weick (1998).

26. Moorman and Miner (1998a, b) described the role improvisation plays in aiding new product development teams.

27. Hatch (1993).

28. Lounsbury, Ventresca, and Hirsch (2003); see also Lounsbury (2005).

29. Drazin, Glynn and Kazanjian (2004:162).

30. Lave and Wenger (1991).

31. Brown and Duguid (1991).

32. Gongla and Rizzuto (2001).

33. Examples include Meyer and Rowan (1977); Hirsch (1986); Grant, Keenoy and Oswick (1998); Cunliffe (2001); deHolan and Phillips (2002).

34. Shotter (1993).

35. Cooper and Burrell (1988).

36. Clegg (1990).

37. Ferguson (1984); Martin (1990); Eisenstein (1995); Gherardi (1995).

38. Ashcraft (2001).

39. Farmer (1997).

References

Argote, Linda (1999) *Organizational Learning: Creating, Retaining, and Transferring Knowledge.* Boston, MA: Kluwer Academic Press.

Ashcraft, Karen L. (2001) Organized dissonance. Feminist bureaucracy as hybrid form. *Academy of Management Journal*, 44/6: 1301–22.

Barley, Stephen R. and Tolbert, Pamela (1997) Institutionalization and structuration: Studying the links between action and institution. *Organization Studies*, 18: 93–117.

Blau, Peter M. and Schoenherr, Richard A. (1971) *The Structure of Organizations.* New York: Basic Books.

Bourdieu, Pierre (1990) *The Logic of Practice.* Cambridge: Polity Press (first published in 1980).

Brown, J. S. and Duguid, P. (1991) Organizational learning and communities of practice: Towards a unified view of working, learning, and innovation. *Organization Science*, 2/1: 40–57.

Burns, Tom and Stalker, George M. (1961) *The Management of Innovation.* London: Tavistock Publications.

Clegg, Stewart (1990) *Modern Organizations: Organization Studies in the Postmodern World.* London: Sage.

Cooper, Robert and Burrell, Gibson (1988) Modernism, postmodernism and organizational analysis: An introduction. *Organization Studies*, 9/1: 91–112.

Cunliffe, Ann L. (2001) Managers as practical authors: Reconstructing our understanding of management practice. *Journal of Management Studies*, 38/3: 351–71.

Cyert, Richard M. and March, James G. (1963) *A Behavioral Theory of the Firm.* Englewood Cliffs, NJ: Prentice Hall.

de Holan, Martin and Phillips, Nelson (2002) Managing in transition: A case study of institutional management and organizational change in Cuba. *Journal of Management Inquiry*, 11: 68–83.

Donaldson, Lex (1996). The normal science of structural contingency theory. In S. R. Clegg, C. Hardy. and W. R. Nord (eds.), *Handbook of Organization Studies*. London: Sage, 57–76.

Drazin, Robert, Glynn, Mary Ann, and Kazanjian, Robert K. (2004) Dynamics of structural change. In M. S. Poole and A. H. Van de Ven (eds.), *Handbook of Organizational Change and Innovation*. New York: Oxford University Press, 161–89.

Eisenstein. H. (1995) The Australian femocratic experiment: A feminist case for bureaucracy. In M. M. Ferree and P. Y. Martin (eds.), *Feminist Organizations: Harvest of the New Women's Movement.* Philadelphia: Temple University Press, 69–83.

Emirbayer, Mustafa and Mische, Ann (1998) What is agency? *American Journal of Sociology*, 103/4: 962–1023.

Farmer, David. J. (1997) The postmodern turn and the Socratic gadfly. In H. T. Miller and C. J. Fox (eds.), *Postmodernism, 'Reality' and Public Administration*. Burke, VA: Chatelaine Press, 105–17.

Feldman, Martha (2000) Organizational routines as a source of continuous change. *Organization Science*, 11: 611–29.

—— and Pentland, Brian T. (2003) Reconceptualizing organizational routines as source of flexibility and change. *Administrative Science Quarterly*, 48: 94–118.

Ferguson, Kathy E. (1984) *The Feminist Case against Bureaucracy*. Philadelphia: Temple University Press.

Galbraith, Jay (1973) *Designing Complex Organizations*. Reading, MA: Addison-Wesley.

Gherardi, S. (1995) *Gender, Symbolism, and Organization Cultures*. Newbury Park, CA: Sage.

Giddens, Anthony (1979) *Central Problems in Social Theory: Action, Structure and Contradiction in Social Analysis*. Berkeley: University of California Press.

—— (1984) *The Constitution of Society*. Berkeley: University of California Press.

Gongla, P. and Rizzuto, C.R. (2001) Evolving communities of practice: IBM Global Services experience. *IBM Systems Journal*, 40/4. http://www.research.ibm.com/journal/sj/404/gongla.html (accessed October 23, 2003).

Grant, David, Keenoy, Thomas, and Oswick, Cliff (eds.) (1998) *Discourse + Organization*. London: Sage.

Greiner, Larry (1972) Evolution and revolution as organizations grow. *Harvard Business Review*, 50: 37–46.

Grinyer, P. H. and Yasai-Ardekani, M. (1980) Dimensions of organizational structure: A critical replication. *Academy of Management Journal*, 23: 405–21.

Hage, Jerald (1974) *Communication and Organizational Control: Cybernetics in Health and Welfare Settings*. New York: John Wiley & Sons Inc.

Hatch, Mary Jo (1993) The empty spaces of organizing: How improvisational jazz helps redescribe organizational structure. *Organization Studies*, 20: 75–100.

Hirsch, Paul (1986) From ambushes to golden parachutes: Corporate takeovers as an instance of cultural framing and institutional integration. *American Journal of Sociology*, 91: 800–37.

Huber, George (1991) Organizational learning: The contributing processes and the literatures. *Organization Science*, 2: 88–115.

Kamoche, Kenneth, Cunha, Miguel P., and da Cunha, J. V. (2002) (eds.) *Organizational Improvisation*. London: Routledge.

Katz, Daniel and Kahn, Robert L. (1966) *The Social Psychology of Organizations*. New York: John Wiley & Sons Inc.

Lave, J. and Wenger, E. (1991) *Situated Learning: Legitimate Peripheral Participation*. Cambridge: Cambridge University Press.

Lawrence, Paul R. and Lorsch, Jay W. (1967) *Organization and Environment: Managing Differentiation and Integration*. Boston, MA: Division of Research, Graduate School of Business Administration, Harvard University.

Lounsbury, Michael (2005) Institutional variation in the evolution of social movements: Competing logics and the spread of advocacy groups. In G. F. Davis, D. McAdam, W. R. Scott, and M. N. Zald (eds.), *Social Movements and Organization Theory*. Cambridge: Cambridge University Press.

—— Ventresca, Marc J., and Hirsch, Paul M. (2003) Social movements, field frames and industry emergence: A cultural-political perspective on US recycling. *Socio-Economic Review*, 1/1: 71–104.

Mansfield, Roger (1973) Bureaucracy and centralization: An examination of organizational structure. *Administrative Science Quarterly*, 18: 77–88.

March, James G. (1991) Exploration and exploitation in organizational learning. *Organization Science* 2: 71–87.

—— and Simon, Herbert A. (1958) *Organizations*. New York: John Wiley & Sons Inc.

Martin, Joanne (1990) Deconstructing organizational taboos: The suppression of gender conflict in organizations. *Organization Science*, 1: 339–59.

McKelvey, William (1982) *Organizational Systematics*. Berkeley: University of California Press.

Meyer, John W. and Rowan, Brian (1977) Institutionalized organizations: Formal structure as myth and ceremony. *American Journal of Sociology*, 83: 340–63.

Mintzberg, Henry (1981) Organizational design: Fashion or fit? *Harvard Business Review*, 59/1: 103–16.

—— (1983) *Structure in Fives: Designing Effective Organizations*. Englewood Cliffs, NJ: Prentice Hall.

Moorman, Christine and Miner, Anne S. (1998a) The convergence of planning and execution: Improvisation in new product development. *Journal of Marketing*, 61: 1–20.

—— (1998b) Organizational improvisation and organizational memory. *Academy of Management Review*, 23: 698–723.

Nelson, R. R. and Winter, Stanley G. (1982) *An Evolutionary Theory of Economic Change*. Cambridge, MA: Harvard University Press.

Parsons, Talcott (1947) *The Theory of Social and Economic Organization*. Glencoe, IL: Free Press.

Pugh, Derek S. and Hickson, D. J. (1979) *Organizational Structure in Context*. Westmead, Hants: Saxon House.

——— and Hinings, C. R. (1969) An empirical taxonomy of structures of work organizations. *Administrative Science Quarterly*, 14: 115–26.

——— and Turner, C. (1968) Dimensions of organization structure. *Administrative Science Quarterly*, 13: 65–105.

Ranson, Stewart, Hinings, Robert, and Greenwood, Royston (1980) The structuring of organizational structures. *Administrative Science Quarterly*, 25: 1–17.

Riley, Patricia (1983) A structurationist account of political culture. *Administrative Science Quarterly*, 28: 414–37.

Rousseau, Denise (1978) Characteristics of departments, positions, and individuals: Contexts for attitudes and behaviors. *Administrative Science Quarterly*, 23: 521–40.

Scott, W. Richard (1992) *Organizations: Rational, Natural, and Open Systems* (3rd edn.). Englewood Cliffs, NJ: Prentice Hall.

Shotter, John (1993) *Conversational Realities: Constructing Life through Language*. Thousand Oaks, CA: Sage.

Stene, E. (1940) An approach to the science of administration. *American Political Science Review*, 34: 1124–37.

Weber, Max (1946) *From Max Weber: Essays in Sociology* (ed. Hans H. Gerth and C. Wright Mills). New York: Oxford University Press (translation of original published 1906–24).

——(1947) *The Theory of Social and Economic Organization* (ed. A. H. Henderson and Talcott Parsons). Glencoe, IL: Free Press (translation of original published 1924).

Weick, Karl (1998) Improvisation as a mindset for organizational analysis. *Organization Science*, 9: 543–55.

Yoshino, Michael Y. and Fagan, Perry L. (2003) The Renault-Nissan Alliance, HBS case 9-3-30023.

Further reading

Bacharach, Samuel B. and Aiken, Michael (1977) Communication in administrative bureaucracies. *Academy of Management Journal*, 20: 356–77.

Bouchikhi, H., Kilduff, M. K., and Whittington, R. (forthcoming) (eds.) *Action, Structure and Organizations*. Coventry: Warwick Business School Research Bureau.

Braun, P. (2002) Digital knowledge networks: Linking communities of practice with innovation. *Journal of Business Strategies*, 19: 43–54.

Chia, Robert (1996) *Organizational Analysis as Deconstructive Practice*. Berlin: de Gruyter.

Cohen, Michael D. and Bacdayan, P. (1994) Organizational routines are stored as procedural memory: Evidence from a laboratory study. *Organization Science*, 5: 554–68.

Doz, Yves (1988) Technology partnerships between larger and smaller firms: Some critical issues. *International Studies of Management and Organization*, 17/4: 31–57.

Galbraith, Jay R. (1995) *Designing Organizations: An Executive Briefing on Strategy, Structure and Process*. San Francisco, CA: Jossey-Bass.

Gergen, K. J. (1992) Organization theory in the postmodern era. In M. Reed and M. Hughes (eds.), *Rethinking Organization: New Directions in Organization Theory and Analysis*. London: Sage.

Ghoshal, Sumantra and Bartlett, Christopher A. (1990) The multinational corporation as an interorganizational network. *Academy of Management Review*, 15: 603–25.

Hage, Jerald, Aiken, Michael, and Marrett, C. B. (1971) Organization structure and communications. *American Sociological Review*, 36: 860–71.

Jaques, E. (1990) In praise of hierarchy. *Harvard Business Review*, Jan.–Feb.: 127–33.

Koh, Sarah (1992) Corporate globalization: A new trend. *Academy of Management Executive*, 6: 89–96.

Mintzberg, Henry (1979) *The Structuring of Organizations: A Synthesis of the Research*. Englewood Cliffs, NJ: Prentice-Hall.

Parker, Barbara (1996) Evolution and revolution: From international business to globalization. In S. R. Clegg, C. Hardy, and W. Nord (eds.), *Handbook of Organization Studies*, 484–506.

Parsons, Talcott (1947) *The Theory of Social and Economic Organization*. Glencoe, IL: Free Press.

Perrow, Charles (1986) *Complex Organizations: A Critical Essay* (3rd edn.). New York: Random House.

Powell, Walter W. (1990) Neither market nor hierarchy: Network forms of organization. *Research in Organizational Behavior*, 12: 295–336.

Scott, W. Richard (1975) Organizational structure. *Annual Review of Sociology*, 1: 1–20.

Swan, J., Scarbrough, H., and Robertson, M. (2002) The construction of 'communities of practice' in the management of innovation. *Management Learning*, 33: 477–96.

Tosi, Henry L. (1974) The human effects of budgeting systems on management. *MSU Business Topics*, Autumn: 53–63.

Windeler, Arnold and Sydow, J. (2001) Project networks and changing industry practices: Collaborative content production in the German television industry. *Organization Studies*, 22/6: 1035–60.

5 Technology

Techne is the Greek root of our modern words technical and technology but, in contrast to contemporary meanings, ancient Greeks used this term to refer to the skill of the artist. Of course en route from the artists of ancient Greece to our times, the meaning of *techne* was shaped, in turn, by artisans during the Middle Ages, craft workers in the pre-industrial era, and industrial age production engineers.

At each of these stages of development *techne*'s early association with art became more obscured by modern tendencies to objectify, for example by equating technology with the tangible tools, equipment, machines, and procedures by which work is accomplished. Recent shifts toward post-industrial mindsets, however, move industrial understandings of technology back in the direction of *techne*'s original meaning by re-invoking its relationship to power/knowledge or else to craftsmanship and artistry. For example, Nissan fused its industrial technology with the post-industrial by giving marketing a key role in product design to ensure that every aspect of the way it builds cars is artfully infused with the spirit of its brand to 'Shift_ thinking.'[1]

In contrast to the tools and techniques orientation the modern perspective favors, the symbolic study of technology emphasizes, not what technology produces, but how technology itself is produced by social construction and enactment. From this perspective technology is both an outcome of social processes and a process of ongoing learning and design activity. It often relies upon the historical or ethnographic study of technology under construction and technology-in-use.

Because technological design builds behavioral demands directly into production systems, managers and designers can magnify their control over workers through the production technologies they choose. For this reason many critical postmodernists believe technologies impose discipline on those who use them by providing the means to monitor and control behavior. Concerns about privacy and security create images of the evil purposes to which technology can be put, but technology also unleashes powerful forces to combat these negative effects. For example, social media enables people to organize, lobby, and take collective action based on their own interests rather than the interests of those who claim authority over them. The futuristic thinking of other postmodernists sees technology fusing with organization to produce 'cyborganizations.'

Each of these ideas will be examined as we follow the development of the concept of technology within each of the three perspectives, starting with the modern.

Modernist definitions of technology and three typologies

Automotive firms design and manufacture cars and trucks, hospitals care for sick people, and universities educate citizens. Just so, modern organization theorists believe, the purpose an organization fulfills intimately links its technology to its environment (see Figure 5.1). Every organization employs a specific **technology**, or interrelated group of technologies, defined as the means it uses to transform inputs into products or services.

The concept of technology can be applied to any analytical level you choose, from organization to units, jobs, and tasks. At the organization level technology typically refers to the **core technology** that secures an uninterrupted flow of resources that sustains the organization. If an organization employs more than one core technology, as happens in conglomerates like GE, Charoen Pokphand, or Tata that combine unrelated businesses, you will need to perform separate analyses on each one and then analyze the relationships between them (or lack thereof).

At the unit level of analysis you can identify different technologies operating within any one organization that support the core, as do those of purchasing, marketing, accounting, personnel, finance, and sales functions. Unit level technologies of course can be broken down still further into technologies operating at the task level, such as those for maintaining machinery, assembling products, handling complaints, planning budgets, purchasing supplies, or producing reports, to name only a few possibilities.

You might describe a university's core technology as research and education, or simply knowledge production. A richer image of this technology would be formed by separately analyzing how knowledge production is accomplished across the various departments and in each classroom, research laboratory, and administrative office that constitutes the university. The technologies of all these units could be further analyzed at the task level by focusing, for example, on the technologies of teaching (e.g., techniques of classroom engagement and examination), research (e.g., research design and data collection), and administration (e.g., student recruitment and matriculation). Of course any of these could be analytically broken down and examined in even greater detail.

Because many technologies operate simultaneously at all levels within every organization, the term technology can generate confusion if you are not careful to define your level

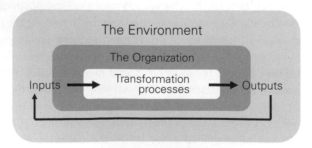

Figure 5.1 The organization as a technical system for transforming inputs into outputs

The technology of the organization is connected to the environment by its need for resource inputs and a market for the product and/or service that forms its output. The uninterrupted consumption of its output stream, shown by the arrow from outputs back to inputs in this modernist model, ensures new resource inputs will be provided to the organization.

of analysis. You also need to be aware of differences between service and manufacturing technologies. The addition of services to the thinking of organization theorists interested in technology highlights three distinctive characteristics of **services**: services are (1) consumed at the same time they are produced, (2) intangible, and (3) cannot be stored in inventory.

Consider the example of a news organization whose service involves providing customers with access to information. Because information only becomes news when it is communicated, news is consumed at the moment that it is produced. It is intangible in the sense that it occurs in the act of communication rather than in the form a specific act of communication takes (e.g., newspaper, broadcast). Because what is news today will not be news tomorrow, news cannot be stored.

Contrast the news with an automobile. Automobiles are not consumed as they are produced, but rather can be stored for months or years without losing too much of their value—they can be sold and resold years after their date of manufacture. Some models even gain value over time. Nonetheless, many aspects of the product of an automobile manufacturing technology are similar to those of a service technology. For example, the value of the style and design of most automobiles dissipates rapidly with the introduction of new models.

The distinction between service and manufacturing technologies can be difficult to maintain beyond a superficial categorization of particular types of businesses (e.g., by industrial codes that separate manufacturing and service organizations into different categories). When you undertake a more detailed analysis of an organization's technology you will notice that the outputs of most technologies have both service and manufacturing characteristics. For example, the warranty that accompanies newly manufactured automobiles is a promise of service that attaches to many automotive products, making them combinations of products and services. Or consider how banks often refer to the services they offer as products. Treating a service like a product encourages attending to packaging and other concerns associated with manufactured goods. For their part, numerous manufacturing firms have become obsessed with customer service.

The cross-fertilization of ideas between the domains of service and manufacturing technologies indicates that the distinction so often made between them is not a clean one. Nonetheless, the distinction contributed much to the early development of modernist theories of technology.

Types of technology

Early modernists focused on comparing the core technologies of manufacturing organizations. As knowledge about technology developed beyond industrial applications, modern organization theorists extended and refined their typologies to encompass first service and then task level technologies. Developing ways of measuring and comparing technology types and levels of analysis contributed new variables to contingency theory to reveal that the performance of a given social structure is not just contingent on the environment, but on technology as well. Joan Woodward, James Thompson, and Charles Perrow are the modernists chiefly responsible for adding the concept of technology to organization theory.

Woodward's typology

Although Joan Woodward, a British sociologist, was among the first organization theorists to draw attention to the importance of technology, her initial research question did not concern technology at all. At the time Woodward designed her study the legacy of the classical management school dominated organization theory. Differences of opinion over which of the proposed ways of organizing was best captured the imaginations of researchers and, in this context, Woodward decided to design what for that time was a large sample scientific study to find out once and for all which organizational arrangements produce the highest levels of performance.

Woodward surveyed 100 manufacturing organizations operating in the vicinity of South Essex, England. Her survey measured relative levels of performance (above average, average, and below average for their industry), average span of control, number of management levels, degree of centralization in decision-making practices, and management style. Woodward expected to find that one constellation of these classical management variables consistently related to high levels of performance, thus she was quite surprised when her analysis revealed no significant relationships.

Such an unexpected result could not be presented without explanation so Woodward sought an answer by trying different approaches to her data. At one point she grouped companies according to their level of technical complexity, which she defined as the degree of mechanization in the core manufacturing process. This move revealed the pattern that made Woodward famous. Her analysis showed that structure was related to performance after all, but only when the type of core technology used by the organization was taken into account as a key contingency. That is, the best structure for an organization (i.e., one associated with high performance) depended upon the core technology employed.

Woodward's scale of technological complexity, which she developed to describe the technologies used in her sample of organizations, is shown in Figure 5.2. On the left side of the figure you will see how her scale was broken up into three parts to provide a simple typology consisting of (1) unit or small batch technologies, (2) large batch or mass production, and (3) continuous processing.

Unit and small batch technologies produce one item or unit at a time; or a few items all at once. A small amount of product, whether unit-by-unit or in a batch, is produced from start to finish and then the process begins again. Custom-made clothing, such as a tailored suit or theatrical costume, is usually the product of unit production technology. Other products typically produced in this way include original works of art, designer glassware, commercial or custom building projects, and engineering prototypes. Wine is produced using small batch technology—a quantity of wine is produced in one lot. Small batch technologies are also found in traditional bakeries and most college classrooms. In both unit and small batch technologies workers typically participate in the whole production process start to finish and so have a fairly complete understanding of the technology being used. Woodward's study showed that organizations that use unit and small batch technologies are more successful when they have smaller spans of control, fewer levels of management, and when they practice decentralized decision making—characteristics associated with organic organizational forms.

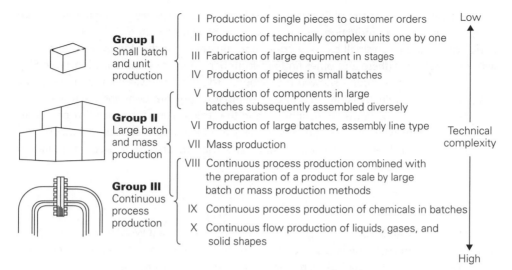

Figure 5.2 Woodward's original typology showing how she arrived at the technical complexity scale

Source: Woodward (1958). Crown copyright is reproduced with the permission of the Controller of HMSO.

Large batch or mass production technologies produce great quantities of identical products using highly routinized and often mechanized procedures. These technologies involve breaking the total production process into many discrete steps that can be performed either by human hands or machines. An automobile assembly line is an example of mass production technology while steel production is an example of large batch technology. In large batch and mass production technologies workers repetitively perform a subset of the tasks involved in producing output. For instance, mass production workers are often physically located in positions adjacent to others whose activities are sequentially related to their own—the person on one side of them performs the task that precedes theirs, and the person on their other side performs the task that follows theirs. Woodward's study showed that organizations using large batch and mass production technologies are more successful when their managers have larger spans of control and when they practice centralized decision making—characteristics associated with mechanistic forms of organizing.

Whereas mass production is a series of discrete tasks performed sequentially, **continuous processing** is a series of non-discrete transformations occurring in a sequence. Consider the examples of oil refining and waste treatment. In these cases, raw material (crude oil, raw sewage) is fed into one end of the process and, as it flows continuously through the system, contaminants and other unwanted substances are removed until the desired degree of refinement is reached (refined oil, treated sewage). In continuous processing, humans tend equipment that affects the transformation automatically, whereas in mass production direct human intervention is involved in at least some parts of the production process. Woodward's study showed that the patterns of organizing in successful continuous processing organizations were similar to those for unit and small batch technologies in that they had smaller spans of control and decentralized decision making; however, they required more levels of management than either small batch or mass production technologies due to the greater technical complexity of the manufacturing process.

In general, Woodward found that the highest levels of performance among her firms were achieved when mass production technologies were combined with mechanistic organizational forms, and when small batch or continuous processing technologies were combined with organic forms (these and other findings from her study are summarized in Table 5.1). However, subsequent studies showed that Woodward's typology was limited in two ways. First, her study examined mainly small and medium-sized organizations and the moderating relationship she found between technology and the structure–performance link proved to be less important when organizational structures are large and therefore more complex. Second, Woodward had ignored the technologies used to provide services, a limitation Thompson sought to overcome.

Thompson's typology

In the late 1960s American sociologist James Thompson stretched Woodward's typology to include both manufacturing and service sector technologies.[2] Thompson's theory rested on distinguishing between long-linked, mediating, and intensive technologies.

Long-linked technologies encapsulate both the mass production and continuous processing categories Woodward defined. Thus automobile assembly lines as well as technologies for producing chemicals and generating electrical power fit the category of long-linked technology. Thompson used the descriptive term long-linked because all technologies of this type involve linear transformation processes in which inputs enter at one end of a long series of sequential steps from which products emerge at the other end.

Table 5.1 Findings from Woodward's study linking technology to social structure

Structural dimension	Technology		
	Unit production	Mass production	Continuous process
Levels of management	3	4	6
Span of control	23	48	15
Ratio of direct to indirect labor	9:1	4:1	1:1
Administrative ratio	low	medium	high
Formalization (written communication)	low	high	low
Centralization	low	high	low
Verbal communication	high	low	high
Skill level of workers	high	low	high
Overall structure	organic	mechanistic	organic

Source: Woodward (1965). By permission of Oxford University Press.

Mediating technologies serve clients or customers by bringing them together in an exchange or other transaction. Banks, brokerage firms, and insurance companies all operate using mediating technology that links the participants by helping them locate one another and conduct their transactions, often without ever having to physically meet. For example, banks use mediating technology to bring together savers who want to invest money and borrowers who want to take out loans. Banking technology mediates between savers and borrowers by providing a location for both types of customers, and by providing standardized procedures to facilitate their mutual benefit, in this case, interest payments for savers and funds for borrowers. eBay links sellers and buyers through mediating technology providing software applications often involving further mediation from a financial services provider such as PayPal or a credit card company.

Intensive technology occurs in hospital emergency rooms, research laboratories, and in project organizations such as those typical within the construction industry and engineering firms. Intensive technologies require coordinating the specialized abilities of two or more experts in the transformation of a usually unique input into a customized output. Each use of intensive technology requires on-the-spot development and application of specialized knowledge to new problems or unique circumstances.

Thompson's typology was grounded in the open systems model of organization according to which a core technology is open to its environment on both the input and output sides (see Figure 5.1). This model drew Thompson's attention to the inputs to the technical process and the outputs it produced. He observed that some technologies use highly standardized inputs and outputs (e.g., traditional mass production automobile manufacturing assembles nearly identical parts into nearly identical automobiles), while in others unstandardized inputs are used to produce unstandardized outputs (e.g., hospital emergency rooms transform diseased or injured patients into stabilized patients for discharge or ready to be input into other hospital services).

In addition to input and output standardization, Thompson also recognized that technologies differed depending upon their transformation processes. He characterized some technologies as standardized in their processing of inputs into outputs (e.g., automobile assembly workers perform the same tasks repeatedly), and others as having little process standardization (e.g., emergency room personnel respond to the unique needs of each patient as they come through the door).

Thompson's theory can be summarized using a two-by-two matrix classifying core technologies according to their standardization of inputs/outputs and their standardization of transformation process (see Figure 5.3). The four cells of the matrix represent Thompson's three types of organizational technologies, plus one extra: (1) standardized inputs/outputs with standardized transformation processes describe long-linked technologies, (2) unstandardized inputs/outputs with standardized transformation processes describe mediating technologies, (3) unstandardized inputs/outputs with unstandardized transformation processes describe intensive technologies, and (4) standardized inputs/outputs with unstandardized transformation processes.

It is interesting to speculate about why Thompson ignored the fourth cell of this matrix—standardized inputs/outputs with unstandardized transformation processes. The absence of a description of this category is probably due to the enormous inefficiency Thompson would have associated with such a technology. Imagine producing a standard product with

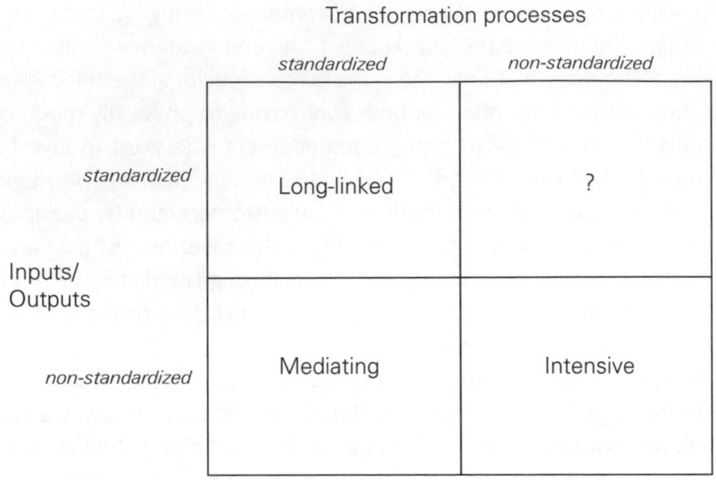

Transformation processes

	standardized	non-standardized
standardized	Long-linked	?
non-standardized	Mediating	Intensive

Inputs/Outputs

Figure 5.3 Two-by-two matrix showing Thompson's typology of technologies
Source: Based on Thompson (1967).

standard inputs, and doing so in a different way every time. While such technologies do exist (e.g., building design prototypes for manufacturing processes, brainstorming innovative ideas), Thompson, a modernist who was obsessed with applying norms of rationality, may have deliberately ignored this type of technology, thereby making way for Perrow to take another stab at creating an all-encompassing typology.

Perrow's typology

Whereas Woodward's and Thompson's typologies only considered core technology, American sociologist Charles Perrow dropped from the organizational to the task level of analysis to develop his framework.[3] Perrow began by defining the variability and analyzability of tasks as the means of differentiating technologies (see Figure 5.4).

Task variability refers to the number of exceptions to standard procedures encountered in the application of a given technology. **Task analyzability** is the extent to which, when an exception is encountered, there are known methods for dealing with it. Although Perrow defined task variability and task analyzability at the level of tasks, these two variables have been used to characterize technologies at the unit and organizational levels of analysis. Arraying task variability and task analyzability in a two-by-two matrix produces four technology types Perrow named routine, craft, engineering, and non-routine.

Routine technologies are characterized by low task variability and high task analyzability. The traditional automobile assembly line that illustrates Thompson's long-linked technology and Woodward's mass production category also fit Perrow's routine technology category. Clerical work is another example, this one representing a service technology. Filing clerks, for instance, encounter few exceptions to their standardized work practices and when they do there is almost always a known method of resolution, such as hierarchical referral (i.e., ask the boss).

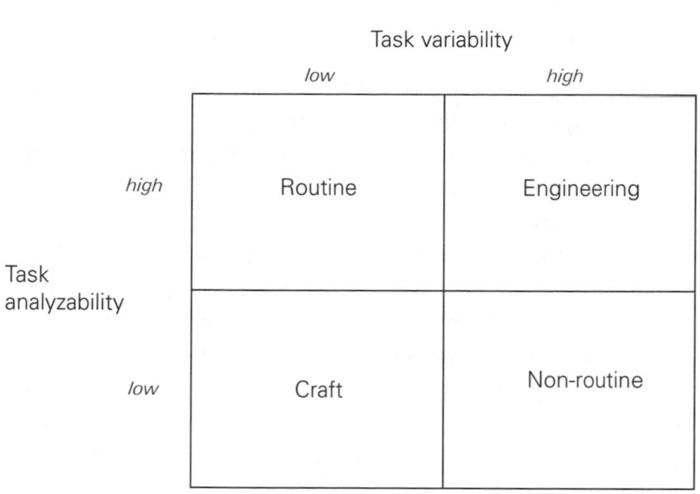

Figure 5.4 Two-by-two matrix showing Perrow's typology of technologies
Source: Based on Perrow (1967).

Craft technology describes conditions of low task variability and low task analyzability. Construction work is a craft technology. The construction worker encounters few exceptions to standard procedures but when exceptions do arise, such as mistakes in planning or unavailable materials, a way of dealing with them must be invented. Most forms of artistic production provide other examples of craft technology, as does locating water for drilling wells. In craft technologies intuition and experience become extremely important, as happens when standard geological solutions to finding water fail. Although standard procedures usually work in craft technologies, when exceptions occur (e.g., an artist runs out of canvas or paint, no water is found using scientific prediction), there are few known solutions upon which workers can rely. In these conditions experience, intuition, and improvisation play important roles.

Engineering technologies occur where high task variability combines with high task analyzability. The technologies of laboratory technicians, executive secretaries, accountants, and most engineers fit the engineering category. In engineering technology many exceptions to standard practices arise but employees possess the knowledge needed to solve these problems. Often the knowledge required by engineering technologies comes from advanced and highly specialized training, thus the presence of a great deal of professional work usually indicates an engineering technology in use.

Perrow labeled as **non-routine technology** those characterized by high task variability and low task analyzability. These conditions occur, for instance, in research and development departments, aerospace engineering, and in design and prototype laboratories. Perrow's non-routine category overlaps Woodward's unit and small batch technologies and has commonalities with Thompson's intensive category as well as his missing category of standardized input/outputs and unstandardized transformation processes. The high number of problems encountered in non-routine technologies, and the lack of known methods for solving them, place employees using these technologies in a more or less constant state of uncertainty.

Using the three typologies

Even though the three typologies discussed so far overlap, you should still begin a modernist technology analysis by applying all three in order to maximize the information available to you. Using all three will force you to consider the six dimensions that collectively underpin these types: technical complexity, routineness of work, standardization of inputs/outputs, standardization of transformation processes, task variability, and task analyzability. Although you may ultimately conclude you do not need all of these dimensions to adequately describe the technology you are studying, until you try them out on your organization you will not know which are most helpful. Many times I have been surprised by the insight provided when I applied a theory I did not initially believe would help me.

To see how to apply the typologies, consider a company that manufactures buses. A chassis is brought in at one end of the factory and moves down the assembly line where axels, an engine, the body, interior trim, and so on are added. Your initial assessment might be that the core technology at the organizational level of analysis is *long-linked* (Thompson). You can see that it is not *large batch* (Woodward), because even though there are 50 buses at various stages of completion on the assembly line—ten are for one customer, five for another customer, two for another—each order has different requirements for heating, air conditioning, internal features, and external trim, making it a *small batch* technology (Woodward).

Closer analysis of bus manufacturing at the unit level reveals that the Chassis and Suspension Department can be characterized by *routine* technology (Perrow) because task variability is low (the only variation is the choice of two chassis lengths) and task analyzability is high (there are standardized methods for positioning and bolting the suspension on the chassis). The Internal Trim Department, however, is characterized by *engineering* technology because task variability is high (different customers want different seating configurations, heaters, handrails, doors, lights, decals, etc., situated in different places) as is task analyzability (there are known procedures and methods for dealing with these differences).

The bus-manufacturing example highlights the complexity of analyzing the technology of an organization and the danger of ignoring one or more levels of analysis. By focusing only on core technology at the organizational level you lose the interesting details of technological diversity that emerge in analyses conducted at the unit and task levels. The loss can be justified on the grounds of the power of abstraction to make generalized comparisons across organizations, but you should not forget what you give up in the bargain.

As you focus on the interesting details that appear at the unit or task levels of analysis you will probably want to combine several different types from among the typologies. By encouraging you to think multi-dimensionally this technique will both stretch your imagination and strengthen your ability to perform modernist technology analysis. But remember to take great care with levels of analysis; it is easy to switch levels without being aware that you are doing so. Level switching is often illuminating but if you lose your bearings it will be hard to avoid confusion.

Technology in the symbolic perspective

Symbolically inclined organization theorists believe that, like every other aspect of organizations, technology is socially constructed. Thus technology does not only refer to physical objects like raw materials and equipment, but also to symbols including words, images, and metaphors. It is not just focused on task activities, but also on interactions between people and technology, and interpretation becomes as important as knowledge in understanding technology.

New (computer-based) technologies

In her 1988 book *In the Age of the Smart Machine* Shoshona Zuboff analyzed what at the time were called new technologies, a category referring to computer-based technologies such as those found in microelectronics, satellite communications, lasers, expert systems, robotics, and multi-media. She characterized the use of new technologies as requiring more interpretive processes than do traditional technologies, because processes involving computers involve manipulating symbolic representations (information or data) rather than tangible objects.

Karl Weick's theory of new technology derives from his examination of the role cognition, particularly interpretation, plays. Computer-mediated technology, typical of continuous production processes but also found in less complex technologies, allows operators to monitor production processes without ever touching, or in some cases even seeing, the product. What operators are able to know about what is happening inside computer-mediated processes is based on interpretations of symbolic representations provided as computer output (often in the form of numeric or graphic displays), and this information may or may not align with what is actually taking place out of sight. Weick characterized the ways new technologies differ from the technologies identified by Woodward, Thompson, and Perrow, in terms of their being stochastic, continuous, and abstract.[4]

Stochastic events are unexpected interruptions. While older technologies also occasion stochastic events (e.g., boilers sometimes blow up for no apparent reason), operators of new technologies experience these interruptions much more often. But the frequency with which stochastic events take place does not necessarily lead to learning, because each of these events is the unique product of dense interactions among the parts of a complex system. Thus the **stochastic** nature of new technologies means that their processes and underlying causes and effects cannot be well understood by their operators.

New technologies are often operated nonstop, which is to say they are **continuous** processes, but in ways never anticipated by Woodward, Thompson, or Perrow. One feature of computer work is the constant need for the revision and updating of both hardware and software. Computer technicians and programmers working with a continuous technology must change that technology while it is in operation. For example, in order to make flight reservations 24 hours a day, 7 days a week, 52 weeks a year, airlines must process data continuously; if the data processing system were to stop, even for short periods, chaos could ensue resulting in double bookings or the reporting of inaccurate flight times or incorrect destinations. Their continuous nature pushes new technologies to a much higher level of complexity compared to those described by Woodward, Thompson, and Perrow.

Compared to old technologies where you can see the moving parts of a machine or shadow a service provider, the working processes of computer-mediated technology are **abstract** and often hidden from view inside computers and other machines. Understanding new technologies therefore presents an operator with a highly abstract model that is once or twice removed from what the technical process is doing. Differences arising between the two processes—one in the head, the other in the computer—can lead to misunderstanding, error, and the possibility of conflicting interpretations of what things mean when a malfunction occurs. This has always been a problem for those who work with computers. Because a computer's hardware is operated via software that can never map the hardware's processes completely, there is always room for error and misunderstanding of what the underlying process is doing.

The stochastic, continuous and abstract qualities of new technology add a new level of complication to technology that makes them qualitatively different from even the most complex technologies described by Woodward, Thompson, and Perrow. Weick's theory thus complements dimensions of technology like non-routineness, standardization, and technical complexity. One implication of the stochastic, continuous, and abstract nature of new technologies is that they make **reliability** a big issue, which brings with it questions about how best to organize for high reliability. The importance of high reliability when using new technologies is perhaps most evident when applications of new technology involve dangerous activities, such as nuclear power production or air traffic control.

Perrow studied the dangers of new technology in his 1984 book *Normal Accidents*, an empirical exploration of technological failures such as the 1979 partial core meltdown of the nuclear reactor at Three Mile Island in the US. In it Perrow defined the failures of new technology he observed as impossible to anticipate, unique, and random. He explained their unpredictable behavior and the inability to analyze their failures as the result of an interaction between technical complexity and tight coupling. In Perrow's theory system **complexity** produces unexpected interactions between components, while **tight coupling** between those components involving human reactions to the unexpected system interactions means that the conditions ripe for failure escalate rapidly. The inevitability of the consequences of complexity interacting with tight coupling that Perrow saw in new technology prompted him to call their failures normal accidents.

In his analysis of the partial meltdown of the nuclear reactor at Three Mile Island, Perrow argued that the simultaneous failure of two fairly minor safety devices embedded in a complex, tightly-coupled system misled those involved in their attempts to intervene. According to Perrow, the dense interactions between components of the complex technical systems controlling the plant made it impossible to deduce the cause of the problem, and there followed a series of inappropriate interventions that created a series of further mechanical failures that increased the confusion of the operators. Mechanical failure interacting with human limitations escalated to the point of near disaster.

Perrow's morose conclusion was that prevention of normal accidents is unlikely because we will never be able to understand the underlying interaction effects of complexity and tight coupling well enough or fast enough to intervene effectively. That failures such as the 1986 meltdown at the Chernobyl nuclear facility in Ukraine and the 2010 oil spill in the Gulf of Mexico continue to plague us does little to disconfirm Perrow's view. However, Perrow does caution us not to overextend his theory by applying it to human moral failure, which is how he assessed the 2008 global financial crisis.[5] Bankers claiming not to have understood the complex interactions of tightly coupled financial instruments, in his view, paper over the real cause of the crisis—unrestrained human greed.

The social construction of technology

Though Weick and Perrow move into symbolic territory by giving interpretation a role in technology, their theories still harbor objectivity in that they define dimensions and variables with which to objectively test the explanatory power of their theories. Moving further into the realm of social construction theory requires seeing how non-technical concerns such as cultural norms and expectations shape technology. In contrast to how technology is portrayed in the modern perspective, social constructionists view technology, not as a pure application of science to productive work, but rather as the product of social, cultural, and economic factors in the environment.

The theory of the **social construction of technology** (SCOT) promoted by Dutch professor of science and technology Wiebe Bijker in collaboration with British sociologists John Law and Trevor Pinch, among others, describes how technologies are shaped by complex socio-cultural trade-offs.[6] Bijker and Pinch, for example, proposed an evolutionary model of technological innovation that exposed the role of social construction in the development of bicycling technology. According to their model technological innovation introduces variation to a population of products, following which users select those to be retained and those abandoned, thereby influencing which technologies will be selected from those on offer.

To demonstrate their theory they traced technological innovations in the bicycle industry. At one crucial point in bicycle innovation history that occurred in the early 1900s, they discovered that women cyclists who wore long dresses demanded certain modifications to the bicycle frame. Response to their demands produced a type of bicycle that was unappreciated by other users whose demands for stability and speed were met by competitive models, thus presenting the market for bicycles with considerable variation.

According to Bijker and Pinch, the bicycle we use today represents the evolutionary success of one of those technologies but their analysis revealed that social rather than purely scientific forces shaped the selection process. Moreover, the selected bicycling technology then influenced society and culture by helping to change attitudes toward women wearing trousers. In other words, strong preferences for speedier bicycles led to favoring one technology over others, but having established itself, the favored technology influenced society and culture to reduce the negative impact on women.

While a number of SCOT theorists focus on the macro level of technological innovation, as Bijker and his colleagues did, others examine interpretive processes that influence technological developments at the organizational or unit levels of analysis. Julian Orr's ethnographic study of the work of photocopier repair technicians at Xerox provides an example.[7] In order to explore how meaning is negotiated around technology, Orr, a researcher at the Xerox Palo Alto Research Center (now PARC), immersed himself in a community of Xerox photocopier repair technicians. He and the technicians attended classes at repair school, hung out at lunch, and went on service visits; all the while Orr audio taped their interactions and kept field notes. He also studied customers/users, their organizations, and the copy machines they used.

Orr concluded from his study that copy machines have both a technical and a social presence. Their technical presence—which is built into the machines—is constituted by mechanical and electronic technologies that require specific behavioral responses from their technicians and users. However, individual machines also have their own histories and ways of behaving, for example, some have a history of breakdowns, others make unique noises. This means that users and technicians often become attuned to the way they experience a particular machine and, even though they have an operating manual, they may need to improvise when interacting with these machines.

Orr discovered the social aspect of technology by observing conversations about copiers. For example, he observed technicians and customers negotiating the meaning of technical problems and the appropriate use of the technology the machines offered. Furthermore, Orr noted that technicians discussed their work among themselves, sharing knowledge and constructing their identities as competent technicians by showing off their skill in handling problems and carrying out successful repairs. Their regularized interactions resulted in the development of a community of practice and formed a subculture within Xerox. Thus Orr's study not only highlighted the socially constructed and situated nature of technical work and technology but also affirmed that the concepts of technology, social structure, and organizational culture influence each other.

You should recognize that the socially constructed nature of technology may be hidden from its users. Although much of the face-to-face collaboration Orr studied took place in the work setting, employees believed that most of their communication was mediated by their computers.[8] All employees at Xerox were linked through an intranet and everything they emailed to one another was documented by computer programs. However, much of the sharing and interpretation of information concerning work improvements and problem solving took place in their informal, spontaneous face-to-face gatherings.

Orr's findings indicate that managing technology (old or new) is not just about the technology itself, but also about the interactions and interpretations made by people using the technology. Furthermore those involved may be unaware of the interpretations they make or their consequences, raising concerns about technology that the critical postmodern perspective explores.

Postmodernism and technology

Postmodernists interested in a critical approach to technology trace their concerns about its abusive potential to German philosopher Martin Heidegger, an existential phenomenologist whose work falls within the symbolic perspective, as does his claim that the essence of technology lies in the manner in which it is used (particularly how we unlock its potential) and how we allow it to shape who we are.[9] However, in *The Question Concerning Technology*, Heidegger raised provocative questions about the relationship between technology and the self that resonate with the critical postmodern perspective. Much as Weber warned us that bureaucracy can become an iron cage, Heidegger saw grave danger in technology because, while it offers many seductions, it can also imprison us if we allow ourselves to become subservient to its needs.[10]

Following Heidegger's lead, postmodern organization theorists have studied how technology controls behavior by disciplining organizational members, and how managers gain power by controlling these technologies. Notice that, as we move into the postmodern perspective, there is a subtle shift in the use of the concept of technology. The linguistic turn of postmodernism is in evidence as the controlling practices of those who manage are turned into technologies of control by postmodern critics who want to reveal how technology affects the humans it serves.

Technologies of control and representation

Because technological design builds behavioral demands directly into production systems, managers and designers can exercise control over workers through the technologies they impose. Technologies discipline workers who must conform to their physical and often mental and emotional demands in order to perform their jobs.

Even more unsettling may be the perniciously seductive nature of technology that can cause us to lose our grip on what is real and imprison us in illusion. For example, while most postmodernists portray technology as a form of overt control, others comment on its ability to addict us to mass consumption or other aspects of modern ways of living. Consider how many people are bombarded daily by media and Internet images selling lifestyles and identities they are encouraged to consume and then communicate to others, enticing them to do the same. It is not much of a leap of imagination to move from here to the cinematic nightmare of technologically imprisoned lives portrayed by futuristic films like *Blade Runner*, *Minority Report*, and *The Matrix*.

In *The Postmodern Condition* Lyotard offered an explanation of how the technology of post-industrial capitalism has shifted social values away from truth and justice toward efficiency and rationality. The value for optimal performance achieved by minimizing energy expended while maximizing output is often enacted, he claimed, by decisions about the value of a person, department, or institution that are based primarily on their contribution to efficiency. Because character traits such as integrity and fairness are not clearly related to efficiency, the social values of truth and justice are neglected. The efficiency logic is often bolstered by the institutional myth that efficiency serves rationality. Once these ideas take hold, the more efficient and rational seeming the organization, technology, or person, the more power they acquire, but also the more firmly the system that defines power in terms of efficiency and rationality imprisons them.

Defining the terms by which power is bestowed leads us from consideration of technologies of control to an interest in the technologies of representation. If the way in which success, fame, celebrity, and other versions of power are defined marks out the road to their achievement, then representation itself becomes a technology for manipulating power and exercising control over others. It was in this sense that British organizational theorists Rod Coombs, David Knights, and Hugh Willmott equated information technology (IT) with managerial control.[11]

Coombs, Knights, and Willmott argued that IT is a means to direct thought and action in organizations and to discipline members for noncompliance with the desires or expectations of managers. They argued that the seeming objectivity of performance data conceals the fact that the categories into which data are collected and from which they are reported impose values on those who work within the system. For example, being forced to report the number of patients served per day in a hospital subtly reinforces a value for speedy processing, often at the expense of the value for quality care. Doctors, nurses, and administrators who feel pressured by the desire to keep their jobs and their self-esteem also feel pressure to buy into the speedy processing of patients.

The critical view recognizes that employees are not powerless within this system; they can resist control via sabotage (e.g., entering false data into the information system), non-responsiveness (e.g., refusing to react to feedback from the system), or joking (e.g., as a psychological defense against changing their values). However, the critique emphasizes the alignment between most modern technology theories and the interests of management. It was in this latter sense that Lyotard predicted that in the future the only knowledge valued will be that which can be translated into information for analysis and dissemination by computers. Power struggles will occur, not over the control of geopolitical territory as in the past, but over the control of information.

Lyotard ends *The Postmodern Condition* by predicting that the computerization of society will either lead to totalitarian control of the market system and the production of knowledge, or to greater justice. He warned that the path to greater justice only opens with free public access to information, as illustrated by the open source movement in computing that demands open access to the source codes from which computing applications are built. The movement alters technology at all levels from reorganization of computing and software industries, to enactment of specific open source applications such as the Linux operating system, and the Mozilla Firefox and Google Chromium web browsers.

Today we can do just about anything through virtual exchanges conducted over the Internet without any direct contact between us. The terror this future brings with it can be anticipated in the growth of cyberveillance—computer programs that can track every keystroke you make, every website you access, and that can hack your online accounts in order to capture your identity and security codes. Postmodernists acknowledge, however, that computer technology also encourages democracy and is a useful tool of economic, environmental, and political resistance. Social movements can provide information to mobilize and organize people across the globe.

Cyborganization

Technologies of representation can be employed to make organizations and actions appear to be real when they are not. Symbols and images have the power to produce a simulacrum, for example as is done by computer games involving three-dimensional virtual realities and other sensory experiences. Because they give users the illusion of having an objective experience, they can claim to invent a reality detached from objective existence. Postmodernists fascinated by the idea of 'cyborganizations' make a less radical break with reality that still subscribes to futurist visions of human dependence on technology. The points of contact between humans and machines are emphasized by the idea of the cyborg popularized in science fiction films like *Robocop* and *The Terminator*.

The term cyborg was coined by Manfred Clynes, a space scientist who researched ways to free astronauts from routine maintenance tasks in space, but it was American feminist Donna Haraway who wrote about cyborgs in a way that caught the attention of organization theorists. Haraway proposed using the cyborg myth, in the postmodern sense of a hybrid—something at once human and machine, simultaneously natural and artificial, mind and body, male and female, in other words a complete postmodern denial of all dichotomizing polarities.

In *Simians, Cyborgs, and Women: The Reinvention of Nature*, Haraway defined cyborgs as 'a kind of disassembled and reassembled, postmodern collective and personal self.'[12] She claimed that, by being embodied in one technologically enhanced creature, dualisms break down permitting old, stale social–political standoffs to be reconfigured. In this way Haraway applied cyborg imagery to the exploration of alternative realities to encourage embracing contradiction, deconstructing boundaries, and opening new connections—all of which mark the positive contributions made by the postmodern perspective and in particular the role that feminist techno-science plays in specifying the positive implications of high-tech culture for humankind.

According to British organization theorists Martin Parker and Robert Cooper, cyborganization, a contraction of cybernetic and organization, brings Haraway's cyborg myth into organization theory. Cybernetics is a branch of systems theory that focuses on communication and control in humans and machines. It contributes to organization theory when it defines patterns of information or activity as organization. One of the primary contributions of cybernetics has been its insistence on viewing organization as the outcome of bipolar forces of stability/instability and order/disorder. Cyberneticists not only acknowledge the complexity of bipolarity, they introduce the notion of complicity such as occurs when humans partner with machines in man–machine hybrids, which of course are cyborgs.

Cooper related Haraway's cyborg myth to developments in information theory suggested by American mathematician Norbert Weiner. According to Weiner: 'A piece of information, in order to contribute to the general information of a community, must say something substantially different from the community's previous stock of information.'[13] The implication of Weiner's insight, according to Cooper, is that information systems, which postmodern organizations increasingly are, thrive on their openness to novelty and surprise.[14]

If we are to appreciate cyborganizations, it becomes clear that we must see organizations as bound to their technologies, not just in their core production processes but through and through. Think of all the computers, video equipment, photocopiers, communication and transportation devices, manufacturing gear, and so on that make up most organizations. In these terms, can you think of any organization today that is not a cyborganization?

Actor network theory

The modernist view of scientific knowledge as the product of explaining, hypothesizing, and experimentation, is upended by actor network theory (ANT), which instead regards scientific knowledge as a social construction and understands scientific work as constructing data, composing texts, and negotiating with other scientists. Knowledge from the ANT theorist's perspective is a product of actor networks that organize various interacting materials (machines, people, buildings, concepts, written documents). This view of science, contributed by Michel Callon and Bruno Latour among others, was based on ethnographic studies of science in action.[15]

In their influential studies both Latour and Collon observed that actors never act alone but always in conjunction with things, for example scientists conduct science with petri dishes and telescopes. Consequently actor network theorists place actors within a network of other actants, a term borrowed from French semiotician Algirdas Julien Greimas to embrace both those who act and that which is acted upon, including humans and non-humans. In ANT any act carried out implies a network of interacting actants as driving a car requires a driver, the car, a road, driving regulations, a license, and so forth. The term actor-network arises from the belief that it is the network, not the actor alone, that performs an act, whether this be an act of science, technology, organization, or any other socio-material phenomenon.

In a key study that laid the groundwork for ANT, Latour spent two years doing an ethnographic study of how research was conducted at the Salk Institute for Biological Studies in California. In his words, by focusing on how science is conducted, he: 'was trying to account for the various ways in which truth is built.'[16] In 1979 Latour and British sociologist Steve Woolgar presented the Salk study, in *Laboratory Life: The Social Construction of Scientific Facts*, in which they concluded that what Latour had observed involved a lot more power and politics than was normally acknowledged within the scientific community.

The book provoked considerable controversy, not only because it claimed that scientific work is socially constructed from a 'seething mass of alternative interpretations' and from 'the confrontation and negotiation of utter confusion,' but also because practitioners of normal science expected research focused on science to be conducted using objective scientific methods, not qualitative ethnography borrowed from the social sciences. Even more unsettling for some, ANT employed postmodernism's tactic of decentering the subject. By defining societies, technologies, and organizations as effects of the interacting heterogeneous materials circulating within them, ANT had made humans just another element in the network, neither more nor less important than any other.

ANT depends upon two main assumptions. First, the social world is materially heterogeneous, in other words, buildings, machines, actors' bodies, written documents, other physical objects, and talk are all involved in the process of socio-technical ordering, which includes making sense of, constructing, and maintaining the network. Second, the elements of an actor network only achieve meaning and identity in relation to other elements, they do not have a fixed existence independent of these relationships. Known in ANT as the principle of relationality, this idea resonates strongly with the linguistic ontology of postmodernism, with the main difference being that ANT leans more heavily on materiality, at least that of some network elements.

Based on these assumptions, organization theorists use ANT to study organizations as networks of relationship between human and nonhuman actants (technical, physical, natural, body, thought, text, etc.). The human actor is no more or less important than any other material, but acts as the translator who builds coherence and organization from all the bits and pieces. Network objects are fluid and many of the ways that network materials adapt to particular circumstances are invisible.[17]

Take the example of a company manufacturing high-pressure mercury lamps used for street lighting. Decreased demand for mercury lamps and growing demand for the higher quality, more efficient natural light provided by metal halide lamps convince production and design engineers to modify their company's existing machine so that it will produce the new type of lamp. The physical shape and design of the machine, its components, raw material inputs, operating procedures, operator behavior, problem-solving activities and interactions, quality standards, and so on will change as these elements of the network interact and try to organize and adapt themselves to the demands of manufacturing and supplying the new product.

ANT competes with the related ideas of social construction of technology (SCOT) and social network theory. Whereas SCOT presents technology and people as interacting but separate entities, in the ANT perspective as stated by Latour: 'Society and technology are not two ontologically distinct entities but more like phases of the same essential action.'[18] In ANT technology achieves meaning and thereby exists because of relationality (between people, work, artifacts, and so on) and therefore it must be studied and managed as an integral part of the actor network. Similar to social network theory, ANT focuses on the relationships between elements in the network rather than on the elements themselves, but unlike social network theory, ANT theorists adopt the assumptions of interpretive epistemology presumed by their ethnographic methods. Additionally, decentering human actors satisfies one of the conditions of postmodernism.

Combining technology, social structure, and environment

Advocates of the normative approach to technology want to know how the use of new technologies, such as social media, affect the way an organization should be designed and managed. Modernist organization theorists who have examined the relationship of new technology to social structure claim that computer technologies and communication networks have made classical organizational and work designs obsolete. For example, new technologies reduce the need for physical proximity, hierarchical controls, and the face-to-face mechanisms of integration (e.g., supervision, liaison roles, co-located teams), and have enabled the work of virtual organizations and other co-acting groups.

New technologies can also lead to greater decentralization of decision making because data are more readily available—integration occurs through electronic linking, increased spans of control, and decreased hierarchical levels. Software programs correct errors and make the exchange of greater amounts of information easier and faster.[19] But examining changes in the relationships between social structure, technology, and the environment demands that we understand their historical patterns.

In this final section I will review some important history concerning changing ideas about the role of technology and its relationship to structure and environment, starting with the story of how Woodward brought technology into organization theory and thereby helped to found contingency theory.

The technological imperative

Woodward's influential study ushered in the idea that technology determines which sort of organizational structure is most effective. Belief in this idea came to be known as the **technological imperative**—that is, choosing a technology determines the preferred organizational structure. That technology could predict the success of a given structure would lead others to formulate contingency theory, but meanwhile organization theorists intent on replicating and extending Woodward's research, found evidence that undermined belief in the technological imperative.

One set of scholars known as the Aston Group, because they worked at Aston University in the UK, presented empirical evidence that the influence of technology on structure depends on the size of the organization; the smaller the organization the greater the significance of technology for the structure–performance relationship.[20] The Aston researchers explained that when organizations consist of little beyond their core technology, as was the case for the relatively small organizations studied by Woodward, then technology has a significant and possibly determining effect on social structure. But as organizations become more complex this relationship disappears.

Another way to interpret the Aston studies is to recognize that social structures relate to all the technologies in use, which for some units and their employees will not be the core technology of the organization, but the technology of their unit. In small organizations most employees are directly involved with the core technology, for example, a small welding company will employ mainly welders with perhaps one staff person. In large organizations many employees rely on technologies that are not directly related to the core. Thus, the overall characteristics of social structures in larger organizations reflect the greater differentiation and integration of a wider array of technologies than do social structures in small organizations. This means that in large organizations the relationship between the core technology and the general characteristics of the complex social structure that organizes all the different units with their different technologies will be harder to determine. Technology and structure are still significantly related, but the relationship is vastly more complicated in large organizations than it is in small ones.

Technical complexity, uncertainty, and routineness

You will recall that Woodward distinguished technologies by their technical complexity, measuring this variable as the extent to which machines perform core transformation processes. In relating technical complexity to structural arrangements, Woodward noticed that technologies at both extremes of her scale (unit and continuous processing technologies) were best served by organic structures, while technologies in the middle range (large batch, mass production) performed better with a mechanistic structure.

Woodward explained this pattern using the concept of the **routineness of work** involved in different types of technology. Woodward noticed that both unit and continuous processing technologies involved work that was non-routine relative to the work associated with mass production, which was routine. Unit and continuous process technologies are therefore better suited to organic structures, she reasoned, because they are more compatible with non-routine work. On the other hand, she predicted that mass production technologies would be better suited to mechanistic structures because these structures encourage and support routine work.

It may help you to remember the relationship Woodward discovered between the routineness of work and technical complexity if you picture the inverted U-shaped curve shown in Figure 5.5. Consider, for example, a graphic art firm that serves clients by designing logos and producing finished artwork for use in magazines and on websites (a unit/small batch technology having low technical complexity but requiring fairly non-routine work). Compare this organization with a manufacturer of standardized electrical components whose raw materials and manufacturing processes vary little across time (a mass production/large batch technology with high routineness of work and moderate complexity). Now compare both of these to a nuclear power plant where most of the work done by humans consists of monitoring machines (a continuous processing technology with high technical complexity and low routineness due to the non-routine nature of work when problems arise).

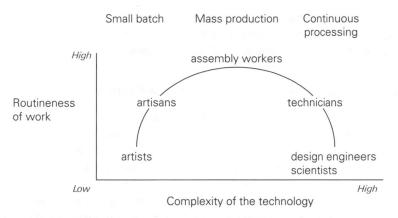

Figure 5.5 The relationship between routineness of work and technical complexity

Woodward's findings indicated that both unit and continuous processing technologies are associated with low routineness, while mass production technologies have high routineness; thus the relationship between routineness of work and technical complexity takes the inverted U shown in this figure.

The graphics design firm needs to be much more responsive to client needs and flexible in relation to how work is accomplished than does the manufacturing company. And although most work in a nuclear power plant is highly routine, when the equipment malfunctions workers must be ready for anything. For this reason they keep their structure flexible to allow them to confront the stochastic need for extremely non-routine activity.

Although Perrow categorized technologies on a different basis than did Woodward, he too noted the importance of routineness when he included routine and non-routine as two types of technology. Perrow refined Woodward's conceptualizations of the routineness of work, by breaking the dimension of routineness into the sub-dimensions of task variability and analyzability, which enhanced the predictability and accuracy of applications of technology theory to organizational design. Refining theoretical relationships like this grounds many developments within the modern perspective such as adding a new contingency to those already proposed.

For example, Perrow's interest in non-routineness led him to focus on technology as a determinant of uncertainty in organizations. According to Perrow, technology contributes to uncertainty either through variations in the quality or availability of inputs to the transformation process or through the variable nature of the transformation process itself. When uncertainty is high it becomes difficult to design a structure to support the activities of the organization because the activities that are required are not always known in advance.

Perrow's and Woodward's discussions of the effects of technology are like two sides of a single coin. Both explain the links between technology and social structure in terms of the routineness and non-routineness of work. However, whereas Woodward was the first to propose the relationship between technology and social structure, Perrow sought a more thorough explanation for it. Like Perrow, Thompson looked for deeper understanding of the links between technology and social structure, but in contrast to Perrow, did so with greater emphasis on social structure.

You can see the positivist drive to accumulate knowledge here—first Woodward discovered the importance of technology in understanding how organizational structure and performance are related, then Thompson added service technologies to extend the theory beyond manufacturing organizations, and finally Perrow elaborated the differences between technology types when they are viewed from the unit and task levels of analysis.

Task interdependence and mechanisms of coordination

Following Woodward and Perrow's emphasis on variability in the routineness of work, Thompson recognized that the work processes associated with a technology vary in the extent to which they are interrelated. He called this variable **task interdependence** to emphasize the issue of dependence on others for the accomplishment of tasks. Thompson related the task interdependence created by technology to different possible coordination mechanisms that could be designed into an organization's social structure. His work on task interdependence identified links between different forms of coordination and the mediating, long-linked, and intensive technologies framed by his typology.

In a mediating technology a number of offices or officials perform their work tasks almost independently of one another, at least so far as actual work flows between units is concerned. Therefore, little direct contact is needed between units (or individuals). Thompson used the term **pooled task interdependence** to refer to cases in which the output of the organization is primarily the sum of the efforts of each unit (see Figure 5.6).

Take banking as a prime example of mediating technology. Banks mediate between borrowers and savers or investors, and their mediation can be accomplished simultaneously by several bank branches that operate almost independently of one another. Day and night shifts on an assembly line, franchised restaurants, and the different departments of a university, or a large retail store provide additional examples of organizational units whose work is typified by pooled task interdependence.

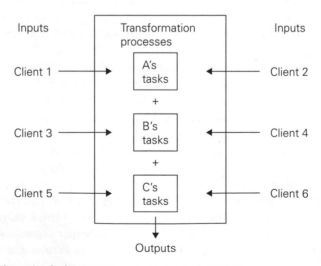

Figure 5.6 Mediating technologies generate pooled task interdependence

Notice that A, B, and C's joint product forms the output of the organization, yet these three units can operate more or less independently of one another.

According to Thompson, groups operating with pooled task interdependence demand very little in the way of coordination. The coordination required to achieve a coherent organizational identity or to ensure that services are consistent across units can, for the most part, be accomplished through the use of **rules and standard procedures** for routine operations. For example, rules and standard procedures for tasks such as opening bank accounts, investing in certificates of deposit or mutual funds, and applying for and approving loans and lines of credit produce sufficient coordination for a bank to integrate the activities of its branches.

Long-linked technology involves both pooled and sequential task interdependence. For instance, several assembly lines can operate at once in a manner that leaves them practically independent of one another; in this regard the different lines are pooled in the sense that their outputs are aggregated into the total output of the organization. However, within each line interdependence is more complex because each worker is dependent on the work of others located at positions prior to theirs on the line. If workers early in the process are not performing their tasks properly, then the work of those further down the line suffers. This is called **sequential task interdependence** because the work tasks are performed in a fixed sequence (Figure 5.7).

The sequential nature of task interdependence found in long-linked technologies requires more **planning and scheduling** than does pooled interdependence. Again consider the assembly line as an example. All work tasks must be designed and workers assigned and scheduled to work together in order for the assembly line operation to function properly. Because any break in the line can interrupt production, careful planning of tasks and scheduling of workers is imperative. Of course, in addition to coordination by plans and schedules, rules about coming to work on time and procedures to follow when something on the line has created a problem are also part of coordinating this type of technology.

The scope of the task within an intensive technology is too large for one individual to perform the transformation alone, so there is need for an exchange of information between workers during the performance of their tasks. Thompson describes this as **reciprocal task interdependence**. In a restaurant, for example, the kitchen staff and the wait staff have reciprocal interdependence because the kitchen is dependent upon the wait staff to provide orders, and the wait staff is dependent upon the kitchen staff to provide meals prepared to the customers' satisfaction. The primary difference between sequential and reciprocal task interdependence is that, where long-linked technologies involve work flows that move in one direction only, intensive technologies involve reciprocal work flows (see Figure 5.8).

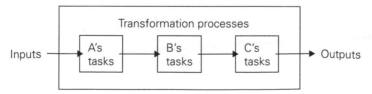

Figure 5.7 Long-linked technologies are associated with sequential task interdependence

This type of technology generates an unbalanced relationship where A experiences the least dependence and C the most, with B's dependence being less than C's but more than A's.

Coordinating the tasks central to the operation of an intensive technology requires **mutual adjustment** on the part of the individuals or units involved due to the reciprocal nature of their task interdependence. When intensive technologies involve immediate reciprocal coordination, mutual adjustment takes the extreme form of teamwork. In teamwork, work inputs to the transformation process are acted upon simultaneously by members of the work team, rather than passing inputs back and forth as is the case for less intensive forms of reciprocal task interdependence.

Take the case of an emergency room surgical operation. A surgeon needs to be able to continuously exchange information with the anesthesiologist, assisting doctors, and nurses during the performance of the operation. Thus, intensive technologies require joint decision making and either physical co-location or a direct channel of communication such as a satellite link or other instantaneous communication device.

Be sure to notice that intensive technology also involves pooled and sequential task interdependence. Mutual adjustment, planning, scheduling, rules, and procedures all contribute to the ability of experts to perform when and where their services are required. For example, emergency room doctors have scheduled work hours and rules to follow, ranging from established surgical procedures to wearing a beeper when they are on call. Notice how, as task interdependence increases from pooled to sequential to reciprocal, mechanisms of coordination get added to the organization (see Table 5.2). Pooled interdependence only requires rules and procedures, but sequential interdependence uses rules, procedures, and

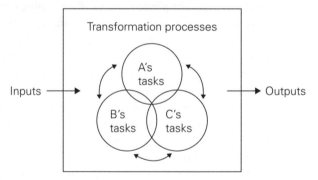

Figure 5.8 Intensive technologies create reciprocal task interdependence

A, B, and C are mutually dependent; thus this type of technology generates the highest levels of task interdependence.

Table 5.2 As task interdependence increases, increasingly sophisticated coordination mechanisms will be added to those already in use by an organization

Task interdependence	Rules and procedures	Schedules and plans	Mutual adjustment
Pooled	x		
Sequential	x	x	
Reciprocal	x	x	x

Source: Based on Thompson (1967).

scheduling, while reciprocal interdependence uses all these forms of coordination plus mutual adjustment.

Information processing and new technologies

Jay Galbraith, an American organization theorist, proposed that complexity, uncertainty, and interdependence place demands on an organization to process information in order to coordinate activities.[21] Galbraith claimed that it is demands for **communication** that shape the structure of the organization. He argued that technical complexity leads to structural complexity, uncertainty promotes organic forms, and interdependence increases demands for coordination *because* these factors increase the communication load carried by an organization. It is the communication load, however, that directly affects how people interact and thus the organization's social structure.

According to Galbraith, the effects of technology and the environment on social structure are mediated by communication. Notice the similarity between Galbraith's and Woodward's theories. Just as Woodward identified technology as a mediating factor in the structure–performance relationship, Galbraith argued that communication mediates the relationships between technology and structure, and environment and structure. This progressive elaboration and refinement of distinctions and relationships is another way modernist organization theorists develop new contingency theories.

Perrow's elaboration of the routineness of work scale, his addition of uncertainty as a response to technology, and Galbraith's proposal that communication mediates the relationship between technology and social structure all led to developments within contingency theory. But the shackles of contingency thinking would be broken for the first time when symbolism came into view, and one of the first efforts to bring modern and symbolic perspectives together, Giddens's structuration theory, proved inspiring to organization theorists interested in technology.

Technology and structuration

Many critical postmodernists believe that the material properties of technology force us to behave in ways predetermined by the equipment technology provides, for example the physical components of a computer force us to sit in front of a screen for hours on end. Because technology similarly programs interactions among workers, they conceptualize social structure as embedded in technology. Others, adopting SCOT or ANT, believe that social structures and technology emerge *from* those interactions. For example, the mobile and yet interconnected lives that caused computer technology to adapt, taking the form of laptops, tablets, and smartphones move collaboration and teamwork toward the virtual.

Accepting both these points of view, **adaptive structuration theory** proposed examining **technology-in-use**.[22] Adopting this approach, American organization theorist Wanda Orlikowski found that individuals often use technology quite differently. Graphic artists and accountants, for example, use different software programs; and some people type with two fingers while others use all ten. Orlikowski argued that individual usage constitutes differences in what objectively might seem like the same technologies as they identify and use different features, develop their own style of interacting with technology, and base their sensemaking on technologically mediated data. Thus humans give meaning and shape to technology as it shapes them through the mediation of practices.[23]

A technology-in-use may be resistant to change as we develop habits and then attribute them to the system, but it may change as we modify the technology or improvise new practices. In another study Orlikowski observed how different groups in a multinational consulting firm used a software program called Notes. She found that technology staff used Notes extensively and often customized it to their own needs. Routines they enacted around the Notes technology included electronic discussions, information sharing, and cooperative troubleshooting—a collaborative technology-in-use. However, most consultants used the software minimally, enacting a more limited version of the technology-in-use. These users had little knowledge about Notes and were skeptical about its value in helping them do their jobs. So, even though the technology was technically the same for both groups of users, practices varied across contexts depending upon the users' levels of interest and the practical, institutional, and interpretive limits of the technology they perceived.

According to the theory of technology-in-use, structure emerges from both the physical properties of technology and the ways we interact with and construct that technology. As Orlikowski put it: 'Technology is physically constructed by actors working in a given social context, and technology is socially constructed by actors through the different meaning they attach to it and the various features they emphasize and use.'[24] This can be seen across the field of information technology (IT) and in the practices of dotcoms and social media companies like Google and Facebook, where technology and social structure emerge as people improvise their use of technology while they produce the technologies still others will use. In these organizations, the product is not necessarily a concrete object, but may be a database, website or information-processing routine. In this technologically oriented application of structuration theory the methods of production are interwoven with the end product as people use the technology for their own purposes as well as those of the organization.

The global village: Technology and globalization

Concerns about unlimited and surreptitious control, or breaches of privacy and security, create images of the evils to which technology-in-use can lead, but technology also unleashes powerful forces to combat these negative effects by providing support for freedom and democracy. Postmodern theorists interested in the liberating potential of technology concentrate on understanding and enhancing its ability to transform the world. Some, for example, see new technology creating a global village tied together by strong social bonds that work even when large geographical or cultural distances separate people.[25]

Others believe that new technology and social media will play yet to be fully understood roles in social and cultural developments taking place around the world. Even though these developments are still underway, we know that new technology-enabled social media were used by those who enacted the Arab Awakening and by members of the Occupy movement to help them organize, lobby, and take collective action, sometimes reaching around the globe to find inspiration as well as social, technical, and financial support from like-minded others. It remains to be seen how the uses of new technology in combination with the ever-changing conditions and trends in the environment will affect the shapes and forms organization and organizing take on in the future.

Summary

From the modernist perspective, technology is typically defined in terms of its:

- Objects—products, services, and the tools and equipment used in their production.
- Task activities and processes—the methods of production.
- Knowledge needed to develop and apply equipment, tools, and methods to produce a product or service.

In organization theory the term technology refers not only to technologies that contribute directly to organizational output, but also to technologies that indirectly maintain this function (e.g., purchasing, sales, accounting, internal communication), and to technologies for adapting the organization to its environment (e.g., economic analysis, market research, strategic planning, external communication). To avoid confusion, organization theorists use the term **core technology** to mean the transformation processes by which the organization's products and services are produced. Large diversified organizations often have multiple core technologies, but every form of work has a technology that can be defined at the unit or task level. Thus, the modern perspective on technology describes the set of interacting and interdependent technologies on which an organization depends.

Although modernist theories give us an image of technology as lying inside organizational boundaries while environment stays outside, these two concerns are closely connected in the modernist perspective. First of all, the knowledge needed to operate a technology is normally produced outside the organization's boundary and imported, except when basic research is conducted internally, as is sometimes done in R&D departments. Second, tools and many production processes are imported in the form of hardware, software, and skilled or educated employees. The environment provides the technological ingredients of an organization just as it provides the material resources upon which the organization depends for its survival. Technology and other resources are scattered about in a more or less random fashion until a portion of the environment becomes organized, that is, until resources and technologies are combined by organizations to provide outputs to satisfy the environment's needs or demands.

A different image of technology is offered by the symbolic perspective. Drawing on subjectivist ontology suggests studying how technology is constructed and used within a socio-cultural context of symbolic interaction and meaning making. While some engage in ethnographic studies, those who believe in the social construction of technology (SCOT) often use historical analysis to build theory about how social, cultural, and economic contexts link resources and people to shape technological innovations. Both provide views of how the social organization of society influences the shape of technology and its products. This raises the question of how society, in its turn, is shaped by technology. The theme of society being shaped by technology is taken up in postmodern theories of technology, such as those that critique management systems as technologies of control, or present ideas like cyborganization and the global village.

Key terms

technology

   core technology

services

technical complexity

unit and small batch production

large batch or mass production

continuous processing

long-linked technology

mediating technology

intensive technology

task variability

task analyzability

routine technology

craft technology

engineering technology

non-routine technology

new (computer-based) technologies

   stochastic

   continuous

   abstract

reliability

normal accidents

complexity and tight-coupling

social construction of technology (SCOT)

technologies of control and representation

cyborganization

actor network theory (ANT)

technological imperative

routineness of work

task interdependence

   pooled

   sequential

   reciprocal

coordination mechanisms

   rules and standard procedures

   planning and scheduling

   mutual adjustment

communication

adaptive structuration theory

technology-in-use

Endnotes

1. See more about Nissan's Shift campaign and its relationship to corporate identity at: http://www.nissan-global.com/EN/COMPANY/SHIFT_/index.html (accessed February 18, 2012).

2. Thompson (1967).

3. Perrow (1967, 1986).

4. Weick (1990).

5. Perrow (2011).

6. Bijker, Hughes, and Pinch (1987); Bijker and Law (1992).

7. Orr (1996).

8. Mangrum, Fairley, and Weider (2001).

9. Heidegger (1993: 341).

10. In spite of the threat technology poses, Heidegger believed that the closer we come to the danger, the more likely we are to ask critical questions that will allow us to avoid disaster. Furthermore, by questioning its effects, we not only avoid the shackles of technology, but we open new horizons.

11. Combs, Knights, and Willmott (1992).

12. Haraway (1991: 163).

13. Weiner (1954), cited in Parker and Cooper (1998: 214).

14. Cooper and Law (1995: 268), cited in Parker and Cooper (1998: 219–20).

15. Collon (1986); Latour (2005); see also Law (1992).

16. Latour and Woolgar (1979: 36).

17. deLaet and Mol (2000); Law and Singleton (2003).

18. Latour (1991: 129).

19. Huber (1990); Lucas and Baroudi (1994).

20. Pugh et al. (1963).

21. Galbraith (1973).

22. DeSanctis and Poole (1994); Griffiths (1999).

23. Orlikowski (2000).

24. Orlikowski (1992: 406).

25. McLuhan and Powers (1989).

References

Bijker, Wiebe E. and Law, John (1992) (eds.) *Shaping Technology/Building Society: Studies in Sociotechnical Change*. Cambridge, MA: MIT Press.

——Hughes, Thomas P. and Pinch, Trevor (1987) (eds.) *The Social Construction of Technological Systems: New Directions in the Sociology and History of Technology*. Cambridge, MA: MIT Press.

Collon, Michel (1986) The sociology of an actor-network: The case of the electric vehicle. In M. Collon, J. Law, and A. Rip (eds.), *Mapping the Dynamics of Science and Technology*, Houndmills: Macmillan, 19–34.

Coombs, Rod, Knights, David, and Willmott, Hugh (1992) Culture control and competition: Towards a conceptual framework for the study of information technology in organizations. *Organization Studies*, 13: 51–72.

Cooper, R. and Law, J. (1995) Organization: Distal and proximal views. *Research in the Sociology of Organizations*, 13: 237–74.

de Laet, M. and Mol, A. (2000) The Zimbabwe bush pump: Mechanics of a fluid technology. *Social Studies of Science*, 30: 225–63.

DeSanctis, G. and Poole, M. (1994) Capturing the complexity in advanced technology use: Adaptive structuration theory. *Organization Science*, 5: 121–47.

Galbraith, Jay (1973) *Designing Complex Organizations*. Reading, MA: Addison-Wesley.

Griffiths, T. L. (1999) Technology features as triggers for sensemaking. *Academy of Management Review*, 24/3: 472–88.

Haraway, D. J. (1991) *Simians, Cyborgs and Women: The Reinvention of Nature*. New York: Routledge.

Heidegger, M. (1993) The question concerning technology. In D. F. Krell (ed.), *Martin Heidegger: Basic Writings from Being and Time (1927) to the Task of Thinking (1964)*, London: Routledge, Kegan and Paul, 307–41.

Huber, G. (1990) A theory of the effects of advanced information technologies on organizational design, intelligence, and decision making. *Academy of Management Review*, 15/1: 47–71.

Latour, Bruno (1991) Technology is society made durable. In John Law (ed.) *A Sociology of Monsters: Essays on Power, Technology and Domination*, London: Routledge, 103–31.

—— (2005) *Reassembling the Social: An Introduction to Actor-Network Theory*. Oxford: Oxford University Press.

—— and Woolgar, Steven (1979) *Laboratory Life: The Social Construction of Scientific Facts*. Beverley Hills, CA: Sage.

Law, John (1992) Notes on the theory of the actor network: Ordering, strategy and heterogeneity. *Systems Practice*, 5: 379–93.

—— and Singleton, Vicky (2003) Object lessons. Centre for Science Studies, Lancaster University. http://www.lancs.ac.uk/fss/sociology/papers/law-singleton-object-lessons.pdf (accessed July 12, 2005).

Lucas, H. C. and Baroudi, J. (1994) The role of information technology in organizational design. *Journal of Management Information Systems*, 10/4: 9–24.

Lyotard, Jean-François (1979) *The Postmodern Condition: A Report on Knowledge*. Minneapolis: University of Minnesota Press.

Mangrum, S., Fairley, D., and Weider, L. (2001) Informal problem solving in the technology-mediated workplace. *Journal of Business Communication*, 38/3: 315–36.

McLuhan, M. and Powers, B. R. (1989) *The Global Village: Transformations in World Life and Media in the Twenty-first Century*. New York: Oxford University Press.

Orlikowski, W. J. (1992) The duality of technology: Rethinking the concept of technology in organizations. *Organization Science*, 3: 398–427.

—— (2000) Using technology and constituting structures: A practice lens for studying technology in organization. *Organization Science*, 11/4: 404–28.

Orr, J. E. (1996) *Talking about Machines: An Ethnography of a Modern Job*. Ithaca, NY: Cornell University Press.

Parker, Martin and Cooper, Robert (1998) Cyborganization: Cinema as nervous system. In J. Hassard and R. Holliday (eds.), *Organization Representation: Work and Organizations in Popular Culture*. London: Sage, 201–28.

Perrow, Charles (1967) A framework for comparative organizational analysis. *American Sociological Review*, 32/2: 194–208.

—— (1984) *Normal Accidents: Living with High-risk Technologies*. New York: Basic Books.

—— (1986) *Complex Organizations: A Critical Essay* (3rd edn.). New York: Random House.

—— (2011) *The Next Catastrophe: Reducing Our Vulnerabilities to Natural, Industrial and Terrorist Disasters*. Princeton, NJ: Princeton University Press (hard cover edition published in 2007).

Pugh, D. S., Hickson, D. J., Hinings, C. R., MacDonald, K. M., Turner, C., and Lupton, T. (1963) A conceptual scheme for organizational analysis. *Administrative Science Quarterly*, 8: 289–315.

Thompson, James (1967) *Organizations in Action*. New York: McGraw-Hill.

Weick, Karl E. (1990) Technology as equivoque: Sensemaking in new technologies. In Paul S. Goodman, Lee S. Sproull, and Associates (eds.), *Technology and Organizations*, San Francisco, CA: Jossey-Bass, 1–44.

Woodward, Joan (1958) *Management and Technology*. London: Her Majesty's Stationery Office.

—— (1965) *Industrial Organization: Theory and Practice*. London: Oxford University Press.

Zuboff, S. (1988) *In the Age of the Smart Machine: The Future of Work and Power*. New York: Basic Books.

Further reading

Coyne, R. (1995) *Designing Information Technology in the Postmodern Age*. Cambridge, MA: MIT Press.

Haraway, D. J. (1997) *Modest-Witness@Second-Millennium.FemaleMan-Meets-Oncomouse: Feminism and Technoscience*. New York and London: Routledge.

Latour, B. (1987) *Science in Action*. Cambridge, MA: Harvard University Press.

Law, J. (1991) (ed.) *A Sociology of Monsters: Essays on Power, Technology and Domination*. London: Routledge.

Law, J. and Hassard, J. (1999) *Actor Network Theory and After*. Oxford: Blackwell.

MacKenzie, D. and Wajcman, J. (1985) (eds.) *The Social Shaping of Technology*. Milton Keynes: Open University Press.

Pinch, T. J. and Trocco, Frank (2002) *Analog Days: The Invention and Impact of the Moog Synthesizer*. Cambridge, MA: Harvard University Press.

Scott, W. Richard (1990) Technology and structure: An organizational-level perspective. In Paul S. Goodman, Lee S. Sproull, and Associates (eds.), *Technology and Organizations*. San Francisco: Jossey-Bass, 109–43.

Zeleny, Milan (1990) High technology management. In H. Noori and R. E. Radford (eds.), *Readings and Cases in the Management of New Technology: An Operations Perspective.* Englewood Cliffs, NJ: Prentice-Hall, 14–22.

Organizational culture

According to British sociologist Chris Jenks, the concept of culture originally referred to the cultivation of crops, but sometime during the nineteenth century social scientists extended the idea to include the cultivation of human beings.[1] Following this trajectory, anthropologists and sociologists contributed much to the study of culture, and their work both extended the modern perspective and introduced the symbolic perspective to organization theory.

In 1871 British social anthropologist E. B. Tylor provided one of the earliest and most influential definitions of culture as 'that complex whole which includes knowledge, belief, art, morals, law, custom, and any other capabilities and habits acquired by man as a member of society.'[2] At the time, anthropology was focused on explaining how humans differ from other animal species, and culture served as an initial answer. Fascinated by Charles Darwin's highly popular theory of evolution, they reasoned that, if humans develop along some sort of evolutionary continuum, as Darwin showed for other animal species, then studying the evolution of human culture should reveal new information about the human species.

The idea that human cultures evolve along an evolutionary continuum was supported by the reports of travelers to distant lands who had encountered people untouched by modern civilization. It was believed that studying these 'primitive' cultures would bring insight into human evolution. Anthropologists set off to study various tribes of native people for extended periods of time, learning to speak their languages and documenting their daily lives in hopes of learning what advanced cultures might have looked like in earlier periods of their evolution.

As evidence from anthropological studies mounted over the course of several decades, the idea that so-called primitive cultures were inferior to advanced cultures became increasingly difficult to sustain. The colonialism that had accompanied the anthropologists precipitated one of the earliest moves within social science toward critical postmodernism via the critique of colonialism; but long before postmodernism invaded anthropology, the differences between cultures produced an important refinement in the definition of culture—the study of culture had become the study of cultures, not the one but the many.

This shifting of attention from the similarities all humans share to their cultural differences led American cultural anthropologist Melville Herskowitz in 1948 to alter Tylor's early definition of culture to: 'the total body of belief, behavior, knowledge, sanctions, values, and goals *that make up the way of life of a people*.'[3] Conceptualizing culture as 'the way of life of a people' opened the door to defining organizational culture as the way of life within an organization.

This chapter begins with definitions of organizational culture and issues such as levels of analysis, subcultural silos, and cultural strength. There follows a history describing how organizational culture arrived within the symbolic and modern perspectives of organization theory pretty much at the same time but in very different ways. The tensions between the modernists' highly normative theories proposing to explain how culture can be managed, and symbolic efforts to understand symbolism and cultural change, fed postmodern critiques of culture as a concept and reflections on the dangers of theory and theorizing.

Definitions: culture, subculture, silos, and cultural strength

The most widely used definitions of organizational culture appear in Table 6.1. You will probably notice that all of these definitions refer to something held in common among group members, variously described as some combination of shared meanings, beliefs, assumptions, understandings, norms, values, and knowledge.

The concept of sharing invoked by most definitions of organizational culture suggests widespread agreement or consensus among cultural members, but on closer examination you can see that the practice of sharing reveals the importance of maintaining differences. Think of sharing a meal with your friends or family—you may prepare the meal together in the same kitchen using common ingredients and cooking tools, yet each of you eats a different portion of the food prepared and enjoys the experience in your own way.

Cultures allow for similarity and agreement on some matters, but they also rely upon differences. They need to accommodate disagreement without making it impossible to maintain collective identity. In other words, cultures place diverse humans within a shared framework of belonging, which they express through a multitude of artifacts and symbols, only a key few of which do they all acknowledge.[4] And even when a symbol *is* widely shared it will most likely carry multiple and conflicting meanings.

In this sense, you might consider culture a distributed phenomenon. Culture is distributed among the people who hold the values, beliefs, meanings, expectations, and so on, of which culture is constituted. In turn, the value and significance attributed to the distinctive contributions of group members as they interact constructs culture and creates the coherence needed to form and maintain a collective identity.

The definitions given in Table 6.1 all apply equally well to organizations and to organizational subcultures. According to American organizational ethnographers John Van Maanen and Stephen Barley, a **subculture** is a subset of an organization's members that identifies itself as a distinct group within the organization based either on similarity or familiarity.[5] Subcultures based on similarity arise from shared professional, gendered, racial, ethnic, occupational, regional, or national identities. Subcultures based on familiarity develop when employees interact frequently, as they often do when they share space and equipment such as particular areas within a factory or office building, a canteen, copy machine, and water cooler.

Another way to look at subcultures, suggested by American organizational researchers Caren Siehl and Joanne Martin, is to define them by the ways in which they relate to each other.[6] Because of the way power is distributed in most organizations, top management

Table 6.1 Selected definitions of organizational culture

Elliott Jaques (1952: 251)	'The culture of the factory is its customary and traditional way of thinking and doing of things, which is shared to a greater or lesser degree by all its members, and which new members must learn, and at least partially accept, in order to be accepted into service in the firm.'
Andrew Pettigrew (1979: 574)	'Culture is a system of publicly and collectively accepted meanings operating for a given group at a given time. This system of terms, forms, categories, and images interprets a people's own situation to themselves.'
Meryl Reis Louis (1983: 39)	'Organizations [are] culture-bearing milieux, that is, [they are] distinctive social units possessed of a set of common understandings for organizing action (e.g., what we're doing together in this particular group, appropriate ways of doing in and among members of the group) and languages and other symbolic vehicles for expressing common understandings.'
Edgar Schein (1985: 6)	'The pattern of basic assumptions that a given group has invented, discovered, or developed in learning to cope with its problems of external adaptation and internal integration, and that have worked well enough to be considered valid, and, therefore, to be taught to new members as the correct way to perceive, think, and feel in relation to these problems.'
John Van Maanen (1988: 3)	'Culture refers to the knowledge members of a given group are thought to more or less share; knowledge of the sort that is said to inform, embed, shape, and account for the routine and not-so-routine activities of the members of the culture . . . A culture is expressed (or constituted) only through the actions and words of its members and must be interpreted by, not given to, a fieldworker . . . Culture is not itself visible, but is made visible only through its representation.'
Harrison Trice and Janice Beyer (1993: 2)	'Cultures are collective phenomena that embody people's responses to the uncertainties and chaos that are inevitable in human experience. These responses fall into two major categories. The first is the substance of a culture—shared, emotionally charged belief systems that we call ideologies. The second is cultural forms—observable entities, including actions, through which members of a culture express, affirm, and communicate the substance of their culture to one another.'

typically creates the dominant subculture, which many refer to as the **corporate culture**, even though it might be more accurate to call it the corporate subculture. Siehl and Martin characterized the possible relationships between corporate and other subcultures as **enhancing**, when a subculture enthusiastically supports the corporate culture's values, beliefs, norms, and expectations; **orthogonal** when it maintains independence from the influence of the dominant subculture, but not in ways that create conflict; and

counterculture, when a subculture actively and overtly challenges the values, beliefs, norms, and expectations of the dominant subculture.

As an example of counterculture, Siehl and Martin cited John De Lorean who in the 1960s headed up a division of General Motors that refused to play by the company's rules yet was tolerated because it was profitable and brought an edge to GM's otherwise conservative line of cars. De Lorean was so admired by other executives at GM that, before he left to start his own company, he was promoted to VP of all car and truck divisions and was considered a serious candidate for CEO. Countercultures and their leaders play important and often creative roles in the organizational cultures that they challenge, which is why they are tolerated, at least for a time, within their organizations.

Subcultures are neither good nor bad per se. Their value to the organization depends upon the influence they exercise. The De Lorean counterculture afforded GM much needed creativity. But subcultures can also undermine coordination and limit communication between parts of an organization, a problem given the metaphoric name **silos**, a term borrowed from agriculture where it refers to tall cylindrical, self-contained storage units used to preserve harvested corn. When applied to organizations the metaphor describes strong organizational subcultures whose self-containment makes collaboration between them difficult or impossible and can lead to unproductive conflict.

The concept of **strong culture** helps explain the problem of organizational silos. American researchers Jennifer Chatman and Sandra Cha defined strong culture in terms of two variables: agreement about what is valued and the intensity with which values are held within a culture.[7] Strong cultures are the product of high agreement combined with high intensity. Applying the concept to subcultures suggests that, when high intensity and agreement produce strong subcultures the strength of the subcultures undermines that of the overall organizational culture, leading to poor communication and lack of coordination; in other words, you get silos.

A history of organizational culture in organization theory

With the publication of his book *The Changing Culture of a Factory* in 1952, British sociologist Elliott Jaques became the first organization theorist to describe an organizational culture. Jaques justified including the culture concept in organization theory by noting that the focus on organizational structure had led researchers to ignore the human and emotional elements of organizational life. His work inspired organizational scholars like Barry Turner and Andrew Pettigrew in the United Kingdom, who were soon joined by Pasquale Gagliardi in Italy, Gareth Morgan and Peter Frost in Canada, and Lou Pondy and Linda Smircich in the United States, among others. Together these scholars made a persuasive case for studying organizational culture by focusing on the role symbolism plays in organizational life, and by doing so began forming a subculture within organization theory.

At first, no one in the mainstream of modern organization theory took much notice of organizational symbolism. Then, in the late 1970s and early 1980s, several books on corporate culture appeared on bestseller lists in the United States including William Ouchi's *Theory Z* and Terrence Deal and Allan Kennedy's *Corporate Cultures: The Rites and Rituals of Corporate Life*. Tom Peters and Robert Waterman's *In Search of Excellence*, the most successful of the lot, topped the *New York Times* bestseller list for months following its release and was even turned into a series of TV programs.

The popular appeal of books proposing culture as an explanation of superior organizational performance stunned and seduced much of the academic community, which, up until then, had never seen any of its concepts attract much popular attention. Academics interested in organizational culture read and studied these books, along with Edgar Schein's more academic but equally influential *Organizational Culture and Leadership*, which appeared around the same time.[8]

Much of the early work on organizational culture was normative in orientation. Culture was treated as something to be managed; a tool to enhance organizational effectiveness and competitiveness. For example, Peters and Waterman promoted the idea that strong cultures breed excellence, while Ouchi made the case for culture as a desirable alternative to both market mechanisms and bureaucracy for the control of organizations.[9] Meanwhile organizational culture researchers who adopted the symbolic perspective began expressing doubts about the ease with which organizational cultures might be manipulated to managerial ends.

In the late 1970s and early 1980s, a few small conferences on organizational symbolism were held in Europe and the United States. These gatherings attracted a curious mix of scholars from fields ranging from organization theory and sociology, to anthropology, psychoanalysis, and folklore. Their meetings often involved creating playful rituals filled with symbols that evoked their phenomena of interest right in their midst. A movement was soon underway, attracting lots of fresh recruits. Special issues of mainstream academic journals devoted to organizational culture appeared and the fledgling Standing Conference on Organizational Symbolism (SCOS) soon dwarfed its parent organization the European Group for Organization Studies (EGOS), one of Europe's prestigious academic associations. At the Academy of Management in the US, sessions on organizational culture began to multiply rapidly.

Many organizational culture researchers embraced qualitative methods that were descriptive rather than explanatory in purpose. Culture was difficult to define in operational terms that captured the nuances of meaning involved in understanding symbolism. Ethnography became the most common method used—a combination of participant observation and in-depth unstructured interviews. Symbolic researchers hoped that the reputation of ethnography in cultural anthropology and interpretive sociology would satisfy the demands for rigor coming from skeptics, but most modernists remained unconvinced, suspicious of ethnography's origins in the humanistic social sciences. Battle lines were drawn and a war ensued, fought primarily over the legitimacy of qualitative methods for conducting organizational research.[10]

The war was waged most publicly at conferences, though it also showed up in the editorial review processes of academic journals and in faculty discussions about who would and would not be granted tenure. Through presentations at conferences and papers submitted to journals, researchers adopting the symbolic perspective eventually forged a base of support as they created a strong counterculture within organization theory.

It was largely through research on organizational culture that the symbolic perspective became established. However, this does not mean that modernists gave up their claim to culture. On the contrary, some of the earliest and most long lasting organizational culture theories were rooted in the still dominant modern perspective.

The modernist perspective in organizational culture theory

Dutch organization theorist Geert Hofstede explored national influences on organizational culture through differences he first observed in the international subsidiaries of IBM. His enormously influential work defining dimensions of difference between cultures around the world was complemented by work being done at the same time by American social psychologist Edgar Schein. Both of these theorists tapped the modern perspective, but while Hofstede remained faithful to modernist ambitions to measure and study cultural differences quantitatively, Schein's theory crossed over to inspire at least some symbolic organizational culture researchers. Meanwhile efforts to define variables and measure organizational culture continue, illustrated by the popular Organizational Culture Inventory (OCI).

National cultural influences on organizations

Organizational cultures have a two-way relationship with the environments in which they are found and from which they recruit their members. Employees who join an organization come pre-socialized to a certain extent by cultural institutions such as family, school, community, and religion. They carry aspects of national, regional, industrial, occupational, and professional cultures into the organization by melding their values and identities with those of the organization.[11] Meanwhile organizations influence the local, regional, and national cultures to which they contribute. For example, the many entrepreneurial computer companies that produced the regional culture of California's Silicon Valley in the 1970s, eventually reshaped organizational cultures everywhere through their technological innovations and the appeal of their youthful, nerdy, 24/7 organizational cultures.

Sometimes an organizational culture clashes with the culture of a place where it locates. The controversial opening in 1992 of a new Disneyland theme park in France illustrates the difficulties organizations may face when operating in cultural settings that are unfamiliar to them. Before construction of the park even got underway, Euro Disney was criticized as an assault on French culture. It was seen as a symbol of the American way of life that French critics feared would Americanize their children. Then, as French employees were recruited and trained, labor unions protested against Disney's strict dress code claiming that it undermined French individualism. They accused Disney of indoctrinating cast members, pointing to the company's rules regarding smiling and appearing to be sincere all day.

Eventually Disney adapted the Paris theme park somewhat to accommodate French culture. For instance, female employees were allowed to wear bright red lipstick to work and wine was served in Euro Disney's many restaurants. Remarkably, given the influence of critical opinion, the theme park was renamed Disneyland Paris in 1994. Clearly Disneyland Paris, operating within France, brought French values and employment practices into the larger company.

Although the Disneyland example clearly shows the effects of national culture on an organization, later developments in the story show just how interwoven an organizational culture and its environment can become. When Disneyland Paris threatened bankruptcy in 2005, instead of rejoicing at the failure of this widely resisted American icon, the French government offered the American company a substantial loan to keep Disneyland Paris open in order to avoid the loss of 35,000 French jobs. With acceptance of its dependence on

Disneyland, the park became a part of France in a way that allows Disneyland Paris a deeper connection to French culture than the one the French initially feared.

Hofstede's approach to organizational culture is derivative of the idea that organizations are subcultures of larger cultural systems. In the late 1970s Hofstede studied the influence of national cultures on IBM.[12] At the time of the study IBM operated in seventy countries, the forty largest of which Hofstede used for his study. IBM's annual employee surveys conducted from 1967 through 1973 provided Hofstede with his data.

Using IBM data, Hofstede constructed measures of work-related values that he then compared across countries. Further analysis revealed four dimensions of national cultural difference operating within IBM's organizational culture: power distance, uncertainty avoidance, individualism vs. collectivism, and masculinity vs. femininity (see Figures 6.1 and 6.2). The findings supporting these dimensions have been replicated in populations of commercial airline pilots, civil service managers, and consumers. A fifth dimension of long- versus short-term orientation was revealed by Hofstede's research on Asian cultures.[13]

Power distance refers to the extent to which the members of a culture are willing to accept an unequal distribution of power, wealth, and prestige. Hofstede's data showed that low power distance characterized countries like Denmark where inequalities of status are difficult to accept. For instance the Danish Jante Law (*Janteloven*) proclaims that no individual should have more than, or stand out in any noticeable way from, other Danes. When Danes try to put themselves forward as more prestigious or powerful than others they are quickly reminded that they are no better than anyone else.

Organizations from high power distance cultures, such as Brazil, Singapore, and the Arabic countries, rely heavily on hierarchy. Their unequal distributions of authority are accompanied by a lack of upward mobility. When organizations from higher power distance cultures attempt to impose their authority structures on subsidiaries from lower power distance cultures like Denmark, difficulties generally follow. Similarly Danish managers face problems when they try to use egalitarian leadership practices to control international subsidiaries in countries noted for high power distance. Such cultural mismatches, according to Hofstede, result from different cultural norms and expectations.

In high power distance cultures subordinates expect to be told what to do; for them hierarchy is an existential inequality. In low power distance cultures, hierarchy is considered an inequality of roles created for convenience rather than reflecting essential differences between people, thus subordinates in low power distance cultures expect to be consulted by their superiors. As a consequence of these contradictory expectations, for example, the ideal boss in a low power distance culture is a resourceful democrat, whereas in a high power distance culture the best boss is likely to be a benevolent autocrat.

Uncertainty avoidance can be defined as the degree to which members of a culture avoid taking risks. Hofstede argued that different societies have different levels of tolerance for uncertainty and that these differences show up in a variety of ways. In low uncertainty avoidance cultures, for example, people are more accepting of innovative ideas, differences of opinion, and eccentric or deviant behavior, whereas in cultures with high uncertainty avoidance these things are resisted or even legislated against. Rules, regulations, and control are more acceptable in high than in low uncertainty avoidance cultures and Hofstede claimed that organizations in these cultures have more formalization and standardization, whereas organizations in cultures with low uncertainty avoidance dislike rules and resist formalization and standardization.

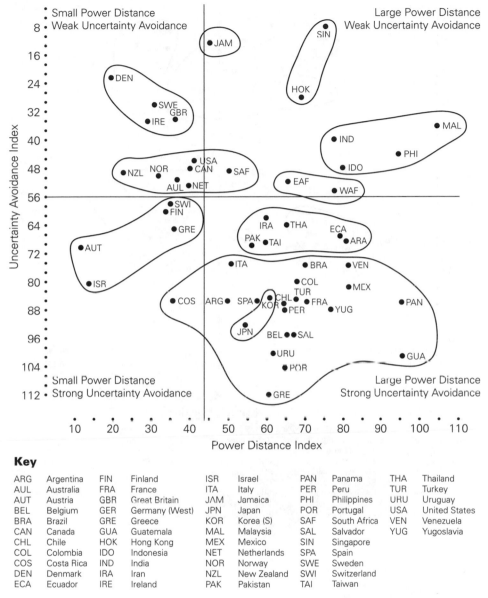

Figure 6.1 Position of countries on Hofstede's uncertainty avoidance and power distance dimensions

Source: Hofstede (2001: 152). Reprinted by kind permission of Geert Hofstede.

In his original study Hofstede found that uncertainty avoidance was highest in the IBM employees from Greece, Portugal, and Japan, while it was lowest in those from Singapore, Hong Kong, and Sweden. You can contrast this with the results of a later study (see Figure 6.2) in which Greece, Portugal, and Guatemala topped the list, while Singapore, Jamaica, and Denmark anchored the low end of the scale. Using Hofstede's insights about uncertainty avoidance you can perhaps better understand the Greek people's resistance to change and

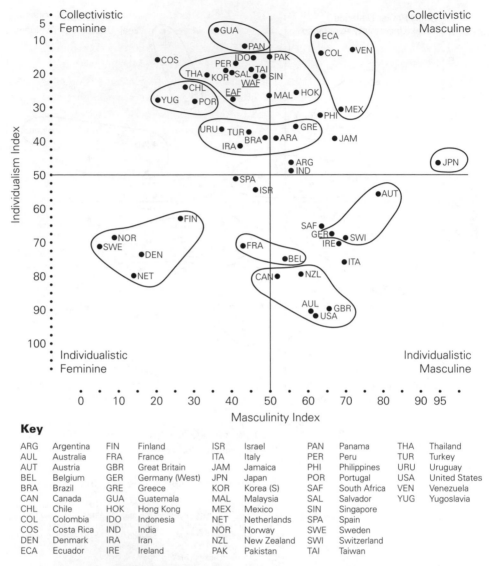

Figure 6.2 Position of countries on Hofstede's individualism and masculinity dimensions

Source: Hofstede (2001: 294). Reprinted by kind permission of Geert Hofstede.

the uncertainty it brings appeared in their responses to European Union calls for reform during the Greek debt crisis of 2010–12.

→ **Individualism versus collectivism** involves the degree to which individuals in a culture are expected to act independently of others in their society. In highly individualistic cultures, individual rights are paramount. You will find evidence of individualism versus collectivism in the ways in which people live together (e.g., alone, in shifting partnerships, tribes, or nuclear families) and in their religious beliefs (e.g., whether or not an individual can have a personal relationship with the supernatural).

Hofstede pointed out that in cultures such as the United States individualism is seen as a source of wellbeing, whereas in Chinese or Mexican cultures it is seen as undesirable and alienating. This orientation toward individualism or collectivism has implications for the sorts of relationships preferred within different cultures. Relationships between members of individualistic cultures are loose and individuals are expected to take care of themselves. By contrast, in collectivist cultures, cohesive groups (e.g., extended families) give individuals their sense of identity and belonging, demanding considerable loyalty in return.

Individualism versus collectivism helps to explain why those from collectivist cultures find the highly adverse reactions among many US citizens to calls for universal health insurance so unfathomable. On the other hand, the progress made toward providing more social services may indicate a shift in the US toward a more collectivist culture. Related to this distinction, Hofstede claimed that, in individualistic cultures like the US, tasks take precedence over relationships, whereas relationships prevail over tasks in organizations from collectivist cultures, like those of Asia.

You can imagine the sort of difficulties created when an organization from an individualistic culture imposes its task-focused control systems on an acquisition located in a collectivist culture. The acquirer may well be legitimately puzzled in ways captured by the question: 'Why don't they just do what they are told?' By the same token, when an organization from a collectivist culture acquires a company in an individualistic culture, you will likely hear frustrated cries from the acquired along the lines: 'Why don't they just tell us what they want us to do?'

→ Hofstede's **masculine versus feminine** designations for culture refers to the degree of separation between gender roles in a society. For example, in highly masculine cultures such as Japan, Austria, and Venezuela, men are expected to be more assertive and women more nurturing. In Sweden, Denmark, Norway, and the Netherlands, cultures that score high on the feminine dimension, gender differences are less pronounced. The highly masculine cultures in Hofstede's studies tended to place emphasis on work goals having to do with career advancement and earnings, and their members celebrated assertiveness, decisiveness, and self-promotion, while members of organizations in feminine cultures were likely to ridicule assertiveness and to undersell themselves.

The feminine cultures in Hofstede's studies favored work goals concerning interpersonal relationships, service, and preserving the physical environment, their members valued quality of life and intuition. Not surprisingly Hofstede found that women held more professional and technical jobs and were treated more equally in highly feminine cultures than in cultures high on the masculinity scale. You have to wonder, in light of recent changes in the gender roles of many countries, if there is not a shift to the feminine side underway globally, seen in the rise of service sector economies and spreading concerns about sustainability and social justice.

Long-term versus short-term orientation describes cultural differences in predilections for thrift and perseverance as well as respect for tradition. According to Hofstede countries that score highly on long-term orientation believe that hard work will lead to long-term rewards. In these countries it will also likely take longer to develop new business, particularly for foreigners.[14] Organizations from cultures characterized by a short-term orientation face fewer challenges to change.

The importance of Hofstede's research is not only that it identified specific, measurable, national cultural differences but also that it revealed organizational culture to be a mechanism through which societal cultures influence organizations. The national cultural traits identified by Hofstede can be seen as part of the web of meaning that provides context for organizational culture and the recent addition of the fifth dimension of long-term versus short-term orientation suggests there are potentially even more ways to define national cultural influence. Nonetheless, Hofstede's dimensions wrap a context around organizational level theories of culture such as that presented by American social psychologist Edgar Schein.

Schein's theory of organizational culture

According to Schein, a set of basic assumptions forms the core of a culture (see Figure 6.3). This core manifests as values and behavioral norms that cultural members recognize, respond to, and maintain as they use them to make choices and take action. Culturally guided choices and actions produce the artifacts of a culture, including among many other things the products organizations manufacture and the services they provide.

Basic assumptions represent what members of a culture believe about their reality; however, since they are typically taken for granted, you rarely find cultural members who can state their culture's basic assumptions. Try to imagine what a fish thinks about water and you get an idea of the limited awareness most people have of their basic assumptions. But even lying beneath ordinary awareness, basic assumptions and beliefs penetrate every part of cultural life and color all forms of human experience. As Schein put it, basic assumptions influence what members of a culture perceive, think, and feel.

Their unquestioned yet pervasive character is why it is likely that you will only become alive to cultural differences when you live for an extended period in a foreign culture. When your assumptions lead you to engage in inappropriate behavior or to misinterpret someone else's behavior, the workings of your native culture become more obvious to you. Because you are using the wrong assumptions to explain what is going on in the foreign culture, your experiences of surprise will encourage you to observe more attentively and ask questions. If your investigation renders you able to release yourself from your native cultural assumptions and try on those of your host culture, you will slowly become able to explain the differences and this will lead you, not only to function more effectively in the culture you are visiting, but to understand your native culture more deeply. Even though it may still be difficult to put

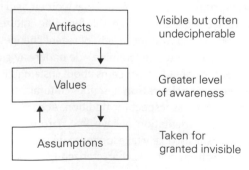

Figure 6.3 Schein: Three levels of culture

Source: Adapted from *Organizational Culture and Leadership* (p. 14) by E. H. Schein. Copyright 1985 Jossey-Bass Inc., Publishers, San Francisco. All rights reserved.

anybody's cultural assumptions into words, you will nonetheless become savvy about culture and better at moving gracefully between cultures.

According to Schein, a culture's assumptions pervade the next level of culture—values. **Values** are the social principles, goals, and standards that cultural members believe have intrinsic worth. They define what the members of a culture care about most and are revealed by their priorities. Because they also guide cultural members in their assessments of right and wrong, a culture's values are sometimes equated with its morality or ethical code.

Although values are more accessible to consciousness than basic assumptions they are not always top of mind. Nonetheless, cultural members are able to recognize their values fairly easily and when someone challenges their culture in some fundamental way, such as breaking with convention, they often become quite upset. When organizational values are challenged, that challenge most often comes from marginal members of the organization such as newcomers, artists, or revolutionaries—or from outsiders like a new CEO hired by a board of directors to shake things up. For example, in the 1960s, being marginal and challenging mainstream cultural values was a part of the youth counterculture, or the 'hippie' subculture as it was known in the US (see Figure 6.4).

A great deal of research conducted from within the modern perspective has been devoted to specifying the values various organizational cultures hold (e.g., for customers, employees, socially or environmentally responsible behavior). However, according to Schein, the important issue is the influence cultural assumptions and values, taken as a whole, have on perceptions, behavior, and emotional states. One significant influence that cultural values exercise on organizational members takes place through defining norms and expectations for behavior.

Figure 6.4 Challenges to cultural values most often come from marginal members of the culture such as newcomers, revolutionaries, or outsiders

Norms are the unwritten rules and common body of knowledge that allow members of a culture to know what is expected of them in a wide variety of situations, including how to coordinate their behavior with that of others in acts of organizing. Norms communicate expectations regarding many types of social behavior such as talking in movie theaters, cutting in line, and standing at football games. Organizational norms communicate important information, for example, when you should inform your boss of potential problems, what sort of clothing you should wear to work, and when it is appropriate to display emotion.

While in some organizations these matters are spelled out by formal rules and regulations (a point of overlap between culture and social structure), in most they are left unstated and communicated informally via the normative pressures of culture, such as the disapproving looks used in some cultures, or in others by looking away. The contrast between a look of disapproval and looking away indicates just one of many differences that combine to make each culture an expression of its constellation of assumptions, values, norms, and expectations.

While values specify what is important to the members of a culture, norms establish what sorts of behavior to expect from oneself and others. In short, values define what is valued, while norms make clear what it takes to be considered normal or abnormal. The link between values and norms is that the behaviors that norms sanction (either through rewards or punishments) can be traced to outcomes that are valued. For example, norms about not talking in movie theaters or cutting in line might be traced to a cultural value for courtesy to others. Norms about wearing business suits and not displaying any emotion while at work might indicate a value for self-discipline. Beware, however, that even though values underpin norms, any given norm can be ambiguous relative to underlying values. For example, a norm for wearing suits at work could indicate a value for self-discipline or for fashion consciousness. The ambiguity of interpretation extends to artifacts.

According to Schein's theory, members of a culture hold values and conform to cultural norms because their culture's underlying assumptions and beliefs nurture and support these norms and values. The norms and values, in turn, encourage activities that produce cultural artifacts. **Artifacts** are manifestations or expressions of the same cultural core that produces and maintains the values and norms; however, their greater distance from the core can make it even more difficult to interpret their cultural significance unambiguously.

A few years ago a sign displayed in the foyer of a new neighborhood cinema that I visited in the United States informed patrons that, in contrast to other cinemas they may have frequented, talking during the screening of a film was permitted in this establishment. The cinema attracted a clientele that liked to express their reactions to movies vocally, and thus they violated the then dominant American cultural norm of silence during movies. The sign—an artifact produced by the organization—named an otherwise unspoken dominant cultural norm and, by doing so, drew a symbolic boundary around this counterculture that encouraged those who entered to acknowledge and accept the countercultural norm. I imagine that the sign was the product of more than one angry misunderstanding that erupted among patrons of the establishment who did not realize they had entered a counterculture.

Artifacts like the cinema sign are unusually tangible indicators of cultural norms, values, and assumptions; you normally need to study many artifacts before you will recognize the cultural patterns that reveal the deeper layers of culture. Most cultures do not post conspicuous signs to orient newcomers like the cinema did! To gain access to the deeper levels of a culture you must train yourself to observe artifacts and how members use them. Categories of artifacts to include in your observations consist of objects, verbal expressions, and activities. Table 6.2 shows several examples of each.

A good exercise to try involves thinking of an organizational culture you know and listing as many of each artifact type that come to mind. Use the scheme in Table 6.2 to jog your memory for any artifacts you have overlooked. If possible visit the organization. You will find your heightened sensitivity to culture will cause you to see many more artifacts than you are able to remember off the top of your head. This experience should convince you of the hidden power of culture operating beneath ordinary awareness in your daily life.

Once you have a few dozen artifacts, start sifting through them for patterns that suggest values and maybe even an assumption or two. But beware of a common tendency to impose your own cultural values on those of the group you wish to study. Learning to separate your values from those of the culture you want to understand will take time. It will help if, as you proceed with your analysis, you talk to cultural members and allow them to challenge your emergent understanding until gradually you gain deeper insight. Working on forming your interpretations alongside members of the culture will expose you to the subjective richness of cultural knowledge.

One way you will know you are making headway in a cultural analysis is when your data surprise you. Surprise indicates that you are getting beneath the surface of cultural artifacts by learning how the locals understand their world in ways that differ from your own. You will

Table 6.2 Artifacts of organizational culture

Category	Examples
Objects	Art/design/logo
	Architecture/décor/furnishings
	Dress/appearance/costume/uniform
	Products/equipment/tools
	Displays of posters/photos/memorabilia/cartoons
	Signage
Verbal expressions	Jargon/names/nicknames
	Explanations/theories
	Stories/myths/legends and their heroes and villains
	Superstitions/rumors
	Humor/jokes
	Metaphors/proverbs/slogans
	Speeches/rhetoric/oratory
Activities	Ceremonies/rituals/rites of passage
	Meetings/retreats/parties
	Communication patterns
	Traditions/customs/social routines
	Gestures
	Play/recreation/games
	Rewards/punishments

Source: Based on Dandridge, Mitroff and Joyce (1980); Schultz (1995); Jones (1996).

learn to better appreciate your own culture as well as the one you are studying when you realize that previously unexamined aspects of your own culture create your surprise at another's interpretations of objects, behavior, or words.

The organizational culture inventory

Robert Cooke and J.C. Lafferty exemplify the quantification in organizational culture research associated with the modern perspective. These researchers developed the Organizational Culture Inventory (OCI) in the 1980s as a means to measure the extent to which an organizational culture is supported by each of twelve different behavioral norms.[15] Factor analysis of survey responses to a 120-question inventory provided by members of a variety of organizations revealed three types of organizational culture each supported by four norms. Constructive organizational cultures are distinguished by achievement, self-actualizing, humanistic-encouraging, and affiliative norms. Passive-defensive organizational cultures embrace approval, conventional, dependent, and avoidance norms. And aggressive-defensive organizational cultures are supported by oppositional, power, competitive, and perfectionistic norms.

Subsequent studies employing the OCI yielded significant correlations between the three culture types and various outcomes. For example, constructive cultures have been significantly and positively correlated with employee motivation and job satisfaction, teamwork, and the quality of customer service, whereas passive-defensive cultures appear negatively correlated with the same variables. Aggressive-defensive cultures yield few significant correlations with the same measures but show significantly positive correlations with stress levels and negative correlations with quality of work relations and customer service.[16]

Although modernist studies of culture such as those based on the OCI provide knowledge that is readily translatable into normative prescriptions for management, they are limited to studying dimensions of organizational culture that are predefined by the researcher and are common to numerous cultures. Modernist studies are therefore unlikely to present the surprises that occur when researchers encounter a new culture. This is where the symbolic perspective offers an advantage over the modern—symbolic researchers personally enter cultural territory to develop subjective knowledge about their phenomena of interest.

Symbolic organizational culture research

In the early 1960s, Anselm Strauss and his research team studied hospitals using participant observation methods and an analytical approach they developed called **grounded theory** because the theory was built from empirical observations.[17] In their hospital study they learned that staff and patients negotiated patient care regimens and in doing so mutually created and maintained a sense of order, which the researchers labeled **negotiated order**. They noted that, although the hospital's rules and hierarchies needed to be considered in explaining staff behavior, negotiated order better accounted for the way the hospital actually functioned.

While this research was going on, American cognitive sociologist Harold Garfinkel, employing **ethnomethodology**, developed interpretive epistemological foundations for symbolic culture studies. His 1967 *Studies in Ethnomethodology* reported the results of interpretive field experiments carried out by his students, whom Garfinkel had instructed to challenge commonsense expectations about their everyday life, such as how to shop in a department store or eat a family dinner. He taught the students to first violate prevailing behavioral norms, for example, by negotiating the price of an item in a department store, and then observe and document what happened, including their own feelings and responses to the incident their unexpected behavior created.

You can try this out for yourself. Next time a friend reports going on a date or having a flat tire, pretend not to know what a date is or what it means to have a flat tire. Maintain your naivety throughout no matter how uncomfortable you become. Then document your feelings in the situation as well as what you observe of the others involved because your feelings of discomfort will uncover subtle subjective cultural expectations and how they influence you. Do not simply assume you know how this will work out—have the actual experience.

Garfinkel argued that engaging in unexpected behavior denies the taken-for-grantedness of shared understanding and catapults participants out of their everyday interpretive frameworks. The students who participated in his research reported the experiments caused confusion, discomfort, and occasional bouts of offence, yet although a great deal of nonsense was produced, the prevailing social order never collapsed entirely. Instead, participants renewed their efforts to reestablish or retain things-as-usual, for example, by saying: 'You are just kidding around, right?' or 'Come back when you are ready to behave normally!'

Based on his ethnomethodological experiments with students, Garfinkel concluded that whatever sense everyday social life makes, its sensibility is a social accomplishment, that is, people conspire to achieve and maintain the taken-for-grantedness of their social lives, even if they do so unwittingly. His concepts of negotiated order and social life-as-accomplishment echo those of enactment and social construction theory and thus complement the definition of culture as constructed by interacting individuals who, in interpreting what is going on around them, collectively create meaning. Seen from within the symbolic perspective, meaning produces culture even as it is the product of culturally informed behavior.

Organization theorists who adopt the symbolic perspective assume an interpretive epistemology, which means they focus on how organizational members make subjective meaning and the roles their subjectivity and meaning making play in socially constructing the workplace. They believe that meaning is dependent on context and, in the case of organizations, culture provides that context.

You have probably had the experience of having your words taken out of context, for example, when someone uses something you have said against you in an argument. Similarly, you may have heard politicians make this claim in defending themselves against criticism by the press or other politicians. This shows that the act of moving cultural symbols from one context to another changes their meaning. In cultural research **contextualizing** means studying artifacts and symbols in the situations and locations in which they naturally occur by observing organizational members using and speaking about them as they ordinarily do. Symbolic culture researchers want to experience the contextualizing effects of organizational culture as its members do, hence their reliance on participant observation and the methods of ethnography, ethnomethodology, and grounded theory.

Symbols, symbolism, and symbolic behavior

According to American sociologist Abner Cohen, **symbols** are 'objects, acts, relationships or linguistic formations that stand ambiguously for a multiplicity of meanings, evoke emotions and impel men to action.'[18] Symbols denote or substitute for something, as when a corporate logo stands for a company. **Denotation** refers to a symbol's instrumental use as a signifier, for example, holding up a white flag to indicate surrender. But symbols also carry connotative meanings. **Connotation** refers to the expressive uses of a symbol, as when an American flag is waved or burned, or a corporate logo is transformed into a joke or criticism of the company it signifies. For example, the Canadian magazine *Adbusters* published an image featuring a saddled but riderless horse grazing near headstones in a colorless snow-covered cemetery. Beneath the image Philip Morris's familiar advertising slogan was appropriated to chillingly declare: 'Marlboro Country.'

Because symbols such as the Marlboro Cowboy can bear multiple connotations, they remain ambiguous, always open to new meaning being made with them, as *Adbusters* did by associating the Marlboro imagery with an absent and presumably dead cowboy. Symbolic researchers, therefore, place as much attention on the processes by which meaning is constructed as on the specific meanings that symbols carry. According to John Van Maanen: 'To study symbolism is to learn how the meanings on which people base actions are created, communicated, contested, and sometimes changed.'[19] To see how this works requires looking into the relationship between symbols and artifacts.

Any artifact can become a symbol, but not all artifacts do. According to Canadian organization theorists Gareth Morgan and Peter Frost and their American colleague Lou Pondy: 'Symbols are created and recreated whenever human beings vest elements of their world with a pattern of meaning and significance which extends beyond its intrinsic content.'[20] For instance, we can see that a national flag is a symbol by the responses given to it by members of the culture that it represents. It can be used symbolically at one moment (saluting it, flying it over your home, painting it on your face, burning it in protest) and not at the next (when the flag is tucked away in a drawer or you wash the paint from your face). As these examples show, what makes an artifact a symbol is its use to make or communicate meaning.

Notice that observing an artifact being used as a symbol does not necessarily equate to knowing the symbol's meaning. Discovering the meaning of a symbol involves interpreting it within the cultural context of its use. I remember being mildly alarmed by the number of Danish national flags I saw on display when I moved to Denmark in 1990. In the liberal US subculture in which I grew up such behavior would have indicated an uncomfortable level of nationalism. When I encountered Danish flags displayed not only outside public buildings, but inside homes and offices, and even on birthday cakes, I wondered what was going on. Yet my Danish friends seemed puzzled when I asked them about their 'flag waving' (a term widely used in my native culture but unfamiliar to them). They told me the Danish flag was a normal part of everyday life and would be a matter for comment for them only if it were absent. Thus my surprise tipped me off to one of many cultural differences between the US and Denmark.

Whereas artifacts may be the most accessible elements of culture because they appear as tangible objects, behaviors, or verbal expressions, you need to remember that artifacts lie furthest from the cultural core and can be easily misinterpreted by those who are culturally naïve, such as you will be whenever you enter a new culture. If studying cultural meaning interests you then sensitize yourself to misunderstandings like my encounter with Danish flags, as these can lead to profound cultural insights. Having these insights generally requires questioning insiders about specific elements of observed culture that surprise you, as I did with my Danish friends. Understanding culture requires both observation and interviewing skills.

Also remember that, while tangible symbols-as-artifacts are often shared, the meanings they carry may, and usually do, differ among the members of a culture. The potential for multiple and even contradictory meanings is what makes symbolism and its cultural context both so rich and so difficult to control. For those who produce an artifact with a symbolic purpose in mind, a particular meaning may be clear, but once others adopt the artifact and thus engage in their own symbolization, they will express their meanings when they use it rather than adhering strictly to the originating intent. Consider the Mercedes logo. Intended by its maker to symbolize prestige, it has also been used to symbolize overindulgence or the injustice of being poor. While executives can exercise considerable control over the design and display of corporate artifacts, the symbolic meanings with which these artifacts become associated are far less easy to control.

American cultural anthropologist Clifford Geertz's persuasive method of thick description led many organization theorists to the symbolic perspective. But, as some modern organization theorists might put it, he did so in the way the Pied Piper led the children of Hamlin—by being remarkably seductive.

Thick description

In the early 1980s, organization theorists enamored of Geertz's highly acclaimed book *The Interpretation of Cultures* carried symbolic cultural anthropology into the mainstream of organization theory. Those researchers disenchanted with positivist epistemology and quantitative methods used Geertz's success to legitimize their interests in organizational symbolism and culture, and his methodology to guide their research.

Geertz concisely and evocatively described the conceptual foundation of the symbolic approach and boldly differentiated it from positivism in an opening salvo stating: 'Believing, with Max Weber, that man is an animal suspended in webs of significance he himself has spun, I take culture to be those webs, and the analysis of it to be therefore not an experimental science in search of law but an interpretive one in search of meaning.'[21] This bold statement suggested that Weber, often claimed by modernists to be one of their own, could also be called upon to render support for the symbolic perspective.[22]

Thick description is a form of ethnography focused on symbolic human behavior observed in its context and described in enough detail to make the behavior and its cultural context meaningful for the reader.[23] Geertz credited British philosopher Gilbert Ryle with the term thick description, and Geertz borrowed Ryle's distinction between a wink and a twitch to explain the difference between **symbolic** and **non-symbolic behavior**. Both involve contractions of the eyelid, but a twitch is involuntary, while a wink means something (e.g., I like you or I acknowledge our conspiracy). To get at the difference requires digging beneath the surface of behavior to the inferences and implications made by those who give and receive winks versus those who merely twitch.

Culturally contextualized symbolic behavior requires thick description because the phenomenon itself is so rich. **Thick description** is all about digging beneath surfaces to discover symbolic meaning in order to show culture at work, as Geertz's story of a Balinese cockfight so admirably demonstrates. One of the important aspects of Geertz's storytelling for organization theory is its revelation of the narrative underpinnings of not just ethnographic writing, but all forms of research reporting. No sooner had Geertz's ideas infiltrated organization theory then organizational researchers began studying organizational stories, storytelling, and narrative. Somewhat later they would apply thick description to themselves, examining academic theorizing and writing practices.

Organizational stories and storytelling

The simplest way of defining organizational narrative is as a story of real events with a plot and characters that reveal an organization's culture and distinctive practices by providing an experience of what they are like. Stories were an early interest for symbolic organization theorists like American social psychologist Joanne Martin and her students Martha Feldman, Sim Sitkin, and me because it was widely believed that stories were one way organizational cultures expressed their unique identities. In a 1983 article we reported on our analysis of stories collected from numerous corporate biographies.[24] Contrary to our expectations, **content analysis** showed that nearly all the stories in the biographies we read were variants of the same seven story themes:

> What happens when a higher status person breaks a rule?
> Is the big boss human?
> Can a little person rise to the top?
> What will get someone fired?
> What happens when the organization asks someone to move?
> How will the boss react to mistakes?
> How will the organization deal with obstacles?

We called our article 'The Uniqueness Paradox in Organizational Stories' because our main finding indicated that stories claiming cultural uniqueness rested on non-unique story types.

American folklorist Michael Owen Jones was quick to point out that taking a narrative approach to culture demands more than just collecting and analyzing the content of stories—it involves engaging with **storytelling**.[25] The cultural significance of stories lies as much in the teller's expressive artistry and the listeners' responses, as it does in the content of the story told, as Jones explained:

> During 'narrating' . . . a speaker communicates not only through linguistic channels (words) but also through paralinguistic and kinesic ones (intonation, change in pitch, body language). Moreover, the speaker responds to listener feedback by digressing, explaining, repeating, emphasizing, elaborating, abbreviating, dramatizing, and so on . . . Participants in a narrating event infer multiple, even quite different meanings from the varied cues; much depends on their experiences, feelings, and concerns in the present circumstances (the situational context that makes this narrating a 'situated event'). Therefore, it is misleading to refer to 'a story' or 'the story' as if it has an independent existence. It is inadequate to document 'stories' as linguistic entities with no regard for other channels of communication that convey information and affect responses. And it is misguided to assume that the event has a single meaning for participants.[26]

The uniqueness paradox study and other story studies undertaken at the time were vulnerable to Jones's criticism. To overcome this limitation American organization theorist David Boje looked at storytelling in the everyday work life of an office supply company. Boje's study contributed the concept of the **storytelling organization** defined as a 'collective storytelling system in which the performance of stories is a key part of members' sense making and a means to supplanting individual memories with institutional memory.'[27] One of the surprises Boje's study revealed came from his description of **terse storytelling**, which occurs when participants share a common history by working together. Much like the joke about the prisoners who know each other's jokes so well they simply call out a number and everyone laughs, terse stories are abbreviated to such an extent that outsiders may not realize storytelling has taken place.

In another approach to storytelling, organizational researchers study the use of storytelling by leaders. American communication scholar Ellen O'Connor, for example, studied the start-up of a high tech research organization in Silicon Valley.[28] She spent the better part of a year immersed in daily organizational life, attending meetings and discussions, talking to organizational members, and reading their memos and emails. Based on her observations, O'Connor concluded that the success of the start-up had depended in part on the narrative competence of its founder, that is, his ability to weave together plot and character to create a coherent and persuasive story shared and acted upon by other organizational members. In addition O'Connor identified three different types of narratives used within the organization: personal narratives including the life history, dreams, and visions of the founder; generic narratives that created the company, for example, business plans and strategy; and situational narratives or histories of critical events that explain why things were done in certain ways within the organization.

O'Connor's observations about the narrative competence of entrepreneurs was corroborated by an interpretive study Monica Kostera, Andrzej Koźmiński, and I conducted using interviews with CEOs published in *Harvard Business Review*.[29] Whereas nearly all the CEOs in a sample of thirty interviews showed signs of narrative competence, the interviews of those who founded a company were constructed almost entirely of personal narrative. Like all the CEOs in the sample, the entrepreneurial founders relied heavily on the epic form of storytelling, but they demonstrated much greater skill using other story types and were more likely to blend different types together to form highly complex stories. The typology of story types we used traces back to Aristotle (see Table 6.3).

To illustrate our application of this Aristotelian approach, consider the comic-epic story told by Masayoshi Son, founder and CEO of Japan's Softbank:

> When I first started the company, I only had two part-time workers and a small office. I got two apple boxes, and I stood up on them in the morning as if I was giving a speech. In a loud voice, I said to my two workers, 'You guys have to listen to me, because I am the president of this company.' I said, 'In five years, I'm going to have $75 million in sales. In five years, I will be supplying 1,000 dealer outlets, and we'll be number one in PC software distribution.' And I said it very loudly.
>
> Those two guys opened their mouths. They stood up and opened wide their eyes and mouths, and they thought, this guy must be crazy. And they both quit.
>
> That was in 1981. About a year and a half later, we were supplying 200 dealer outlets. Now we supply 15,000. In ten years, we've gone from two part-time employees doing software

Table 6.3 Aristotle's typology of stories

	Comic	Tragic	Epic	Romantic
Protagonist	Deserving victim, fool	Undeserving victim	Hero	Love object
Other characters	Trickster	Villain, helper	Rescue object, assistant, villain	Gift-giver, lover, injured or sick person
Plot focus	Misfortune or deserved chastisement	Undeserved misfortune, trauma	Achievement, noble victory, success	Love triumphant, love conquers misfortune
Predicament	Accident, mistake, coincidence, the unexpected or unpredictable	Crime, accident, insult, injury, loss, mistake, repetition, mis-recognition	Contest, challenge, trial, test, mission, quest, sacrifice	Gift, romantic fantasy, falling in love, reciprocation, recognition
Emotions	Mirth, aggression, scorn	Sorrow, pity, fear, anger, pathos	Pride, admiration, nostalgia	Love, care, kindness, generosity, gratitude
Function in business	Amusement	Catharsis	Inspiration	Compassion

Source: Hatch, Kostera and Koźmiński (2005), based on Gabriel (2000).

distribution and making about $12,000 to 570 employees doing software distribution, book and magazine publishing, telephone least cost routing, system integration, network computing, and CAD-CAM and making about $350 million.[30]

The comedic element of Son's story arises from this entrepreneur positioning himself as the deserving victim of the misfortune of losing his first two employees. To generate the epic effect, Son then repositions himself as heroically enduring the trials of starting up a company and achieving success. His initial mistake becomes but one early encounter in a much longer quest. According to Aristotle, this comic-epic story should provoke a combination of scorn and admiration in the listener that encourages amusement but also inspires. It also shows off the sophisticated storytelling of this successful entrepreneur as he makes skillful use of complex story forms.

Narrative and reflexivity in organization studies

Alasdair MacIntyre, a British moral philosopher, proposed narrative as a way of knowing, an epistemology, reasoning that all social life is narrated, as is evidenced, for example, by the existence of life stories.[31] MacIntyre claimed that our individual narratives give meaning to and construct our lives, yet, because we live within organizational, social, and historical contexts, our lives are intertwined with organizational, social, and historical narratives. In other words, in many respects, our story is part of the organizational and societal stories it contributes to.

Narrative is epistemic in that it is a way of knowing that includes knowing ourselves. Using narrative epistemology means believing that humans develop knowledge by listening and telling stories to one another and to themselves. One implication of this epistemological assumption is that we can learn about organizations by studying the stories and accounts of organizational experience that organizational members tell. Thus MacIntyre placed a philosophical foundation under the organizational storytelling and narrating research tradition forming at the time.

Polish-born Swedish organization theorist Barbara Czarniawska took on the challenge MacIntryre laid down by proposing a theory of narrative identity formation based on the organizations she had studied in the Swedish public sector.[32] She compared the stories she heard about privatization and computerization to soap operas traced out in multiple intersecting plotlines involving numerous characters enacting a series of challenging adventures and interpersonal conflicts that continued without end even as the multiple storytellers used their stories to tell themselves and others who they were. According to Czarniawska, the complex plot lines and multiple characters of soap opera-like organizational narratives weave in and out of, always unfinished, organizational lives.

In addition to conceptualizing organizations as ongoing narratives, organizational culture researchers have used narrative epistemology to study theorizing as a narrative act. American organization theorist John Van Maanen was one of the first to use this reflexive approach. His book *Tales of the Field*, which distinguished realist, confessional, and impressionist tales, encouraged organizational researchers to examine their narrative practices and attend to the influence their narrative choices have on the stories they tell, namely their theories and the research reports they write.[33]

In an article that built on Van Maanen's work, I described how narrative theorists challenge the distinction between fiction and non-fiction such that, from the perspective of social science:

> research design involves creating the roles of subject and observer, establishing a context, and determining a sequence of actions and events. This suggests comparing the social scientist with an author of fiction who develops character, situation and plot. Furthermore, although research reports may demonstrate scientific achievement, the act of reporting is a narrative act.[34]

My study applied narrative theory developed by French literary theorist Gerard Genette who advanced the idea that narrative emerges from the conjunction of a story, its narrator, and an act of narration. Genette defined the relationship between the narrator and the story as perspective, while that between the narrator and the narrative act he called voice (see Figure 6.5). I translated narrative perspective and voice into the questions: 'Who sees?' and 'Who says?'

Perspective defines the position from which the narrator observes the phenomenon under investigation as either inside or outside its boundaries, the narrative equivalent of the distinction between subjective and objective ontological positioning. **Voice** depends upon whether or not the narrator appears as a character in the story told, which determines whether narrative reflexivity is admitted into the story.

Also following in Van Maanen's footsteps, Karen Golden-Biddle and Karen Locke analyzed the strategies authors of several well-regarded organizational ethnographies employed to make their accounts convincing.[35] Their **rhetorical analysis** revealed three dimensions the research reports they studied had in common – authenticity, plausibility, and criticality.

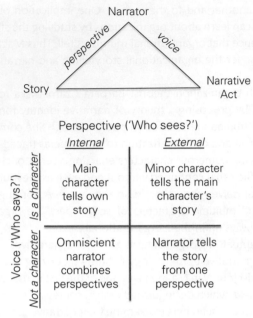

Figure 6.5 Basic elements of Genette's narrative theory and the relationships between them that constitute narrative position at the intersection of perspective and voice

Note that reflexivity is only possible for the narrator or researcher when she or he becomes a character in the story they tell.

Source: Based on Genette (1980: 186) who credits Brooks and Warren (1943: 589).

Golden-Biddle and Locke argued that **authenticity** convinces readers of the author's presence in the field and of their grasp of how those studied understood their world by offering details about everyday life, describing the relationship the author formed with informants and how data were extracted from them, and giving an account of their personal biases. They claimed that **plausibility** convinces readers of a study's contribution and importance by making unorthodox methods (how ethnography was viewed at the time) seem normal, by legitimating contestable assertions, and by building dramatic anticipation.

Criticality, the third of Golden-Biddle and Locke's criteria for convincing readers of the value of an ethnographic study, causes readers to probe their own previously unexamined assumptions or question the prevailing attitudes and beliefs of their field. While they found authenticity and plausibility necessary to convince readers to accept an ethnographic study, they found criticality the most promising for achieving wholesale acceptance of the symbolic approach within organization theory.

The theater metaphor: Dramaturgy and performativity

Erving Goffman, a Canadian sociologist, borrowed ideas from drama theory to explore how Shakespeare's saying 'All the world's a stage/And all the men and women merely players' applies to life in social organizations. Goffman believed that individuals shape themselves and their social realities through performances that are similar to how dramatists and actors compose and present stories on a stage in front of an audience.[36] Goffman developed his dramaturgical approach while studying a mental hospital wherein he discovered that the social order of the hospital depended upon doctors, nurses, and patients all acting out roles for each other on an institutional stage.

American sociologist Michael Rosen used Goffman's dramaturgical approach to analyze a cultural ritual created by an American advertising agency. The annual ritual was known in the company as Breakfast at Spiro's, the name of the restaurant where it took place.[37] He described the symbols, dress, language, and pictures on display at the corporate breakfast he attended, and also how different groups and individuals manipulated these symbols to communicate meanings that reinforced their individual and organizational identities and enacted the organization's hierarchy.

For example, Rosen observed that different groups of employees dressed differently for the occasion—whereas clerical workers and creative people did not appear to be restricted by a dress code, employees looking for promotion and rewards wore suits of a particular type. Speeches were made by senior executives (all wearing the right suits) and their remarks reinforced images of control and benevolence, as when the Chairman of the Board talked about how some employees' attitudes caused problems requiring changes in personnel, and then presented ten-year service awards to loyal employees. Rosen claimed that, juxtaposed in this way, the awards symbolized conformity to company rules and reinforced the agency's hierarchical values. The same symbolism informed employees how to declare their membership in the firm's creative subculture by not dressing or behaving like those in charge.

As Rosen's study illustrates, **dramaturgy** is concerned with the theatrical elements of a performance such as acting, costumes, staging, masks, props, and scenery. It builds on a metaphor connecting aspects of the theater with organizing. For example, both acting and organizing depend upon specifying roles for actors to play, and both troupes of actors and businesses are called companies. Performance features prominently in the discourses of theater and organization alike, as in references to the performance of an actor, a play, or an organization, all of which are assessed through processes of critical review.

Similarities between theatrical and organizational performance caused some dramaturgically inclined organizational researchers to adopt the notion of **performativity** introduced by British linguist John L. Austin in his book *How to Do Things with Words*. As opposed to using words simply to convey information, Austin defined performatives as words which, when uttered, perform an action (e.g., 'I thee wed,' 'You're fired!').[38] Performativity moved dramaturgical studies of organizations toward the postmodern perspective.

Starting as a student of the theater metaphor but quickly moving into the realm of performativity, British organization theorist Heather Höpfl, a former theatrical stage manager in the UK, pointed out many similarities between the subjective experience of actors performing their craft and the world of work. Her studies examining dramaturgical and performative aspects of customer service in airline crews and employment agencies showed that when customer service employees embody corporate values, they leave a part of themselves aside, just as dramatic actors do.[39] On this basis Höpfl formulated a critique of organizational practices and procedures governing customer experience performances and thereby adopting the critical postmodern perspective.

Höpfl argued that the costs of role performance, for dramatic and corporate actors alike, must be measured in terms of the hypocrisy, degradation, stress, and emotional burnout that performing demands. Quoting the radical eighteenth-century French philosopher Denis

Diderot she provocatively compared an actor to a prostitute, saying that the actor is like 'the whore who feels nothing for the man she is with, but lets herself go in his arms anyway as a demonstration of her professional competence.'[40]

According to Höpfl: 'Diderot's actor is an instrument or an empty vessel, capable of playing any or all characters precisely because his/her own character is eradicated and sensibilities obliterated in the pursuit of professional craft.' She considered the implications for those who manage organizations for whom 'the achievement of a flexible and well-rehearsed work force which can move easily between a variety of roles with skill is considered to be a desirable accomplishment.'[41] It is this attitude on the part of management, she claimed, that both exploits and masks the actor's pain.

To demonstrate that performing in the theatrical sense is a familiar aspect of many service jobs, and to give an example of the pain customer service inflicts on organizational performers, Höpfl described a group of airline employees she observed in the act of overplaying their roles.

> In 1998, on a scheduled flight from Warsaw to Heathrow, I witnessed an extraordinary performance by the cabin crew that resembled a sixth-form review. The cabin crew donned the duty free articles they were selling and one of the male cabin crew members pushed his trolley up the aisle in an ostentatiously camp manner, wearing a silk headscarf and Rayban sunglasses, with a small teddy bear mascot waving from his breast pocket. The female member of the crew who accompanied him gestured and pointed like a magician's assistant. I have never seen anything like it in many years of flying. Another cabin crew member announced that this was the floorshow and the passengers broke into spontaneous and sustained applause. At the end of the performance, the crew took their bows. I was struck by the inevitable logic of the performance requirement of the organization which takes performance to this extreme. Without doubt, these crewmembers were acting beyond the call of their roles. This example provides an insight into what occurs to a lesser degree in everyday organizational performance in a less immediate and obvious way. Its significance lies in what is revealed by the extreme variant. This has much in common with the notion of the theatre of the absurd in which the production of the action is made transparent in its performance.[42]

Höpfl's last point about performance rendering the production of action transparent is what is meant by the term performativity as it is used in the postmodern perspective.

Postmodernism and organizational culture

Postmodern organization theorists rely heavily on a different metaphor than that of the theater—the text. For them, texts are ongoing interpretive performances of meaning and everything, including an organization, is a text. They borrow most of their ideas about organizations as texts from post-structural literary theory, a rich source of postmodern concepts and theory.

Bulgarian-born French linguist Julia Kristeva introduced a theory of intertextuality that has been particularly influential on those applying the metaphor of the text to organizations.[43] **Intertextuality** derives from the assumption that no text exists in isolation. All texts are interwoven with other texts to which they refer (e.g., by quotation, allusion, description, inscription) and that provide some of their meaning. Thus, the question of the original meaning of a text as intended by its author is nonsense because discourses produce and are produced by many interwoven texts whose multiple authors and readers continuously (re)read and (re)write them.

Applying intertextuality to organizations transforms organizational culture, identity, symbols, actions, and actors into texts that create one another via mutual ongoing referencing.[44] In this regard Czarniawska's empirical descriptions of organizational soap operas in the Swedish public sector is an application of Kristeva's theory. However, while Czarniawska's organizational soap operas offer a non-linear, open-ended version of storytelling, the narratives she described are still mutually coherent enough to be understood. Full-blown postmodernism undermines such holistic aspirations and celebrates instead the fragmentation of meaning and coherence.

Culture as fragmentation

Some culture researchers focus on the ways in which organizational cultures are inconsistent, ambiguous, and in a constant state of flux. In this view alliances or coalitions never stabilize into subcultures and certainly not into an integrated culture because discourse and its focal issues are always changing. In this spirit American organizational researchers Debra Meyerson and Joanne Martin provided an image of organizational culture as **fragmentation** to offset what they regarded as overly consensual views of organizational culture they categorized as **unity** (to indicate a unifying set of values and beliefs) and **differentiation** (i.e., subcultural).[45] As Martin put it:

> when two cultural members agree (or disagree) on a particular interpretation of, say, a ritual, this is likely to be a temporary and issue-specific congruence (or incongruence). It may well not reflect agreement or disagreement on other issues, at other times. Subcultures, then, are reconceptualized as fleeting, issue-specific coalitions that may or may not have a similar configuration in the future. This is not simply a failure to achieve subcultural consensus in a particular context; from the Fragmentation perspective this is the most consensus possible in any context.[46]

While fragmentation studies have much in common with postmodernism, Martin claimed that postmodern cultural studies often go beyond fragmentation to assert that reality (and therefore culture) is an illusion.[47] In spite of her disagreement with postmodernists over whether culture is an illusion, Martin agreed that organizational culture is just one more way for those in power to mask their manipulation and control of others. She followed critical postmodern organizational culture researchers into textual deconstruction, using this technique to show the power relations hidden by a culture's unspoken understandings.

Deconstructing organizational culture

Some critical postmodern organizational theorists challenge Grand Narrative in organizations and organization theory by criticizing the ideological function of modernist narratives and stories, including modernist theory and modernist writing styles. One of these, American communication scholar Dennis Mumby, suggested that organizational narratives lead to a systematic distortion of organizational culture because they reproduce and maintain particular meanings that support existing relationships of dependence and domination.[48]

Deconstruction exposes the ideological nature of organizational stories by showing how they privilege particular groups and exclude others. For example, Martin deconstructed a story told by the CEO of a multinational corporation. The CEO's story told about a young woman who arranged her Caesarean section so that she could be virtually present at the launch of a new product she had been instrumental in developing by using a closed circuit television the company provided for the purpose.[49]

Martin argued that the primary beneficiary of the act reported by the CEO was not the woman but the company because the woman's involvement in the launch event enhanced the company's productivity rather than the wellbeing of her child. Martin further suggested that what the CEO referred to as the company's culture of concern actually controlled and supported gender discrimination by blurring the boundary between public and private life, thus enabling the organization to appropriate some of the time the woman otherwise would have devoted to her new family member.

Other interpretations of the story told by the CEO are possible, of course. For example, the woman in the story might claim to have seen herself giving birth to two progeny at the same time—one her child and the other the new product—hence she may have welcomed having access to both events from her hospital room. A more critical reading might counter that this version gives evidence of the mother's false consciousness, and round and round we could go; however, the content of interpretations such as these is not the main point.

Deconstructive readings such as Martin's reveal the possibilities of dominance and other forms of power (such as the woman's creative power to give birth *and* to help develop a new product) without the necessity to settle the matter of which interpretation wins. It is the unending struggle for domination through the control of meaning that critical postmodernists seek to reveal. The point of deconstruction is to sensitize you to this ongoing power struggle, which, according to postmodernists, is where organizing takes place.

Deconstruction can also reveal the illusions created by hollow and ambiguous identity claims, rituals, and other meaningless organizational symbols. Recall how Michael Rosen's study of Breakfast at Spiro's revealed this organizational ritual as involving acts of imitation (e.g., parroting desired feelings rather than having those feelings) that seduced members into conformity with management ideology. Another deconstructionist, Australian sociologist Douglas Ezzy, suggested that organizational cultures claiming to value trust and family are contradicted by rewards for individual achievement rather than cooperation, and by layoffs during hard times.[50] He argues that workers who trust and invest themselves in an organizational culture that controls and then abandons them have fallen prey to illusion.

Similarly, in interviewing members of the Engineering Division of a US electronics company, Israeli organizational ethnographer Gideon Kunda noticed that workers complained it was difficult to maintain a boundary between what they described as their organizational and their true selves.[51] His informants described working long hours developing innovative technologies in a culture of fun that, ironically, they themselves produced at the expense of their personal lives. He noted that many of them suffered burn-out showing that organizational culture represses and controls workers who believe in its illusions.

Culture and change: A return to the normative

What managers most often want to know about their organization's culture is how to change it. Regardless of the perspective adopted, all organization culture researchers acknowledge that top managers are powerful members of an organization's culture. And, because power grants them a disproportionate share of attention, their behavior becomes a role model for others, their words are carefully attended, and their directives obeyed. But what is recommended to managers on the basis of culture theory differs markedly according to the perspective adopted.

Symbolic organization theorists believe the opportunity to influence other members of the organization does not necessarily guarantee that the words and actions of executives will be interpreted as intended or that they will have the intended effects. They accuse modernists who represent culture as a management tool of being unrealistic about the potential to control the interpretations and behavior of employees, who are the ones most directly engaged with the organization's culture and thus most able to change it or to resist change. Critical postmodernists go further than their symbolic colleagues in resisting the modernist culture-as-tool view; they cut to the quick by challenging the ethics of managerial control.

Modern perspective: Culture as control

Modernists claim that if culture shapes behavior via norms and values, then it should be possible to manage the culture of an organization in such a way that desired behavior is more or less guaranteed. They believe cultural control comes, for example, through recruiting and hiring practices aimed at finding value-compatible employees, socialization, and training that inculcates employees with organizationally preferred norms and values, and rewards that reinforce conformity to management demands.[52]

American organization theorist William Ouchi introduced one of the strongest notions of culture as control with his concept of clan control, part of a general typology of organizational control mechanisms that also included market and bureaucratic control.[53] The role of culture is clear in **clan control**, which depends upon the socialization of new organizational members such that they internalize cultural values, goals, expectations, and practices that will drive them to desired levels of performance. Ouchi noted that, once internalized, implicit understandings direct and coordinate employees' behavior and cause them to internally monitor their own behavior and that of others. In clan control, managers take charge of cultural norms and expectations and make certain that all organizational members accept and internalize them. Once established, culture then controls employees on behalf of the managers who control the culture. It should be a simple matter of redirection to change a culture whose management employs clan control.

Schein's theory also supports modernist normative ambitions to control culture but Schein presented a more sophisticated rendering of the management of culture change. Based on his theory of culture as assumptions, values, and artifacts, Schein claimed that organizational cultures only change when new values are introduced by the decree or example of top management. But Schein notes that only when the new values are absorbed into unconscious assumptions will the culture actually change, giving employees a controlling role as well.

Members of the culture must personally experience the benefits of proposed new values for cultural change to take hold.

Normatively speaking, Schein believed the main organizational benefits of culture change come either through environmental adaptation or internal integration, and several modernist American researchers provided insight into how culture differentially serves adaptation and/or integration. Studying the performance effects of strong cultures in a population of over 200 corporations, John Kotter and James Heskett found that cultural strength was significantly related to organizational performance overall.[54] But when cultural values supported organizational adaptation to the environment, the relationship became even stronger. Culture significantly influenced organizational performance when it either helped the organization to anticipate or adapt to environmental change (positive effect) or interfered with its adaptation (negative effect). In other words, when cultures do not support adaptation, cultural strength can interfere with performance, but when culture and the need for adaptation are aligned, cultural strength boosts performance.

Absorbing culture into contingency theory Dan Denison proposed that an organization's strategy, culture, and environment need to be aligned if an organization is to achieve high performance.[55] Denison found that organizations operating in rapidly changing environments performed best if they valued either flexibility and change (Denison called this adaptability culture), or participation and high levels of organizational commitment (involvement culture). In stable environments, successful organizations possessed either a shared vision of the future (mission culture), or had strong values for tradition and conformity (consistency culture). Adaptability and mission cultures according to Denison's theory are externally focused, while involvement and consistency cultures focus internally. Denison's work supports Schein's normative statement about the two main benefits of culture being external adaptation and internal integration; however, Schein did not treat these as mutually exclusive, a puzzle that remains to be studied further.

Symbolic perspectives on change: Culture as strategy and identity

Those taking the symbolic perspective want to convince managers to observe, listen, and respond to what employees say and do as a means of engaging in the interpretive processes that form, maintain, and change culture. They believe managers are managed *by* cultural influences even while they are trying to manage their organizations from within one or more cultural contexts.

Normatively, the symbolic perspective warns managers that the biggest mistake they can make is to think that the corporate subculture they generate is equivalent to the organization's culture. To know the organization's culture and subcultures they must engage with employees. When corporate and organizational cultures differ, managers can fail to recognize the ways in which their efforts to change the organization work against rather than with collective understandings of organizational identity and norms for how things should be done.

Italian organization theorist Pasquale Gagliardi combined Schein's notion of culture as assumptions and values with the concepts of strategy and identity to forge his theory that an organization's primary strategy is to protect the organizational identity, which in turn is defined by its cultural assumptions and values (see Figure 6.6).

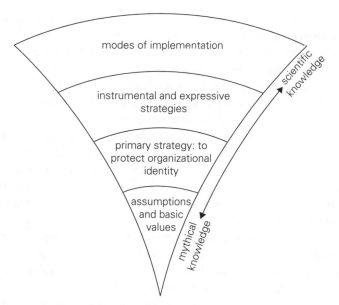

Figure 6.6 Gagliardi's fan model of culture in relation to strategy and identity
Source: Gagliardi (1986).

Gagliardi argued that organizations develop and implement a range of secondary strategies to serve the primary strategy of protecting their identity. These can be either instrumental or expressive. **Instrumental strategies** are operational in nature; they direct attention to the attainment of specific measurable objectives. **Expressive strategies** operate in the symbolic realm and protect the stability and coherence of shared meanings so that group members can maintain a collective self-concept and offer a recognizable identity to the outside world.

Secondary strategies can be *both* expressive and instrumental. For example, an advertising campaign can be designed to present the organizational identity to its external audiences (expressive) at the same time that it helps to sell the company's products (instrumental). Similarly a move to an open plan office may reflect a strategy to improve communication efficiency (instrumental) *and* to symbolize an increase in the importance of teamwork (expressive). According to Gagliardi, changes in behavior, technology, symbols, and structure occur through implementation of secondary strategies. The most effective strategies in his view are identity-laden expressions of organizational culture.

Based on his theory Gagliardi offered descriptions of three outcomes of cultural change efforts he observed in his consulting work with organizations. He described each cultural change outcome as the result of a different relationship between culture and strategy. When strategies align with existing organizational assumptions and values cultures do not really change, they only appear to do so by incorporating a new artifact or two. Deep change is avoided because in such **apparent change** the organization formulates and implements its secondary strategies from within the confines of its existing culture and identity.

When strategies are in conflict with assumptions and values, culture is either overthrown by being replaced or destroyed, or the strategy is resisted and never implemented. In either case, according to Gagliardi, no deep cultural change occurs. It may be obvious why cultural resistance produces no change, but the case of revolutionary change requires explanation. In **revolutionary change**, a strategy is imposed, usually through the entry of outsiders who destroy most of the culture's symbols and bring new ones to take their place. This can occur, for example, when the organization is acquired by a firm with a significantly different culture, or when a beloved founder is replaced by someone who overturns the founder's philosophy. In these cases, Gagliardi argued, it is 'more correct to say that the old firm dies and that a new firm, which has little in common with the first, was born.'[56]

Cultural change only occurs when a strategy is different but not incompatible with existing assumptions and values. In this case the culture is extended by addition of the new assumptions and values introduced by the strategy, thus Gagliardi called it **incremental change** (see Figure 6.7). Borrowing from Schein's theory Gagliardi explained, if the new strategy meets with success, then the incremental change in values it brings about will be absorbed into the organization's set of assumptions.

Gagliardi advised that incremental changes of cultural values, assumptions, and identity are more likely to occur if they are supported by storytelling and mythmaking, two elements drawn from the symbolic perspective, as was his concept of expressive strategies. But Gagliardi only alluded to the symbolic and interpretive processes by which cultural change occurs. My own theory of the dynamics of organizational culture was an effort to move further in this direction.

The dynamics of organizational culture

Like Gagliardi's theory, my cultural dynamics model was built on Schein's theory of culture as assumptions, values, and artifacts. Cultural dynamics theory, however, focuses not on these elements per se, but on the organizing processes connecting them (see Figure 6.8).[57]

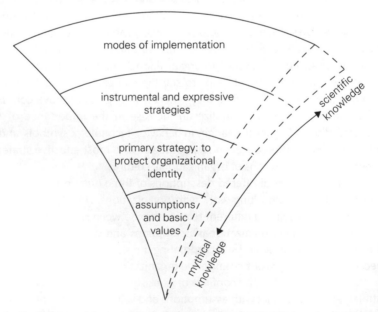

Figure 6.7 Gagliardi's fan model stretched to include new cultural assumptions and values
Source: Gagliardi (1986).

This idea arose from trying to understand the unnamed arrows linking assumptions with values, and values with artifacts in Schein's model. At one point I flipped Schein's diagram onto its side and split the two sets of arrows apart, making room to insert symbols opposite values (compare Schein's model in the center of Figure 6.8 to the cultural dynamics model that encircles it). Introducing symbols added the symbolic perspective of Schein's model, while naming the arrows emphasized the cultural processes of manifestation, realization, symbolization, and interpretation of interest to me.

In the upper left-hand quadrant of the cultural dynamics model, assumptions manifest as values that create expectations about the world and guide action. **Manifestation** can be illustrated by examining the assumption that humans are lazy:

> According to the cultural dynamics perspective, this assumption produces expectations of laziness, which lead to perceptions of lazy acts. These perceptions, in combination with other manifesting assumptions, color thoughts and feelings about these acts. For instance, in an organization that assumes that success depends upon sustained effort, laziness is likely to be considered in a negative light, and perceptions of laziness along with negative thoughts and feelings about it can easily develop into a value for controlling laziness. Meanwhile the laziness assumption also works to inhibit expectations of industrious acts (because humans are lazy, why would they act in this way?), and perceptions, thoughts, and feelings about these acts will be constrained. This inhibition suppresses a value for autonomy (because

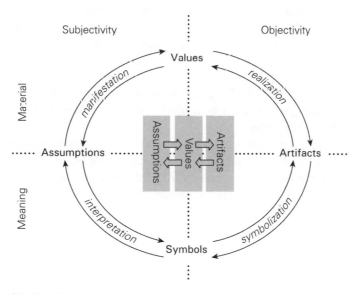

Figure 6.8 Hatch's cultural dynamics model

This model shows four interrelated processes of manifestation, realization, symbolization, and interpretation that continuously spin stable features of culture along with cultural change. The top half of the model shows how culture becomes material in artifacts produced by behavior inflected with and reflective of assumptions and values. In the bottom portion of the model cultural meaning making transforms artifacts into symbols that either support or challenge assumptions. The dotted line separating the right and left sides of the figure indicates that while artifacts appear in the domain of objectivity, assumptions seem to disappear into the subjective domain; symbols and values lie between these domains and share some of the properties of each.

Source: Hatch (1993). Permission granted by Academy of Management.

giving lazy people autonomy will almost certainly lead to little or no effort being exerted), which further supports the value for control by eliminating a potentially competing force from the value set. That is, although autonomy would be compatible with an assumption that organizational success depends upon effort, the laziness assumption interferes with an effort/autonomy value set and supports an effort/control value set.[58]

Once culture influences action by manifesting values, value-based action produces cultural artifacts (e.g., objects, events, verbal statements, texts). The production of artifacts is referred to as the **realization** process because it is by this process that images grounded in assumptions and values are made real by being given tangible forms. To carry on with the laziness example:

> An assumption that the organization is filled with laggards contributes to a value for control that enhances the likelihood that certain social and material forms will appear. For instance, time clocks, daily productivity reports, performance reviews, and visually accessible offices are acceptable ideas in a culture that values controlling laziness. Proactive realization is the process by which manifest expectations are made tangible in activity. Thus, time clocks might be installed, daily activity reports requested and filed, performance assessed, and visually accessible offices built, all as partial means of realizing the expectation of 'how it should be' in an organization assumed to be filled with laggards.[59]

The top half of the cultural dynamics model shown in Figure 6.8 describes the manifestation and realization processes by which artifacts are created; the bottom half describes what happens once artifacts are made part of the organization's cultural inventory and become available for symbolization and interpretation. In the upper half of the model, assumptions and values shape activity such that artifacts are created and maintained, while in the lower half organizational members choose some (but not all) of the available artifacts and use them to symbolize their meanings to themselves and to communicate them with others.

The process by which symbols are fashioned from artifacts is called **symbolization**. For example, an organization's beautiful new open plan office building might be used by members of top management to communicate an image of the organization as participative and inclusive. Meanwhile, at lower levels in the hierarchy, time clocks, daily activity reports, and the behavior of managers tell employees that they are not trusted, leading them to feel resentment and experience exclusion. In this case the employees who attach their negative feelings to the artifacts of time clocks and activity reports produce symbols that counteract those of top management.

Through the selection and expressive uses of symbols to represent ideas and feelings, **interpretation** processes forge meaning and significance within everyday organizational life. As time moves on, the four processes of manifestation, realization, symbolization, and interpretation combine to influence what people assume and value about their culture from moment to moment and thereby produce, maintain, and change the artifacts and symbols that materialize its meaning.

Returning to the earlier example, the appearance of an obviously hardworking individual challenges the basic assumption of laziness bringing the possibility of new meaning into the culture. Of course it may happen that the symbol of the hardworking individual is simply reinterpreted to fit into existing assumptions, for instance, by making an excuse for the aberration ('his twin daughters are ready for college and he really needs a promotion so he is kissing up to the boss'). In that instance, stability will win out over change. But change is also possible, and when it occurs it is by the mechanism of confrontation with symbols that do not fit the assumed reality. Suppose the same hardworking individual wins a $50,000,000 lottery and keeps on working. This additional information brings the assumption of laziness into question, and now people start to assert against the normal view that at least some workers have initiative. If this questioning leads people to distinguish lazy and hardworking individuals, perhaps a new employee selection process will take hold that eventually changes the employee base, organizational behavior, and the artifact pool that represents cultural symbolic resources for the future, and so on.

Notice how cultural processes work in two directions: for instance, interpretation uses assumptions to help determine the meaning of symbols, but allows symbols to either maintain or challenge existing assumptions. Maintenance of assumptions, which is tantamount to **cultural stability**, occurs when interpretations support what is already expected. But interpretations sometimes run counter to expectations. **Cultural change** comes when assumptions are symbolically challenged within the interpretation process and this starts a chain of effects extending back throughout the processes of the model. Forces for stability and change co-exist within cultural dynamics as described by the model, and are ongoing and interrelated.

Managers desiring to change an organization using cultural dynamics theory would need to take part in the processes described by the model. An attempt to intentionally introduce change usually begins with the processes of realization and symbolization when management introduces a new idea through language and other artifacts that are new to the culture (do not forget that physical objects and behavioral manifestations are also powerful communicators) which then may be symbolized and interpreted by those who will either carry the change forward or deny it any influence. If the symbols made by interpreting artifacts align with existing organizational assumptions and values, change should be relatively easy but not very deep, as Gagliardi predicted for apparent change.

However, change in line with existing assumptions and values may not be what management wants. Change then involves introducing less comfortable ideas into the organization and change agents must recognize that their control over the process diminishes as others confront the new artifacts and make their own interpretations, not only of these artifacts, but of the intent of the change agent. Symbolic significance will accrue throughout all of this meaning-making activity, contributed by many others than those who initiated the change.

Normatively speaking, cultural dynamics theory places the manager inside the processes that create, maintain, and change organizational culture. It suggests that much of the power attributed to leaders lies in their sensitivity to their own symbolic meaning within the cultural contexts in which it is produced and maintained by others. Leaders have tremendous influence within organizations, as modernists and postmodernists alike point out, but the symbolic perspective insists that a leader's ability to effectively mobilize this influence depends upon their knowledge of and relationship with the culture, and their respect for and responses to the interpretive acts of others.[60] In this way cultural dynamics combines modern and symbolic perspectives.

Postmodern perspective: A different normativity

Those adopting the symbolic perspective conceptualize culture as the context within which management is socially constructed as either effective or not, leaving room for the idea that enlightened management could yet exercise control over culture. Postmodernists want none of this and push beyond what they regard as the illusion of management control, enlightened or otherwise. Normatively inclined postmodernists promote the benefits of relinquishing managerial control in favor of encouraging individual creativity and freedom, and licensing workplace democracy. More often, however, they choose to deconstruct any theory of culture they encounter, regarding it as another Grand Narrative needing to be exposed for the abuses of power it hides.

As the field of organizational culture studies shifted in the direction suggested by the text metaphor for organizing, researching culture per se gradually disappeared from organization theory, replaced by taking a cultural perspective on just about every other phenomenon of interest to the field. This change, brought about by developments within postmodernism, amounts to full acceptance of the symbolic perspective in organization theory today at the same time that it renders it somewhat invisible.

Research focused explicitly on culture is not really gone, however, rather culture research has taken up residence in the academic field of marketing where those studying corporate branding have used it to make organizational inroads into their theorizing.[61] Needless to say, postmodern organization theorists have put up resistance to this disappearing act by focusing attention on the phenomenon of being branded, how employees can effectively resist this new form of domination, and hidden control over their organizational practices and cultural identities.[62]

Summary

An organization can be viewed as a culture in its own right, as a set of subcultures contained within the organization, or as subculture(s) operating within national culture(s). Examples of each of these levels of analysis were given in this chapter, but it is important to bear in mind the many ways these levels work together. For example, if you only pay attention to cultural forces at the environmental or societal level, and do not consider culture at the level of the organization, you will miss much of what makes an organization distinctive and differentiates it from other organizations—its organizational culture and identity. Likewise, if you only focus on the organizational culture and ignore its subcultures, you may miss the tensions and contradictions organizational members confront in trying to understand and manage their organizations.

Modernists follow those adopting the symbolic perspective in believing that assumptions and values influence behavior through their expression in norms and values and that culture is communicated through artifacts including stories, symbols, tradition, and customs. The difference between the two perspectives on organizational culture comes from the way their proponents define knowing and what counts as knowledge about culture. The symbolic perspective defines culture as a context for meaning making and interpretation in which cultural understanding permits you to know an organization and the various uses made of its physical, behavioral, and verbal symbols. The modern perspective, on the other hand, interprets knowledge about culture as a tool of management, and culture itself as a variable to be manipulated to enhance the likelihood of achieving desired levels of organizational performance.

Postmodernists find numerous ways to challenge the notion that organizations have or are cultures. Some use postmodern literary theories like intertextuality to suggest that the idea of shared understanding is an illusion and, therefore, so is organizational culture. Others spend their research energy deconstructing organizational narratives to unmask the power struggles that they believe explain organizational life. Still others develop metaphoric forms of analysis based in literature and drama to describe the performativity of organizing and to extend the boundaries of organization theory beyond both the natural and the social sciences to embrace the humanities and the arts.

Normative interests in organization theory push culture theorists to advise managers on culture change. While Schein explains how changing values and artifacts induces change at the level of assumptions, Gagliardi and Hatch regard normative demands for tips on culture change as less easy to fulfill. Gagliardi describes real culture change at the level of deep assumptions as only possible via incremental additions of new values, and cautions that revolutionary change throws away existing culture while apparent change can fool you into thinking a change has occurred when it has not. Meanwhile Hatch's cultural dynamics theory explains cultural stability and change as intertwined outcomes of always ongoing processes of manifestation, realization, symbolization, and interpretation into which managers must embed themselves if they are to influence culture successfully. Postmodernists decry all efforts to manipulate employees and call instead for deconstructing culture along with managerial control, cultural or otherwise.

Key terms

subculture

   enhancing

   orthogonal

   countercultural

corporate culture

silos

strong culture

national cultural differences

   power distance

   uncertainty avoidance

   individualism vs. collectivism

   masculine vs. feminine

   long-term vs. short-term orientation

Schein's theory of culture

   basic assumptions

values

norms

artifacts

Organizational Culture Inventory (OCI)

grounded theory

negotiated order

ethnomethodology

contextualizing

symbols

   denotation/instrumental meaning

   connotation/expressive meaning

   symbolic and non-symbolic behavior

thick description

content analysis

organizational stories

storytelling

storytelling organization

terse storytelling

epic, comic, tragic, romantic stories

narrative

narrative epistemology

perspective and voice

rhetorical analysis

authenticity

plausibility

criticality

theater metaphor

dramaturgy

performativity

intertextuality

culture as unity, differentiation, fragmentation

deconstructive readings

clan control

Gagliardi's culture change theory

instrumental vs. expressive strategies

apparent change

revolutionary change

incremental change

Hatch's cultural dynamics theory

manifestation

realization

symbolization

interpretation

cultural stability and change

Endnotes

1. Jenks (1993).
2. Tylor (1871/1958: 1).
3. Herskowitz (1948: 625).
4. Ortner (1973).
5. Van Maanen and Barley (1984).
6. Martin and Siehl (1983); Siehl and Martin (1984); see also De Lorean and Wright (1979).
7. Chatman and Cha (2003).
8. Schein (1984); see also Schein (1983, 1991, 1992, 1996, 2000).
9. Ouchi (1979); Peters and Waterman (1982).
10. Martin and Frost (1996); see also Hatch and Yanow (2003).
11. Phillips, Goodman, and Sackmann (1992).
12. Hofstede (1997, 2001).
13. Hofstede and Bond (1988).
14. Lurie and Riccucci (2003).
15. Cooke and Laferty (1987).
16. Cooke and Szumal (2000: 157-9).
17. Strauss et al. (1963, 1964).
18. Cohen (1976: 23).
19. Van Maanen (2005: 383).
20. Morgan, Frost, and Pondy (1983: 4-5).
21. Geertz (1973: 5).
22. Schroeder (1992).

23. Geertz (1973); see in particular the first chapter of 'Thick description: Toward an interpretive theory of culture', 3–30.

24. Martin et al. (1983).

25. Jones (1996). A similar critique was raised by Boland and Tenkasi (1995).

26. Jones (1996: 7).

27. Boje (1991, 1995).

28. O'Connor (2000).

29. Hatch, Kostera, and Koźmiński (2005).

30. Webber (1992).

31. MacIntyre (1984: 205).

32. Czarniawska (1997).

33. Van Maanen (1988); see also Sandelands and Drazin (1989); Golden-Biddle and Locke (1993, 1997); Hatch (1996); Czarniawska (1999).

34. Hatch (1996: 360).

35. Golden-Biddle and Locke (1993).

36. Goffman (1959) built his notion of dramaturgy on Burke's (1945) dramatism.

37. Rosen (1985).

38. Austin (1962).

39. Höpfl (2002: 262).

40. Diderot (1773) cited in Hopfl (2002: 255, 258).

41. Höpfl (2002: 262).

42. Höpfl (2002: 258–9).

43. Kristeva (1984).

44. Notice the similarity to Derrida's use of the term *différance* to explain the fluid meaning of words; by a similar logic, intertextuality explains the fluid meaning of texts.

45. Meyerson and Martin (1987); Martin (1992, 2002).

46. Martin (1992: 138).

47. For a postmodern take on culture, see Bauman (1973/1999) who describes culture doing a disappearing act in the mixing and matching of global societies. See also Schultz (1992) for commentary on the postmodern perspective and its image of culture as fragments seen in a broken mirror.

48. Mumby (1988).

49. Martin (1990).

50. Ezzy (2001).

51. Kunda (1996).

52. Kilmann, Saxton, and Serpa (1986); O'Reilly (1989); O'Reilly, Chatman, and Caldwell (1991).

53. Ouchi (1979).

54. Kotter and Heskett (1992). Cultural strength was rated by financial analysts and managers of competing firms. An average cultural strength score was computed for each firm in the sample and correlated with indicators of organizational performance, including average yearly return on investment, changes in net income, and changes in the firm's market capitalization.

55. Denison (1990).

56. Gagliardi (1986: 125).

57. Hatch (1993, 2004). Hatch (2010) links the cultural dynamics model with the dynamics of organizational identity, building even further on Gagliardi's work.

58. Hatch (1993: 662).

59. Hatch (1993: 667).

60. Hatch (2000).

61. Hatch and Schultz (2008).

62. Alvesson (1990); Kärreman and Rylander (2008); *Scandinavian Journal of Management* (forthcoming), special Issue on 'being branded.'

References

Alvesson, M. (1990) Organization: From substance to image? *Organization Studies*, 11: 373–94.

Austin, J. L. (1962) *How to Do Things with Words*. New York: Oxford.

Bauman, Zygmunt (1973/1999) *Culture as Praxis*. London: Sage.

Boje, David (1991) The storytelling organization: A study of story performance in an office-supply firm. *Administrative Science Quarterly*, 36: 106–26.

—— (1995) Stories of the storytelling organization: A postmodern analysis of Disney as Tamara-land. *Academy of Management Journal*, 38: 997–1035.

Boland, Richard J., Jr. and Tenkasi, Ramkrishnan V. (1995) Perspective making and perspective taking in communities of knowing. *Organization Science*, 6/4: 350–73.

Brooks, Cleanth and Penn Warren, Robert (1948) *Understanding Fiction*. New York: Crofts.

Burke, Kenneth (1945/1969) *A Grammar of Motives*. Berkeley: University of California Press.

Chatman, Jennifer A. and Cha, Sandra Eunyoung (2003) Leading by leveraging culture. *California Management Review*, 45/4: 20–66.

Cohen, Abner (1976) *Two Dimensional Man: An Essay on the Anthropology of Power and Symbolism in Complex Society*. Berkeley: University of California Press.

Cooke, R. and Lafferty, J. (1987) *Organizational Culture Inventory (OCI)*. Plymouth, MI: Human Synergistics.

Cooke, Robert A. and Szumal, Janet L. (2000) Using the organizational culture inventory to understand the operating cultures of organizations. In N. Ashkanasy, C. Wilderom and M. Peterson (eds.), *Handbook of Organizational Culture and Climate*. Thousand Oaks, CA: Sage, 147–62.

Czarniawska, Barbara (1997) *Narrating the Organization: Dramas of Institutional Identity*. Chicago, IL: University of Chicago Press.

—— (1999) *Writing Management: Organization Theory as a Literary Genre*. Oxford: Oxford University Press.

Dandridge, Thomas C., Mitroff, Ian, and Joyce, William F. (1980) Organizational symbolism: A topic to expand organizational analysis. *Academy of Management Review*, 5: 77–82.

De Lorean, John Z. and Wright, J. Patrick (1979) *On a Clear Day You Can See General Motors*. Grosse Pointe, MI: Wright Enterprises.

Deal, Terrence E. and Kennedy, Allan A. (1982) *Corporate Cultures: The Rites and Rituals of Corporate Life*. Reading, MA: Addison-Wesley.

Denison, Daniel R. (1990) *Corporate Culture and Organizational Effectiveness*. New York: John Wiley & Sons Inc.

Ezzy, D. (2001) A simulacrum of workplace community: Individualism and engineered culture. *Sociology*, 35: 631–50.

Gabriel, Yiannis (2000) *Storytelling in Organizations: Facts, Fictions, and Fantasies*. Oxford: Oxford University Press.

Gagliardi, Pasquale (1986) The creation and change of organizational cultures: A conceptual framework. *Organization Studies*, 7: 117–34.

Geertz, Clifford (1973) *Interpretation of Cultures*. New York: Basic Books.

Genette, Gerard (1980) *Narrative Discourse: An Essay in Method* (J. E. Lewin, trans.). Ithaca, NY: Cornell University Press.

Goffman, Erving (1959) *The Presentation of Self in Everyday Life*. Garden City, NY: Doubleday.

Golden-Biddle, Karen and Locke, Karen (1993) Appealing work: An investigation of how ethnographic texts convince. *Organization Science*, 4: 595–616.

—— (1997) *Composing Qualitative Research*. Thousand Oaks, CA: Sage.

Hatch, Mary Jo (1993) The dynamics of organizational culture. *Academy of Management Review*, 18/4: 657–63.

—— (1996) The role of the researcher: An analysis of narrative position in organization theory. *Journal of Management Inquiry*, 5: 359–74.

—— (2000) The cultural dynamics of organizing and change. In N. Ashkanasy, C. Wilderom and M. Peterson (eds.), *Handbook of Organizational Culture and Climate*. Thousand Oaks, CA: Sage, 245–60.

—— (2004) Dynamics in organizational culture. In M.S. Poole and A. Van de Ven (eds.), *Handbook of Organizational Change and Innovation*. Oxford: Oxford University Press, 190–211.

—— (2010) Material and meaning in the dynamics of organizational culture and identity with implications for the leadership of organizational change. In N. Ashkanasy, C. Wilderom, and M. Peterson (eds.), *The Handbook of Organizational Culture and Climate* (2nd edn.). Thousand Oaks, CA: Sage, 341–58.

—— Kostera, M. and Kózmiński, A. K. (2005) *The Three Faces of Leadership: Manager, Artist, Priest*. London: Blackwell.

—— and Schultz, M. (2008) *Taking Brand Initiative: How Corporations Can Align Strategy, Culture and Identity through Corporate Branding*. San Francisco, CA: Jossey-Bass.

—— and Yanow, D. (2003) Organization theory as an interpretive science. In C. Knudsen and H. Tsoukas (eds.), *The Oxford Handbook of Organization Theory: Meta-theoretical Perspectives*. Oxford: Oxford University Press, 61–87.

Herskowitz, Melville J. (1948) *Man and His Works: The Science of Cultural Anthropology*. New York: Alfred A. Knopf.

Hofstede, Geert (1997) *Cultures and Organizations: Software of the Mind* (rev. edn.). New York: McGraw-Hill.

—— (2001) *Culture's Consequences: Comparing Values, Behaviors, Institutions and Organizations across Nations* (2nd edn.). Thousand Oaks, CA: Sage.

—— and Bond, M.H. (1988) The Confucius connection: From cultural roots to economic growth. *Organizational Dynamics*, 16/4: 4–21.

Höpfl, Heather (2002) Playing the part: Reflections on aspects of mere performance in the customer–client relationship. *Journal of Management Studies*, 39: 255–67.

Jaques, Elliott (1952) *The Changing Culture of a Factory*. New York: Dryden Press.

Jenks, Chris (1993) *Culture*. London: Routledge.

Jones, Michael Owen (1996) *Studying Organizational Symbolism*. Thousand Oaks, CA: Sage.

Kärreman, Dan and Rylander, Anna (2008) Managing meaning through branding: The case of a consulting firm. *Organization Studies*, 29: 103–25.

Kilmann, R., Saxton, M., and Serpa, R. (1986) *Gaining Control of the Corporate Culture*. San Francisco, CA: Jossey-Bass.

Kotter, John P. and Heskett, James L. (1992) *Corporate Culture and Performance*. New York: Free Press.

Kristeva, Julia (1984) *Revolution in Poetic Language* (Margaret Waller, trans.). New York: Columbia University Press.

Kunda, G. (1996) *Engineering Culture*. Philadelphia, PA: Temple University Press.

Louis, Meryl Reis (1983) Organizations as culture-bearing milieux. In L. Pondy, P. Frost, G. Morgan, and T. Dandridge (eds.), *Organizational Culture*. Greenwich, CT: JAI Press, 39–54.

Lurie, Irene and Riccucci, Norma M. (2003) Changing the 'culture' of welfare offices: From vision to the front lines. *Administration & Society*, 34/6: 653–77.

MacIntyre, Alasdair (1984) *After Virtue: A Study in Moral Theory*. Notre Dame, IN: University of Notre Dame Press.

Martin, Joanne (1990) Deconstructing organizational taboos: The suppression of gender conflict in organizations. *Organization Science*, 1: 1–22.

—— (1992) *Cultures in Organizations: Three Perspectives*. New York: Oxford University Press.

—— (2002) *Organizational Culture: Mapping the Terrain*. Thousand Oaks, CA: Sage.

—— Feldman, Martha, Hatch, Mary Jo, and Sitkin, Sim (1983) The uniqueness paradox in organizational stories. *Administrative Science Quarterly*, 28: 438–53.

—— and Frost, Peter (1996) The organization culture war games: A struggle for intellectual dominance. In S. R. Clegg and C. Hardy (eds.), *Studying organization: Theory and Method*. London: Sage, 345–67.

—— and Siehl, Caren (1983) Organizational culture and counterculture: An uneasy symbiosis. *Organizational Dynamics*, Autumn: 52–64.

Meyerson, Debra and Martin, Joanne (1987) Cultural change: An integration of three different views. *Journal of Management Studies*, 24: 623–47.

Morgan, Gareth, Frost, Peter J., and Pondy, Louis R. (1983) Organizational symbolism. In L. R. Pondy, P. J. Frost, G. Morgan, and T. C. Dandridge (eds.), *Organizational Symbolism*. Greenwich, CT: JAI Press, 3–35.

Mumby, Dennis K. (1988) *Communication and Power in Organization: Discourse, Ideology and Domination*. Norwood, NJ: Ablex Publishing.

O'Connor, Ellen S. (2000) Plotting the organization: The embedded narrative as a construct for studying change. *Journal of Applied Behavioral Science*, 36/2: 174–93.

O'Reilly, Charles (1989) Corporations, culture, and commitment: Motivation and social control in organizations. *California Management Review*, 31: 9–25.

—— Chatman, Jennifer, and Caldwell, David (1991) People and organizational culture: A Q-sort approach to assessing person–organization fit. *Academy of Management Journal*, 16: 285–303.

Ortner, S. B. (1973) On key symbols. *American Anthropologist*, 75: 1338–46.

Ouchi, William G. (1979) A conceptual framework for the design of organizational control mechanisms. *Management Science*, 25: 833–48.

—— (1981) *Theory Z: How American Business Can Meet the Japanese Challenge*. Reading, MA: Addison-Wesley.

Peters, Thomas J. and Waterman, R. H. (1982) *In Search of Excellence: Lessons from America's Best Run Companies*. New York: Harper & Row.

Pettigrew, Andrew (1979) On studying organizational culture. *Administrative Science Quarterly*, 24: 570–81.

Phillips, Margaret E., Goodman, Richard A., and Sackmann, Sonja A. (1992) Exploring the complex cultural milieu of project teams. *PMNetwork*, 6/8: 20–26.

Rosen, Michael (1985) Breakfast at Spiros: Dramaturgy and dominance. *Journal of Management*, 11: 31–48.

Sandelands, Lloyd and Drazin, Robert (1989) On the language of organization theory. *Organization Studies*, 10/4: 457–78.

Schein, Edgar H. (1984). Coming to a new awareness of organizational culture. *Sloan Management Review*, 25: 3–16.

—— (1991) Organizational culture. *American Psychologist*, 45: 109–19.

—— (1992/1985) *Organizational Culture and Leadership* (2nd edn.). San Francisco, CA: Jossey-Bass.

—— (1996) Culture: The missing concept in organization studies. *Administrative Science Quarterly*, 41: 229–40.

—— (2000) Sense and nonsense about culture and climate. In N. M. Ashkanasy, C. P. M. Wilderom and M.F. Peterson (eds.), *Handbook of Organizational Culture and Climate*. Thousand Oaks, CA: Sage, xxiii–xxx.

Schroeder, Ralph (1992) *Max Weber and the Sociology of Culture*. London: Sage.

Schultz, Majken (1992) Postmodern pictures of culture: A postmodern reflection on the 'Modern notion' of corporate culture. *International Studies of Management and Organization*, 22: 15–36.

—— (1995) *On Studying Organizational Cultures: Diagnosis and Understanding*. Berlin: Walter de Gruyter.

Siehl, Caren and Martin, Joanne (1984) The role of symbolic management: How can managers effectively transmit organizational culture? In J. D. Hunt, D. Hosking, C. Schriesheim, and R. Steward (eds.), *Leaders and Managers: International Perspectives on Managerial Behavior and Leadership*. New York: Pergamon, 227–39.

Strauss, Anselm, Schatzman, Leonard, Ehrlich, Danuta, Bucher, Rue, and Sabshin, Melvin (1963) The hospital and its negotiated order. In Eliot Friedson (ed.) *The Hospital in Modern Society*. London: Free Press of Glencoe, 147–69.

—— (1964) *Psychiatric Ideologies and Institutions*. New York: Free Press.

Trice, Harrison M. and Beyer, Janice M. (1993) *The Cultures of Work Organizations*. Englewood Cliffs, NJ: Prentice-Hall.

Tylor, Edward Burnett (1958) *Primitive Culture: Researches into the Development of Mythology, Philosophy, Religion, Art and Custom*. Gloucester, MA: Smith (first published in 1871).

Van Maanen, John (1988) *Tales of the Field: On Writing Ethnography*. Chicago, IL: University of Chicago Press.

—— (2005) Symbolism. In N. Nicholson, P. G. Audia, and M. M. Pillutla (eds.), *The Blackwell Encyclopedia of Management* (2nd edn.). London: Blackwell, 383.

—— and Barley, Stephen R. (1984) Occupational communities: Culture and control in organizations. In B. M. Staw and L. L. Cummings (eds.), *Research in Organizational Behavior*. Greenwich, CT: JAI Press, vi. 287–366.

Webber, A. M. (1992) Japanese-style entrepreneurship: An interview with SOFTBANK's CEO, Masayoshi Son. *Harvard Business Review*, Jan.–Feb.: 93–103.

Further reading

Alvesson, Matts and Berg, Per Olaf (1992) *Corporate Culture and Organizational Symbolism: An Overview*. New York: Walter de Gruyter.

Ashkanasy, Neal M., Wilderom, Celeste P. M., and Peterson, Mark F. (2010) (eds.) *Handbook of Organizational Culture and Climate*, 2nd Edn. Thousand Oaks, CA: Sage.

Brown, Richard Harvey (1987) *Society as Text: Essays on Rhetoric, Reason and Reality*. Chicago, IL: University of Chicago Press.

Dandridge, Thomas C., Mitroff, Ian, and Joyce, W. F. (1980) Organizational symbolism: A topic to expand organizational analysis. *Academy of Management Review*, 5: 77–82.

Eisenberg, Eric M. and Riley, Patricia (1988) Organizational symbols and sense-making. In G. M. Goldhaber and G. A. Barnett (eds.), *Handbook of Organizational Communication*. Norwood, NJ: Ablex.

Frost, P., Moore, L., Louis, M., Lundberg, C., and Martin, J. (1985) (eds.) *Organizational Culture*. Beverly Hills, CA: Sage.

——(1991) (eds.) *Reframing Organizational Culture*. Newbury Park, CA: Sage.

Gabriel, Yiannis (2004) (ed.) *Myths, Stories and Organizations: Premodern Narratives for Our Times*. Oxford: Oxford University Press.

Gagliardi, Pasquale (1990) (ed.) *Symbols and Artifacts: Views of the Corporate Landscape*. Berlin: Walter de Gruyter.

Hatch, M.J. (2010) Culture Stanford's way. In Claudia Bird Schoonhoven and Frank Dobbin (eds.), *Stanford's Organization Theory Renaissance, 1970–2000, Research in the Sociology of Organizations*, Vol. 28, Emerald Group, 71–96.

Johansson, B. and Woodilla, J. (2005) *Irony and Organisations: Epistemological Claims and Supporting Field Stories*. Frederiksberg: Copenhagen Business School Press.

Linstead, Stephen and Grafton-Small, Robert (1992) On reading organizational culture. *Organization Studies*, 13: 331–56.

Mangham, I. L. and Overington, M. A. (1987) *Organizations as Theater: Social Psychology and Dramatic Performance*. Chichester: John Wiley & Sons Ltd.

Martin, Joanne (1982) Stories and scripts in organizational settings. In A. Hastorf and A. Isen (eds.), *Cognitive and Social Psychology*. London: Routledge, 255–305.

Pfeffer, Jeffrey (1981) Management as symbolic action: The creation and maintenance of organizational paradigms. In L. L. Cummings and B. M. Staw (eds.), *Research in Organizational Behavior*, 3: 1–52.

Pondy, Lou, Frost, Peter, Morgan, Gareth, and Dandridge, Tom (1983) *Organizational Symbolism*. Greenwich, CT: JAI Press.

Schein, Edgar H. (1999) *The Corporate Culture Survival Guide*. San Francisco, CA: Jossey-Bass.

Smircich, Linda and Calas, Marta (1987) Organizational culture, a critical assessment. In F. Jablin, L. Putnam, K. Roberts, and L. Porter (eds.), *The Handbook of Organizational Communication*. Beverly Hills, CA: Sage, 228–63.

Turner, Barry A. (1990) (ed.) *Organizational Symbolism*. Berlin: Walter de Gruyter.

Williams, Raymond (1983) *Keywords: A Vocabulary of Culture and Society* (rev. edn.). New York: Oxford University Press.

Young, Ed (1989) On naming the rose: Interests and multiple meanings as elements of organizational change. *Organizational Studies*, 10: 187–206.

7 The physical structure of organizations

The very physicality of built space gives organizations objective characteristics that can be measured and correlated with outcomes such as efficiency and performance. This gives the topic great appeal among some modernists, while others think using abstract concepts and theories to explain anything as objective as a building is overkill. However, just because physical structures are tangible does not mean they are not also symbolic, and, even though you can demolish physical structures with a wrecking ball, you can also deconstruct their powerful influences using postmodernism. Physical structure and the space it surrounds are suitable for theorizing from all perspectives.

The interest of organization theorists in physical structure can generally be traced to empirical research carried out at the Hawthorne Works of Western Electric in the late 1920s and early 1930s.[1] Led by Harvard University professor Elton Mayo, the Hawthorne researchers performed a series of field observations and experiments focused, among other things, on learning how changes in the physical environment of work affect worker productivity. In a key experiment subjects were moved into an enclosed workroom where they performed their normal tasks under various manipulated conditions.

For one of the conditions of the field experiment conducted in the special room, researchers systematically increased the amount of available light while measuring the workers' output. As was anticipated, worker productivity increased along with illumination levels. But, to make certain that their experimental manipulation was causing the productivity gains, the researchers systematically reduced illumination levels again. To their surprise, productivity levels continued to rise, even when the workers were operating in near darkness.[2]

The Hawthorne researchers concluded that the workers believed the special room, and the attentions lavished upon them, meant *they* were special, and it was this social effect—later called the Hawthorne Effect—that motivated them. Because these empirical studies made social influences on worker productivity seem more potent than the effects of physical structure, the Hawthorne Studies deflected research interest away from physical structure for quite a long time.

Disinterest in physical structure in organization theory continued even after, in 1950, the influential American sociologist George Homans pointed out that the Hawthorne Effect was triggered by changes to the physical environment of work after all—the famous effect was the result of moving workers to a new room![3] In spite of Homan's efforts to reclaim it, the topic of physical structure remained a theoretical backwater until the 1970s and 1980s when environmental psychologists and human factors engineers revived this line of research; a small group of organization theorists followed their lead.[4]

This chapter departs from modernist definitions of basic elements of physical structure: geography, layout, landscaping, exterior design, and décor. But as you will soon see, the theories and concepts informed by these elements nearly always invite symbolic understanding. For this reason the path this chapter follows wends from mostly modern to increasingly symbolic ideas, never quite being able to draw a clear line between them. Linking the materiality of physical structure to identity will show that it is just as hard to limit the symbolic uses and effects of physical structure to one level of analysis, as it is to contain it in a single perspective. A postmodern figure ground reversal will then turn our attention from physical structures to the spaces they leave empty, pulling into our path concepts of spatiality and embodiment. The chapter ends by overturning the critical postmodern assumption that all buildings breed control, thereby suggesting a possible post-postmodern future.

Organization as arrangement in space and time

American organization theorist Jeffrey Pfeffer, a major proponent of the modern perspective, observed about physical structure that, since humans cannot walk through walls or see through floors, their behavior is shaped by the physical structures they occupy.[5] When you look at walls and floors, and other material components of organizations, from a strictly modern perspective, you see that physical structure both enables and constrains behavior. This section explores the most widely studied of its components: organizational geography, layout, landscaping, architectural features, and décor.

Organizational geographies: Space, time, and place

An organization has a physical presence that extends in space and time. Its **physical geography** contains all those points in space where the organization conducts its business, including not only the locations of facilities owned or operated by the organization, but also locations in which they carry out their business, such as the facilities of partners, customers, suppliers, or other stakeholders.

If you superimpose the physical reach of an organization's activities on a map of the world, like airlines do with their route maps (see Figure 7.1), it will reveal a rough approximation of the **territorial extent** of that organization's physical geography. Of course if the organization you are interested in is NASA, or the China National Space Administration, you will need a bigger map!

Mapping an organization's territorial extent raises the question of **scale**.[6] NASA and the China National Space Administration deal with their physical organizations on an interplanetary and sometimes an intergalactic scale, while most other organizations operate only on a local, regional, national, or global scale. Cities, neighborhoods, buildings, offices, and human bodies offer other scales on which you can imagine and describe the physical structure of organization, each bringing particular concerns into view. For example, if you are interested in geography at the scale of office buildings, office layout will become important.

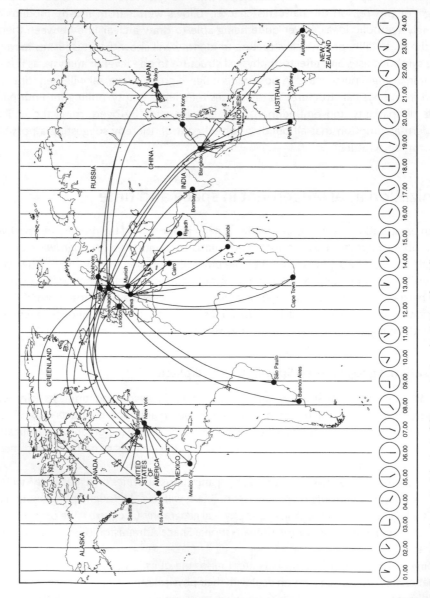

Figure 7.1 Route map showing the territorial extent of the organizational activities of an airline

By measuring territorial extent on any scale, you can examine relationships between physical structure and other aspects of organizing. For example, you will quickly confirm Einstein's theory that space and time are interrelated. Holding all else constant, the more widely an organization's activities are distributed in space, the more time organizational members will devote to travel. The challenges of communicating and coordinating across time zones, providing support during a crisis, exposure to different cultural influences, and disorientation are but a few socio-cultural effects organizations experience with expansive geographies. However, bear in mind that relationships between space and time can be altered by technology; **time-space compression** has followed innovations in electronic communication and improvements in transportation.[7]

Issues of **logistics** related to territorial extent are of particular concern for organizations that deal in physical materials and products. These concerns include: access to various modes of transportation (domestic and international airports, waterways, etc.), distance to markets (including labor, supply, and consumer markets), and the speed and costs of communication, coordination, transportation, and travel. You will want to analyze the logistical implications of an organization's territorial extent in relation to all the connections you identify in a resource dependence analysis, and think about how geographical **location** can be used strategically to manage them. For example, locating near influential stakeholders like customers, regulatory agencies, funding institutions, or universities engaged in relevant basic research offers organizations advantages in terms of managing critical dependencies.

In addition to mapping and analyzing the numerous implications of an organization's geographic distribution you will want to consider pertinent **geographic features** of its locations. In Figure 3.4 we referred to these as the physical sector of the environment. Be sure to consider the features of both physical geography—climate, terrain, and natural resources—and human geography, such as population density, industrialization, urbanization, and the presence (or absence) of different races or ethnic minorities. Features of geography can affect many aspects of organizing.

Take employee recruiting as just one example. Proximity to lakes, mountains, or an ocean, or to the varied attractions of a large urban center, influences the lifestyles of organizational members so the attractiveness of an organization's location will help or hinder it in hiring the employees it most desires. Compare the lifestyles of employees living in Madrid, Johannesburg, Moscow, São Paulo, San Francisco, and Beijing, or compare any of these to what rural locations far from any large metropolitan or industrialized area have to offer. As you can see with recruiting, the effects of organizational geography percolate throughout organizations. For marketing and corporate communication, the features of an organization's geography can affect corporate image, reputation, and organizational identity. For instance, consider the importance of a Wall Street address for an investment firm operating in New York, or a City address for one in London.

That geography combines instrumental and symbolic effects offers just one of many points of contact between the modern and symbolic perspectives as they mingle within the conceptual domain of physical structure. Geographers distinguish these perspectives by differentiating **space and place**. The more instrumental concerns of space (e.g., distances and their logistical effects) contrast with those of place, which involve experiences of and interpretations given to regions of space.[8] You can use the theater metaphor to think of place as a stage on which life's drama unfolds; like the theatrical stage, place provides more than a spatial backdrop for action, it becomes a character in the play.[9]

Most people have strong reactions to familiar place images. To feel this effect watch a film that shows a place where you have lived or visited. Emotional and aesthetic associations with physical spaces or locations produce the symbolic sense of place that makes them meaningful. Combining the physicality of space with the meaning of place makes physical structures and their prominent features into symbols in the same way that other artifacts infused with meaning become symbols.

From the symbolic perspective the artifactual aspects of physical structure become hard to distinguish from culture, while the modern perspective implicates physical structure in social structure and technology. You can see all of these connecting points in layout and landscaping, where you will also find a link to power and the postmodern perspective.

Layout and landscaping

Layout refers to the spatial arrangements of buildings and grounds. Within buildings, it carves up and helps to define interior spaces by determining the placement of objects, especially walls, furnishings, equipment, and employees. When a site has multiple buildings, their **orientation** to one another, including the **landscaping** that physically and aesthetically links them with walkways and vegetation, is another aspect of layout to consider.

When multiple buildings on a site are deliberately arranged to look like a college campus, like Google's Googleplex in Mountain View, California, the symbolic aspects of layout come into view.[10] For example, campus style layouts are typically designed with the intention to offer employees intellectual, emotional, and aesthetic inspiration by referencing university life. In the most effective applications they invite a highly educated workforce to see the organization as a seamless continuation of their earlier learning experiences, and offer nostalgic references to the past that invite them to continue learning. Of course such elegiac sentiments invite critical postmodern deconstruction, pointing out, for example, how references to student life lower employee expectations for power, pay, and privilege.

Office and workstation arrangements and locations of shared facilities such as cafeterias, drinking fountains, restrooms, and meeting rooms, all contribute to internal layout, as does the assignment of people to specific locations, and activities to particular spatial regions. For example, Figure 7.2 illustrates the co-location of similar forms of work activity common in many organizations.

That layout affects coordination can be seen easily in the automated assembly line where individuals and their tools are located at fixed positions along a moving line of partly assembled products. Finding an effective layout involves matching locations with task requirements. Conversely, many inefficiencies and inconveniences will be introduced into a work process if layout is poorly conceived. Whenever workers perform sequential or reciprocally interdependent tasks, their ability to coordinate their activities will be affected by the layout of the workspaces they occupy and the proximity of equipment and co-workers.

All but the smallest organizations face another dilemma of layout—choosing whether to locate managers' offices close to their subordinates, or to group them in one place for ease

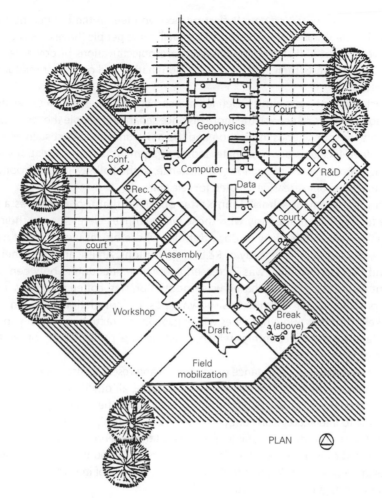

Figure 7.2 Layout of activity regions in a geophysics firm

Source: Doxtater (1990: 121, Fig. 2). By permission of Walter de Gruyter.

of coordination between departments or divisions. The typical choice is to co-locate top executives along with key staff personnel, and then locate other managers' offices close to those they manage. This means that executives must either travel to their subordinates whenever they require face-to-face contact or ask their subordinates to come to them. Such choices involve numerous symbolic implications, such as signaling either the privileges of power or an egalitarian culture, as well as contributing to technical considerations including efficiency and cost effectiveness.

Postmodernists say that physical structure encodes power in a spatial language that speaks unobtrusively. Try making the following conceptual experiment: contrast a large classroom, where you and fellow students are forced to face the teacher because your chairs are bolted to the floor, with a small seminar style classroom where everyone sits around a circular conference table, or with a room that allows the teacher sometimes to arrange the chairs into a circle with no table separating you. Reflect on how you feel in these differently arranged classrooms, but think about others' responses as well; some people thrive on structure, while others thrive without it. If spatial arrangements are objectifications of power relations, as postmodernism suggests, then layout can serve domination and control or reinforce liberty and democracy.

One effect of layout is **proximity**. Defined as nearness in space, proximity has both temporal and social effects. In general the more distance separating people the fewer will be the opportunities for spontaneous interaction and the more time and effort such activities will consume. When locations are proximate and/or equipment is shared, relationships often form through spontaneous interactions, for instance, in the hallway, in a restroom, around the coffee machine, or in areas designated for relaxing.

American management scholar John Kotter observed that top executives and office workers interacted spontaneously with those whose offices were close to theirs, something they were much less likely to do with those whose offices were distant from their own.[11] And, in a ten-year long study of R&D organizations, American researcher Thomas Allen found that performance was increased by chance encounters between members of different project teams who shared washrooms, libraries, coffee machines, or photocopy equipment.[12] Other research has shown a positive correlation between proximity and the likelihood that two employees will engage in interaction, especially interaction involving face-to-face encounters, which most people prefer to all other forms of communication.[13]

The obverse of proximity is distance or separation and research also reveals the influence of these dimensions of layout on behavior. For example, all other factors being equal, the more distance between the workstations of two individuals, the less likely they are to share information or to interact regularly enough to form a relationship. Separation by assignment to different floors or to different buildings decreases the likelihood of interaction even further.[14] Other studies suggest that office location affects the amount and type of information employees process, and is related to the development and use of informal channels of communication such as grapevines and rumor mills.[15]

Task interdependence comes into play in explaining the effects of physical structure on behavior and performance.[16] The need for proximity created by task interdependence places demands on spatial configuration whose physicality constrains how far an organization can go to accommodate task interdependence. This is because there are physical limits as to how many people can be located close together, and no office can have more than two adjacent workspaces along the same hallway.[17]

Proximity, distance, and separation are not the only dimensions of physical structure to interest modernist organization theorists. Openness, visibility, accessibility, and privacy provide another interrelated set. **Openness** and **visibility** come from the lack of physical boundaries such as walls and partitions, and/or their transparency. Locating workstations at fixed points along a factory assembly line, for example, permits easy surveillance of workers by management—it is easy to spot an empty station or someone goofing off.

In offices, typically, openness, visibility, and accessibility are all positively related to each other and negatively related to privacy. **Accessibility** is a measure of how easy it is for others to interact with a person in their assigned work area, while **privacy** offers the ability to regulate interaction with others. A common way of explaining the effects of these variables on office workers involves contrasting open with private office environments.

Open offices have either glass walls, partitions with no doors, or use such things as file cabinets, bookcases, or living plants to visually separate work areas. The openness these office spaces provide their occupants affords limited privacy and enhances accessibility to co-workers and visibility to supervisors. **Private offices** have floor-to-ceiling walls that restrict their visibility to others, usually with a door allowing their occupants full enclosure and the ability to control their accessibility and privacy as they see fit, unless their organization adopts an open door policy!

As the open door policy illustrates, it is important to recognize the limits of design to determine outcomes associated with proximity, openness, visibility, accessibility, and privacy. Physical structures enhance the likelihood of various outcomes rather than determine them. Some of these limitations arise from interpretations embedded in the symbolism of physical space, and others from the influences coming from social structure or technology. For example, regardless of the configuration of their physical spaces, secretaries and other assistants typically experience many interruptions to their work due to the demands of high task interdependence and their relatively low position in most hierarchies. Their service-oriented tasks and relatively low position in the hierarchy combine to make them accessible to co-workers in ways that overwhelm some effects of physical structure.

Physical barriers, such as movable partitions and fixed walls, support, enable, or enhance at least some forms of interaction. In particular, meetings, brief interruptions, confidential conversations, and teamwork have all been shown to occur significantly more often, and for longer periods of time, when co-workers occupy spaces enclosed by walls.[18] However, even though modernist studies show that these forms of interaction are more likely to occur in closed than in open offices, many people continue to believe that open office settings with few or no physical barriers encourage interaction and communication.

One explanation for the belief that open offices encourage communication stays well within the modern perspective. Some groups, especially innovative design teams, claim that the intimate sharing of their workspaces stimulates creativity and supports teamwork. However, enclosure rather than openness seems the most likely explanation here, since the groups in question generally had some sort of physical barrier separating them from the rest of the organization. A second explanation relies upon the symbolic perspective: some people, through symbolic association, conflate the openness of offices and open communication. My study contrasting the effects of open and closed offices sheds some light on this matter.[19]

While my study of knowledge workers in high technology companies in Silicon Valley confirmed that those in open plan offices spent less time interacting with others than did those in closed offices, it also allowed me to observe people at close range and talk to them about why this was so. For instance, in some open offices the occupants created cultural norms prohibiting interference with others' ability to get their work done, sometimes using headphones or traffic lights rigged to glow red to communicate their desire not to be disturbed.

In other open plan offices I studied visibility produced communication efficiencies, for instance, I saw people climb up on their desks to peer out over the vast sea of partitions, which enabled them to ascertain whether potential interaction partners were available. If they were not, the employee would sit back down at the desk to continue what they were doing with minimal interruption to their own or anyone else's work. In contrast, I observed many occupants of closed offices taking a walk to look for desired interaction partners, sometimes bumping into others and conducting spontaneous interactions in the process.

The more or less instrumental explanations my observations offer do not preclude there also being symbolic influences on behavior. Even after being presented with the findings of my study as encouragement to accept management's offer of private offices so as to enhance their communication, the open office inhabitants in my study continued to insist they benefited from the greater communication they enjoyed in their open offices and voted to stay put. I concluded that both instrumental and symbolic influences of physical space were in operation and, in this case, conflicted with rather than supported one another.

The demands of near continuous travel by some executives as well as many other professionals who routinely visit sites away from their home offices have led to an innovation in layout design known as **hot desking**. The practice of hot desking optimizes the use of space by taking advantage of away time and may have been inspired by 'hot racking' of sailors at sea, a reference to sharing bunks. At any given time part of a naval crew is on duty, and as space is severely limited on board any vessel, hot racking provides obvious advantages. Hot desking in organizations, where permanent offices are assigned on an as-needed basis, similarly produces flexibility as well as considerable cost savings.

Hot desking requires many adjustments to work practices. For example, employees must store essential work items in locked trollies they can roll to their assigned workspace, and it helps if they use online storage for documents that can be accessed from anywhere. In an elaboration of hot desking, known as **hoteling**, companies operate a reception desk to handle office allocations and meeting room schedules, and to arrange for secretarial, concierge, and computer support services.

Cost savings accrue to hot desking and hoteling through the minimization of expenses associated with building, supporting, and maintaining office space. The possibility to temporarily co-locate entire groups of employees working together on a temporary project is another advantage. A major disadvantage is that employees lose the symbolic resource of an office to communicate their identity and status. Another is the incessant need for reorientation to find one's way around new spaces, and consequently a certain amount of disorientation. Disorientation can destroy organizational culture and increase stress, when employees find it difficult to relate to others similarly disoriented by not being able to expect anyone to be anywhere.

The converse of disorientation, familiarity is promoted by layouts that encourage repeated face-to-face contact, which can also support subculture formation. Be sure to notice how the socio-cultural effects of physical structure that arise from separating people combine with those that bring them together. This is how physical structures can lend support to silos or subcultural differences even as they enable communication and coordination between different groups of people. The effects of physical structure are rarely as simple as their objectivity can make them seem.

Design features, décor, and dress

Façade, focal points, furnishings, lighting fixtures, ceiling and wall treatments, windows and floor coverings, use of color and form, and displays of anything from tropical foliage and art to advertising, products, and technology, are just some of the features of architectural design and décor found in organizations. They combine to give the sensory environment of an organization's physical structure an aesthetic ambiance, while at the same time providing material objects to be arranged in physical space and symbolic objects with which to forge meaning.

Because design features color and texture experiences in and of spaces, they provoke aesthetic judgments ranging from ugly to nondescript, tolerable, pleasing, beautiful, and inspiring. Of course design features affect more mundane sensory experiences as well, including temperature, air quality, illumination, noise levels, and smells, all of which produce various human physiological responses that can affect performance and attitudes as well as aesthetic judgments. Aesthetic and physiological experiences have entered into theories of how physical structure affects an organization and its inhabitants.

Be aware that aesthetic judgments are heavily influenced by personal taste. For the purposes of organizational analysis your personal preferences are less important than your sensitivity to the fact that organizations evoke aesthetic responses that color the interpretations of employees and other members of the organizational community. Remember that it is their interpretations and reactions that matter when you want to uncover the aesthetic effects of physical structure on organization. But be sure to note how physical structure is affecting you so that you can separate out your reactions from those of others.

The reactions that architectural features of buildings are known or believed to provoke can be used symbolically to express and represent organizational ideas like culture, identity, or strategy. Conversely, knowing that architectural design is used in these symbolic ways means that careful readings of physical structure can reveal an organization's culture, strategy, and so on. Either way you look at it, taking account of the symbolism of physical structure means incorporating interpretation into your concepts and theories, with all the multiplicity of meaning this entails.

Take the simple example of an organization that occupies low-rent facilities and furnishes its offices minimally and inexpensively. Such an organization may be communicating its commitment to a low-cost strategy or telling you that the organization is unconcerned about its physical appearance, or something else entirely, and maybe all this and more. Bear in mind that the meanings of a physical structure, like any other artifact or symbol, are distributed among those whose interpretations construct social reality.

Multiplicity of meaning limits the amount of symbolic control that can be exercised through design, but so too do unintended meanings. Unplanned and emergent aspects of architectural design can impinge on behavioral control. I once toured a newly opened office building with its architect and a corporate executive. As we moved through the space we came upon an oversized golf umbrella hung at a precarious but alluring angle in the large atrium designed as the building's interior focal point and a source of natural light to illuminate workspaces. The umbrella was both a practical means of blocking an unforeseen beam of sunlight that hit a worker's desktop every afternoon, and a colorful addition to an otherwise bland interior.

Buildings are never perfectly designed, and once constructed, do not long remain the same. Seen in this light the umbrella was an emergent feature of living architecture, a spontaneous response to the unplanned effect of the light beam. Knowing this, the architect greeted the umbrella with delight that the occupants of the building were beginning to 'own their space.' Meanwhile the executive bemoaned the loss of the pristine look of the building, and presumably his control over it.

An example of an unintended interpretation of built space comes from the University of Notre Dame in South Bend, Indiana, where I grew up. Notre Dame is famous for the many championship football teams it has contributed to college athletics in the United States. Some years ago this Roman Catholic institution built a large new library building as an architectural focal point for the entire campus, adorning its façade with a beautiful mosaic featuring Jesus Christ (see Figure 7.3). To understand the rest of this story you need to know that, in American style football, when one team scores a goal or 'touchdown' the official in charge indicates the accomplishment by raising his outstretched arms in a gesture similar to that of Jesus as depicted in the mosaic. What apparently no one foresaw when choosing the image is the connection between Christ and football, the two most important symbols of campus culture. It was this connection that produced the mosaic's unintended but nonetheless widely adopted name: Touchdown Jesus.

That décor in building design can both express and reveal a great deal about an organization has been established, but how does décor operate? Scottish architecture critic and

Figure 7.3 Notre Dame library mosaic
Photograph by Joseph C. Fross.

professor of urbanism Witold Rybczynski likened organizational décor to dress in order to explain its technical, social, and perceptual mechanisms:

> The first is technical. Décor, like dress, incorporates fabrics ... [and] ... architecture sometimes directly mimics dress. The garlands in eighteenth-century buildings are sculpted or painted versions of the sashes and flowered ornaments worn by men and women. The ancient Greeks incorporated elements of dress in temple architecture. ... Ancient authors likened the vertical flutes [of Greek colonnades] to the folds in a chiton, or tunic.
>
> The second connection between dress and décor is social. ... Since homes and clothes are timeworn ways in which to convey status, there is a conformity in the types of materials and symbols used to convey social standing. If family coats of arms are displayed, they will be seen on wall medallions as well as on blazer buttons. If gold is treasured, the wealthy will wear gold braid and surround themselves with gilt moldings. If this is considered too flashy, other materials can convey status: stainless steel kitchen appliances and stainless steel watch bracelets. ... In a more general sense—and this has nothing to do with conspicuous consumption—both homes and clothes convey values.
>
> The third connection between dress and décor concerns perception. Architecture, interior decorations, and fashion design are three distinct fields, yet we experience them with the same eye. Whether we look at dress or décor, we bring the same visual bias, the same sensibility, the same taste. This sensibility is not constant. Sometimes we appreciate simplicity, sometimes complexity.[20]

Of course dress becomes indistinguishable from décor when formal dress codes or an informally adopted style of dress join other features of organizational décor to give an organization a particular look and feel. IBM professionals used to be known for their dark suits and white shirts, UPS insists that all delivery personnel wear the same brown uniforms, and costumes are a time-honored feature at Disneyland parks. Although not formally prescribed, the casual attire adopted by those who work in Silicon Valley communicates organizational style through dress, too. Organizational modes of attire, whether voluntary or imposed, formal or informal, communicate organizational, group, and/or individual identities.[21]

Physical structure and organizational identity

Because the physical appearance of an organization is a potent medium in which to create a lasting sense of place, some modernist managers attempt to influence organizational identity, image, and reputation by focusing on their organization's appearance. And just as components of physical structure provide organizational identity markers, so too do they provide employees with symbolic material with which to construct and embellish their individual and group identities.

Symbolic expressions of organizational identity

Wally Olins, globally recognized British co-founder of corporate identity consultants Wolff-Olins and Chairman of Saffron Brand Consultants, has long promoted architecture as a form of corporate communication.[22] For example, he suggested that specific messages can be communicated via architectural design: a very tall building might be used to symbolize an intention to push the organization to higher levels of performance or, in the case of an aerospace engineering firm, to reach for the stars.

You need to recognize, of course, that in some cultures different interpretations hold. For example, American public administration theorist Dvora Yanow described how, in India, executive offices are more likely to be located on lower rather than upper floors of office buildings. She noted as one possible explanation that problems with electricity and unpredictable or nonexistent elevators make accessibility by foot an attractive feature of lower floor locations, another being that, in Hindu traditions, the soul sits in the center of the body (rather than in the head).[23]

You have met the trouble with cross-cultural interpretations many times already: symbols carry multiple meanings. Knowing this, Olins took a further step claiming that, when they are carefully designed to complement each other, dramatic architectural features (façade, roofline, lighting effects, office interiors, decorating themes), product design, company logos, corporate literature (e.g., annual reports, brochures), and styles of dress (uniforms, dress codes) can influence impressions of organizational credibility and character that symbolically reinforce strategic vision as well as corporate identity. Olins's theory is that, when a multiplicity of coherent symbols meets a multiplicity of meaning, architects, designers, and managers have a better chance to shape organizational identity, image, and reputation. His solution is a symbolic extension of the principle of requisite variety from systems theory.

Let's try to combine some theories here. Olins's idea of a brand as packaging for an organization's identity resonates with Rybczynski's theory about architectural décor as dress. If corporate brands are to organizational identity what dress is to décor, then Rybczynski's theory suggests that corporate brands use a combination of technical, social, and perceptual mechanisms to make organizational identities into tactile and fashionable status symbols. Just imagine the field day postmodernists can have with that idea!

Before we get too carried away, let's consider some other symbolic components of physical structure to see how they relate to organizational identity. When people imbue the buildings and grounds of an organization with a sense of place their place associations can contribute to organizational identity.[24] Places can be made memorable with a dramatic building façade, an extraordinary piece of sculpture, a landscaping feature made into a focal point, or some other eye-catching element that becomes associated with the organization. For example, every time I walk into the main courtyard of my publishers at Oxford University Press (OUP), I see the enormous old tree that has been standing there for donkey's years. The notion of 'the tree of knowledge' leaps involuntarily into my mind combining in my imagination with the organization's main product—academic books.

My image of OUP in response to the tree-dominated courtyard is a powerful and highly personal effect of the combined forces of organizational identity and architecture. It contributes both to my sense of OUP as a place, and to my identity as an OUP author. My experience is but one distributed and momentary occurrence within the entire symbolic constellation of OUP identity/image/brand/reputation, a constellation that shifts and changes every time someone encounters and reacts to some part of the whole. From the symbolic perspective, the accumulation of distributed organizational identity/image/brand/reputation components, and the arc of their ever-changing trajectory, produces the social construction we call OUP.

If you feel enthusiasm to harness organizational symbols, as Olins suggested is possible, please remember that interpretations such as those evoked by physical structure can be, not only numerous, but contradictory and surprising. For example, an exquisite new corporate head-quarters building may favorably impress investors ('they must be generating great wealth to afford such a wonderful facility'), customers ('this kind of opulence indicates real staying power'), and community leaders ('what a marvelous aesthetic complement to the community'), while simultaneously being viewed as irresponsible by union leaders ('that money could have gone into better wage packets'), and environmentalists ('a little less squandering on executive perks and more environmental projects might have been possible'). Never assume that the intended meaning designers and executives use to create their architectural designs are the only meanings their designs allow. And bear in mind that insofar as it is a distributed phenomenon, identity, like the effects of physical structure that support it, can never be completely controlled.

Claiming of group identity using territorial boundaries

Shared workspaces define territories that become physically and symbolically associated with the people and processes that inhabit them. As is true among other animal species, humans will mark their territory and defend it. When organizations are divided into multiple territories to accommodate the different activities carried out within them (e.g., marketing, accounting, finance, human resources), their occupants are likely to become territorial about their space, with implications for subcultures and silos

Groups will physically mark their organizational territories with signs, a particular decorative style, or other visual expressions of ownership. These practices provide signals that can be read by others concerning inclusion and exclusion (i.e., who can enter freely and who cannot), what the group wants to be known for (e.g., look at what is hung on walls or otherwise displayed, the style of furnishings and the décor), and where its boundaries lie.

Although there has not been much empirical investigation of the phenomenon, the available evidence suggests that the physical marking of group boundaries is associated with strong group identity in organizations.[25] J.D. Wineman found evidence that the presence of physical barriers around groups (e.g., walls, partitions, furniture) influenced group cohesiveness and interpersonal relationships.[26] He also found that prior cohesiveness compensated for the negative effects of an inadequate physical environment, underscoring the interconnection of the physical and social dimensions of organization structures.

In *Street Corner Society* William Foote Whyte noted that the emergence of street gang subcultures coincided with the marking of territories.[27] What is not known is whether boundaries give groups their strong sense of identity or whether groups in the process of forming a strong identity tend to mark their boundaries. It is possible, of course, these happen simultaneously. Remember too that strong group identity can interfere with inter-group cooperation, which is why silos and subcultural differences can become problematic.

Individual identity markers and personalization

A large office in a privileged location displaying high quality furnishings and fine art is consistently associated with high status for employees of many organizations around the world.[28] Thus, managers of organizations can represent hierarchy and communicate their power and social status using the language of physical geography, layout, and design features. You can reverse engineer some of this meaning back out of physical structure if you want to read individual status or position in the organizational hierarchy. For example, access to more important figures communicates higher status than does access to less important people, the latter being the case for middle managers located close to their subordinates and away from their superiors. Proximity to conveniences like parking spaces or having one's own restroom, coffee machine, or dining area indicates a position at the top of the hierarchy.

Be alert to status markers that may not match your preconceived expectations. In the absence of traditional status indicators, individuals from high power distance culture may improvise symbols of distinction. In one such case the location of cheap coat racks, initially purchased because building designers neglected to install closets in the organization's new building, served to identify the most powerful members of the organization. When the coat racks were first introduced they were made available to anyone who wanted them on a first come, first served basis. Over the course of only a few weeks, however, they migrated into the cubicles of those with the greatest status. In another case, the purchase of work group coffee pots became an informal indicator of status; however, this time the migration was to the offices of lower status employees who were expected to make coffee for their bosses and co-workers.

In organizations with low power distance cultures, high-ranking individuals may choose to personally and symbolically underscore the value for equality by foregoing status markers and other privileges. In organizations you always have to be sensitive to the absence of things as well as to what you see, for example, that a company has no reserved parking spaces.

Another issue involving individual identity expression through physical structure arises in the **personalization of space**. Individuals will sometimes tell you a great deal about their identity through office decoration. Unless prohibited, many will display personal artifacts ranging from family photos, to collections of objects or cartoons, memorabilia, and so on. It can be hard to know what these mean without interviewing those involved, though some postmodernists interpret the personalization of workspaces generically as indicating employee efforts to regain lost control over their self-identity, usurped by their organizations.

Physical structure in theories of organization and organizing

The examples provided in this chapter indicate some of the ways that the interests of the modern, symbolic, and postmodern perspectives intermingle in the study of physical structure. They also show that various components of physical structure straddle the boundaries between, participate in, and extend into technology, social structure, culture, and power. This section presents organization theories explaining how physical structure relates to these other basic concepts of organization theory.

Physical structure and culture: Symbolic conditioning

Think about how you instantly know by your physical surroundings whether you are at home or at work, in your own office, or in someone else's, and how this knowledge triggers various rituals and routines. Or consider the employee who works at home but finds it necessary to dress in a suit and say goodbye to family members before going to work in the next room, all in order to overcome the institutionalized meaning staying at home normally conveys and signal to family members that they are not to interrupt.

These examples illustrate the power of built spaces to symbolically condition expectations and behavior.[29] Such responses can become so automatic that, in the case of practitioners of the Catholic faith, the mere sight of an altar provokes behaviors such as genuflection and making the sign of the cross, often ushering in memories of past religious experiences and the emotions associated with them. Because the stimulus to which such responses have been conditioned is a symbol (the suit and tie or the crucifix on the alter), this sort of conditioning has been called **symbolic conditioning**.

Symbolic conditioning extends to all sorts of organizational behavior. For example, the counter of a McDonald's restaurant indicates that customers should queue up to receive service from employees also conditioned to stand behind the counter and wait on customers in the order in which they present themselves (see Figure 7.4). Other places to look for symbolically conditioned behavior include outside closed office doors, and in and around reception desks, libraries, and meeting rooms.

Symbolic conditioning depends on the formation of unconscious links between physical structure and the normal routines that make up much of daily life both in and out of organizations. For instance the habit of responding to others in an impersonal way is typical of many business cultures and can become symbolically conditioned to the physical surroundings of the workplace. As a result it is not uncommon to find people who want to interact with each other in more personal ways meeting outside their office settings.

Then again, so-called symbolic conditioning may not be purely symbolic, it can be physiological as well. French anthropologist Claude Levi-Strauss discovered that the Bororo tribe in the Amazon built their village along both a north–south axis and an east–west axis that paralleled a river. The tribe used the axes to divide individuals into groups that were expected to follow rules governing such things as who could marry whom (e.g., marriage partners

Figure 7.4 Fast food restaurants symbolically condition customers to line up for service in front of the counter

Notice how when you enter fast food restaurants like McDonald's you automatically engage in the desired behavior of queuing. The appropriate response may be triggered by other customers lining up to be served, however over time the counter alone will prompt the response without your awareness or anyone else's presence.

needed to be from different groups), and where people could reside (e.g., the married couple were to live in the group of the male partner). When missionaries arrived they moved the villagers to another place where the houses were built in rows that did not conform to the axes of the former village. According to Levi-Strauss:

> Disoriented with regard to the cardinal points, deprived of a disposition that gave meaning to their knowledge, the natives rapidly [lost] their sense of traditions as though their social and religious systems were too complex to function without the design made obvious by the disposition of the village.[30]

In organizations that undergo merger or acquisition it is not uncommon for the expected economic benefits of the partnership to go unrealized. Many explain this unfortunate outcome as cultural incompatibility; however, the study of the Bororo suggests that spatial disorientation may be operating, too. Consider that, as companies merge, members of one or both organizations are likely to change their physical locations and surroundings as well as important self-identifying cues in their physical environment. Without familiar physiological and sociological cues to orient them, organizational cultures do not function as expected and, to the extent that this creates stress, it affects productive behavior in ways that can destroy economic value and create conditions ripe for cultural collapse.

Embodied organization theory: Reuniting social and physical structure

That the physiological aspects of spatial orientation affect how and what we know is a central premise of **embodiment theory**, which explains how having a human body influences epistemology.[31] Evidence for physio-spatial knowledge can be found in navigation habits that allow you to drive to work or school by the same route every day without any conscious awareness of your actions, and your ability to pour a cup of coffee without lifting your eyes from your newspaper. It also appears in language when, through metaphor (e.g., happy is up, depressed is down). Humans spatialize their physiological experiences.[32]

Embodied organization theory proposes that, much as human bodies do, the physical structures of organizations embody human experiences as they wrap themselves around and organize activity in the shapes of office buildings and factories. But organizations are also embodied in the sense of being formed from the bodies of employees and stakeholders. Consider, for example, how the Walt Disney Company uses the body types and appearances of its employees, not to mention the physiological responses of its customers, to construct the ride experiences that constitute the offer of Disneyland parks.[33] Those assigned to work as pirates in the *Pirates of the Caribbean* attraction must have pirate-like physiques.

Organizational embodiment theorists join critical postmodernists in seeking to reverse the effects of dichotomies hidden within disembodied modern theories, of which mind/body is but one. Other popular targets include thought/feeling (or cognition/emotion), action/reflection, authority/democracy, and object/subject. Sometimes all that is required is to note how a familiar theory already contains ideas about embodiment, as British organization theorists John Hassard, Ruth Holliday, and Hugh Willmott do when they point out: 'there can be no enactment without embodiment.'[34]

Researchers interested in organizational embodiment complain that organization theory has become too focused on social influences to notice that physiological and spatial components affect organizations, which is what Homans claimed in reference to the Hawthorne Studies all those years ago. But rather than ignoring the social, embodied organization theorists place physical structure—defined as the material embodiment of organizational practices and action—on an equal footing with social structure. Thus one intriguing implication of organizational embodiment theory is that, just as structuration theory reunites social structure with agency, embodiment theory reunites physical structure with organizational action, suggesting an analogy: as agency is to action, so social structure is to physical structure.

Structuration theory's evolution in space and time

Over time, as buildings come to be identified with their inhabitants, they help people construct what they think and feel.[35] In this respect, French sociologist Pierre Bourdieu theorized that buildings are objectified histories in the sense of being 'systems of classifications, hierarchies and oppositions inscribed in the durability of wood, mud and brick.'[36] In the course of his study of the African Berber tribe known as the Kabyle, Bourdieu came to believe that the structure of social relations between the men and women of this society was built into their houses.

For example, Bourdieu described how the Kabyle divided their residences into two sections separated only by a 'small openwork wall half as high as the house.' One section was larger and higher than the other and paved with clay and cow dung that the women polished to a high sheen. This space, regarded as male, was used for human activities like eating and entertaining guests. The smaller space, where animals were kept, was regarded as female. It had a loft where the women and children slept and where tools and animal fodder were stored. According to Bourdieu the Kabyle associated the male space with concepts such as high, light, cooked, dry culture, whereas they associated female space with low, dark, raw, wet nature.

Bourdieu's study clearly evidenced a strong link between social and physical structures, but before buildings can construct what their inhabitants think and feel, they have to be built, for, as British Prime Minister Winston Churchill once famously observed, 'We shape our buildings and afterward our buildings shape us.' American sociologist Thomas Gieryn expanded on the idea that both buildings and meanings evolve in a process that begins with their design. His study of a newly constructed biotechnology research building located on the Cornell University campus in Ithaca, New York provided empirical grounding for his theory:

> The social structure of biotechnology [at Cornell] is shaped by choices made during the design of the building—for example, what people and functional activities are included or excluded, and how are these allocated in architectural space. The finished and occupied building measures a reorganized set of institutional arrangements, interpersonal relations and research practices now routinized and normalized into a more stable, enduring and constraining form. Still, from the day its doors opened, Cornell's Biotechnology Building has become something other than what its designers envisaged and something more than what got built—as users and visitors see in those walls a diverse range of significations.[37]

In theorizing the relationship between buildings and social structure he recognized the link Giddens theorized between structure and agency. Gieryn then contrasted Giddens's agency-oriented view (social structure is produced, maintained, and changed by human interaction) with Bourdieu's theory that the social and physical structures surrounding us define who we are and organize our behavior.

To investigate *how* agency and structure impinge on one another, Gieryn analyzed the evolution of Cornell University's biotechnology building and its meanings. Gieryn defined three phases of this evolution—design, construction, and occupation—and described the relationships between agency and structure he observed in each:

> Design is both the planning of material things and the resolution of sometimes competing social interests . . . [wherein] . . . the interests of powerful voices in the design process are etched into the artifact itself . . . the enrollment of investors, patrons, consumers, managers, eager publics, regulators and vendors is accomplished through the design process [during which] an evolving artifact is shaped to fit the wants and needs of those who must be on board to move it off the drawing board.[38]

Following design, Gieryn explained:

> Some designs get built. What once was a malleable plan—an unsettled thing pushed in different directions by competing interests during negotiation and compromise—now attains stability.[39]

Then, during occupation:

> Once unleashed by designers and builders, artifacts become available for later reconfiguration as they are returned to the hands of human agents for more or less creative redefinition, reevaluation and even re-(or de-)construction.[40]

Gieryn concluded that agency played a predominant role in the design phase of his study, but that the building's physical structure became the dominant force once the building was completed and occupied, which was when the new occupants adapted their behavior to the building's rigid contours. However, at some point after occupation the dominance of physical structure gave way once more to the influence of human agency. As Gieryn put it: 'agency returns to people when the building is narrated and reinterpreted—discursively made anew.'[41]

Although structuration theory suggests that the interplay of structure and agency occurs moment-to-moment (thereby becoming instantiated), Gieryn looked at how structure and agency intermingled over the course of the two years covered by his study. Contrasting Gieryn's theory to those of Giddens and Bourdieu, you begin to suspect that their different understandings of structuration processes are embedded in different **temporal orders**. You see different elements and relationships when you pay attention to what happens over seconds, minutes, or hours, than you see if you attend to what happens weekly, monthly, or annually, and different again if you track events over decades or millennia.

When Giddens theorized structuration processes on the order of instants, he saw more agency than structure, whereas from Bourdieu's historically extended viewpoint structure seemed to dominate agency. Gieryn's approach, midway between these two, was organized around events that transpired over weeks and months, permitting him to analyze (1) structure emerging from agency (design and construction of a building), (2) agents being constrained by their structures (the built space influencing the behavior of the building's occupants), and (3) agents (e.g., occupants, visitors, critics) reconfiguring those structures and their effects via subsequent interpretative activities.

The postmodernism perspective

In the conclusion of his study Gieryn commented on the human tendency to take the commonplace for granted:

> Buildings insist on particular paths that our bodies move along every day, and the predictable convergence or divergence of these paths with those of others is (in a sense) what we mean by *structured* social relations. If buildings silently steer us into associations or away from them, we hardly notice how (or question the rightness of it all).[42]

Gieryn's point resonates with critical postmodern claims that existing physical arrangements make it difficult to imagine other arrangements—we just start taking for granted that things like privacy or accessibility are determined by built spaces and unconsciously deal with their implications. Silence may help to make the associations of certain experiences with particular places meaningful, but it also renders them potentially sinister.

The potential of physical structure to communicate meaning gives designers and the managers who hire them access to symbolic power, for, if physical structures communicate meaning then careful design should be able to suggest, if not outright control, the meanings associated with it. According to advocates of the modern perspective, like Olins, this belief gives architects and designers a strategic role in organizations. For postmodernists, however, it makes them targets for criticism. As British critical postmodernists Gibson Burrell and Karen Dale put it, 'buildings are all about control;' one of their key achievements is to obscure the power they express and maintain.[43]

Reading built spaces like texts and deconstructing them to reveal the power relations they materialize is how many critical postmodernists deal with the topic of physical structures in organization theory. Their methods are similar to those of symbolic theorists who also read built spaces as texts, one clear difference being the focus on power that consumes most critical postmodern readings. But another difference comes through invocations of spatiality.

Postmodern geographers, for example, have accused the vast majority of organization theorists of promoting a-spatial explanations that are both disembodied and disembedded.[44] French postmodern geographer Henri Lefebvre was among the first to accuse Durkheim, Marx, Weber, and their followers of ignoring space to the detriment of their theorizing.[45] Such critiques open social theory for spatial reconstruction, as when British postmodern geographer Derek Gregory claimed that: 'social structures cannot be practiced without spatial structures, and vice versa.'[46]

A similar postmodern critique has been directed at the ways technological control disappears behind the benign appearance of physical structure. The assembly line invented by

Henry Ford is a favorite technological target of deconstruction, which typically begins with the assertion that belief in the factory owners' right to control how work is done, and thereafter the right to control labor, is built right into material aspects of technology that forces workers to perform actions defined by managers at a pace the managers regulate. Thus, postmodernists argue, the assembly line has ideological content that privileges owners and managers over workers, and hides their conflicted interests within the machinery of capitalism.

Repression of conflict occurs, they further argue, because once it is installed the physical presence of line machinery precludes discussion of the right of management to organize work as they have. The choice has already been made and disappears into the machinery. As American economist Richard Edwards described the situation:

> Struggle between workers and bosses over the transformation of labor power into labor was no longer a simple and direct *personal* confrontation; now the conflict was mediated by the production technology itself. Workers had to oppose the pace of the *line*, not the (direct) tyranny of their bosses. The line thus established a technically based and technologically repressive mechanism that kept workers at their tasks.[47]

At the point at which workers accept the mechanized assembly line, the physical structure of the production process organizes social relations of dominance and submission within the hierarchy of owners and workers. Each time the machinery is turned on it both reconstitutes the status quo and suppresses resistance to it.

By seeming innocuous or by being difficult to change, physical structures normalize power relations by fixing them in stone, so to speak. This material fixation parallels the symbolic fixation that occurs through institutionalization. As Burrell and Dale note, the isomorphism and institutional mimesis between organizations and the architectural practices that serve them, forms an alliance that helps to ensure continuity of power and domination through built space. They give the stunning example of the global influence during the first three decades of the twentieth century of German-born American architect Albert Kahn.

Kahn designed factories for the mass-production of automobiles for Packard, Ford, and General Motors in the US, and, under Stalin's auspices, was responsible for all industrial building in Russia until the mid-1930s. Little wonder that his single storied mass production facilities covering acres of land, with their trademark saw-tooth roofs providing daylight on the shop floor, became a defining symbol of the industrial age. As a major instrument of social order and control, Burrell and Dale claim, the Kahn style industrial factory helped to create the identities of workers newly arrived from the farm and thereby forged social changes that would one day resolve into modern capitalism:

> it is important to realize that many of the new entrants to the plants of Detroit and Stalingrad came straight from agrarian roots, may not have spoken the language of the metropolis and were unused to the rhythms of the factory day. The control of their work-space allowed the efficient socialization of the worker in programmes of re-education: they were constructed as a new category of industrial employee.[48]

The alignment of interests between architects and their clients observed in the construction of factories, occurs again in the development of the modern office tower a few years after this. Burrell and Dale reveal how Chicago architects Skidmore, Owings, and Merrill (SOM) exercised a far reaching influence similar to Kahn's through their design of the skyscraper that dominates and defines the skylines of all modern cities today, a particularly influential example of which was the Lever Building SOM designed and built in New York City in 1952. According to Burrell and Dale:

> The success of SOM rests not only on the brilliant projection of corporate capitalism, but also its mimicry of these forces in its own methods and organization. As a house style the model of the Lever Building came cheap . . . Walter Gropius (1955) said that the Lever Building relied upon prefabrication so that 85–90 per cent 'of the whole building was component parts ready-made in a factory, brought to the site and assembled there.' It used mass production methods and components. What also went down well with clients was the opposition in SOM to union or craft power. SOM followed this logic of efficiency and cost-consciousness through into the organization of their own business . . . SOM might be seen as an expression of unalloyed corporate growth: the reflection of the vertical integration of large multinational companies. It embodies a large bureaucratic structure based on hierarchy and a division of labour . . . It did not attack the status quo but reinforced it.[49]

Other postmodernists go beyond deconstructions of power and dominance as naturalized and hidden expressions of physical structures to demand that we learn to control or resist these influences and thereby free ourselves of unwanted influence and avoid abuse. To develop the means to do this they turn to Lefebvre's theory of how the powerful appropriate space to maintain their superiority over others.

Lefebvre argued that, starting with art in the Renaissance, modern thought came under the influence of perspectivism, a way of situating the viewer spatially to give them a vantage point from above. This spatial orientation, Lefebvre claimed, naturalizes hierarchy and other hegemonic practices. You can experience this effect for yourself by looking at an 'upside down' map of the world.[50] Such reorientations give most people an unsettled feeling because their naturalized expectations are undermined.

Postmodernists believe that the very notion of space, which always presents a center and its margins, orients us to domination. At the same time it perpetrates this orienting function, it hides the linguistic tricks it uses in the spatially inflected notions that abound in language—interior/exterior, private/public, local/global, top/bottom, and exclusion/inclusion—and that all intertwine in complex mutually supportive ways to convince us they are true when we see them every day in the way space presents itself.

For example, exclusion/inclusion is built into gated communities that place a society's upper reaches at the center of desire and ambition, while at the other end of the socio-economic spectrum ghettos, slums, and favelas marginalize its bottom rungs. Or consider how, in many organizations, executives commission office buildings that provide them with exclusive executive suites they then use to symbolically reinforce their inclusion within the dominant upper levels of the hierarchy. These examples illustrate the postmodern point that, while built space is socially produced through relations of power, social power is practiced and reproduced through uses of space.[51]

Offering the shopping mall as another example of power embodied by contemporary architecture, organization theorists Martin Kornberger, an Austrian, and Stewart Clegg, from Australia, claimed that: 'Architecture is a powerful means of directing and redirecting our attention, feelings, and thoughts to certain points through the organization of spatial structures,' such as when all pathways in a mall converge on big anchor stores, or how bright lights and big windows direct your view towards whatever is on display.[52]

Kornberger and Clegg claim that this modernist architectural trend toward hyper-control culminates in the bunker, a structure designed to protect its occupants from all harm, but which also imprisons them. Bunker mentality architecture is called terminal building because it marks the logical and physiological extremes to which control through building is taken. As an alternative, Kornberger and Clegg offer the **generative building**.

Generative building denies the architecture-as-control thesis of modern architecture, instead departing from the belief that 'architecture is always ambiguous: it can neither ensure nor hinder freedom.' It encourages 'illegal architects' who 'utilize established power and its architectural manifestations, opening up closed spaces and temporarily closing open spaces, and hijacking designs.' Citing De Certeau, they claim, generative buildings are: 'planned anonymously, emerging spontaneously, changing unpredictably, shaped by the creativity of the users and developed just-in-time.'[53] Instead of territorializing society, generative architecture has the power to re-socialize space in ways that encourage freedom:

> The generative building distinguishes itself from a terminal building in five respects: (dis) order, flexibility, problem generation, movement, and design. The architectural design of a generative building offers a way out of power premised on control into more positive power, away from the panic rooms of terminal architecture towards the design of spaces where surprising things may happen.[54]

Kornberger and Clegg further note that the illegal architects of generative building employ a 'strategy of the void,' an idea presented by Dutch architect Rem Koolhaas who claimed that: 'the most important parts of the building consist of an absence of building.'[55] In Koolhaas's architecture buildings remain deliberately unfinished. Kornberger and Clegg claim that surprise, liberty, and creativity, are harbored in the empty spaces of generative design.

Kornberger and Clegg reveal how the postmodern critique of architecture can itself be overturned by denial of *its* central premise (architecture is control), thereby liberating architecture for further creative development. Could this be one way that reading hegemony in architecture liberates us from its power and domination? Kornberger and Clegg believe we can construct our freedom in the same empty spaces from which post-postmodern generative architecture emerges.

Heinrich Klotz, former director of the German Architecture Museum in Frankfurt similarly described new possibilities of architectural symbolisation' by contrasting postmodern architecture to its modern precursors. But Klotz dealt more explicitly with the symbolics of space and design:

> Whether architects like it or not, a building acts as a vehicle of meaning even if it is supposed to be meaningless. One way or another, it presents a visual aspect. Even the vulgar postwar functionalism that cut the characteristic features of a building to a minimum produced buildings that, as they entered one's visual field, acquired a meaning: An apparently neutral and monotonous uniformity . . . In contrast to the kind of architecture that consciously renounced any symbolic effect since by its own definition in terms of functional efficiency any consideration of meaning was too much, the new trends in architecture are predominantly marked by attempts to draw attention to other contents besides the functional qualities of a building—to contents referring to nonarchitectural as well as architectural contexts.[56]

Postmodern architectural theory points to the possibility of using built space to make symbolic references to organizational meaning per se, and allows doing so in humorous ways that invite paradoxical readings to undermine hierarchical authority at the same time they support it. This is not to say that these possibilities did not exist before postmodernists came along, it is only to say that modernists ignored these possibilities. Of course there is a contributing factor; some of the effects postmodern architects employ are dependent upon construction methods and materials that have evolved with modern technology to make their elaborate structures possible, another irony.

To give just one example of what postmodernism unleashed in architecture, take a look at the Disney Team Building in Burbank, California, designed by American architect Michael Graves.[57] On the façade of this structure, which houses Disney's top executives, stand the Seven Dwarfs frozen into columns supporting the roof. Are they there to cartoonishly invite us to think that Disney employees whistle while they work? Do they in fact encourage employees to whistle on their way in the door? Or is the façade a comment on how Disney's treatment of workers freezes them into statues that support an enormous profit-driven enterprise? Is Disney the self-proclaimed 'Happiest place on Earth,' or is it the Smile Factory Van Maanen described?[58]

Summary

An organization is, in part, a physical entity possessing territorial extent on multiple geographic and temporal scales, comprising a layout of workstations, furniture, equipment, and the human bodies of employees who design and decorate their workspaces with their artifacts and their persons, and produce endless interpretations of what it all means. Physical structure is complexly intertwined with social structure, interwoven with culture and technology, and implicated in outcomes like communication and performance. It is therefore meaningfully material and symbolic in its materiality. Its symbolism carries a multiplicity of meanings that can give the powerful access to meaningful self-expressions of organization through the concrete forms and shapes that built space provides. At the same time it silently shuttles us along pathways designed and built by the powerful. As both physical containers directing human movements, and symbolic resources for the expression of meaning and enactments of power, built spaces invite contention and contestation.

The impressions an organization makes on employees and stakeholders as they respond to and interpret buildings and grounds, particularly when these are architecturally designed to produce a profound visual statement, can reinforce corporate vision and strategy, and signify corporate pride, hegemonic ambition, and a variety of other ideas, both intended and unintended. But the images this impression work leaves on inhabitants may stand in stark contrast to interpretations they form for reasons other than those architectural designers or managers may attempt to impose.

While from the symbolic perspective physical structures of organizations are social constructions open to constantly new meaning making, modernists tend to see them either as meaningless containers with the power to control behavior or, if meaningful, filled with the potential to direct that meaning through carefully controlled design. The postmodern perspective, all the while, treats space as a text to be deciphered and deconstructed, and maybe one day replaced by the freedom it hopes to underwrite and maintain with vigilant deconstruction.

Key terms

spatiality

organizational geography

   geographic distribution

   territorial extent

   scale

   time–space compression

   logistics

   geographic features

   space and place

layout

   orientation

   landscaping

   proximity

   openness/visibility

   accessibility

   privacy

open vs. private offices

hot desking and hoteling

design features

   planned

   unplanned and emergent

décor and dress

symbolic meaning

   intended vs. unintended

   multiplicity of meaning

identity, image, and reputation

   organizational identity expression

   group territorial boundaries

   individual identity markers

   personalization of space

symbolic conditioning

embodiment theory

temporal orders

spatiality

generative building

Endnotes

1. Roethlisberger and Dickson (1939); Mayo (1945).

2. Since the 1970s many social psychologists have disputed the findings of the Hawthorne experiments based on criticisms of the experimental design and of the interpretations given the findings, particularly of the Hawthorne Effect. A useful summary of the criticisms offered by Berkeley Rice (1982) can be found at http://www.cs.unc.edu/~stotts/204/nohawth.html (accessed February 24, 2012).

3. Homans (1950).

4. Elsbach and Pratt (2008) review much of this literature.

5. Pfeffer (1982), who was an early proponent of the inclusion of physical structure studies in organization theory.

6. Taylor and Spicer (2007).

7. Harvey (1990).

8. See Casey (1993, 2002).

9. Godkin (1980).

10. Aerial views of the Googleplex can be seen at (last accessed February 25, 2012): http://network.nature.com/system/photo/000/002/751/googleplex.jpg?1218645567 or http://raymondpirouz.tumblr.com/post/385130526/googleplex-solar

11. Kotter (1983).

12. Allen (1977).

13. Gullahorn (1952); Wells (1965); Gerstberger and Allen (1968); Allen and Gerstberger (1973); Conrath (1973); Szilagyi and Holland (1980).

14. Festinger, Schacter, and Back (1950); Estabrook and Sommer (1972); Parsons (1976).

15. Allen (1977); Davis (1984).

16. Conrath (1973).

17. Daft and Lengel (1984).

18. Oldham and Brass (1979); BOSTI (1981); Oldham and Rotchford (1983); Hatch (1987).

19. Hatch (1990).

20. Rybczynski (2001: 21–25).

21. Rafaeli and Pratt (1993); Rafaeli et al. (1997).

22. Olins (1989, 2003).

23. Yanow (1993).

24. Steele (1981).

25. Richards and Dobyns (1957); Wells (1965).

26. Wineman (1982).

27. Whyte (1943).

28. Konar et al. (1982); Baldry (1999).

29. Berg and Kreiner (1990).

30. Levi-Strauss (1955), cited in Fischer (1997: 24–5).

31. Seamon (1980).

32. Lakoff and Johnson (1980).

33. Van Maanen (1991).

34. Hassard, Holliday, and Willmott (2000: 3).

35. Urry (1991), Yanow (1993).

36. Bourdieu (1981: 305–6), cited in Gieryn (2002: 39).

37. Gieryn (2002: 36).

38. Gieryn (2002: 42).

39. Gieryn (2002: 43).

40. Gieryn (2002: 44).

41. Gieryn (2002: 53).

42. Gieryn (2002: 61).

43. Burrell and Dale (2009: 178).

44. See Yanow (2006) for a thorough discussion of how built spaces mean and a nice summary of Casey's work on the relations between human embodiment and spatial orientation.

45. Lefebvre (1991); see also Soja (1989); Harvey (1990).

46. Gregory (1978: 121).

47. Edwards (1979: 118).

48. Burrell and Dale (2009: 187).

49. Burrell and Dale (2009: 190). For reference to Gropius, see J. Peter (2000) *An Oral History of Modern Architecture*. New York: H.N. Abrams.

50. Find an image of such a map at http://flourish.org/upsidedownmap/

51. Lefebvre (1991).

52. Kornberger and Clegg (2004: 1104).

53. De Certeau (1984); Kornberger and Clegg (2004: 1107–8).

54. Kornberger and Clegg (2004: 1107).

55. Koolhaas (1995: 603).

56. Klotz (1992: 235–6).

57. See http://www.utexas.edu/courses/ancientfilmCC304/lecture1/disney.html for an image of the Disney headquarters building (accessed February 25, 2012).

58. Van Maanen (1991).

References

Allen, T. (1977) *Managing the Flow of Technology: Technology Transfer and the Dissemination of Technological Information within the R&D Organization.* Cambridge, MA: MIT Press.

—— and Gerstberger, P. (1973) A field experiment to improve communications in a product engineering department: The nonterritorial office. *Human Factors*, 15: 487–98.

Baldry, Chris (1999) Space—the final frontier. *Sociology*, 33/3: 535–53.

Berg, Per Olof and Kreiner, Kristian (1990) Corporate architecture: Turning physical settings into symbolic resources. In Pasquale Gagliardi (ed.), *Symbols and Artifacts: Views of the Corporate Landscape.* Berlin: Walter de Gruyter, 41–67.

BOSTI (Buffalo Organization for Social and Technological Innovation) (1981) *The Impact of Office Environment on Productivity and Quality of Working Life: Comprehensive findings.* Buffalo, NY: Buffalo Organization for Social and Technological Innovation.

Bourdieu, Pierre (1981) Men and machines. In Karin Knorr-Cetina and Aaron Cicourel (eds.), *Advances in Social Theory and Methodology.* London: Routledge, 304–18.

Burrell, G. and Dale, K. (2009) Building better worlds? Architecture and critical management studies. In M. Alvesson and H. Willmott (eds.), *Studying Management Critically*, pp. 177–96. London: Sage.

Casey, Edward S. (1993) *Getting back into Place.* Bloomington: Indiana University Press.

—— (2002) *Representing Place.* Minneapolis, MN: University of Minneapolis Press.

Conrath, C. W. (1973) Communication patterns, organizational structure, and man: Some relationships. *Human Factors*, 15: 459–70.

Daft and Lengel (1984) Information richness: A new approach to managerial behavior and organization design. In B. M. Staw and L. L. Cummings (eds.) *Research in Organizational Behavior.* Greenwich, CT: JAI Press, 6: 191–233.

Davis, T. M. R. (1984) The influence of the physical environment of offices. *Academy of Management Review*, 9: 271–83.

De Certeau, Michel (1984) *The Practice of Everyday Life.* Berkeley: University of California Press.

Doxtater, Dennis (1990) Meaning of the workplace: Using ideas of ritual space in design. In Pasquale Gagliardi (ed.), *Symbols and Artifacts: Views of the Corporate Landscape.* Berlin: Walter de Gruyter, 107–27.

Edwards, Richard (1979) *Contested Terrain: The Transformation of the Workplace in the Twentieth Century.* New York: Basic Books.

Elsbach, Kimberly D. and Pratt, Michael G. (2008) The physical environment in organizations. *The Academy of Management Annals*, 1: 181–224.

Estabrook, M. and Sommer, R. (1972) Social rank and acquaintanceship in two academic buildings. In W. Graham and K. H. Roberts (eds.), *Comparative Studies in Organizational Behavior.* New York: Holt, Rhinehart & Winston, 122–8.

Festinger, Leon S., Schacter, Stanley, and Back, Kurt (1950) *Social Pressures in Informal Groups.* Stanford, CA: Stanford University Press.

Fischer, Gustave-Nicolas (1997) *Individuals and Environment: A Psychosocial Approach to Workspace* (trans. Ruth Atkin-Etienne) Berlin: Walter de Gruyter.

Gerstberger, Peter G. and Allen, Thomas J. (1968) Criteria used by research and development engineers in the selection of an information source. *Journal of Applied Psychology*, 52: 272–9.

Gieryn, Thomas F. (2002) What buildings do. *Theory and Society*, 31: 35–74.

Godkin, Michael A. (1980) Identity and place: Clinical applications based on notions of rootedness and uprootedness. In A. Buttimer and D. Seamon (eds.), *The Human Experience of Space and Place*. New York: St. Martin's Press, 73–85.

Gregory, Derek (1978) *Ideology, Science and Human Geography*. London: Hutchinson.

Gullahorn, J. T. (1952) Distance and friendship as factors in the gross interaction matrix. *Sociometry*, 15: 123–34.

Harvey, D. (1990) *The Condition of Postmodernity*. Oxford: Blackwell.

Hassard, John, Holliday, Ruth, and Willmott, Hugh (eds.) (2000) *Body and Organization*. London: Sage.

Hatch, Mary Jo (1987) Physical barriers, task characteristics, and interaction activity in research and development firms. *Administrative Science Quarterly*, 32: 387–99.

––– (1990) The symbolics of office design: An empirical exploration. In Pasquale Gagliardi (ed.), *Symbols and Artifacts: Views of the Corporate Landscape*. Berlin: Walter de Gruyter, 129–46.

Homans, George (1950) *The Human Group*. New York: Harcourt Brace & World.

Klotz, Heinrich (1992) Postmodern architecture. In C. Jencks (ed.), *The Post-modern Reader*. London: St. Martin's Press, 234–48.

Konar, E., Sundstrom, E., Brady, C., Mandel, D., and Rice, R. (1982) Status markers in the office. *Environment and Behavior*, 14: 561–80.

Koolhaas, Rem (1995) *S, M, L, XL*. New York: Monacelli Press.

Kornberger, Martin and Clegg, Stewart R. (2004) Bringing space back in: Organizing the generative building. *Organization Studies*, 25: 1095–114.

Kotter, John P. (1983) *The General Managers*. New York: Free Press.

Lakoff, George and Johnson, Mark (1980) *Metaphors We Live by*. Chicago, IL: University of Chicago Press.

Lefebvre, Henri (1991) *The Production of Space* (trans. D. Nicholson-Smith). Oxford: Blackwell.

Mayo, Elton (1945) *The Social Problems of an Industrial Civilization*. Boston, MA: Graduate School of Business Administration, Harvard University.

Oldham, Greg R. and Brass, Daniel J. (1979) Employee reactions to an open-plan office: A naturally occurring quasi-experiment. *Administrative Science Quarterly*, 24: 267–84.

––– and Rotchford, Nancy L. (1983) Relationships between office characteristics and employee reactions: A study of the physical environment. *Administrative Science Quarterly*, 28: 542–56.

Olins, Wally (1989) *Corporate Identity: Making Business Strategy Visible through Design*. London: Thames and Hudson.

––– (2003) *Wally Olins: On Brand*. London: Thames & Hudson.

Parsons, H.M. (1976) Work environment. In I. Altman and J. F. Wohlwill (eds.), *Human Behavior and Environment: Advances in Theory and Research*. New York: Plenum, i: 163–209.

Pfeffer, Jeffrey (1982) Developing organization theory, organizations as physical structures. In J. Pfeffer (ed.), *Organizations and Organization Theory*. Boston, MA: Pitman, 260–71.

Rafaeli, Anat, Dutton, Jane, Harquail, C. V., and Mackie-Lewis, Stephanie (1997) Navigating by attire: The use of dress by female administrative employees. *Academy of Management Journal*, 40: 9–45.

––– and Pratt, Michael G. (1993) Tailored meanings. *Academy of Management Review*, 18: 32–55.

Rice, B. (1982) The Hawthorne defect: Persistence of a flawed theory. *Psychology Today*, 16/2: 70–4.

Richards, C. B. and Dobyns, H. F. (1957) Topography and culture: The case of the changing cage. *Human Organization*, 16: 16–20.

Roethlisberger, F. J. and Dickson, W. J. (1939) *Management and the Worker: An Account of a Research Program Conducted by the Western Electric Company, Hawthorne Works, Chicago*. Cambridge, MA: Harvard University Press.

Rybczynski, Witold (2001) *The Look of Architecture*. New York: Oxford University Press.

Seamon, David (1980) Body-subject, time-space routines, and place ballets. In A. Buttimer and D. Seamon (eds.), *The Human Experience of Space and Place*. New York: St. Martin's Press, 148–65.

Soja, Edward W. (1989) *Postmodern Geographies: The Reassertion of Space in Critical Social Theory*. London: Verso.

Steele, Fred I. (1981) *The Sense of Place*. Boston, MA: CBI Publishing Company.

Szilagyi, Andrew D. and Holland, Winford E. (1980) Changes in social density: Relationships with functional interaction and perceptions of job characteristics, role stress, and work satisfaction. *Journal of Applied Psychology*, 65: 28–33.

Taylor, Scott and Spicer, André (2007) Time for space: A narrative review of research on organizational spaces. *International Journal of Management Reviews*, 9/4: 325–46.

Urry, John (1991) Time and space in Giddens' social theory. In Christopher G.A. Bryant and David Jary (eds.), *Giddens' Theory of Structuration: A Critical Appreciation*. London: Routledge, 160–75.

Van Maanen, John (1991) The Smile Factory: Work at Disneyland. In P. J. Frost, L. F. Moore, M. R. Louis, C. C. Lundberg, and J. Martin (eds.), *Reframing Organizational Culture*. Newbury Park, CA: Sage Publications, 58–86.

Wells, B. (1965) The psycho-social influence of building environments: Sociometric findings in large and small office spaces. *Building Science*, 1: 153–65.

Whyte, William Foote (1943) *Street Corner Society*. Chicago, IL: University of Chicago Press.

Wineman, J. D. (1982) Office design and evaluation: An overview. *Environment and Behavior*, 14: 271–98.

Yanow, Dvora (1993) Reading policy meanings in organization-scapes. *Journal of Architectural and Planning Research*, 10: 308–27.

—— (2006) How built spaces mean: A semiotics of space. In D. Yanow and P. Schwartz-Shea (eds.), *Interpretation and Method: Empirical Research Methods and the Interpretive Turn*, ch. 20. Armonk, NY: ME Sharpe.

Further reading

Becker, Franklin D. (1981) *Workspace: Creating Environments in Organizations*. New York: Praeger.

Casey, Edward S. (2002) *Representing Place*. Minneapolis, MN: University of Minneapolis Press.

Dale, Karen (2001) *Anatomising Embodiment and Organization Theory*. Basingstoke: Palgrave Macmillan.

—— and Burrell, Gibson (2008) *Spaces of Organization and the Organization of Space: Power, Identity and Materiality at Work*. Basingstoke: Palgrave Macmillan.

Fischer, Gustave-Nicolas (1997) *Individuals and Environment: A Psychosocial Approach to Workspace* (trans. Ruth Atkin-Etienne). Berlin: Walter de Gruyter.

Gagliardi, Pasquale (1990) (ed.) *Symbols and Artifacts: Views of the Corporate Landscape*. Berlin: Walter de Gruyter.

Giddens, Anthony (1985) Time, space and regionalisation. In D. Gregory and J. Urry (eds.), *Social Relations and Spatial Structures*. New York: St. Martin's Press, 265–95.

Jencks, Charles (1977) *The Language of Post-modern Architecture*. London: Academy.

Rappaport, Amos (1982) *The Meaning of the Built Environment*. Beverley Hills, CA: Sage.

Soja, Edward W. (1996) *The Third Place*. London: Verso.

Steele, Fred I. (1973) *Physical Settings and Organization Development*. Reading, MA: Addison-Wesley.

Sundstrom, Eric (1986) *Work Places: The Psychology of the Physical Environment in Offices and Factories*. Cambridge: Cambridge University Press.

8 Organizational power, control, and conflict

Organization theorists who study power agree that this phenomenon pervades all aspects of organizing and therefore needs to be given consideration in theories involving every other concept found in organization theory. Their ideas about power vary considerably, however, and have done so ever since the founding of the field.

Max Weber, for example, assumed that the legitimate hierarchical power of owners and managers gives them the right to control both the means of production and the laborers who employ those means; while Karl Marx saw the use of hierarchical power as an act of domination inviting resistance and producing endless conflict. And where Marx saw conflict as the fundamental condition of organizing, scholars of the classical management school saw cooperation as its main requirement. Aligning these views yet coming from the perspective of cooperation, Mary Parker Follett described the creative potential inherent in power and conflict to promote democratic forms of organization.

Unlike Weber who worried over the 'iron cage' of bureaucracy, and Marx who believed domination and exploitation to be inherent to organization, most early modern organization theorists did not express concern about the ethics of control or their use of power to support it. Like Taylor they were enamored of the prospect of control justified by rationality and efficiency, though some worried a bit when scientific management went so far as to engineer the movements of workers' bodies within precisely controlled work environments. By and large, though, early proponents of the modern perspective assumed, as Weber did, that the use of managerial power to control workers was expected and accepted. American sociologist Arnold Tannenbaum expressed this attitude well when he pronounced unequivocally that:

> Organization implies control. A social organization is an ordered arrangement of individual human interactions. Control processes help circumscribe idiosyncratic behaviors and keep them conformant to the rational plan of the organization. Organizations require a certain amount of conformity as well as the integration of diverse activities.[1]

Marx's theories were never completely excluded from the modern perspective in organization theory, though they often occupied a backwater as advocates of rationality and efficiency rose to prominence and worries over the dark side of power and control subsided. Nonetheless, neo-Marxists who theorized power, control, and conflict as central organizational concepts and adopted the worker's point of view as their primary perspective inspired critical postmodernist and feminist contributions to the theory of power in organizations such as those offering explanations for why women and minorities suffer widespread subordination in most organizations.

Power, politics, and control

Most early modernists thought politics illegitimate in rational organizations where it could undermine the power of authority and threaten management control. Asserting rationality and efficiency as prime directives, the inefficiencies inherent in political behavior made theories about organizational power and politics easy for them to dismiss. Those advocating the political view were not so easily put off, however. Appropriating the methods of the modernists who resisted them, they studied organizational decision making and produced evidence that political behavior in fact occurs in all organizations.

These early theorists of power and politics found the metaphor of the political arena, borrowed from political science, highly useful for describing distributions of organizational power and studying their effects. So transformative were their efforts that by 1980 American sociologists Samuel Bacharach and Edward Lawler were able to state flatly: 'Survival in an organization is a political act. Corporations, universities, and voluntary associations are arenas for daily political action.'[2]

Two Americans, administrative theorist Herbert Simon and political scientist James March, were among the first proponents of political organization theory. Their compelling book *Organizations*, published in 1958, built on Simon's concept of bounded rationality, which was framed as a necessary correction to the overly rational decision-making models that dominated early modernist organization theories. Models describing rational decision making in organizations typically start with defining a problem and then collecting and analyzing all relevant information, following which decision makers generate and evaluate all reasonable alternatives, select a solution based on predefined criteria related to organizational objectives, and implement their choice.

Simon criticized the rational model for wrongly assuming that decision makers agree about organizational goals, possess or can attain all the necessary information to make a rational choice, or have the information processing capacity and the time to process all the complexity in the environment and the problem they face. He claimed these conditions rarely occur in cases of actual decision making in organizations, therefore organizational decision making is rarely rational. In the place of rationality, Simon offered the concept of **bounded rationality**.[3] Under conditions of bounded rationality, March and Simon reasoned, those with the most powerful positions tend to dominate decision-making processes via political behavior that can be quite complex. And, when decision makers are aware of politics, they can manage or manipulate the decision-making process by aligning their interests with others to form a **coalition** in support of a jointly favored position.

Political decision making under bounded rationality works this way: decision makers take stock of their relative power positions in relation to the other decision makers involved in the process. If their forces are not strong enough to overcome opposition, they form a coalition with others who see the advantage of combining their influence. In most cases coalition formation requires behind-the-scenes negotiations to ensure that the interests of all coalition members are considered and it is here that decision-making processes diverge from the rational ideal, often leading to sub-optimal decision outcomes.

The sub-optimality of coalition model decision making is explained at least in part by the negotiated nature of the political process—the give and take required from individual members to reach agreement. What is traded for the sake of making a deal is not always, or even often, beneficial to the overall organization. However, while sub-optimality may be expected to occur, deals are yet beneficial in the sense that they enable decision makers to break deadlocks and take action, which is why, according to March and Simon, bounded rationality pervades organizations.

Following the theories of bounded rationality and coalition formation, power and political processes became more acceptable research subjects in organization theory. Modern organization theorists, however, were still inclined to submerge power and politics in their discussions of organizational control. A good place to start explaining why is to define these key terms.

What is power?

In 1957 American political scientist Robert Dahl defined power with words repeated ever since: 'A has power over B to the extent that he can get B to do something that B would not otherwise do.'[4] A and B can be defined at any level of analysis—individual, group, or organization—but, no matter the level, power is always exercised in the context of relationships between actors. Power never resides in actors; it is always relational.

Authority in particular stands out as a source of power. As Weber argued, an individual's formal authority derives from their structural position in the hierarchy. Its exercise flows downward in an organization, from top to bottom. But formal authority is only one source of individual level power and the others do not work in strictly top-down ways, they also work up the hierarchy, laterally, or cross-organizationally, and may work in all directions at once.

There are many forms of power individuals can draw on in addition to formal authority. They include: personal characteristics (a charismatic personality), expertise (skills, knowledge, or information needed by others), coercive force (the threat or use of fear), control of scarce and critical material resources (capital, raw material, technology, physical space), ability to apply normative sanctions (informal rules and expectations set up by cultural assumptions and values), and opportunity (e.g., access to powerful persons). As American sociologist Melville Dalton showed, these other sources of power provide lower level employees with counterbalancing power in their relationships with those in authority.[5]

Many theorists argue that authority is power from any source that has become legitimized within the organizational setting. The primary difference they see between authority and other forms of power lies in the way power is perceived. In this view authority occurs when the exercise of power becomes both accepted and expected within a given relationship. According to this view, an active distribution and redistribution of power is ongoing among the units and individuals of an organization; but when a particular distribution becomes institutionalized as a normal part of the organization's daily operations, power crystallizes into an authority structure.

An important difference between using authority and using other forms of power is that authority has fewer costs. Using other sources of power usually requires an expenditure of resources such as providing knowledge or personal attention to someone else, or by making commitments or concessions in exchange for support on a given issue (i.e., within coalition-building processes). Once expended, these sources of power cannot be recovered and the power holder must replace them or suffer an eroded power base. By comparison, the exercise of authority, because it is accepted and expected, has fewer costs and in some cases is enhanced through use.

What determines the power of the various social actors? When and how do actors use their power? Much of the research devoted to power in organizations is conducted at the individual level of analysis. Most leads to normative advice telling managers how to maximize their power and use it effectively. Common strategies for developing power within an organization are:

- Creating dependence in others
  - work in areas of high uncertainty
  - cultivate centrality by working in critical areas
  - develop non-substitutable skills
- Coping with uncertainty on behalf of others through:
  - prevention
  - forecasting
  - absorption
- Developing personal networks
- Developing and constantly augmenting your expertise

Common strategies for using power in an organization are:

- Control the information that flows to others
- Control agendas through:
  - issue definition
  - order of issues discussed
  - issue exclusion
- Control decision-making criteria, for example:
  - long- vs. short-term time horizons
  - return vs. risk
  - self-promotion: any criterion favoring your abilities or interests
- Cooptation and coalition building
  - external alliances (e.g., supply chain relationships, interlocking boards of directors)
  - internal alliances
    - promote loyal subordinates
    - appoint committees
    - gain representation on important committees
- Bring in outside experts (consultants) to bolster your position

What is politics?

Jeffrey Pfeffer defined **organizational politics** as: 'those activities taken within organizations to acquire, develop, and use power and other resources to obtain one's preferred outcomes in a situation in which there is uncertainty or dissensus about choices.'[6] Because differing interests are built into organizational structures, each decision represents an opportunity for negotiation and renegotiation in a never-ending stream of political maneuvering that constitutes everyday organizational life.

Seen distributed throughout the organization, Pfeffer's picture of unending organizational politics well suits the metaphor of organizations as political arenas, but also suggests that the dynamics of dominance most often keep control in the hands of those in power. In societies dominated by Western capitalism, postmodernists and feminists point out, these are typically white males, whose disproportion in positions of power across capitalist societies they provide as evidence that the **politics of identity** infiltrates organizations.

Power relationships can create patterns of domination that favor one gender, race, ethnicity, age group, sexual orientation, and/or religious affiliation over others. Of course, there are cultural differences with respect to the specific identities privileged. Age for instance is often a negative characteristic in Western societies, while it is positive in most Eastern cultures. At the societal level, such patterns emerge from the struggle among individuals to define themselves and each other. Societies use these definitions as the basis for distributing power, allowing some identities privileges that others do not enjoy.

Privileging may occur on such a deep level that the favored never recognize how privileged they are by the cultures their dominance allows them to shape in their own image. The negative stereotypes that privileging leaves in its wake cause some members of society to be devalued and discredited in ways only they can tell. Stereotypes serve to make it seem natural to both the privileged and the marginalized that marginalized identity groups take the jobs or occupy the roles that offer the lowest pay and confer the least power and status, while privileged identity groups get all the benefits and maintain control enough to stabilize their position in organizations just as they do in society.

What is control?

American organization theorist William Ouchi, a staunch modernist, stated that the primary responsibility of management is: 'achieving cooperation among individuals who hold partially divergent objectives.'[7] Managers always confront a diversity of interests held by employees who join the organization for different reasons and interpret their roles in ways that may or may not serve organizational objectives. Keeping energy and resources focused is therefore both necessary and problematic. Managerial control practices, according to the modern perspective, align behavior with goals.

Power and control are closely related in that power is often expressed in the form of control. For example, coercion implies the threat of force or physical power to control others. Remuneration or reward power requires control of material resources that are desired or needed by those to be controlled. Normative power controls how cultural members perceive, think, and feel; it is supported by the legitimacy that conformance to cultural values and assumptions bestows.

Based on these three types of control, American sociologist Amitai Etzioni distinguished three types of organizations: coercive power controls prisons and mental institutions, businesses are generally remunerative organizations, and churches, gangs, and volunteer organizations typically take the form of normative organizations. While all three types of control exist in all organizations, Etzioni claimed that every organization is dominated by one of these three defining forms of control.[8]

Theories about organizational power and politics

Theories of organization–environment relations are easy to turn into theories explaining organizational power distributions. Population ecology, for example, explains the distribution of power among the members of a population of organizations in terms of each organization's relative ability to command needed resources. Institutional theory explains the distribution of organizational power within an institutional environment based on conformity to expectations, social norms, and legal regulations. Mimetic, coercive, and normative pressures all elicit conformity from organizations indicating the power of institutional environments to bestow legitimacy. Seen from within organizations the distribution of power among units and individuals was explained by resource dependence theory as the relative ability to manage uncertainty associated with the acquisition of scarce and critical resources. Among these three, resource dependence theory—and its precursor strategic contingencies theory—have been most explicit about the role organizational politics plays.

Strategic contingencies theory

In a study of a state-owned cigarette factory in France, French sociologist Michel Crozier witnessed the influence of uncertainty on power relationships.[9] Crozier discovered that the bureaucratic organization faced little uncertainty because it operated a highly routine technology within a stable environment. In spite of this the maintenance men held an unusual and unexpected amount of power, which they exercised through negotiations with plant managers.

Analysis revealed that the maintenance workers managed a key uncertainty for the organization, namely work delays. When machines broke down production workers who were paid on a piece-rate system lost money, and plant productivity dropped, a crucial factor in managers' performance evaluations. Dependence on the maintenance workers gave them enough power to negotiate for the right to organize their own work, which also allowed them to maintain the dependencies on which their power rested. Crozier reasoned that handling a critical uncertainty confers power to employees able to manage that uncertainty, even if they have low status in the hierarchy. He described his finding in terms of the power of lower level workers.

Findings similar to Crozier's have been reported in studies of universities, where power typically accrues to those departments that have the highest levels of enrollment, produce the most grants, attract the biggest donations, or otherwise bring funds into the university.[10] Such groups use their power to political advantage, for example, to promote one of their members to a top hierarchical position, or to garner control of other areas of critical uncertainty that will further enhance and secure their power base.

Studies such as these inspired strategic contingencies theory, a general theory about why the distribution of power inside organizations relates to uncertainty. According to the theory, individuals or units derive power from their ability to provide something that the organization needs, for example, a high level of performance, an irreplaceable skill, an ability to solve critical problems, or to obtain scarce resources. However, in their elaboration of strategic contingencies theory British organization researchers David Hickson, C.R. Hinings, and their colleagues pointed out that simply handling uncertainty is not enough. Power is linked to the ability of a unit to deal effectively with sources of uncertainty that otherwise would negatively affect the organization to a significant degree.

Hickson and his colleagues suggested three coping strategies organizational units can use to translate uncertainty into power: prevention, forecasting, and absorption. Consider a Human Resources (HR) Department confronting the uncertainty of potential discrimination lawsuits against the company. Prevention might involve developing anti-discrimination policies and training programs; forecasting could be accomplished by collecting, analyzing, and providing information about new legal requirements, recent court decisions, and changes in the definitions of discrimination; and absorption would result from handling discrimination lawsuits arising from the actions of other organizational units.

Remember, coping with uncertainty only generates power for a unit when the task is central to operations of the organization and when no other unit can perform the coping activity (that is, the unit's coping capabilities are non-substitutable). In short, identifying strategic contingencies for developing power in an organization means locating the sources of organizational uncertainty. Converting a strategic contingency into power requires effectively managing the negative consequences of that contingency on behalf of the organization.

Resource dependence theory

Pfeffer and Gerald Salancik reasoned along the lines of strategic contingency theory that dependence on the environment creates uncertainty inside organizations, and uncertainty, in turn, creates opportunities for organizational actors (individuals or units) to garner power.[11] But their resource dependence theory explained that the management of uncertainty produces differential subunit power because not all uncertainties are equally important and not all actors are equally competent.

Even if an actor or unit can cope with an uncertainty on behalf of the organization, another unit or actor may garner more power by coping with an uncertainty involving scarcer or more critical resources. Then, because changes in the environment can alter the mix of uncertainties a company faces, and/or the relative scarcity of its resources, resource dependence can make complex power structures volatile. But, Pfeffer and Salancik noted, politics dampens these effects.

Power dynamics become politicized when subunits are rewarded for dealing with uncertainty by being given bigger budgets, more resources, higher status positions for their members, and so on. The politics of resource dependence involves organizational actors using the resources power puts at their command to legitimate and institutionalize their power rather than to perform the organization's core task. Resource dependence theory recognized that internal political processes occur somewhat independently of environmental contingencies because different individuals and units within the organization make different uses of opportunities to cope with uncertainty, and because already powerful institutionalized units can subvert the resource redeployment and power redistribution attempts of those seeking to use newly acquired power, thereby stabilizing existing structures of power in the face of changing circumstances which can have the effect of making an organization less responsive to its environment.

In later work, Pfeffer pointed out that language and other symbols are important to the dynamics of power relationships because, like other resources, symbols can be appropriated by social actors to support and maintain their power position.[12] Among symbols of authority he listed high salaries and expense accounts, the right to call a superior by his or her given name, the ability to force others to call oneself by title (e.g., General, Detective, Doctor, Professor), executive dining room privileges, reserved parking spaces, and the location, size, and décor of one's office.

Once symbols represent power within a culture, they can be useful in constructing it. The politics of resource dependence can then be extended to symbolic power to explain why employees usually take a keen interest in the physical design of their organizations. The architectural design process becomes politicized by the potential to gain or lose control of symbols of power and identity embedded in buildings. Notice, too, that people can acquire the symbols of power without having any formal authority and yet gain status and power purely from association with symbolic artifacts.

I was once given a very large office because when I joined the university no other offices were available. It never ceased to amuse me to hear someone out in the hall ask who occupied my office in hushed and respectful tones, assuming based on the size of my office that I must be someone important. Knowing that this effect occurs creates competition over status symbols that can be as high, or even higher, than the competition over the formal authority these symbols represent.

The musical comedy *How to Succeed in Business without Really Trying*, a long-standing favorite among business students, satirizes this phenomenon. The story is about a young man who works his way into an organization and then up the corporate ladder by systematically associating himself with the organization's symbols of authority and success (e.g., wearing the right tie, having an office and a secretary). Although believing that symbols are all that is required for power is probably going too far, but it is true that symbols help to establish and maintain power by supporting interpretations of who has power.

Since power is relational, the attribution of power by others is what actually produces power that can then be used to control the power distribution, and the behavior of others.

Theories of organizational control

Managers of organizations constantly face the problem of divergent interests interfering with organizational strategies and goals. Within the modern perspective this ongoing challenge provides the rationale for managerial control, a topic supported by normative concerns to define mechanisms for controlling employees and their managers in order to minimize self-interest and make certain that organizational interests are served.

Table 8.1 summarizes the main points of three theories of control: a cybernetic theory focused on the control of employees, agency theory which presents strategies for controlling

Table 8.1 Three theories of control

	Cybernetic theory	Agency theory	Markets, bureaucracies, and clans
Purpose of control	Identify and adjust for differences between desired and actual performance	Ensure that agents (managers) act in the best interests of owners (capitalists and shareholders)	Minimize transaction costs, achieve cooperation
Control strategies	*Output and behavioral*	*Output and behavioral*	*Output, behavioral, and symbolic*
Control processes	1. Set organizational goals as part of the overall strategic plan 2. Set work targets or standards at each level of the organization 3. Monitor performance (individual and group) against targets 4. Assess and correct deviations	1. Establish a contract between principals (owners) and agents (managers) 2. Obtain information to ensure agents are meeting their contractual obligations and hence are serving the interests of principals 3. Reward agents for fulfilling the demands of the contract	**Market**—comparison of prices and profit as indicators of economic performance (Output control) **Bureaucracy**—compliance with rules monitored by close supervision (Behavioral control) **Clan**—socializing organizational members in cultural values, norms, and expectations (Symbolic control)

managers and executives, and, at the societal level, a framework comparing markets, bureaucracies, and clans as alternative forms of organizational control. As the table indicates, all three make use of output and behavioral control strategies.

Output control strategies are based on work results. They employ measures like the number of products completed, customers or clients served, rejects on an assembly line, processing errors, or customer complaints. But outputs are sometimes hard to measure in such a direct way; for instance, in nursing where the determination of patient health outcomes are complicated by many factors that nurses do not control (e.g., a patient's exercise or dietary habits). However, even when output control strategies are problematic due to ambiguity in defining outputs, advocates of the modern perspective may still use output measures, for example, when a government forces its schools to use standardized achievement tests to assess the quality of teaching in spite of the fact that many factors influence student learning that teachers cannot control.

When output control strategies prove too difficult to apply, **behavioral control strategies** can be useful. Behavior control focuses on how work is performed rather than its outcomes. For example, nurses can be assessed on their demeanor with patients, their accuracy and responsiveness to doctors' orders, or their effectiveness working in a team. Behavioral control works best when behavioral indicators are known to relate to desired outcomes so that measuring behavior is a surrogate for output measures when these are difficult to come by.

When links between behavior and outcome are unclear, ambiguity can frustrate efforts at behavioral control. Difficulties in defining effective behaviors have led some to combine output and behavior control strategies, in the hope that using multiple channels will better direct attention and effort to desired outcomes.

Cybernetic control systems

Cybernetic control systems align organizational and individual goals throughout an organization using resource allocation to direct employee attention to desired activities and communicating performance data to provide corrective feedback (see Figure 8.1). Designing such a system usually starts with setting goals and performance standards and developing the means for measuring outputs and/or behaviors.

Take the case of controlling the performance of faculty members in a university department using cybernetic controls. Performance standards are typically set with reference to goals and expectations such as demonstrated knowledge, enthusiasm, clarity, and skill at managing the classroom. These behavioral measures will likely be assessed with student evaluation and peer review processes that may be complemented by output measures of faculty performance such as the number of research articles published, the amount of grant money generated by research proposals, or the number of students who enroll in the faculty member's classes. Data derived from evaluating employee outcomes and/or behaviors will be combined and used to assess and compare the performance of individual faculty members relative to established goals and/or to each other. Any negative deviation from the desired level of performance is then used for feedback and punishment which can range from the denial of tenure or promotion to the assignment of unpleasant tasks, while positive deviations are recognized and rewarded through promotion and tenure, praise, research fellowships, teaching awards, and so on.

Organizations apply cybernetic control to groups as well as individuals. At the group level measures include things like statistical reports on unit output volumes (e.g., number of students or courses taught by department), quality control data (number of rejected items per 1,000 produced by shift), or occupancy rates (e.g., in a hospital, hotel, or apartment complex). Data from measures like these are then used to provide feedback to units and individuals about their performance relative to goals and targets, and to determine rewards and punishments, including increasing or decreasing resource allocations during the next budget cycle.

Negative deviations between goals and performance will usually be addressed in one of several ways. First, the goal or its measures can be adjusted if it is determined that the deviation is the result of an error in the control system. Second, the individual or group can decide to change their performance by altering their behavior or output level. Often this is encouraged by management through the use of pay or other incentives made contingent on specified levels of performance. Third, workers or units can be replaced or removed if it is determined that they cannot function as required by the system.

Over time, the cybernetic control system is designed to act like the thermostat it emulates—the system can be set to any goals and standards and it will adjust its behavior accordingly. But to change the control system itself requires the intervention of managers who typically

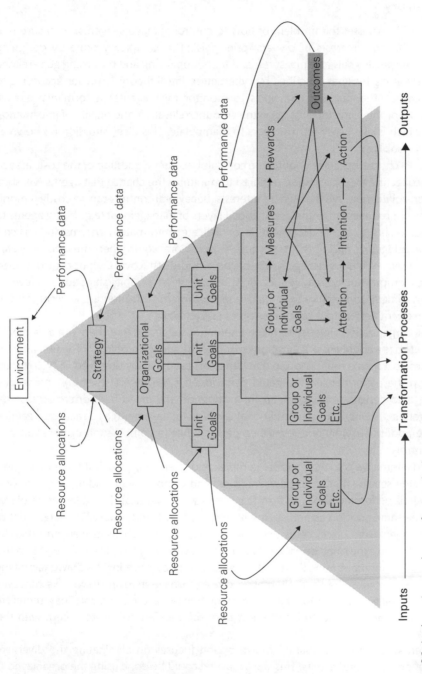

Figure 8.1 A cybernetic control system for organizations

Control processes operating at individual, unit, and the organizational levels of analysis. Notice that strategy connects the control system to the environment so that it can be changed to accommodate changes in the environment or in the intentions of owners and executives.

alter the control system to support new activities when this is deemed necessary or desirable.

Agency theory

Agency theory addresses the problem of how to control managers (agents) to ensure that they act in the best interests of owners (principals). This is typically done by designing contracts that specify goals and measures, and then monitoring and rewarding goal-related performance along the lines described by cybernetic control theory. However, according to agency theorists, the ability of principals to monitor their agents' performance against outcomes like profitability depends upon the amount, relevance, and quality of information available, which is often easy for managers to manipulate. This dicey situation is known as the **agency problem**.

Whether to choose behavior or outcome controls becomes a question of the costs associated with collecting the information required to minimize the chance that agents will shirk their responsibilities to serve the owners' interests. Behavioral controls can be costly if monitoring behavior requires either the use of added layers of management (e.g., hiring agents to watch other agents) or the development of sophisticated information systems, such as cost accounting, budgeting, and formal reporting. As behavioral control becomes too unwieldy or too expensive, output control generally becomes more attractive. Output control is least costly when output can be readily measured (e.g., number of units shipped); however, if outputs are difficult to measure (e.g., quality or customer satisfaction are as important as production quantities), output control becomes less attractive.

American organization theorist Kathleen Eisenhardt suggested that there are a variety of control strategies available to organizations that face the agency problem.[13] The first alternative is to design a simple routine job so that behaviors can be easily observed, and to reward based upon the performance of targeted behaviors (i.e., behavioral control). The second alternative is to design a more complex interesting job and invest in information systems (e.g., budgeting systems, audits, or additional layers of management) as a means of gaining knowledge about behaviors and rewarding performance (a combination of behavior and output controls).

The third alternative is to design more complex and interesting jobs, but use a much simpler evaluation scheme that bases salary increases and/or bonuses (including stock options) on the overall performance of the firm (e.g., profits or revenues). This alternative places agents in the same position as principals with respect to risk and reward. The alignment of rewards for agents and principals is presumed to align their interests as well, and thereby lead agents to make the same decisions that principals would make in their place. When this occurs, the need for monitoring the agents is reduced thus overcoming the drawbacks of the other two alternatives. The third alternative proves to have its own drawbacks however. Agents resist being penalized for things over which they have no control. They therefore demand higher inducements to offset the market risk they are forced to accept with this alternative.

Like alternative three, Eisenhardt's fourth option focuses on eliminating the divergent interests of principals and agents. This she proposed could be done using the organization's culture to control behavior, an idea first presented by Ouchi as clan control.

Markets, bureaucracies, and clans

Ouchi saw markets, bureaucracies, and clans as alternative solutions to the problem of control in organizations.[14] His work extended ideas presented by American institutional economist Oliver Williamson, whose 1975 book *Markets and Hierarchies* had given bureaucracy an intriguing economic explanation. In free markets organizations can command only reasonable prices and profits otherwise competitors take over, but in situations that lack competition, market control mechanisms cannot operate. According to Williamson when markets fail organizations turn to bureaucratic rules and procedures, job specifications, and the hierarchy of authority.[15]

Williamson's theory of market failure explains why many large organizations become bureaucratic. The market can only control behavior when an actor faces the market. For example, subsidiaries, or partners in a law firm or consulting practice can be treated as profit centers whose performance can be assessed by their contributions to profit, or by the prices they can command. But when the contribution to price or profit cannot be clearly assigned to specific individuals or units, the market fails to control behavior inside the organization and bureaucracy becomes necessary to maintain control.

You may think that all public sector and not-for-profit organizations are forced to use bureaucratic control because they do not face market competition. However, many such organizations find ways to incorporate or simulate market control. For example, allowing school choice in a community establishes competition among schools that would otherwise be controlled solely by bureaucratic means. Similarly, bidding out contracts for city services like database management or computer support, forces city departments to compete with external contractors, which creates market or market-like conditions. The reason typically given for such moves is the efficiency and effectiveness of market control mechanisms that keep costs down and quality high through competition, thus negating the need for expensive and demotivating bureaucratic control mechanisms.

In spite of its advantages, questions arise about making decisions strictly on the basis of price and profit where education or police and fire protection are concerned. Do we really want the cheapest schools or a profitable police force? Another concern involves asking government agencies to compete with private sector contractors that may be at liberty to employ minority workers on a part-time basis and provide them no benefits. Should government agencies mimic these practices in order to compete, or should they be expected to provide a living wage and benefits to their employees?

Furthermore, according to Ouchi, both markets and bureaucracies fail when environments are complex and rapidly changing, and uncertainty and ambiguity are consequently high. Under uncertainty and ambiguity, Ouchi reasoned, neither market nor hierarchical control will produce timely adaptation because these control systems depend, respectively, on clear market signals and established rules and procedures. Clear market signals are unavailable and established rules and procedures prove ineffective when environments are complex and rapidly changing. According to Ouchi, these conditions favor clan control.

Chief among the mechanisms of clan control Ouchi counted cultural values, norms, and expectations for defining proper behavior and keeping members focused on organizational objectives. Unlike markets or bureaucracies, clan control requires a fairly high level of commitment to the system by members who frequently sacrifice at least some self-interest to become socialized. But once socialized, internalized cultural understandings help direct, coordinate, and control organizational activities in ways that require much less overt monitoring than do markets and bureaucracies.

Organizations with large numbers of professionals offer particularly good examples of clan control. Because professionals are highly socialized to the norms and expectations of their profession, their commitment to preserving and enhancing their professional reputation helps to control their behavior. However, professional commitment can diverge from the interests of the organization, and when this happens professionals typically sacrifice organizational interests to maintaining their professional identities. So, while professionalization may be a good model of clan control, simply employing professionals is not equivalent to creating clan control in an organization.

Ouchi observed that all organizations employ a combination of the three forms of control, although each organization favors one over the others and this preference correlates with other organizational characteristics. For example, Ouchi observed that the social systems of clan controlled organizations were the most highly developed, while market-controlled organizations were the least, with bureaucracies falling in between. The opposite relationship held for his observations of information systems: market-controlled organizations possessed the most highly evolved information systems (e.g., for tracking prices and profits), while clan-controlled organizations seemed to demand less from theirs, with bureaucracies again falling into the middle.

Comparisons of market, bureaucracy, and clan control suggested to Ouchi that type of control aligned with the control strategies each employed. The prices and profits of market control provide output control measures. In contrast to the market's reliance on output control, bureaucratic control focuses on behavior, particularly decision making. Behavior is controlled in bureaucracies through the use of rules and regulations governing decisions plus procedures for applying them. The hierarchy of authority similarly directs and controls behavior from the bottom to the very top of the organization.

That market-controlled organizations employ output control strategies, and bureaucracy relies upon behavioral control, suggested to Ouchi that clan control might produce an altogether different strategy. Drawing on his observations that clan controlled organizations rely less on formal information systems, and more on social systems involving cultural values, he concluded that clan controlled organizations employ strategies of symbolic control. But Ouchi, being a staunch modernist, never paused to reflect on the ethics of this type of control, a concern that was taken up by critical organization theorists.

Critical studies of power and control

Whereas modernist scholars of organizational power and control focus most of their attention on explaining how power gets distributed in organizations and formulating normative advice for using it effectively in the contexts of politics and control, critical and postmodern scholars have been more interested in understanding the ways power relations become embedded in culture, knowledge, and ideology. In the most general terms, critical and postmodern scholars seek to establish humanistic, ethical, and inclusive organizational decision-making processes as alternatives to the rational ideal held by modernists, which they believe privileges the elite.

Based initially on Marx's definition of power as domination, and employing ideas like manufactured consent and systematically distorted communication, critical theorists retain something of the modernist stance when they assume that social, economic, and political structures explain power relationships. However, when challenging mainstream modernist ideologies and assumptions, particularly those favoring instrumental rationality, they align themselves with postmodernists.

Critical theorists question the institutionalization of power within the organizational hierarchy and the assumption that managers have a legitimate right to control others. The negative connotation they attribute to domination raises the Marxist question: why do dominated groups consent to their own exploitation rather than resist it? Many critical theorists study this phenomenon by analyzing the structural mechanisms and communication processes that maintain exploitative relationships. Their ultimate goal is to create communication and decision-making processes that represent the full range of stakeholder interests—including human rights and environmental protection. Starting from a critique of ideology, they follow Marx in defining power as domination, so this critique is a good place to start.

Ideology, managerialism, and hegemony

Wherever you find a group of people systematically expressing belief in a set of ideas you encounter **ideology**. In this sense ideology is sometimes conflated with cultural assumptions, but the two concepts are not substitutes. Ideologies may be expressed as either religious or secular beliefs, but typically they are held with firm conviction and therefore are difficult to question and resilient to attack. While the same may be said of cultural assumptions, culture consists of many other elements than beliefs and is arguably less political, though this is a contentious statement to make to a critical organization theorist and many postmodernists.

Ideologies are of particular interest to critical theory because they are often used to legitimate the domination of one group over another. Critical organization theorists, for example, make many references to **managerialism**, the ideology owners and managers rely upon to justify their right to control workers. Following from Marx's concept of false consciousness, critical theorists argue that workers participate in their own exploitation when they willingly consent to their oppression by buying into managerialism.

Italian Marxist theorist Antonio Gramsci presented an explanation of false consciousness in his theory of hegemony. According to Gramsci workers accept oppression and exploitation because institutional and ideological forms of domination become part of their taken-for-granted everyday reality.[16] **Hegemony** occurs when the practices and values of a culture or institution align with and maintain existing systems of wealth and power. Hegemonic practices never overtly coerce anyone, instead they lull you subtly and incessantly into regarding as normal and natural the established ways of thinking and talking that privilege the elite.

This gentle coercion can be done linguistically by defining the terms in which everyday organizational realities are constructed. Unguarded and unreflexive acceptance of the language offered by seductive training programs, often led by outside consultants, hides management's involvement in their domination while more or less dictating the terms in which employees will discuss and enact their actions and decisions. Even when the language programmed into the organization employs terms like participation, involvement, engagement, and empowerment, critical theorists see hidden interests of managers operating beneath the surface.[17] This type of control can be considered the linguistic equivalent of factory architecture and machinery that silently controls shop floor workers.

Inspired by Japanese statistician Genichi Taguchi and American W. Edwards Deming, business programs like total quality management (TQM), business process re-engineering (BPR), and Motorola's trademarked Six Sigma Practices offer critical theorists some of their most compelling examples of hegemony. These programs use statistical measurement to control outcomes such as costs and variability in manufacturing and other business processes including software development, sales, and service delivery. Participants are guided by language that uses terms such as quality control, defects (errors), continuous improvement, customer involvement, excellence, and some rendition of Deming's Plan-Do-Check-Act Cycle. Six Sigma practices even assign identity labels—black belts and green belts—to distinguish participants' performance levels and to harness their achievement to program goals. All of this measurement and linguistic labeling is aimed at getting employees to accept a highly controlling environment with minimal resistance.

Three faces of power

The silent and consequently hidden aspects of hegemonic power are similar to what Steven Lukes, a British political and social theorist, called the **third face of power**. Lukes claimed that different faces of power show up in decision making, in non-decision making, and in the ability to shape the preferences and perceptions of others without their awareness.[18] The first face of power involves a forum, such as an organization or parliament, where various actors or groups fully and equally participate in every aspect of decision-making processes. The second face, non-decision, occurs when the powerful limit or prevent the involvement of the less powerful in making decisions. For instance, the powerful might manipulate the way issues are defined, determine what issues appear on meeting agendas (and which do not), suppress discussion of undesired alternatives, or interpret silence as agreement.

Lukes's third face of power incorporates Gramsci's notion of hegemony. This face of power is revealed when social practices shaping the desires and behavior of the dominated work against their interests and cause their oppression. Lukes's theory is that, by giving active consent to hegemonic interests, workers collude in their own domination. This can lead to paradoxes. For example, employees granted greater autonomy at work can end up relinquishing more self-interest to benefit the organization. In a study of a knowledge-intensive firm, Deetz found that employees worked long hours and under-reported the hours that they worked, slept at worksites to maximize the time they could devote to work, and dealt with aggressive and sometimes abusive clients, all in the name of autonomy.

Gramsci suggested that to change hegemonic power relationships, one needs to understand how power is constituted through structures and practices. Acts of resistance do not have to take the form of open rebellion and can be quite subtle, such as withdrawing effort and attention, or engaging in dishonesty, theft, or sabotage. Stories of injustice and oppression, if told and shared by organizational members, can also perform acts of resistance,[19] as illustrated in the following excerpt from a research conversation with a female manager in a large US organization.[20]

Issues of diversity are very personal and unless you confront them in a personal way, organizations just aren't going to get anywhere. It's not about how do I get [me] to fit into this white, male oriented organization, because there is going to come a point at which I say 'No, I'm not going to give up who I am to do that' . . . And in meetings they use baseball and football metaphors—so I thought 'I'm not using any sporting metaphors, I'm creating my own.'[21]

Notice how the manager in the example openly confronted her need to resist hegemonic practices like using male-privileging metaphors to exclude her from organizational conversations, or suppressing her interests in service to theirs. Her acts of resistance include telling her story and introducing her own metaphors to counter those used by her male colleagues.

Labor process theory and the deskilling of labor

American sociologist Harry Braverman introduced labor process theory with the idea that the owners of the means of production (capitalists) control work by systematically **deskilling** labor through job fragmentation and routinization, practices introduced under Taylor's Scientific Management.[22] The deskilling of labor continues, he argued, until the work is so simple that very little training is required. Thus it becomes easy for managers to replace workers who put up resistance to the hegemonic power of management and in this way erode the workers' power base to the point where they feel resistance is futile. When this occurs, control over the labor process shifts from workers to management. Deskilling allows owners to drive down the price of labor to enhance their profits but also exploits and degrades workers and contributes to their alienation from work and the workplace. It is the opposite story to the one Dalton and Crozier told about the power of lower level employees.

Graham Sewell, an Australian organizational theorist, illustrated labor process control in his study of teams in an electronics organization.[23] Sewell found that control was maintained through electronic quality tests at various stages of an assembly process. The resulting quality data were symbolically displayed over each employee's workstation using traffic lights: red meant the team member had exceeded quality error allowances, amber that they were within an acceptable range of error, and green that he or she had made no quality errors. This practice led not only to management control through vertical surveillance, but also to self-discipline and intense peer pressure in the form of horizontal surveillance. Sewell's study showed that the horizontal control team members exerted upon each other by expressing their approval or disapproval was far more potent than the vertical control exerted by the managers.

Communicative rationality

German social philosopher Jürgen Habermas claimed that modern society is dominated by scientific, technical, and administrative experts organized into institutions that focus their attention on the most technically-efficient and rational way of achieving goals.[24] This technocratic ideology invades our everyday life and ignores humanistic concerns for individual and social development. Defining **instrumental rationality** as goal achievement through efficient means, Habermas presented the **communicative rationality** of debate, open discussion, and consensus as an alternative. He claimed that instrumental rationality distorts or undermines communicative rationality through the widespread acceptance and use of its logic of efficiency.

Consider this example. You are invited to a meeting of all departmental employees to discuss how work could be more productive and satisfying. The discussion ranges from streamlining procedures to eliminating the duplication of work that causes uncertainty and conflict between department members. Someone suggests that the department manager give an employee-of-the-month award with a bonus for attaining results above targets. Another person suggests weekly meetings to clarify individual responsibilities and share information. Departmental members might be able to come to some consensus about which of these proposals would make their work life better and feel good about their involvement in the process.

Habermas would argue that communication was systematically distorted during the meeting just described. First, those in power framed the discussion with their initiating question, which presumed a distinction between productivity and work satisfaction, suggesting these are competing concerns and may require tradeoffs between them. Second, those in charge had the possibility to distort communication by responding only to suggestions that supported instrumental rationality, thus ignoring the workers' interests while making them feel as though their interests were given consideration by being raised in the first instance.

From a Habermassian perspective, systematically distorted communication is an implicit form of manipulation and control because it privileges one ideology over others, involves deception (of self or other), and precludes sincere and ethically informed conversation. In this example the goal of the meeting was not to create a satisfying workplace by exploring a range of possibilities through open discussion and mutual understanding (i.e., communicative action), but a way for those in authority to take advantage of employee ideas to obtain consensus (although false) on how to improve productivity.

Workplace democracy

Although suggestions for achieving workplace democracy run the gamut from participation and stock ownership, to worker cooperatives and labor-managed firms (LMFs), it is the latter form of organization that most directly challenges capitalism by embracing democratic principles and promoting collective property ownership. Cooperatives are independent non-profit groups organized by and for the benefit of their members. They have a long history.

One of the earliest cooperatives, established over 250 years ago, was Benjamin Franklin's Philadelphia Contributionship for the Insurance of Houses from Loss by Fire. The New Mexico Rural Electric Cooperatives, another example, is a cooperative of cooperatives—one generating electricity and nineteen others handling its distribution. The plywood industry of the Pacific Northwest was taken over by several independent cooperatives formed by local workers when the plants became unprofitable.[25] Many towns have food and day care cooperatives.

A group of British weavers formed the Rochdale Equitable Pioneers Society in the UK based on the seven cooperative principles that underlie most cooperatives in existence today. These principles include ownership and governance by employees, decisions reached by the democratic vote of all employees, and the distribution of economic surpluses among employees in an equitable way, such as based on pay grade or hours worked. Those who promote cooperative organization argue that worker ownership leads to more socially responsible and community-based decision making and creates a supportive network.

One of the largest and most successful cooperatives in the world is Mondragón founded in the mid-1950s in the Basque region of Northern Spain. This worker-owned organization consists of over one hundred industrial, agricultural, housing, educational, financial, and distribution cooperatives.[26] Its notable features include an initial capital contribution by all new members, restrictions on the ratio of pay between the highest and lowest paid workers, and the rule that the cooperative's earnings may be distributed only as wages or pensions—no dividends are paid.

Feminist and postmodern perspectives on power and control

The themes of ideology and hegemony are tightly interwoven with power and control throughout critical theories and their ideas have proven attractive to feminist and postmodern theorists who sought to expose and then overturn these effects in organizations. Exposure began with the critical concept of stratification and the theory of dual labor markets.

Stratification and dual labor market theory

Using labor market analysis, researchers have provided considerable evidence that high paying, powerful, and prestigious positions are inequitably distributed in modern organizations, with numerous studies demonstrating an extreme disproportion of white males holding these positions in many capitalistic societies. Interpreting this pattern as labor market stratification, American labor economists Peter Doeringer and Michael Piore proposed dual labor market theory.

Doeringer and Piore's theory argues that the market for labor is composed of primary and secondary sectors.[27] High wages and good career opportunities are typical in the primary sector, while the secondary sector is marked by lower wages and poor employment conditions, such as a lack of job security, and limited or no benefits. Doeringer and Piore explained this stratification of opportunities by suggesting that, to remain competitive, employers must have a steady supply of qualified workers who can maintain the firm's technological advantage in the marketplace. This means that they must pay top wages and provide substantial benefits to employees who have desired skills and education. Employers offset the costs of their primary sector workforce by employing unskilled workers to perform less central tasks for less pay in poorer working conditions.

Dual labor market theory explains stratification, but not the disproportion of white males in the primary sector. To put it bluntly, it cannot be that only white males are technically qualified for primary sector jobs. Why are women, ethnic minorities, and both the young and the elderly so underrepresented in the primary sector of the labor market and so over-represented in the secondary? Because dual labor market theory only considers the economic and technological reasons for labor market stratification, it misses important explanations that can only be found by considering cultural, social, physical, legal, and political factors.

Barbara Czarniawska and Swedish organization scholar Guye Sevón applied narrative analysis to the biographies of four female scientists to explore the stratification phenomenon by focusing on places where women managed to infiltrate the primary labor market. Each was the first woman in the country where she lived to be named to a professorial chair at a university.[28] To explain how these women came to hold their positions in this male-dominated primary sector of the labor market Czarniawska and Sevón proposed the concept of double strangeness—the women were not only non-male, but all were foreigners in the country in which they achieved the recognition of being awarded a chaired professorship.

Because the women they interviewed had all faced competition for their posts from similarly qualified women nationals, Czarniawska and Sevón proposed that these female academics' foreignness cancelled the negative implications of their womanhood rendering these talented women less threatening to those already in power than were similarly qualified colleagues who were not foreigners. Either that or their universities were facing political, regulatory, social, and/or cultural pressure to correct the gender imbalance in their faculties. In that case foreign women, having lower status and less access to power than women nationals, would be seen by many of their male colleagues as the lesser of two evils.

Gender studies in organization theory

One popular feminist theory about why organizations are gendered holds that private life is characterized by caring and a sense of community associated with the feminine, while public life fits the expectations set by rationality and competitiveness, characteristics associated with the masculine. A number of feminist scholars have argued that the separation of male and female domains and the practices associated with them (e.g., working outside the home versus child rearing) reinforces a binary view of gender that underpins the everyday actions and interactions of both men and women in the workplace. Men are considered natural decision makers and leaders, while women are expected to be nurturing and play supporting roles. Gendering thus reproduces traditional societal relations of domination and subordination between men and women.

Calls to undermine the ongoing and taken-for-granted ways organizations produce and reproduce gendered outcomes led feminists to look beyond explanations for why women and other minorities are not better represented in the primary sector. Simply replacing male with female practices, after all, would not end stratification; it would only replace one dominant group with another, and anyway was not likely to happen in the competitive world of corporations. Although the feminist literature is far from homogeneous, deconstructing and overturning the practice of constructing gender as part of organizational life became a priority for some who turned their attention on the 'systematic forces that generate, maintain, and replicate gendered relations of domination.'[29]

Joan Acker, an American sociologist, based her work on the feminist theory that language is gendered because meaning circulates around a network of images that have distinctive male or female associations.[30] If language is gendered, then organizations must be gendered as well in that they produce and are the discursive products of gender-based power relations. This is because masculine ways of doing things are inherent in structural, ideo-logical, and symbolic aspects of organization as well as in the everyday interactions and practices of organizing. On this basis Acker proposed the concept of **gendered organizations**.[31]

Building on Acker's work, others have suggested that masculinity is deeply embedded in bureaucracy by its focus on hierarchy, the impersonal application of rules, and the separation of work and private life. For example, several organization theorists maintain that hierarchy is premised on the assumption of a masculine elite that depends on a feminized support staff, and careers based on one's continued commitment to the organization.[32]

While you may hear as a counter argument to the masculine domination of the workplace that women's interests are well represented in organizations through such policies as those establishing women's advisory committees, in effect this amounts to unequal representation. Such committees are explicitly separated from the dominant male structure, which has the effect of both stigmatizing women and keeping them outside the inner circle of power. With the ambition of overcoming this situation, both scholars and activists have proposed creat-ing alternatives to bureaucracy that reflect 'women's ways of organizing.' In practice such organizations have proven effective, particularly in the areas of health care and domestic violence.

At the level of jobs rather than organizations, other feminist scholars explore gendered work in organizations and its construction. For example, in her study of female engineers Joyce Fletcher suggested that definitions of work have a masculine bias. In a high-tech organization she found that the characteristics and behaviors worthy of promotion were autonomy, technical competence, self-promotion, individual heroics, and being able to quantify issues. Relational practices (which she associated with feminine belief systems) included watching over the wellbeing of a project, contributing to programs, mutual empow-ering, and collaborative teamwork, all of which were undervalued or ignored. Inspired by Foucault, Fletcher claimed such biased practices had the effect of disappearing relational practices by interpreting them as inappropriate for work and/or as a sign of weakness.[33] Fletcher found that the female engineers themselves, while wanting to work differently, col-luded in the disappearing act by warning their female colleagues not to openly engage in relational behaviors.

Feminist theorist Karen Ashcraft and communication scholar Dennis Mumby—both American—articulated a feminist communicology of organization in which they suggested that researchers explore how meanings and identities are created inter-subjectively in embodied everyday communication.[34] They used the example of airline pilots to show that the construction of pilot identity is tied into various discourses of gender involving cultural icons and stories of male fliers (e.g., Superman); stories of romantic ladybird female pilots (e.g., Amilia Earhart); the discursive production of an ideal technically capable professional white masculine pilot by the commercial aviation industry; the separation of professional/commercial pilots and lady-fliers by questioning the ability of women to fulfill their duties because of family obligations or lack of physical strength; and the reconstruction of the mas-culine pilot as the adventurous, rugged yet civilized professional. Ashcraft and Mumby sug-gested that these discursive practices, woven together over time, produced gendered identity among airline pilots through the unobtrusive exercise of power.

If current gendered constructions lead to devaluing women's work and to keeping women out of power, it follows in the name of justice that these constructions be changed. Feminist organization theorists propose using their own research politically to produce this change by giving voice to women and minorities; making room for multiplicity by exposing and overturning unitary representations and replacing them with representations inclusive of gender, race, ethnicity, age, and class; and by changing the subjects and objects (audiences) that their research targets. For example, studying and writing for women, people of color, indigenous people, the working class, youth and the aged, rather than dominant white males exposes and overturns dominant assumptions.

Disciplinary power, surveillance, and self-surveillance

As part of his study of how power and control have changed over time, Foucault compared modern prisons to the public executions and tortures commonly used in earlier times, when most societies were ruled by sovereign power (e.g., as in a monarchy).[35] His comparison highlights the difference between overt repression and the subtle and inconspicuous forms of power and control modern societies rely upon for social control. Foucault claimed that modern power and control is disciplinary by nature and can be found not only in prisons, but in hospitals, schools, and factories.

Stan Deetz applied Foucault's concept of disciplinary power to organizations when he claimed that many organizational forms of power and control are inescapable and unobtrusive. He linked the internalization of disciplinary power to organizational culture and clan control when he noted that disciplinary power arises from the ways in which values, ideals, and beliefs are shared and become part of everyday life. According to Deetz, 'Disciplinary power resides in every perception, every judgment, every act. . . . It is not just the rule and routine which becomes internalized, but a complex set of practices which provide common-sense, self-evident experience and personal identity.'[36] His description of knowledge workers who worked excessive hours, slept in their offices, and willingly served abusive clients and customers exemplified the disciplined control of the modern business world.

Foucault claimed that modern societal forms of control evolved alongside the development of psychology as a body of knowledge that legitimated the systematic observation and evaluation of people. This knowledge and these methods, he argued, empower the professionals who use them to control subordinated populations. This intertwining of power and knowledge led Foucault to his concept of power/knowledge. Key to understanding the role psychology played in creating disciplinary control is the widespread acceptance of the idea of normalcy as the goal and ideal of human behavior. Foucault's theory of disciplinary power is that those who decide who is normal and control the treatment of those they label abnormal, use their power/knowledge to discipline others through technologies of control such as incarceration, hospitalization, education, and management.

Foucault's theory of disciplinary power rests on his observations about how surveillance led to self-surveillance, a historical development he traced to an eighteenth-century prison design called the Panopticon. First described by Jeremy Bentham, the Panopticon has a central guard tower around which prison cells are arranged in a circle. The tower is constructed so that prisoners cannot see into the guard tower, but guards can observe everything that goes on in the cells. Prisoners in the Panopticon constantly conform to the rules and behave in the desired way because someone *might* be watching them. In Bentham's words:

> the more constantly the persons to be inspected are under the eyes of the persons who should inspect them, the more perfectly will the purpose of the establishment have been attained. Ideal perfection, if that were the object, would require that each person should actually be in that predicament, during every instant of time. This being impossible, the next thing to be wished for is, that, at every instant, seeing reason to believe as much, and not being able to satisfy himself to the contrary, he should *conceive* himself to be so.[37]

Foucault used the Panopticon to explain that surveillance generates self-surveillance through two mechanisms: the gaze and interiorization. The practice of observation that Foucault called **the gaze** sets up the expectation of surveillance. Then anticipation of the gaze, or the **interiorization** of its psychic force, leads to self-monitoring. Since the self-monitoring prisoner only requires potential surveillance, the control system based on disciplinary power/ knowledge operates without the overt repression of pre-modern control systems. The psychological presence of authority subtly and inconspicuously controls self-monitoring subjects, and it works whether those subjects are prison inmates, hospital patients, school children, or assembly line workers.

British organization theorist Barbara Townley argued that in organizations the gaze is embedded in tools used by human resource managers such as interview protocols, psychological tests, performance appraisals, and assessment centers.[38] Insofar as individuals anticipate the use of these techniques and respond in expected ways, they help to construct the disciplinary control system even as they submit to it. Similarly, Townley claimed, job descriptions, training programs, and the technologies workers employ to do their work lead to the interiorization of expectations. Thus the gaze and interiorization as practiced by HR professionals and those who submit themselves to their methods normalize disciplinary power in organizations.

Foucault believed disciplinary power to be neither inherently good nor bad. In addition to its potential for abuse, he saw its possibilities to produce pleasure, with the implication that we might not want to resist all disciplinary practices. Think about the discipline you adopt to learn a subject matter (also called a discipline!) wherein you allow disciplinary power to transform your subjectivity and often your body for the sake of gaining knowledge. For instance, as you 'take the subject matter in' pathways in your brain are reshaped and your body adapts to the chair in which you study. You will similarly find the effects of disciplinary power in sports, the arts, health and wellness, and parenting. Of course discipline has its dark side, as when expectations aimed at appearance cause people to diet obsessively or risk disfiguring themselves with unnecessary plastic surgery, but disciplinary power and control are not good or bad per se.

Organizational theorists who build on Foucault's theory examine the micro-practices of power and how these may be influenced by broader strategies of power at an institutional and societal level. For example, Australian organization theorist Stewart Clegg studied the power created through techniques of discipline and production that reinforce the status quo.[39] He identified three **circuits of power**: the episodic (daily interaction), dispositional (socially constructed rules), and facilitative (systems and mechanisms including technology, work, rewards). These three intersect and can lead to the empowerment or disempowerment of groups. For example, if a group of workers have knowledge about a particular technology on which others depend (facilitative circuit), they will be empowered in relation to other groups and will be able to negotiate outcomes to their advantage within the episodic and dispositional circuits. Think about Crozier's maintenance workers in the French cigarette factory.

Following Foucault, Burrell argued that, if contemporary organizations both reflect and maintain the disciplinary power of society by categorizing, analyzing, and normalizing us, or by making us focus on productivity or efficiency to the exclusion of our other interests, then modern organization theory is paradoxically complicit in reproducing the chains that critical postmodernists seek to break.[40] The reigning truth of the modernist perspective, capitalism, is based on the idea that profit can be generated through the efficient management of productive resources. Good modernist knowledge therefore addresses how efficiency can be achieved. Organizational hierarchies, technologies, culture, architecture, and processes like training and performance appraisal should all be designed to support this truth. Experts who create this knowledge are powerful because they influence what is done by whom and how, as well as who gets rewarded or punished. As long as modernism prevails in mainstream organization theory, proponents of symbolic and postmodern perspectives will be excluded whenever they resist the assumptions and philosophical position of the dominant discourse.

Theories of organizational conflict

Along lines suggested by Marx, some modernists see conflict as an inevitable aspect of organizing. Their models invoke other aspects of organizing—environment, social and physical structure, technology and culture—to explain why conflict arises and offer normative advice about how to deal with it. Although the organizational conflict theories presented below arose within the modern perspective, with the knowledge you now possess about critical, feminist, and postmodern theories of power, politics, and control, you should be able to adapt these frameworks to embrace the symbolic perspective, and you may even be ready to deconstruct them.

Organizational performance and levels of conflict

Organizational conflict has most often been defined as the struggle between two or more individuals or groups in an organization, or between two or more organizations in an environment. In general, conflict is produced by a state or condition that favors one group of actors over others and emerges when one or more actors perceive the efforts or outcomes of others as interfering with their own. American social psychologists Daniel Katz and Robert Kahn defined conflict as 'a particular kind of interaction, marked by efforts at hindering, compelling, or injuring and by resistance or retaliation against those efforts.'[41]

One widely accepted modernist theory of conflict proposes that both too little and too much conflict result in poor organizational performance, whereas performance is optimized by an intermediate level of conflict, as shown by the curvilinear relationship depicted in Figure 8.2. The normative implication of this theory is that conflict should be managed so as

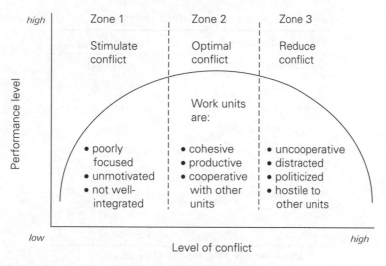

Figure 8.2 The curvilinear relationship between conflict and performance

Strategies for conflict management differ depending on whether the organization is experiencing too little or too much conflict. Characteristics typical of those experiencing conflict in each zone are described beneath the curve.

to produce the benefits of optimal stimulation of ideas and fresh points of view and to strengthen intragroup cohesiveness, while minimizing the negative effects of uncooperative behavior or open hostility.

Because group cohesiveness stimulates productivity, some organizations intentionally create competition between units to maximize their productivity. The price of this extra productivity, however, can be poor cooperation and communication between groups. The tradeoff between the productive influences of inter-unit competition and the negative effects that conflict can generate needs to be managed and much conflict theory is focused on providing normative advice for both reducing and encouraging conflict. Some ways to reduce organizational conflict are shown in Table 8.2.

There are many ways to stimulate conflict in organizations, including:

- Acknowledge repressed conflict
- Role model functional conflict through open disagreement and collaborative responses
- Alter established communication channels
- Hold back information
- Overcommunicate
- Deliver deliberately ambiguous messages
- Differentiate activities or outcomes among subordinates
- Challenge the existing power structure [42]

To make effective use of normative advice about managing conflict, you need a clear understanding of the situation you are facing. This is where the theory of inter-unit conflict comes in handy.

Table 8.2 Ways to reduce conflict in organizations

Recommended action	Implicit strategy
Physical separation	Avoidance
Increase resources	Avoidance
Repress emotions and opinions	Avoidance
Create superordinate goals	Collaboration
Emphasize similarities	Smoothing
Negotiate	Compromise
Appeal to higher authority	Hierarchical referral
Rotate jobs	Structural change
Physical proximity	Confrontation

Source: Based on Robbins (1974); Neilsen (1972); Pondy (1967).

The inter-unit conflict model

Explaining conflict in organizations is tricky because humans employ numerous psychological defense mechanisms and conscious strategies in order to disengage from overt conflict, including avoidance, smoothing, compromise, problem solving, and hierarchical referral (examples are given in Table 8.2). Thus, overt conflict does not occur every time the opportunity for conflict presents itself. You will find that explanations for specific instances of conflict are easily constructed in retrospect, but predicting when overt conflict is going to occur before it actually happens is much more difficult.

The model explaining inter-unit conflict shown in Figure 8.3 helps explain why organizations produce so many instances of conflict that Marx could believe that was their fundamental condition. The normative value of the model should become obvious as you work through the framework provided by American organization theorists Richard Walton and John Dutton, based on their study of conflicts between the sales and production departments of two firms.[43] You will grasp its value as a diagnostic tool most easily by reading it backwards, that is, from right to left. It will also help you to think of a specific example of organizational conflict you have experienced or witnessed and apply the model to it as you work your way through its components.

Observable indices and local conditions

A range of behaviors you might observe in a conflict situation appears on the right side of Figure 8.3. Ranging between the two extremes of open hostility and complete avoidance of interaction, they constitute only the surface layer of organizational conflict. You may find some of the behaviors described, like lack of cooperation and avoidance of interaction, difficult to observe at first; their presence may be more felt than seen, but with some experience you will become more sensitive to its full range of expression. Once you have observed behaviors indicating the presence of conflict, you should look to the nine local conditions described below to see how many of them apply to the conflict you are analyzing.

Figure 8.3 A model showing possible sources of inter-unit conflict

Conflict is seen to be related to local conditions that are more deeply embedded in environment and organizational contexts.

Source: Based on Walton and Dutton (1969).

Interpersonal differences

Not all people get along with each other. You will encounter many individual differences in organizations—for example, differences in authoritarianism and sociability, self-esteem, and the diversity of gender, race, ethnicity, age, or socioeconomic background—any of which can provide a reason for conflict. When you observe conflict under these conditions it can be hard not to attribute it to merely individual differences. You may be tempted to simply blame one party or the other and take sides without considering other factors.

In organizations taking sides is not likely to be effective, since the vast majority of conflicts found there are not simply the result of interpersonal differences, but rather arise from conditions at the group, organizational, and/or environmental levels of analysis. In fact, many people who truly have personal conflicts with one another routinely work together in organizations everywhere, proving that this factor alone is unlikely to account for all dimensions of a conflict that is underway. One or more of the remaining local conditions are likely to be involved.

Group characteristics resulting from differentiation

Each internally differentiated unit of an organization performs a different task and/or copes with a different segment of the environment. These differences become conditions ripe for conflict when units develop distinct discourses, subcultures, and identities. Expecting differentiated units to coordinate their activities and share resources and opportunities can magnify the risk of conflict and its intensity. Some organizations add layers of management or additional units to bridge relations between conflicted parties, but this only multiplies the opportunities for future conflict among now more numerous organizational units.

American sociologist William Foote Whyte studied a classic situation of conflict between the wait staff and cooks in a restaurant.[44] Whyte found the two groups differed markedly in their flexibility, their time horizons, and the results for which they were held accountable. Wait persons followed strict routines in order to be efficient enough to give adequate attention to all of their customers, while cooks remained flexible so they could adapt to the unpredictable flow of customer orders coming into the kitchen. Wait persons generally kept track of time in terms of the stages of a meal, whereas cooks thought in terms of shifts (e.g., lunch, dinner). Customers evaluated wait staff on their efficiency, demeanor, accuracy in taking orders, and skill in serving food, while cooks were evaluated on their culinary achievements. These differences defined unique characteristics of the subcultures to which the wait staff and cooks belonged and these characteristics made communication and coordination between them difficult.

Goal incompatibility

Goals defined at the highest levels of an organization must be translated and divided between the units and positions of the organization so that a variety of activities will ultimately be performed to achieve the overall strategy (see Figure 8.1). Once the goals have been translated to the operational level, however, it is often the case that tradeoffs are revealed.

For example, marketing departments typically state their goals in terms of sales to customers, which are enhanced by responsiveness to customer demands for services, such as fast delivery or customized product designs. A manufacturing unit, on the other hand, will usually specify its goals in terms of cost savings and production efficiency. Since their goals may be incompatible with marketing's responsiveness to customer requests, there is plenty of opportunity for disagreement and hostility to develop.

Task interdependence

As James Thompson explained, there are at least three different forms of task interdependence and each implies different amounts and types of conflict. Pooled task interdependence produces minimal direct conflict because interdependent units have little reason to interact as they pursue their goals and interests independently of one another.

Reciprocal task interdependence is a different story. It demands almost continuous interaction and therefore offers unlimited opportunities for conflict. However, conflict in these conditions tends to be moderated by the incentive to manage relationships well. Because each actor or group depends upon the others to achieve its objectives, open conflict hinders both parties simultaneously. In practice reciprocal task interdependence tends to produce periods of smooth interaction punctuated by periods of intense conflict because, when reciprocal interdependence breaks down, rapid escalation usually occurs on both sides.

Sequential task interdependence is the case where one unit is highly dependent on another but the dependency is not reciprocated. The more independent unit has little incentive to respond to the interests and demands of the dependent unit, setting up the conditions for chronic conflict between them.

Rewards and performance criteria

When performance criteria and rewards are not carefully coordinated between units they can damage the combined performance of the entire organization and lead units to refuse to cooperate. Consider the problem of giving exams to multiple sections of students taking the same course during the semester. One way to ensure that students in earlier sections will not reveal the questions to students in later sections is to inform them that all examinations will be graded on the same standard, and that if students in later sections improve their own scores because they know the questions in advance, it will be at the expense of students who did not have this advantage.

Notice how creating conflict between students leads to elimination of cooperation between them. Also be aware that while this strategy may increase fairness in the grading system, such strategies may be counterproductive from the viewpoint of encouraging information-sharing and the formation of cooperative study groups that benefit all students and the classes they attend.

Common resources

Dependence on a common pool of scarce resources often provokes conflict. Competition, for example over operating funds or capital allocations, physical space, shared equipment, and centralized staff services can produce conditions ripe for conflict.

Consider how your frustration level increases with the length of the queue for using a shared copy machine or one of a limited number of computer terminals in the library. When two groups both face pressure to work rapidly, claims about their relative need for access to shared resources can quickly escalate into open hostility or seething rage.

Status incongruity

Asking groups with significantly different statuses to coordinate their activities produces another condition that can lead to conflict. The imbalance of status is not problematic as long as higher status groups influence lower status groups; however, if lower status groups must initiate activities or exercise influence over higher status groups, then conflict is likely. Whyte observed this conflict condition in the restaurant where wait staff routinely initiated activity for cooks by giving them customer orders. Similar status incongruity was observed when engineers directed a higher status research group to do routine testing.[45] In both of these cases the inversion of a status hierarchy led to breakdowns in inter-unit cooperation.

You may observe conflict of this sort in required classes on organizational behavior (OB) in business schools. Grades in these classes often invert the status hierarchies of business schools that give more status to the quantitatively gifted than to those having other abilities, like the people skills that OB classes reward. This inversion frequently leads to conflicts between finance students and their organizational behavior professors and also contributes to devaluing this subject in business school cultures dominated by finance majors admired by other students for their higher earning potential.

Jurisdictional ambiguities

Jurisdictional ambiguities occur with unclear delineation of responsibility when credit or blame is at stake. Situations in which it is unclear who deserves credit or blame present an opportunity for units to come into conflict as each tries to take credit from, or assign blame to, the other. A lost order in a busy restaurant kitchen is a problem that triggers this sort of conflict when wait staff and cooks each can claim the other is at fault. Whyte showed that the addition of food servers to buffer communication between wait staff and cooks eased this conflict but only when this new group was given responsibility for tracking all orders, thus eliminating the ambiguity of who was at fault for a lost order.

Communication obstacles

When units speak different languages, they are less likely to agree on issues of mutual concern and more likely to attribute the lack of agreement to intransigence and self-interest by the other party. They may fail to understand it as the result of two groups looking at things in incompatible ways. Take the example of resident doctors and hospital administrators. Conflicts between these groups can often be traced, at least in part, to the different ways in which they communicate. Each of their discourses (medical vs. administrative) depends upon language that serves the unique purposes of their group, but as each group uses its preferred terms the other group feels its interests are being marginalized, a situation that can provoke resistance and hostility. Similar communication obstacles are famous sources of conflict between university departments whose faculties are professionally committed to producing well-differentiated (and some would say impenetrable) discourses.

Environment and organization as contexts for inter-unit conflict

It is now time to consider the deeper patterns that relate observable conflict and its local conditions to the environment and to aspects of the organization that relate to the core concepts of organization theory. Grasping the larger picture will help you put conflict in its proper perspective, even when those around you are caught in the grip of negative emotions.

Environment

The principle of isomorphism suggests that organizations attempt to match the complexity and rate of change in their environments by internal differentiation into specialized units and by adaptation to environmental change. Changing environmental conditions are often experienced as uncertainty within the organization, and groups that develop greater capacities for coping with the uncertainty can thereby alter organizational power relations between themselves and other units. Altered power relations can shift control over, as well as the need for resources, reward distributions, relative status, jurisdictions, and so on. Thus, complexity and change in the environment of an organization can contribute to any or all of the local conditions for conflict reviewed above.

Strategy

A growth strategy for an organization leads to increases in size and differentiation with effects similar to those just related to environmental complexity and change, including an increase in internal complexity and changes in the existing power structure. If growth involves mergers, acquisitions, or joint ventures, then adaptation to new units and the cultures they bring with them will also put strains on the organization that can contribute to conflict. Strategies involving downsizing contribute to conflict by creating the perception of shrinking resources, which provokes competition over what remains to be divided. When jobs are on the line, competition becomes fierce. Thus, strategies that affect organizational size in either a positive or a negative direction can magnify the effects of some or all of the local conditions for conflict. On the other hand, periods of abundance can mask conflict, so in these periods you may not find it easy to observe conflict even when it exists.

Technology

The organization's tasks are defined in large measure by its choice of technology, and changes in technology mean changes in the tasks assigned to units and their members. Since the assignment of tasks influences the amount and type of interdependence between units of the organization, technologies set up at least this local condition for organizational conflict. But technology can influence other local conditions as well, for example, status incongruity (e.g., when a new technology is introduced technical experts often need to instruct higher level organizational members in its use), reward criteria (new tasks demand different control structures), and even group characteristics (as when computers were new and organizations added information technology specialists to their organization structures).

Social structure

The creation and maintenance of a hierarchy of authority defines the basis for vertical conflict in the organization, while the division of labor separates the organization in a way that presents opportunities for horizontal conflict. Thus, choices about social structure lay a foundation for all the local conditions of conflict.

Organizational culture

When subcultures develop in opposition to dominant cultural values they are likely to create conflict, as in the case of countercultures. Divergence in basic assumptions between subcultures can help to explain the communication obstacles that arise in many organizations, such as incompatible discourses and silos. Differing basic assumptions can also produce incompatible goals, for example the assumption that science is a communal activity that requires sharing research findings within the scientific community brings research and development scientists into conflict with the corporate legal department that assumes *not* sharing research findings is the best way to protect the organization from patent infringement or industrial espionage.

Physical structure

Differences in the size, location, quality, or style of physical spaces assigned to different units can feed feelings of superiority or inferiority. These conditions can contribute to all the local conditions for conflict or may increase sensitivity to conflicts inherent in other contextual factors. Layout of physical facilities and location can produce or eliminate communication obstacles and affect the level of conflict that is due to task interdependence. Physical proximity contributes to conflict when it makes otherwise conflicted groups accessible to one another, while physical distance can reduce opportunities for engaging in conflict behavior but may introduce a communication obstacle.

Applying the inter-unit conflict model

There are probably endless ways to combine the factors producing a context in which conflict may or may not overtly occur, and many other scenarios than those discussed can be formulated, but you should by now see how the model works as a diagnostic tool. While not all factors will be present in every case of conflict you encounter, it is always a good idea to check them all to be sure not to miss something important.

But the inter-unit conflict model is useful in another, less normative way that starts by reading Figure 8.3 from left to right. Try imagining the organization embedded in its environmental context, responding with strategy, social and physical structure, technology, and culture to changes that constantly bring new potential conflicts into play. In this sense the Walton and Dutton inter-unit conflict model presents a theory of organization that builds directly on Marx's notion of conflict as central to organizing.

As an organization theory consider also how the inter-unit conflict model can be used to elaborate the five circles of Figure 1.1. By placing importance on how the parts of the organization align or not to produce the issues (including conflicts) faced daily in organizations, Figure 8.3 shows how the lives that organizational members lead map onto the ways an organization unfolds through everything people think, say, and do, as structuration theory claims. But do not forget that the use of conflict to change organizations is a political act that depends upon the use of power and the ability to control others—and that power and control, like conflict itself, may be suppressed and hidden from view. Thus do the themes of power and control ceaselessly intertwine with conflict, just as all three are part of organizing.

Summary

When politics is needed to overcome legitimate differences in preferences for goals or methods, then the coalitional model of decision making is of great value in resolving conflicts and moving organizations forward to take action. Politics loses its organizational usefulness, however, when it is applied to situations in which these conditions do not hold. This does not mean that politics will never be misapplied in organizations. A seasoned organizational politician can create conflict out of nearly any situation and will do so if the stakes are high enough. The bad feelings you may have experienced surrounding political maneuvering in organizations most likely stem from counterproductive applications of politics within organizational decision-making processes and the consequent occurrence of conflict that such behavior can produce. However, you should recognize the useful aspects of both political behavior and conflict, as well as their risks.

Modernist views suggest that the political process is most effectively managed by seeking a balance between too little and too much political activity, channeling political action into situations where it will be of value, and discouraging it when conditions favor other decision-making activities. However, critical, postmodern, and feminist studies remind you to be self-reflexive about the judgments you make as to what are useful and what are disruptive uses of political action. If managers only permit political discourse around issues that do not challenge *their* claims to authority and autonomy, then suppression of voices within the organization is likely to occur. Since suppression can affect productivity, particularly where innovation is important, even the most modern of managers will do well to reflect honestly on their motivations concerning political actions—their own and those of other members of the organization. Postmodernism encourages managers to understand that power is part of everyday social relationships and can lead to unintended consequences and repressive practices that dehumanize and mechanize the self. By revealing these practices, along with the gendered nature of organizations, more ethical and responsive forms of organizing can be created.

For critical and many feminist organizational scholars, power is evident in the domination of one group over another and is reflected in social, economic, and class structures. Seen from this perspective, organizations are networks of power relations that exist within broader historical, ideological, economic, and social conditions. The focus of these organization theorists is on the oppression of workers by owners and managers, and how capitalist ideology is maintained by all members of society without the necessity of their awareness that this is what they are doing. These scholars examine the material differences and injustices associated with the control of one group over another—with control being exercised through the deskilling of work (labor process theory) and by workers giving their active consent to the policies, practices, and requirements of management (hegemony and false consciousness). While some critical theorists focus on a theoretical critique, others have carried out empirical studies of how power relationships are produced and maintained in organizational practices and these merge with the perspective of postmodernists who study the effects of voice and other acts of resistance within the context of everyday organization life, often using the ethnographic methods introduced by culture researchers.

Critical theorists have studied taken-for-granted inequalities lying within ideologies, the negative effects of instrumental reasoning on human beings and the planet, false consciousness, and systematically distorted communication. By doing this they attempted to ensure that all interests are heard and no one's interest dominates. As you have seen, postmodern scholars use concepts of difference and fragmentation to study conflicts between alternative constructions of reality and the marginalization of groups of people. They believe that by bringing conflict and resistance into the open, they can reclaim a space for marginalized voices. Meanwhile, modernist approaches carry on viewing conflict as a manageable tool for leveraging worker and organizational productivity.

Table 8.3 summarizes the core ideas of the chapter by presenting modern, critical, and postmodern conceptions of power, control, and conflict.

Table 8.3 Modern, critical, and postmodern conceptions of power, control, and conflict

	Modern	Critical	Postmodern
Locus of power	Hierarchy, knowledge, and skill to solve key organizational problems	Social, economic, and political institutions and ideologies	Everyday social relationships, and discursive and non-discursive practices
Basis of power	The unquestioned and unchallenged right to control production work and workers	A democracy of stakeholder interests; challenges owner/shareholder's right to profit	Disciplinary power embedded in taken for granted, discursive and non-discursive practices
View of organizations	Rational and/or political arenas	Systems of exploitation, domination, and resistance	Producers and products of disciplinary power
Goal	To improve organizational efficiency and effectiveness	To emancipate dominated groups and develop democratic and humanistic forms of communication and decision making	To interrogate practices that lead to self-disciplinary behaviors and the marginalization of groups and individuals
Implications for control	Use of market, bureaucracy, or clan (cultural) control mechanisms	Use of hegemony and systematically distorted communication; employees must consent to their own exploitation	Use of disciplinary technologies and self-surveillance; requires both 'The Gaze' and interiorization
View of conflict	Counter-productive and should be managed by those in power to maximize performance	Inevitable consequence of capitalism's social and economic inequalities; necessary for resistance and the overthrow of the powerful, and for radical change	Emerges within the network of power relations as groups contest the right for some to frame others' reality and subjectivity

Key terms

bounded rationality

coalition

power

conflict

conflict resolution strategies

    domination

    compromise

    integration

organizational politics

politics of identity

control

strategic contingencies theory

resource dependence theory

symbolic power

output control strategies

behavioral control strategies

cybernetic control

agency theory

agency problem

market control

market failure

bureaucratic control

clan control

ideology

managerialism

hegemony

third face of power

labor process theory

deskilling

instrumental vs. communicative rationality

workplace democracy

stratification

dual labor market theory

gendered organizations

disciplinary power

surveillance and self-surveillance

the gaze

interiorization

three circuits of power

episodic

dispositional

facilitative

conflict and performance

conflict reduction

conflict stimulation

inter-unit conflict model

Endnotes

1. Tannenbaum (1968: 3).
2. Bacharach and Lawler (1980: 1).
3. Simon (1957, 1959); March and Simon (1958); see also Cyert and March (1963) and March (1978).
4. Dahl (1957: 203).
5. Dalton (1959); see also Mechanic (1962).
6. Pfeffer (1981b: 7).
7. Ouchi (1979: 845); see also Ouchi and McGuire (1975).
8. Etzioni (1975).
9. Crozier (1964).
10. Hickson et al. (1971).
11. Salancik and Pfeffer (1977); Pfeffer and Salancik (1978); Pfeffer and Moore (1980).
12. Pfeffer (1981a).
13. Eisenhardt (1985).
14. Ouchi (1979).
15. Williamson (1975).
16. Gramsci (1971).
17. Alvesson and Willmott (1996: 98).
18. Lukes (1974).
19. Deetz (1998).
20. Gabriel (2000).
21. Cunliffe (1997).
22. Braverman (1974).
23. Sewell (1998).

24. Habermas (1971).
25. Craig and Pencavel (1992).
26. Mondragón has recently deviated from cooperative principles by hiring non-member workers and centralizing decision making http://www.geo.coop/huet.htm
27. Doeringer and Piore (1971).
28. Czarniawska and Sevón (2008).
29. Ibid. 139.
30. This part of Acker's theory traces to Ferguson (1994).
31. Acker (1992: 249); see also Calás and Smircich (1992, 1999).
32. For example, see Grant and Tancred (1992) and Martin, Knopoff, and Beckman (1998); see also Huff (1990–2009).
33. Fletcher (1998).
34. Ashcraft and Mumby (2004).
35. Foucault (1980a, 1980b).
36. Deetz (1992: 37).
37. Bentham (1787).
38. Townley (1994).
39. Clegg (1989).
40. Burrell (1988).
41. Katz and Kahn (1966: 615).
42. This list is based on Robbins (1974).
43. Whyte (1949).
44. Seiler (1963).
45. Walton and Dutton (1969).

References

Acker, Joan (1992) Gendering organizational theory. In A. J. Mills and P. Tancred (eds.), *Gendering Organizational Theory*. Newbury Park, CA: Sage, 248–60.

Alvesson, M. and Willmott, H. (1996) *Making Sense of Management: A Critical Introduction*. London: Sage.

Ashcraft, K. L. and Mumby, D. K. (2004) *Reworking Gender: A Feminist Communicology of Organization*. Thousand Oaks, CA: Sage.

Bacharach, Samuel B. and Lawler, Edward J. (1980) *Power and Politics in Organizations*. San Francisco, CA: Jossey-Bass.

Bentham, J. (1995) Panopticon; or the inspection-house. In J. Bentham (ed.), *The Panopticon Writings* (Miran Bozovic, edn.) London: Verso, 29–95 (originally published 1787, also found at: http://cartome.org/panopticon2.htm

Braverman, Harry (1974) *Labour and Monopoly Capital: The Degradation of Work in the Twentieth Century*. New York: Monthly Review Press.

Burrell, G. (1988) Modernism, post modernism and organizational analysis 2: The contribution of Michel Foucault. *Organization Studies*, 9: 221–35.

Calás, M.B. and Smircich L. (1992) Using the 'F' word: Feminist theories and the social consequences of organizational research. In A. J. Mills and P. Tancred (eds.), *Gendering Organizational Theory*. Newbury Park, CA: Sage, 222–34.

——— (1999) From 'the woman's' point of view: Feminist approaches to organization studies. In S. R. Clegg and C. Hardy (eds.), *Studying Organization: Theory and Method*. London: Sage, 212–51.

Clegg, S.R. (1989) *Frameworks of Power*. London: Sage.

Craig, B. and Pencavel, J. (1992) The behavior of worker cooperatives: The plywood companies. *American Economic Review*, 82: 1083–106.

Crozier, Michel (1964) *The Bureaucratic Phenomenon*. London: Tavistock.

Cunliffe, Ann L. (1997) Managers as practical authors: A social poetics of managing and the implications for management inquiry and learning. PhD Thesis, Lancaster University, UK.

Cyert, Richard M. and March, James G. (1963) *A Behavioral Theory of the Firm*. Englewood Cliffs, NJ: Prentice-Hall.

Czarniawska, Barbara and Sevón, Guye (2008) The thin end of the wedge: Foreign women professors as double strangers in academia. *Gender, Work & Organization* 15: 235–87.

Dahl, Robert A. (1957) The concept of power. *Behavioral Science*, 2: 201–15.

Dalton, Melville (1959) *Men Who Manage.* New York: John Wiley & Sons Inc.

Deetz, Stanley A. (1992) Disciplinary power in the modern corporation. In M. Alvesson and H. Willmott (eds.), *Critical Management Studies.* London: Sage, 21–45.

—— (1998) Discursive formations, strategized subordination and self-surveillance. In A. McKinlay and K. Starkey (eds.), *Foucault, Management and Organization Theory.* London: Sage, 151–72.

Doeringer, Peter B. and Piore, Michael J. (1971) *Internal Labor Markets and Manpower Analysis.* Lexington, MA: Heath.

Eisenhardt, Kathleen M. (1985) Control: Organizational and economic approaches. *Management Science*, 31: 134–49.

Etzioni, Amitai (1975) *A Comparative Analysis of Complex Organizations.* New York: Free Press.

Ferguson, Kathy E. (1994) On bringing more theory, more voices and more politics to the study of organization. *Organization*, 1: 81–99.

Fletcher, Joyce (1998) Relational practice: A feminist reconstruction of work. *Journal of Management Inquiry*, 7: 163–88.

Foucault, Michel (1980a) *The History of Sexuality*, Vol. 1. *An Introduction* (trans. R. Hurley). London: Penguin.

—— (1980b) *Power/Knowledge: Selected Interviews and Other Writings by Michel Foucault, 1972–1977* (ed. C. Gordon). New York: Pantheon.

Gabriel, Yiannis (2000) *Storytelling in Organizations: Facts, Fictions and Fantasies.* Oxford: Oxford University Press.

Gramsci, Antonio (1971) *Selections from the Prison Notebooks* (trans. Q. Hoare and G. Nowell-Smith). New York: International.

Grant, Judith and Tancred, P. (1992) A feminist perspective on state bureaucracy. In A. J. Mills and P. Tancred (eds.) *Gendering Organizational Theory.* Newbury Park, CA: Sage, 112–28.

Habermas, Jürgen (1971) *Toward a Rational Society.* London: Heinemann.

Hickson, David J., Hinings, C. R., Lee, C. A., Schneck, R. E., and Pennings, J. M. (1971) A strategic contingencies theory of intra-organizational power. *Administrative Science Quarterly*, 16: 216–29.

Huff, Anne S. (1990–2009) Wives—of the organization. http://www.harzing.com/huff_wives.htm (accessed April 7, 2012).

Katz, Daniel and Kahn, Robert L. (1966) *The Social Psychology of Organizations.* New York: John Wiley & Sons Inc.

Lukes, Steven (1974) *Power: A Radical View.* London: Macmillan.

March, James G. (1978) Bounded rationality, ambiguity, and the engineering of choice. *Bell Journal of Economics*, 9: 587–608.

—— and Simon, Herbert A. (1958) *Organizations.* New York: John Wiley & Sons Inc.

Martin, Joanne, Knopoff, K., and Beckman, C. (1998) An alternative to bureaucratic impersonality and emotional labor: Bounded emotionality at the Body Shop. *Administrative Science Quarterly*, 43: 429–69.

Mechanic, David (1962) Sources of power of lower participants in complex organizations. *Administrative Science Quarterly*, 7: 349–64.

Neilsen, Eric H. (1972) Understanding and managing conflict. In J. W. Lorsch and P. R. Lawrence (eds.), *Managing Group and Intergroup Relations.* Homewood, IL: Irwin and Dorsey.

Ouchi, William G. (1979) A conceptual framework for the design of organizational control mechanisms. *Management Science*, 25: 833–48.

—— and McGuire, Maryann (1975) Organizational control: Two functions. *Administrative Science Quarterly*, 20: 559–69.

Pfeffer, Jeffrey (1978) The micropolitics of organizations. In M. W. Meyer and Associates (eds.), *Environments and organizations.* San Francisco, CA: Jossey-Bass, 29–50.

—— (1981a) Management as symbolic action: The creation and maintenance of organizational paradigms. In B. M. Staw and L. Cummings (eds.), *Research in Organizational Behavior.* Greenwich, CT: JAI Press, 3: 1–52.

—— (1981b). *Power in Organizations.* Boston, MA: Pitman.

—— and Moore, William L. (1980) Power in university budgeting: A replication and extension. *Administrative Science Quarterly*, 25: 637–53.

—— and Salancik, Gerald R. (1978) *The External Control of Organizations: A Resource Dependence Perspective.* New York: Harper & Row.

Pondy, Louis R. (1967) Organizational conflict: Concepts and models. *Administrative Science Quarterly*, 12: 296–320.

Robbins, Stephen P. (1974) *Managing Organizational Conflict: A Nontraditional Approach.* Englewood Cliffs, NJ: Prentice-Hall.

Salancik, Gerald R. and Pfeffer, Jeffrey (1977) Who gets power—and how they hold on to it: A strategic contingency model of power. *Organizational Dynamics*, 5: 3–21.

Seiler, J. A. (1963) Diagnosing interdepartmental conflict. *Harvard Business Review*, 41: 121–132.

Sewell, G. (1998) The discipline of teams: The control of team-based industrial work through electronic and peer surveillance. *Administrative Science Quarterly*, 43: 397–429.

Simon, Herbert A. (1957) *Models of Man.* New York: John Wiley & Sons Inc.

—— (1959). Theories of decision-making in economics and behavioral science. *American Economic Review*, 49: 253–83.

Tannenbaum, Arnold S. (1968) *Control in Organizations.* New York: McGraw-Hill.

Townley, B. (1994) *Reframing Human Resource Management: Power, Ethics and the Subject at Work.* London: Sage.

Walton, Richard E. and Dutton, John M. (1969) The management of interdepartmental conflict. *Administrative Science Quarterly*, 14: 73–84.

Whyte, William F. (1949) The social structure of the restaurant. *American Journal of Sociology*, 54: 302–10.

Williamson, Oliver E. (1975) *Markets and Hiera.* New York: Free Press.

Further reading

Burawoy, M. (1979) *Manufacturing Consent: Changes in the Labor Process under Monopoly Capitalism.* Chicago, IL: University of Chicago Press.

Czarniawska-Joerges, Barbara (1988) Power as an experiential concept. *Scandinavian Journal of Management*, 4: 31–44.

Emerson, R. M. (1962) Power-dependence relations. *American Sociological Review*, 27: 31–40.

Gherardi, Silvia (2007) *Gendertelling in Organizations: Narratives from Male-dominated Environments.* Copenhagen: Copenhagen Business School Press.

Kanter, Rosabeth Moss (1977) *Men and Women of the Corporation.* New York: Basic Books.

March, James G. (1994) *A Primer on Decision Making: How Decisions Happen.* New York: Free Press.

McKinlay, A. and Starkey, K. (1998) (eds.) *Foucault, Management and Organization Theory.* London: Sage.

Mills, Albert J. and Tanered, Peta (1992) (eds.) *Gendering Organizational Theory.* Newbury Park, CA: Sage.

Pettigrew, Andrew (1973) *The Politics of Organizational Decision-making.* London: Tavistock.

Pringle, Rosemary (1988) *Secretaries Talk: Sexuality, Power and Work.* London: Verso.

Simon, Herbert A. (1979) Rational decision making in business organizations. *American Economic Review*, 69: 493–513.

Wildavsky, Aaron (1979) *The Politics of the Budgeting Process* (3rd edn.). Boston, MA: Little, Brown.

Part 3

Looking Back and Looking Forward

This book has thus far told a story of how the normal science of organization theory defined by the modern perspective was revolutionized by the proponents of symbolic and postmodern perspectives. Because such a story must remain forever incomplete the concluding chapters that make up Part II will begin introducing additional ideas into it. Few of these ideas are really new, although all have something new to contribute, a concept, a theory, or a perspective that, lending itself to organization, extends them both. In my mind, the ideas presented in Part III collectively set the stage for organization theory's next act.

Of course there are many more promising ideas than there are pages left in this book, so I began my search for the content of Part III by selecting ideas that have the greatest likelihood of transforming into the next core concept, theory, or perspective to be accepted within the mainstream. Then I added some wild cards. As I wrote about them the mixture of these ideas began to form their own connections, so in a way these last two chapters reflect my theorizing process. You may or may not be able to reverse engineer my theorizing practices from what is written, but if you are interested in how I work, here you may find some clues.

Part 3

Looking Back and
Looking Forward

9 Theory and practice

The tension between theory and practice, introduced by combining economic and sociological theory with the normative interests set forth by classical management scholars during its prehistory, has been present in organization theory for nearly a century. It is still going strong. This chapter introduces pragmatism, a theoretical perspective some credit with being the source of this tension, and others see as its future. Next we consider ways in which organization theory has provided practical guidance to managers in their efforts to design organizations and how the question of organizational design is morphing into interest in the new organizational forms emerging in response to the complexity and dynamism of our globalizing world. Organizational change will be tracked through a similar course alteration as it becomes less a question of managing or leading change and more one of coming to terms with the dynamics of organizing, becoming what today in organization theory is addressed through concepts like institutional entrepreneurship. The chapter ends on two of pragmatism's most obvious but not yet well developed contributions to organization theory—practice theory and process theory—both of which will provide context and vocabulary for addressing the topics presented as Chapter 10.

Is pragmatism the new normative perspective?

American pragmatist philosopher John Dewey believed that all knowledge was the product of human inquiry, which he defined as the search for practical solutions to the challenges life presents. Dewey grounded his **pragmatism** in the belief that what and how we know—our ontology and epistemology—and our motivation to seek or create knowledge, derive from our practical nature.[1] Everything we do, including organizing, theorizing, and philosophizing, we do because we find it useful in some way or other. Thus the proven usefulness of an idea became pragmatism's key criterion for determining what is to be considered knowledge and granted the status of truth. An important implication of this central pragmatic idea is that truth and knowledge are always provisional, they shift and change with experience, which itself is ongoing, plural, and equivocal.

Charles Sanders Peirce and William James, who founded pragmatism, developed their views by rejecting modern philosophy.[2] Specifically, they rejected the idea of scientific progress, the search for absolute truth, and modernism's dependence on the duality of thought. For example, they opposed what Dewey once described as 'the spectator theory of knowledge' adhered to by many modern philosophers. Pragmatic belief that all knowing derives from doing made it imperative that knowers involve themselves in the production of knowledge, rather than being passive observers.[3]

Practicing what his theory taught him, Dewey applied pragmatism to education.[4] He believed that if learning is the product of lived experience, then education should provide students with opportunities to learn in the context of doing things. Teachers were to facilitate learning by putting students into practical situations and helping them discover what works for them. To contradict the implications of the spectator theory of knowledge, Dewey recommended that educators cultivate imagination and respect the inseparability of inner and outer ways of knowing, in other words, objective materials were to be regarded always and everywhere intertwined with subjective meaning.[5] It is in this sense that the experienced object and the experiencing subject form a pragmatic unity, as do other dualistic oppositions of modernism when viewed from the perspective of pragmatism, such as mind/body, stability/change, and structure/agency. In these beliefs, pragmatism anticipated postmodernism by nearly a century.

Modernist organization theorists thus far have mainly used pragmatism to reassert the practical side of the theory/practice duality in organization theory. By reining back what many modernists experience as esoteric postmodern ideas, some see in pragmatism a needed corrective to the chaos of multiplicity threatening to undermine modernism's dominance. On the other hand, as already noted, many postmodernists see pragmatism as further support for their aims and ambitions. Mutual acceptance gives pragmatism the potential to move organization theory beyond old and tired debates to explore new or at least different territory.

One way to think about pragmatism's potential might be to compare how each of our three perspectives would respond to the pragmatically inspired question raised by Kurt Lewin's maxim: if there is nothing so practical as a good theory, what, exactly, makes a theory practical? For advocates of the modern perspective there is an obvious answer: practicality is to be found in the ability of a theoretical explanation to indicate useful solutions to practical problems such as how to structure an organization, respond to environmental or technological change, or create a culture that supports the strategic direction set by management. However, when symbolic or postmodern perspectives press us to find practicality in theoretical understanding or critical appreciation, what to regard as useful theory is less obvious. What do these perspectives offer that can be considered practical?

The problem we face is not that understanding and appreciation have no practical value, it is that their usefulness is of an ontologically and epistemologically different order than that of explanation. Knowing why something works lends itself to controlling outcomes. But one does not seek to use their understanding of phenomena to control them, understanding provides insight and a deeper feeling for the thing, the person, or the process at which understanding is directed. Similarly appreciation is not oriented to the control of outcomes or even to insight, it is oriented to the unfolding of possibility through, as Dewey would have it, artistry, intention, and imagination.[6] These different approaches to the practical require adjusting expectations and actions to the kind of theory and the sort of practice being engaged. Understanding and appreciation are simply not practiced in the same way that explanation is. Remember that just because a theory's practical value is not realized intellectually does not mean it has none. Practical value can as easily be actualized by feeling, hearing, or seeing, by engaging in action (i.e., learning tacitly by doing), and by exercising empathy, imagination, artistry, and intuition.

To better accommodate pragmatism to organization theory, I will now look backward at two ways that organization theory has been applied to the practice of organizing—organizational design and change. Looking forward, I then attempt to reformulate these ideas in ways that make them more compatible with new developments within the field, specifically practice theory and process theory.

How do you design an organization?

Today globalization and other changes in organizational environments and technology demand new solutions to the perennial problem of how to organize. Contingency theory implies there are many valid solutions, but formulaic efforts to determine what design works best in a given situation have proven unsatisfactory. To get into some of the technicalities modernists cite to explain these shortcomings, the complexity of the phenomenon, coupled with difficulties in defining and measuring all possible contingencies, prohibit mathematical models from converging on clear solutions. Nonetheless a combination of theory and practice has produced certain generic organizational designs that offer the main choices practitioners face.

Theories of **organizational design** are normative by nature in that they seek to address the problem of intentionally selecting and implementing organizational structures and proc-esses to enhance organizational performance. Modernists have traditionally led the field in normative influence, while the main contribution of the symbolic perspective has been to urge organizational designers to be sensitive to the culturally embedded meanings that con-textualize all social orders and to the symbolism of representations like the organization charts often used to communicate different organization designs. Studies of the human con-sequences of organizational design for everyday experience have aided postmodernist efforts to bring the interests of those subjected to organizational design into focus, along with any processes establishing hegemony or leading to exclusion or marginalization. Post-modernists critique organization design in order to prescribe ethically desirable alternatives to structuring practices, such as workplace democracy, or to call for resistance and subter-fuge as escape routes defying an organization's restrictions on individual freedoms.

From a modernist perspective a good organizational design optimizes organizational per-formance by balancing elements or dimensions of social structure such as differentiation and integration. Modernists often use criteria such as efficiency and effectiveness to judge competing design solutions. For instance, organizational design is deemed effective if it guides the attention of employees to the differentiated activities that fulfill an organization's strategy, if it promotes ease of integration among all employees, and supports and coordi-nates their activities. A design is efficient if it minimizes the time, effort, and resources needed to achieve organizational goals.

Careful analysis of an organizational design will reveal where efficiency and effectiveness are not achieved and organizational design changes can be implemented to address these problems. Bear in mind, however, that every social structure has gaps resulting from the practical impossibility of perfectly integrating a complex and highly differentiated organization. Conflicts resulting from gaps should therefore not necessarily be interpreted as bad; they may function in ways that allow an imperfect social structure to work in spite of its imperfections.

Organization theorists and managers alike use **organization charts** to get a quick impression of an organizational design. Organization charts are tools for mapping the structure of roles and responsibilities distributed throughout an organization and can be useful for redesigning an organization structure as well. They provide a fairly clear representation of the hierarchy of authority and a general idea of the division of labor, but, organization charts do *not* offer much information about coordination mechanisms, informal relationships (although some can be represented with dotted lines), or the distribution of power that flows outside the formal hierarchy.

Generic organizational designs

There are several generic organizational designs that organization theorists and managers use as templates for designing organizational structures. Modernists have conducted much research over the years that enables them to characterize these organizational designs in relation to the theoretical concepts of social structure, technology, environment, conflict, control, and culture, and to relate these characteristics to performance outcomes that practitioners like to measure. The primary findings from these studies are offered along with descriptions of each design, and an organization chart showing a generic or actual example is offered where appropriate.

Simple organization

Extremely small and/or highly organic organizations often appear to have little if any formalized social structure or rules; their typically emergent organizational design is best described as simple. Simple designs characterized by completely flexible social relationships with limited differentiation evidence almost no hierarchy. There is little need for delegation and little opportunity for specialization in a simple organization since everyone works, more or less, side-by-side to get the job done.

In a simple organizational design the assignment of tasks determined by management decree or by mutual agreement is open to direct and informal coordination and supervision that occur as part of the flow of activity with those in authority being constantly available for consultation and instruction. Simple organizational designs are characteristic of newly formed organizations (e.g., an entrepreneurial venture) or permanently small organizations (e.g., a traditional, one-dentist dental practice). They also occur within prototype laboratories, product design or project teams, in cross-functional management groups, and in many subunits of large organizations, or they can result from de-differentiation of one or more of the structures produced by the following organizational designs.

Functional organization

Organizations that grow too complex to be administered using a simple design usually adopt a functional design to cope with the increased demands of differentiation. Functional designs

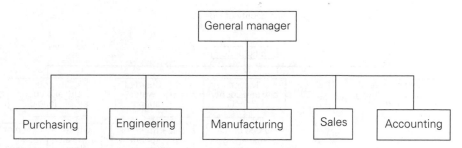

Figure 9.1 An organization chart showing a functional design

are so called because they group activities according to a logic of similarity in work functions (the nature of the work people perform). But functional similarity usually also implies high levels of task interdependence and common goals. For instance, the functions of a typical manufacturing organization include jobs grouped into units that are responsible for production, sales, purchasing, personnel (or human resource management), accounting, and engineering, and may also include the functions of finance, marketing, R&D, public relations, communication, and facilities management (Figure 9.1). Within each of these functions, people do similar kinds of related or interdependent work tasks and strive to accomplish a particular set of goals. You will find functional designs in common use among many government organizations, as you can see in the organization chart for the city and county of Honolulu (Figure 9.2).[7]

Functional designs maximize economies of scale resulting from specialization and thus are efficient in the sense that they limit duplication of effort. The logic of functionally designed organizations is highly transparent to employees who can easily recognize the connections between the tasks performed within their function and the tasks others perform (e.g., marketing work is easily differentiated from accounting or manufacturing work). The downside of the functional differentiation of work tasks is that employees may develop greater loyalty to their function than to the organization as a whole, leading to the problem of functional silos.

Functional designs give the top manager tight control in the sense that she or he is the only person whose position gives them the big picture with respect to what everyone else in the organization is doing. This tight control, however, can also be a major shortcoming. For example, as the solitary pinnacle of authority, the top manager can easily become overburdened with decision-making responsibilities, particularly when the organization starts to grow. And, because no one else in the organization has the same breadth of perspective and responsibility, if the top manager is suddenly lost, other managers in the organization will likely be ill prepared to take over.

Multi-divisional (M-form) organization

In developmental terms, the organization that outgrows a functional design will often turn to the multi-divisional form (M-form, for short) as a means to alleviate overburdened decision makers. The M-form is essentially a set of separate functionally structured units that report to a headquarters staff (see Figure 9.3). Division management of each functionally structured

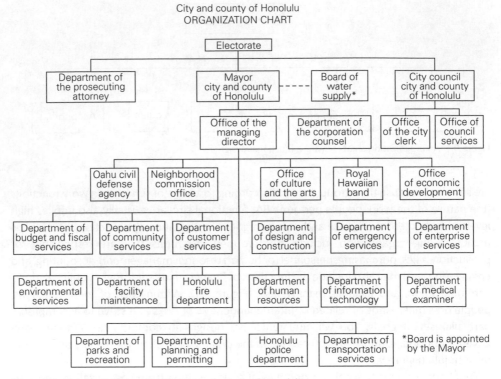

Figure 9.2 Organization chart for the city and county of Honolulu

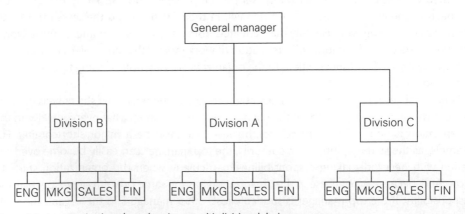

Figure 9.3 An organization chart showing a multi-divisional design

unit is responsible for managing its own day-to-day internal operations (e.g., production scheduling, sales, and marketing), while the headquarters staff assumes responsibility for financial controls and long-range strategic developments.

M-form organizations group people, positions, and units in one of three ways: by similarities in products or production processes, customer type, or geographical region of activity.

For example, the NASA Glenn Research Center has four Directorates (Aeronautics, Research and Technology, Space, and Engineering and Technical Services) each of which is subdivided into product divisions.[8] British Telecommunications (BT) is divisionalized by customer type, with divisions that include BT Global Services (worldwide business services and solutions), BT Retail (residential and end-business customers), BT Wholesale (telecommunications networks, sales of network capacity and call terminations to other carriers), BT Exact (network design, telecommunications engineering, IT systems, and other services to BT businesses), and BT Openworld (international mass-market Internet), all of which are managed by the holding company BT Group plc.[9] The United States Geological Survey (a Department in the US Department of the Interior) is divisionalized on the basis of three geographic regions: Western, Central, and Eastern.[10]

When they are treated as profit centers, multi-divisional designs allow for a type of accountability that is not possible in functional designs; each division can be assessed in comparison with its competitors on the basis of performance in the marketplace, whereas the higher level of interdependence among groups in a functional design makes this type of accountability impossible. However, you should recognize that, within each division of an M-form organization, the problem of functional accountability remains. Nonetheless, M-form organizations are usually able to offer enhanced responsiveness to the needs of customers because the specialization of the organization allows greater focus on the businesses each division operates.

Sometimes companies operate divisions in different industries rather than just divisionalizing products within an industry. Such organizations are known as conglomerates or holding companies. Conglomerates are usually formed by merger or acquisition of other organizations, although not all mergers and acquisitions result in conglomerates. The reasons for forming a conglomerate are generally financial, involving investment opportunities rather than concern for technical economies or market advantages such as are produced by vertical and horizontal integration, which can also be achieved through merger or acquisition. Since the core activities of the conglomerate often consist of unrelated technologies operating in different environments, all information must be reduced to a common denominator in order for top executives to make the comparisons that drive their budgeting decisions. The common denominator is profitability, and therefore concern for profit becomes the driving force within these organizations.

As with other M-forms, strategy at the corporate level of a conglomerate focuses on managing resource flows into divisions, which is accomplished using capital investment and budgeting procedures and by creation, acquisition, or divestment of divisions. Business-level strategy and operating decisions are delegated to divisional heads. The main difference between the conglomerate and other M-forms is that top executives of conglomerates come to view their organizations almost entirely in financial terms, rather than in terms of providing goods or services to a particular market or environment. This way of thinking trickles down to the rest of the organization, for example, by creating enormous concern for budgeting decisions, and thus middle managers learn to focus much of their attention on the financial reports that they provide as input to budgeting decisions, sometimes at the expense of other aspects of the business.[11] (Figure 8.1 showed a generic example of this sort of control system with resources flowing from the environment downward to all levels of the organization while the reporting of how budgeted resources were converted to performance flows in the opposite direction.)

Most if not all outcomes within the divisions of a conglomerate depend upon decisions concerning how profitability is to be calculated, and arguments over these calculations abound. For example, when divisions sell products to one another, conflicts occur over transfer prices. This is because one division's costs are another division's revenues. The irony of the M-form is that, for all their emphasis on profit, M-forms generally turn out to be less profitable than their functional equivalents, in part due to the resources diverted to waging political battles.[12] A greater irony is that the financial management model developed within conglomerates has become an institutionalized feature of many organizations that use other types of design. In spite of the evidence that the M-form is usually less profitable than other designs, institutional pressures supporting this type of structure cause many managers to prefer the M-form. That and the fact that, generally speaking, the bigger the organization, the fatter the salary top executives demand, which also undercuts the M-form's profitability.

Another reason that M-form organizations are not as profitable as those using functional designs is that instead of one sales, accounting, production, and purchasing department, the M-form organization has one of each for every division. To the extent that some of the work of these departments is redundant, M-form organizations will be more costly to operate. This redundancy can only be reduced by centralizing some functions (e.g., sales force, supply chain); however, coordination costs are high and the advantages of responsiveness to the market will be lost if the organization moves too far back toward a fully centralized functional design. The costs of integrating multi-divisional structures are also greater. Top management must coordinate across several divisions that are often geographically separated. Increased complexity is costly in terms of control loss, travel, and demands for communication.

In spite of the drawbacks, the M-form has several advantages to recommend it. The first of these is size. Multi-divisional organizations consistently grow larger than their functional counterparts. Size gives organizations a competitive advantage in that large organizations have greater influence on their environment and usually occupy more central positions in their inter-organizational networks than do small organizations. Larger organizations can typically hire the best executives because most are attracted to the power and influence large organizations command, not to mention the salaries they offer. Furthermore, the resources that are under the control of large organizations give them more opportunities to broaden their competitive activities both domestically and abroad. The M-form also provides better training for future executives than does the functional structure—divisional managers operate with roughly the same perspective and set of responsibilities as would the president of a functionally designed organization, and headquarters staff acquire broad-based experience that is unlikely to be gained within the functional form.

Matrix organization

The matrix design was developed with the intention of combining the efficiency of the functional design with the flexibility and responsiveness of the M-form (Figure 9.4). You can think of the matrix organization as having two structures, each of which is the responsibility of a different group of managers. Managers on the functional side of the matrix are

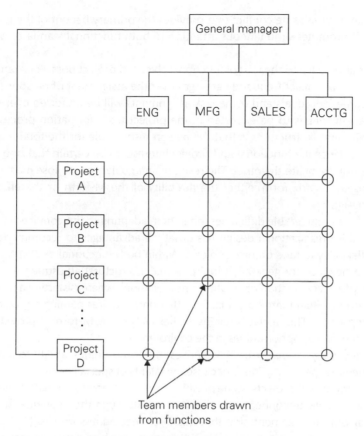

Figure 9.4 An organization chart showing a matrix design

responsible for allocating specialists to projects, helping them maintain their skills and acquire new ones, and monitoring their performance with respect to the standards of their functional specialty.

Managers on the project side of the matrix are responsible for overseeing specific projects: planning the project, allocating resources, coordinating work, monitoring task performance, and ensuring project requirements and deadlines are met. The goal of project managers is to bring the project to completion on time and within budget.

The greatest difficulty in using the matrix design lies in managing the conflict built into the dual lines of authority to which employees working inside the matrix are subjected. Functional managers will expect their matrix employees to meet the requirements of their specialty, while project managers want them to adjust to the requirements of the rest of the project team and meet or exceed customer expectations. Thus matrix employees confront the, often contradictory, expectations of performing complex tasks to high quality specifications while at the same time facing pressure to minimize costs and meet tight schedules. When employees serve on more than one project team, they face the additional pressure of conflicting demands from multiple project leaders. You should recognize, however, that it is this same conflict that provides the primary benefit of the matrix structure in that it promotes simultaneous attention to both functional standards and project demands.

Conflict is also built into the jobs of functional chief and project boss. For example, at this level in the matrix conflict frequently emerges over the assignment of persons to projects. Obviously some individuals and some task assignments will be preferred over others and political maneuvering is to be expected in the project team formation process. Another challenge with matrix structures is that the person responsible for the total matrix design will need to balance the functional and project interests to be certain that one side of the matrix does not dominate the other. The result of an imbalance is to lose most of the benefits of using the matrix form, either the flexibility of the M-form or the efficiency of a functional design.

In spite of the considerable difficulties inherent in adapting to the conflicts and pressures of a matrix, this organizational design has offsetting advantages to recommend it. One is enormous flexibility to take on new projects. Within both functional and M-form designs, starting up a new activity generally requires a major structural adjustment (i.e., adding a responsibility to every function or creating a new division), whereas starting a new project is a common event within matrix organizations that only requires naming a project manager and recruiting a team. Thus a matrix retains the flexibility of the M-form to provide customer service and respond to opportunities in the environment.

Another advantage of matrix designs derives from their unique ability to maximize the value of expensive specialists. This is because the talents of specialists can be pooled for use among a wide variety of projects, some of which may be otherwise unrelated and thus likely to remain structurally unconnected in the M-form. Although the individual specialist will have to deal with the fragmentation that this disconnectedness implies (e.g., working on two or more unrelated projects for project managers who have little concern for the specialists' competing responsibilities), from the perspective of the organization, the sharing out of specialized capabilities creates the considerable efficiency the functional design offers relative to the M-form. This is because where the M-form would hire potentially redundant specialists for each of its divisions, the matrix can more easily use its specialists to their full capacity.

Hybrid designs

The organizational designs already examined represent pure types, and organizations will not always conform to one of these. Hybrid designs are partly one design type and partly another. For example, a research and development division may use a matrix, while other divisions are organized functionally. Hybrids may occur either because designers deliberately mix forms in an attempt to blend the advantages of two or more different types, or because the organization is changing and is only part way to realizing its new structure. Most big companies today are hybrids that combine corporate staff functions, matrices, and divisions. Hybrid forms can be confusing in that the basis of relationships changes as you move from one part of the organization to another. On the other hand, the hybrid form allows the organization the flexibility to adopt the design most appropriate to the varied needs and preferred ways of working of its different subunits.

Strategic alliances and joint ventures

Strategic alliances represent contractual, often long-term, relationships created between different organizations to allow collaboration on new opportunities, such as the development of a new product or technology transfer. Alliances can be formed with or between government organizations or with organizations in the same or different industries or countries, and even between competitors. They can take the form of joint ventures or contracts (e.g., licensing arrangements, supplier and distributor contracts) and involve two or more organizations cooperating to design, produce, and distribute a product or service. In a joint venture (JV), a separate organization (the JV) is created to manage the relationship, whereas in a contractual alliance there is no new organization, at least not formally speaking. Companies operating within both alliances and joint ventures help their partner organizations utilize the parents' strengths, reduce uncertainty, learn, minimize costs, share risk, and facilitate low-cost entry into new markets.

Nissan and Renault exemplify a successful alliance between two global automotive manufacturers, headquartered respectively in Japan and France. These organizations are legally separate companies that compete in a few markets but who share manufacturing facilities, automotive designs, and, from time to time, executives. Carlos Ghosn, on loan from Renault to hold Nissan's CEO position during its remarkable turnaround, now heads up both Renault and Nissan.

Airbus is an example of a joint venture. This European consortium of French, German, Spanish, and UK companies was established in the 1970s to enable the Europeans to share development costs and compete with much larger US aircraft manufacturers. In 2001 Airbus became a single company incorporating the joint stock of EADS and BAE. Based in Toulouse, France, the company is managed by an executive committee of ten members and so far has captured about 50 percent of the global aircraft market.[13]

Multinational corporations (MNCs) and global matrix organization

In these days of increasing international competition, many organizations are strategically positioning themselves to take advantage of global opportunities. An organization that desires to move beyond a purely domestic orientation to operate on a multinational or even a global scale will confront the need for structural adaptation. This is because the new orientation will require the organization to engage in new activities that put differentiation pressures on existing structures.

For example, a functionally designed organization that merely wants to market its products or services abroad, or wants to take advantage of low-cost labor to produce products for home markets, will generally form a new department to handle the details of import and export, usually by subcontracting with experts in the markets in which the organization wants to be involved. At this stage the organization is really not multinational because it remains committed to the logic of its domestic business, but it has started the differentiation process by adding a new structure.

As experience with non-domestic markets accumulates, the organization will typically become aware of additional opportunities abroad and become more experienced at addressing them, at least in one or a few of its foreign locations. At this point many of the activities that were originally subcontracted will be brought in-house and an international division will be formed. Notice that the M-form structure adopted at this stage allows the organization to maintain essentially a multi-domestic orientation. That is, it acts like a firm operating domestically in several national markets simultaneously, similar to the way a conglomerate operates in several industries at the same time.

When the activities of the firm can no longer be separated into either domestic or international units, and the international division is replaced by a multinational product or geographic M-form structure in which all units engage in the coordination of international activities, the multinational corporation (MNC) appears. This shift typically occurs when international sales become the main source of organizational revenues and as suppliers, manufacturers, and distributors from a variety of countries form an interdependent inter-organizational network on a truly multinational scale. As with conglomerate M-forms, an organization can achieve a multinational structure either through internal growth, or through joint ventures, mergers, and/or acquisitions.

The multinational product or geographical divisional form confronts the same drawbacks as do domestic M-form organizations. The desire to be more efficient and flexible leads to global matrix structures like that depicted in Figure 9.5. In a global matrix there are managers of geographic regions and of products or product groups such that local units are organized both by interests in corporate effectiveness related to serving a particular region of the world and by interests in developing the corporation's knowledge and efficiency in regard to production across regional markets. Each of the local units can be fully operational companies in their own right, and the array of the units that comprise the MNC may be a hybrid of any of the other designs described here.

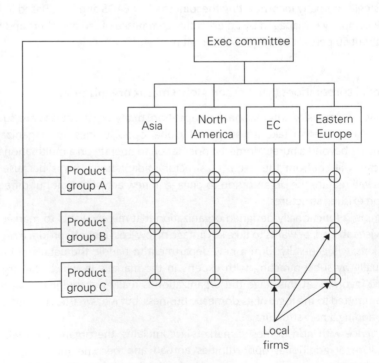

Figure 9.5 The global matrix

Obviously, a major drawback of MNCs and global matrices are their often mind-boggling complexity. Even with electronic communication and rapid transportation between most destinations, the coordination problems these organizations create stretch modernist organization designs to their limit. As complexity increases through demands for attention to more than the two or three dimensions that can be represented in an organization chart, the fragmentation and incoherence about which postmodernists write becomes increasingly apparent.

Here, an image of fragmented organizations as networks of loosely connected interests operating without Grand Narratives of overarching corporate strategy overtakes the idyllic images of planning and control offered by modernist organization theory. The importance of symbolism also becomes hard to deny, as symbols may be the only means of forming webs of social or cultural relationship between network partners. Think of Benetton's controversial 'United Colors of Benetton' international advertising campaign, for example, whose images challenge people to think about responding to human injustice, or accepting interracial or homosexual couples.[14] The meanings and interpretations of these symbols are unlikely to be controllable worldwide, but they nonetheless can become the focus of network identity around which relationships among network partners cohere.

Networks and virtual organizations

Non-hierarchical relationships comprised of human points of contact, called nodes, form a network structure. Organizationally, networks link headquarters with subsidiaries, and units with each other, their stakeholders, and their employees. Networks are typically represented by maps showing a set of linked nodes, such as Figure 3.3 that showed an inter-organizational network.

Virtual organizations are networks whose connections take place primarily or entirely via electronic media, as opposed to face-to-face interaction. For example, the market created on eBay lets buyers and sellers negotiate exchanges without ever making contact except through the Internet. Wikipedia, an online encyclopedia, is another virtual organization, this one comprised of user volunteers who edit one another's entries and socialize new contributors all done online.[15] Of course, some virtual networks, like online dating services, exist to create a means for people to meet non-virtually, so you can also find hybrid blends combining virtual organization with a traditional network.

Networks of organizations are most likely to form when organizations face rapid technological change, shortened product lifecycles, and fragmented, specialized markets. In networks, needed assets are distributed among several partners such that it is not a single organization within the network that produces products or services, but rather the network as a whole that is the producer or provider. Most, if not all, vertical communication and control relationships are replaced with lateral relationships and partnerships among several organizations in these networks.

Benetton is an example of a network organization. It is comprised of hundreds of small clothing manufacturers and thousands of franchised sales outlets arrayed around a central distribution channel with a common information and control system. Some of the manufacturers within the Benetton network were spun off the original Benetton operation, while others joined the network because their small size would otherwise have left them out of the international fashion market in which Benetton firms participate. In addition to managing distribution channels (which are also part of the network) Benetton provides its suppliers with technical manufacturing expertise, much of the necessary equipment, and sometimes capital, and handles marketing efforts for the network.

Within a network structure, partners are linked by supplier–customer relationships that resemble a free market system. That is, goods are bought and sold between network partners just as they would be on the open market. In this way competitive pressures on the supplying partners keep downward pressure on prices. Also, the use of market mechanisms to coordinate activities eliminates much of the need for the vertical hierarchy of traditional organizations and this reduces administrative overhead. These characteristics of network organizations reduce their overall costs and increase efficiency and profitability, which help keep the network competitive. The German TV industry provides an example of a network of temporary project-based organizations.[16] When a broadcaster commissions a TV program producers bring together mostly independent writers, directors, camera people, actors, and other media specialists to work on the project. The collaboration ends when the program is completed.

There are some advantages associated with networks: they encourage information sharing, liberate decision making, and inspire innovation. Also, networks are capable of extremely rapid information exchange because they can process information in multiple directions at the same time. Rapid information exchange enables network partners to exploit opportunities before non-networked competitors even become aware that they exist. Relative independence of decision making allows experimentation and learning, and new learning can be rapidly diffused throughout the network. By enhancing the spread of information and bringing together different logics and novel combinations of information, networks provide the conditions for innovation.

On the other hand, a simple economic relationship between network partners can lead to exploitation by partners who gain control of critical information or resources, such as by key suppliers who are able to create and take advantage of dependencies in the larger system (i.e., charging higher prices once demand for their products is generated by the rest of the network). In these situations, one segment of the network holds the rest hostage for higher profits. This is where networks developed upon more than economic relationships have an advantage. For instance, relationships built on friendship, reputation, or shared ideology may prove more effective due to their greater ability to generate trust and cooperation.

Many of the advantages networks enjoy depend upon members working voluntarily together to innovate, solve problems of mutual concern, and coordinate their activities. This demands a level of organizational teamwork that cannot be taken for granted. Networks create webs of information exchange and mutual obligation that can provide a foundation for deeper relationships, but these relationships are not automatic—they must be managed. Network partners may undermine network effectiveness by pursuing self-interest and middle managers and technical specialists within network organizations may not always be enthusiastic about cooperation. Probably the greatest challenge in managing network relationships is developing and maintaining an organizational identity and sense of purpose in the face of geographic and/or cultural diversity and loosely coupled interests and activities.

New forms of organizing

Some pundits predict that organizations will soon outsource nearly all their activity, leaving behind only a shell of their former corporate selves. Many manufacturing activities in the industrial organizations of the West have already been outsourced and executives are left to oversee managers supervising consultants who hire workers on a temporary basis to do the remaining work. The consultants, in turn, work for global service organizations supported by multiple intersecting networks of scientists, engineers, and other knowledge workers operating via proprietary intranet servers. Elsewhere, of course, the outsourced activity may be done by organizations designed in traditional ways (e.g., simple, functional, M-form), but some will adopt new designs.

Some say that business models are morphing through crowdsourcing, hacking, and other emergent processes into platforms for organizing the work of anonymous freelancers who are contracted and paid on a project-by-project basis, much as craft workers were in pre-industrial economies. Freelancers can find projects, submit work, and receive pay, all over computer monitored electronic devices connected to the Internet permitting networks to operate 24/7 from locations spread all over the Earth and one day, maybe, beyond. As these changes take hold, some believe, traditional old economy organizations will recede into the background or may disappear altogether.

But even as some organizations disappear, others emerge. For example, new kinds of unions offer freelancers group rates on health insurance and other benefits, and organize quasi office parties to fill the social needs created by the isolation, alienation, and fragmentation of working conditions typical in the new economy. At the same time various actors within the institutional environment of global business are organizing around a perceived need to control the biggest corporations, mainly by forming NGOs or joining global social movements to save the planet, eradicate poverty or fight for human rights. Some say that the mix and match pastiche of the conditions of work life in the new economy coupled with reorganization of the institutional field will reshape organizations rather than leading to their demise.

What comes next is a matter of speculation, but recent changes in the global environment due to growing concerns over sustainability and human rights that have led to political activism operating on a scale never before seen, appear to be creating the conditions for the emergence of organizational forms that combine the properties of virtual and network organizations with social movements. Consider that today, many employees have interests in society as well as in the organizations for which they work. Individuals who express their societal interests while at work push organizations into the role of servant to society or to humankind more generally, as opposed to being merely vehicles for expressing the economic and technological interests of the most powerful. This is what some people hope will be the consequence of the shift from industrial (old economy) to post-industrial (new economy) societies.

Figure 9.6 shows four diagrams representing the shifting roles organizations and organizing play as we move from industrial (old economy) to post-industrial (new economy) societies. The triangle in panel 1 of the figure represents an organization-as-entity doing the work of producing goods and services in the old economy. The many small grey blobs are various stakeholders, some of whom have direct access to the organization indicated by their position inside the triangle, think about key customers and major shareholders, or important

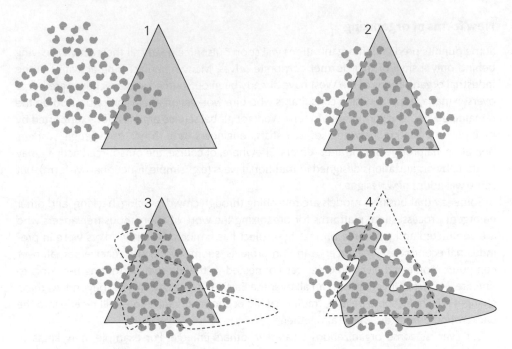

Figure 9.6 How organizations form and reform around the activities and interests of people who contribute raw material, energy, action, influence, culture, and capital

Panel 1 shows a traditional organization, while the situation in panel 2 emerges as increasing numbers of stakeholders gain access to the organization and its resources. In panel 3 parts of the organization have reorganized around interests shared by employees and other stakeholders to produce temporary structures that ooze and change as interests and people come and go. In panel 4 these once temporary alignments and relationships solidify into one or more new but still organic organizations as the boundary around the former traditional organization recedes into the background or melts away altogether.

Source: Hatch, M.J. (2011) *Organizations: A Very Short Introduction*. Oxford: Oxford University Press.

suppliers. Other stakeholders take positions outside the boundaries of the triangle in that they are more marginal from the organization's point of view, including those activists and special interest groups that may pressure the organization to change its behavior or ethics regarding environmental and social responsibility.

In panel 2, more and more stakeholder interests have been taken into account inside the organization by its different functions—marketing to serve customers, HR to serve employees, finance to serve the capital markets, PR to handle media and community relations, communication to manage public opinion expressed in corporate image or reputation, and so on. As time passes the relationships forged between insiders and outsiders give outsiders access to the organization bringing them, or at least their engaged interests, within its walls. This can be seen today in organizations like LEGO Group that create new products and train new employees with the help of LEGO fans who volunteer to work as product designers and ambassadors inside the LEGO organization.

When you compare panels 1 and 2 you see the invasion of the organization by many more blobs. For a time the purposes of the panel 2 organization may become befuddled by the influence of so many competing interests attracted by the appeal of engagement, an effect compounded by the organization's pursuit of legitimacy in the eyes of all its stakeholders. If corporate interests prevail, the organization will return to the state depicted in panel 1; it will have resisted the pressures of adaptation to the new economy. Alternatively, the scenario shown in panel 3 could unfold as the organization discovers new ways to respond to its stakeholders, some designed by them.

Organizations described by panel 3 will find it difficult to differentiate employees from other actors as stakeholder engagement provides access to the internal workings and resources of the organization placing some organizational members outside the organization's walls and bringing increasing numbers of external stakeholders within them. As this happens, employees and other stakeholders join forces and build relationships that allow them to act on extra-organizational interests even as they serve those of the organization. In some cases, for example, corporate social responsibility (CSR) becomes a key concern leading to a new business model less focused on doing well (e.g., making a profit) and more on doing good (i.e., serving society). New boundaries emerge within and around the triangle in panel 3 as stakeholders align with employees around common interests and together engage in activities realizing them using corporate resources and capabilities.

IBM's Corporate Service Corp provides an example of panel 3 organizing. IBM Service Corp volunteers serve the corporate vision of creating a Smarter Planet by living in an impoverished community they pledge to serve for six to twelve months. There they take on projects co-designed with local residents to apply IBM competencies to solving the community's most urgent problems. A critic might see this as an attempt by IBM to grow its market, but from the point of view of community members, it is an opportunity to take advantage of the resources and capabilities of this massive corporation. Panel 3 shows how, as insiders and outsiders join forces, the boundaries of an organization like IBM start to shift, reshaping its identity and culture as well as its social and physical structures.

If alliances between society and business, such as those encouraged by the IBM Corporate Service Corp, were to become institutionalized then one more shift would occur. In panel 4 the solidified yet organic shape of the boundary around the aligned stakeholder interests depicts a different organization growing within and later potentially emerging from the first. The now dotted line around the triangle indicates the possible disappearance of the older form, perhaps taking bureaucracy with it.

If organizing continues to produce new emergent properties, institutionalization will become less and less likely. The new boundaries shown in panel 4 will not hold and organizing as depicted by the organic shape in the center of panel 3, along with the disappearing boundary around formal organization in panel 4, will prevail. In this view, temporary organizations emerge from and melt back into networks whose boundaries are never clear for long. Even if a few old economy organizations persist, they will most likely take the form of virtual shells of their former selves, temporarily populated by constantly changing hordes of new economy freelancers. This does not mean, however, that the cultural dynamics of people working together will cease, only that the temporary nature of organizing will replace our static appreciations (e.g., structure) with more liquid forms. And of course, there is no reason to believe that these organic, temporary, interest-driven forms of organizing cannot co-exist with old school corporations in symbiotic or parasitic relationships that produce offsetting urges to exploit one another.

Whether we get a proliferation of dynamic organizings, like the organic shapes in the center of panels 3 and 4 in Figure 9.6, or whether we fall back into panel 1 or 2 style organizations, remains to be seen. But with ideas like lines of flight and hactivism, to be considered next, you can begin to see where innovative opportunity lies and what its emancipating benefits and costs might be relative to traditional ways of organizing.

Designerly approaches to organization design

Recently the fields of design and design management have begun describing ways in which designers approach organizational design. Often the visual skills designers possess become focal in commentary and research about design work, but more important may be the capacity for empathy and aesthetic imagination, and the performative and interactive skills designers cultivate by working intensely with clients.

In general, designerly approaches replace classical organization development (OD) practices with activities informed by the studio pedagogy of design fields such as architecture, fashion, and service design.[17] Much of this type of organizational work is just getting underway, but to offer you one tantalizing example: consider how Swedish fashion theorist and designer Otto Von Busch took new economy freedoms with the old economy organizational forms that dominate the fashion industry, and what his designerly way of working implies for organizational innovation and change.

Von Busch bases his design practices, in part, on the work of Gilles Deleuze and Pierre-Félix Guattari. These French philosophers developed the postmodern concept of **lines of flight** to describe escape routes awaiting us within the hierarchy and bureaucracy of the state (see Figure 9.7). These theorists explicitly denied any connection between their concept and the image it evokes for many of the random trajectories of bird flight that occur when a flock is surprised by a hunter firing a shot into their midst. I nonetheless find the mental image of bird flight helpful because, just as the birds will flock together again reunifying their scattered trajectories, so Deleuze and Guattari argued coherence will be (re)established for diverse but culturally connected humans, only to be disturbed once more by the next unexpected event or shock.

But Deleuze and Guattari were not talking about random responses to exogenous shocks; instead they were interested in describing the opportunities ever present within repressive social structures. The key to appreciating their concept lies in the power of lines of flight to **deterritorialize** existing structures by invading their spaces and breaking up stratified systems, such as those of hierarchy, privilege, or habit. In these ways lines of flight escape and thereby undermine the repression of compartmentalized thinking, like that imposed by a discipline or an organization. Such maneuvers release hidden potential and concentrate capabilities in ways that Deleuze and Guattari claimed traverse old patterns of behavior and thought, and connect multiplicities with one another. They compare lines of flight to music that ruptures expected patterns and proliferates in ways comparable to how weeds propagate rhizomatically, that is to say in a dynamic and unpredictable fashion.[18]

Von Busch compared Delueze and Guatarri's description of lines of flight to the mindset required for **hacking**, an idea borrowed from the computer field that he and others apply to fashion. Distinguishing 'hacking' from 'cracking,' he noted that while 'cracking' involves opening a computer program in order to harm or destroy it, 'hacking' builds on existing code in

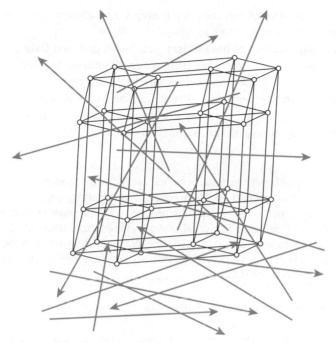

Figure 9.7 Lines of flight

The grid in the background of this figure represents Deleuze and Guattari's notion of the state apparatus from which the lines of flight depicted by the arrows represent escape routes.

Adapted from 'A 5 cube' by Joseph Malkevitch. Reproduced with kind permission.

order to get it to do new things. Using the terminology provided by Deleuze and Guatarri, Von Busch explained:

> The hack itself is an escape, but it is paradoxically also a re-structuring and a reterritorialization, as it builds new forms of relations, relations that are yet open, as in open source code and open protocols. The reterritorialization process is unavoidable so it is crucial to be attentive to how to best affect this process and keep the line of flight intensive, open and accessible.[19]

A self-described hacktivist, Von Busch promotes and studies 'fashion-able' activities that have the intention of playing with fashion in order to change how the industry operates as well as helping people transform their wardrobes into creative things of beauty. One event he helped to organize and facilitated taught participants to hack into the fashion of particular designers by cracking the code of a brand such as Gucci's and then using the hack to produce 'Gucci-fied' fashions that are not copies so much as they are variants of the brand's core attributes and values.

Providing a simple example of how hacking fashion works, Von Busch described Stephanie Syjuco's Counterfeit Crochet Project.[20] This project involved offering instructions for counterfeiting a designer handbag in crochet by first using the enlarge function on a photocopier to make a low resolution image from a photograph of an original bag, and subsequently using the pixilated image as a crochet pattern to produce a playful variant that is not a copy so much as it is a new way of rendering the hacked brand idea (as well as being an ironic comment on the practice of counterfeiting).

In an industrial application of **hacktivism**, Von Busch engaged Dale Sko, a small rural shoe manufacturer in Norway suffering from competitive woes that led the company to gradually reduce its workforce from somewhere around a couple of hundred to ten. It was at this low point in the company's history that Von Busch arrived to engage employees in a workshop involving six prominent Norwegian fashion designers, an established fashion photographer, a stylist, and a shoemaker/teacher. As Von Busch related the story:

> The hope was to create some new approaches to post-industrial production and try to probe 'nonlinear' means of action and co-design, open for spontaneity and crafty interventions during the normally strictly linear production process . . . All the experimentation during the workshop was to be firmly based on collaboration on the factory floor. An ability to merge these roles and create a wider range of possibilities for interaction between the participants would change the flow within the factory, while at the same time create unique designs, using the full skill of all those involved.[21]

The process combined chaos with standard manufacturing technology:

> Operational misuse of the factory equipment, using machines at the wrong moment in the process, assembling pieces in wrong order or using wrong sizes of tools for various elements in production proved to be ways that opened new action spaces . . . [even though t]his can only be done in small quantities [and] still remain within mass-production or economy of scale, and this mix of craft and mass-production is the scale of manufacture for a small factory such as Dale Sko.

Von Busch next described how the Dale Sko workers reacted during the three-day workshop:

> During the first day of the workshop the atmosphere was filled with anticipation and at first the craftsman of the factory seemed slightly skeptical of the working process. Why change? But as the process went on the mood changed. On the first day, all workers went home when the bell rang signaling the end of the working day. But on the last day of the workshop many of the workers stayed after working hours, helping the participants to finish their shoes and chatting.

To explain the role the designers played, he described how one of them worked with the process:

> It is perhaps the works of [designer] Siv Støldal that can be seen as a quintessential modus operandi of this type of hacking. She used the already existing models from Dale Sko, recombined materials and parts into new forms. She changed leather materials, shifted soles between models, and introduced random punched decorations into the designs. But at the same time she preserved the general design of every sub-part intact. With these schemes for individualizing the shoes, every pair became unique. Still preserving the integrity of the traditional models from Dale Sko this model became a point of departure and an instrument for her future collaborations with Dale Sko.

The project attracted media attention that brought important benefits for Dale Sko:

> During the workshop, the project also received an amount of local coverage in the press, radio and TV. Bringing in the eyes of media as well as putting the spotlight on the collaborative working process created a renewed pride in the craft element in the factory. Dale Sko came to be recognized and respected not only for its century old merits but also for its concern to go further, innovate and continue to be a progressive local player with global fashion connections. The media attention became a form of recognition for this hard work and boosted the confidence of the factory . . . The factory, in the past the main employer and gem of the town, now demonstrate[d] an imaginative and innovative spirit with high future ambitions and is now once again the source of local pride.

Other results were equally impressive:

> After the finish of the workshop the traces of the project are still visible today. Støldal has continued her collaboration with Dale Sko and is currently making her fourth collection with them, still using the existing models as a practical point of departure. The new shoes have been shown at the fashion weeks in London, Paris and Tokyo and are for sale in stores in London and other cities. The factory also developed a prototype lab and since the hack has hosted several other designers and interns from fashion schools. In addition, the board of directors of the factory has been changed and one designer as well as the shoemaker/teacher was taken onto the board. In 2008 the project also won a special prize at the European Fashion Awards.

Von Busch claimed that his hack of Dale Sko deliberately mixed modern technology with postmodern ways of organizing. It also shows a designer taking theory into practice by intentionally using lines of flight as inspiration for the design of an intervention meant to change an organization. His intervention demonstrated how hacking can generate creative solutions to problems left behind by modernist industrial organizing practices thereby producing innovation within those very technologies. And, his method of helping an organization escape the constraints of old ways of working, demonstrated a time honored design principle—**frame breaking**. But most important to the discussion of organizational design, Von Busch's hacking practices present a version of organizing that resembles in certain respects the images depicted in panels 3 and 4 of Figure 9.6, and puts some flesh on these new bones.

Organizational change and change management

Two questions practitioners always seem to ask regarding **organizational change** are: what makes organizations change and how can change be managed? Change is an inherent characteristic of most organizations: environments change, organizations grow, innovation produces new technologies, conflicts arise, and so on. For instance, as we have just seen, changes wrought by globalization have woven economies into intricate networks of dependence spinning around capital flows that, in turn, are altering organizational structures all over the world. As a consequence, one of the biggest changes many people perceive today is that the rate of change itself appears to be on the rise. In response, many managers no longer bother about stabilizing their organizations, instead they spend their time trying to change them, or at least keep up with their many changes.

Chronologically the pendulum began swinging from stability to change around the end of WWII when systems theory introduced the idea that organizations depend on their environments. It was then that managers began regarding adaptation as key to organizational survival, and strategy as a mechanism to guide them through necessary change. Along with recognizing the importance of finding and maintaining an organization's strategic 'fit' within its environment, came the need to implement strategy through planned organizational change. Lewin's model of the stages of planned change offered them an answer and provided one of the first normative theories of organizational change.

Lewin's normative model of planned organizational change

In the 1950s, Lewin developed an equilibrium theory based on his belief that social institutions, including organizations, result from a balance of forces, some driving change and the others restraining it. According to Lewin, stability is not only maintained by the forces opposing change, it represents a stalemate between forces for and against change (see Figure 9.8). For Lewin, change was transient instability interrupting an otherwise stable equilibrium and his theory prescribed the inducement of managed instability to bring about planned change. According to his model, planned change involves three separate practical activities: unfreezing, movement, and refreezing.

Unfreezing unbalances the equilibrium sustaining organizational stability, and this is accomplished, according to Lewin, by destabilizing present behavioral patterns sufficiently to overcome resistance to change. For example, locating and then taking advantage of existing stress or dissatisfaction brings about unfreezing by increasing the forces for change

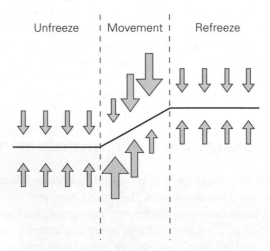

Figure 9.8 Lewin's model of planned organizational change

Change results from disturbances in the force field sustaining organizational stability. Whenever forces favoring change are greater than forces resisting it, the organization will move from one state to another. In planned change, movement can be induced via unfreezing the old equilibrium, moving to a new state, and then refreezing by re-establishing equilibrium at the new position.

Source: Based on Lewin (1951, 1958).

within a system. Unfreezing can also be brought about by lowering resistance, for example, by educating organizational members about the need for change.

Once unfreezing has taken place, **movement** involves influencing the direction of change in the now destabilized system. Strategies for influencing the direction of change include training new behavioral patterns, altering reporting relationships and reward systems, and introducing different styles of management (e.g., replacing an authoritarian with a participative management style).

Movement continues until a new balance between driving and restraining forces is achieved by refreezing. **Refreezing** occurs when new behavioral patterns are institutionalized. An example of a refreezing strategy would be formalizing new recruiting policies to assure that new hires share the organizational culture and work well within the new structure and reward systems as well as with the new managerial style.

A large proportion of the case studies and theoretical discussions of organizational change that comprise the field of OD are formulated in the tradition that Lewin's model inspired. OD provides well-documented illustrations of the unfreezing/movement/refreezing processes. To give just one example, American organization development specialists Leonard Goodstein and Warner Burke applied Lewin's model to analyze changes undertaken at British Airways (BA) in the early 1980s.[22]

Goodstein and Burke claimed that changes at BA were made when two environmental influences combined with poor corporate performance. First, Margaret Thatcher, who was then Prime Minister of Britain, opposed public ownership of business. Second, governments around the world deregulated international air traffic with consequent intense airfare competition among airlines. BA's lack of profitability in the prior years was complicated by the challenges of its impending privatization and the fare wars. For instance, in 1982 the airline lost nearly US$900 million and required large government subsidies that encouraged the Thatcher government to privatize BA. As the noose tightened, BA recognized the need for radical change, which it then undertook from 1982 to 1987. Goodstein and Burke reported that during this period, BA went from government ownership and a bureaucratic command and control culture that was facing huge losses and a decreasing market share, to a privately owned company having a service-oriented and market-driven culture with profits of over US$400 million and a rising market share.

Goodstein and Burke identified many different elements in BA's change effort. First, the company reduced its workforce from 59,000 to 37,000 employees. Second, it welcomed an industrialist as chairman of its board and named a new CEO with a marketing background. These leaders differed considerably from their predecessors, many of whom had been retired Royal Air Force officers. Goodstein and Burke argued that the effect of these new appointments was to signal an imminent change in BA's values. Third, training programs were initiated to help 'line workers and managers understand the service nature of the airline industry.' The combination of workforce reductions, a new top management, and extensive employee training accomplished unfreezing.

Movement was guided through management training programs, changes in structure and reward systems, a new, more user-friendly management information system, and team building. Management training programs helped BA adopt a participative management style that emphasized employee commitment and involvement. Two elements of the unfreezing stage—the cross-functional, cross-level teams that planned the change effort, and reductions in middle management—signaled a participative management style that was symbolically reinforced during the movement process by the introduction of a new user-friendly computer system, profit sharing, and a bottom-up budgeting process. Also during movement, the CEO became a symbol of participation by engaging in question and answer sessions during training programs. Goodstein and Burke claimed that it was in this phase that BA changed its identity from a transportation to a service company. The core idea of emotional labor was a key part of the new service identity and involved developing emotional support systems that allowed employees to offset the burnout that service providers often experience.

BA accomplished refreezing via orientation programs for new employees at all levels, a policy of promoting people who symbolized the new corporate values, and education programs for executives and managers called Top Flight Academies. In addition, performance appraisal and compensation systems were developed around the principle of rewarding customer service and employee development. Meanwhile, new uniforms, refurbished aircraft, and a new logo with the motto 'We fly to serve,' communicated BA's new identity. Continued use of teamwork and data feedback to management helped BA maintain its new participative management style. Of course, as Goodstein and Burke pointed out, moving from a known but undesirable state, to a desired but unknown future state, involved a transition period of disorganization and lowered effectiveness during which, these researchers claimed, courageous and committed leadership offset anger, uncertainty, and fear.[23]

Although Lewin's model specifies a path for introducing desired change into a stable society or organization, it does not tell you much about the ways in which a system responds to the introduction of programmatic change. An early theory proposed by Max Weber provided insight into this process and thus complements Lewin's theory.

Weber's routinization of charisma and the leadership of change

Weber theorized the role that **charismatic leadership** plays in societal change, claiming that new ideas introduced by a charismatic leader are altered as part of their acceptance into everyday life. His theory of the **routinization of charisma** explains why and how revolutionary change in worldviews and their consequent influence on social action occur.[24] Weber defined charisma as:

> a certain quality of an individual personality by virtue of which he is considered extraordinary and treated as endowed with supernatural, superhuman, or at least specifically exceptional powers or qualities. These as such are not accessible to the ordinary person, but are regarded as of divine origin or as exemplary, and on the basis of them the individual concerned is treated as a 'leader.'[25]

The definition of charisma at first blush seems to limit the applicability of Weber's theory. Not many organizational leaders qualify as charismatic, although with the advent of the celebrity CEO there is reason to believe that at least some have attained this level of influence. Think Steve Jobs of Apple or Virgin's Richard Branson. Furthermore, managers aspire to charismatic influence when they attempt to change their organization's culture. The link between the routinization of charisma and organizational change becomes clearer when Weber differentiates charisma from the forces of reason:

[The] revolutionary force of 'reason' works from *without*: by altering the situations of life and hence its problems, finally in this way changing men's attitudes toward them; or it intellectualizes the individual. Charisma, on the other hand, *may* effect a subjective or *internal* reorientation born out of suffering, conflicts, or enthusiasm. It may then result in a radical alteration of the central attitudes and directions of action with a completely new orientation of all attitudes toward the different problems of the 'world.'[26]

What happens after the introduction of the revolutionary influence of a charismatic leader into a society is of particular interest for understanding reactions to planned organizational change. Charisma, or by extension the subjective influence of leadership in organizations, is not direct in its influence because routinization processes adapt charismatic ideas to the needs and interests of those at whom change efforts are directed. Although charismatic leadership may be highly influential, its influence will be routinized during the change process by those who must implement strategic vision through systematization and accommodation, two subprocesses of routinization described by Weber.

Here is how Weber explained routinization. Following the introduction of new ideas by a charismatic leader, disciples champion the charismatic individual's ideas to other members of society. As the actions of the champions spread the leader's ideas throughout society, some of their revolutionary appeal dissipates as the ideas are linked to various mundane aspects of everyday life.[27] Weber called this subprocess **systematization**, because as the ideas spread they are reworked to fit into the existing social system and culture. **Accommodation**, the second part of the routinization process, involves power and politics. Those affected by the new ideas negotiate over how to reinterpret their beliefs and values to accommodate the new ideas and how to implement the new obligations required of them. The politics of these negotiations further shape and alter the charismatic influence as they align the new ideas with the familiar, causing their implementation to conform, more or less, to existing power relations and cultural norms, which makes the new ideas into routine aspects of daily life.

According to Weber, dissipation of the original revolutionary appeal that systematizes charismatic ideas, plus their accommodation within existing power structures and culture, routinizes charisma, thereby embedding change in society even as it renders the changes undertaken mundane. Routinization occurs because the demands of everyday life impinge on followers who not only wish to participate in the society envisioned by the charismatic leader, but also seek to maintain the stability of their social position and their material well-being. Thus Weber claimed charismatic authority as the primary source of change in society, but allowed that its routinization gives members considerable influence within the change process. In his view, the subjects of charismatic authority alter the ideas leaders introduce to suit their everyday life and its political, religious, intellectual, and economic interests.

Although Weber acknowledged that leaders would probably not regard their charisma as dependent on the attitudes of the masses toward them, he claimed that their authority nevertheless rests on how their followers and subordinates regard them. He stated that: 'In general it should be kept clearly in mind that the basis of every authority, and correspondingly of every kind of willingness to obey, is a *belief*, a belief by virtue of which persons exercising authority are lent prestige.'[28] In other words, the beliefs of organizational members determine not only how a leader will be regarded, but who will be regarded as a leader.

With ideas like authority-as-belief, Weber acknowledged the social construction of reality and seems to invite deconstruction for the purpose of change. The routinization of charisma also invites comparison with institutionalization processes. Weber's admission of change through charismatic influence, albeit processed through systematization and accommodation, helps to explain institutional change, an idea that has recently arisen as a primary criticism of institutional theory.

Institutional change and entrepreneurship: What about culture?

Institutional theory has succeeded in explaining how the expectations lodged in institutional environments constrain organizational behavior through coercive, normative, and mimetic pressures and thus stabilize recognizably legitimate structures. But the explanation that actors unreflexively adopt taken-for-granted practices that sustain their legitimacy leaves little room to explain how or why institutions change. Yet we know that some institutions *do* change, that new institutions emerge from time to time, and some even disappear. The central problem with which critics confront institutional theorists is: how can actors innovate when the institutional environment determines their actions and beliefs?

Until recently institutional theorists attributed institutional change to exogenous shocks (e.g., crisis or scandal, disruptive technological innovation, or regulatory change) over which actors had limited if any control. Thus agency within an institutional field was not considered part of the explanation for change. Royston Greenwood, Roy Suddaby, and C. Robert Hinings theorized that such exogenous shocks destabilize the socially constructed consensus of an institutional field by causing actors to question their taken-for-granted assumptions thereby allowing the introduction of new ways of thinking and acting.[29] An example would be the economic crisis faced by the countries of Western Europe in the 1980s that led to the proposal for a European Union.[30]

When structuration theory came along, its positioning of agency appealed to institutional theorists, not only because it offered an answer to the puzzle of change, but because agency provided a means of addressing the normative interests of practicing managers. American institutional theorist Paul DiMaggio was among the first to offer **institutional entrepreneurship** as an endogenous explanation for institutional change rooted in agency.[31] He pointed out that institutional entrepreneurship refers to a process of institutional change enacted by individuals or collectives such as organizations, coalitions, and social movements that partake in the destabilization, creation, diffusion, and/or stabilization of institutions.

How does institutional entrepreneurship explain change? One set of explanations examines differences between emerging and mature institutional fields finding that in emerging fields entrepreneurs do not face existing institutions, they simply build new ones. Under these conditions, institutional theorists argue, actors are motivated to stabilize relationships, meanings, ways of thinking, and practices to reduce uncertainty and develop legitimacy. In mature fields, on the other hand, peripheral actors may see themselves as disadvantaged by existing institutional arrangements and so work to destabilize and change them, while powerful actors may seek to alter current arrangements either to avoid problems or take advantage of new opportunities. For example, the largest accounting firms pioneered new multi-disciplinary ways of working such as adding management consulting activities that produced opportunities for cross-selling additional services to their clients. Subsequently this innovative act of institutional entrepreneurship led to an exogenous institutional shock to the institutional field in the form of the ENRON scandal of 2001, quickly followed by the downfall of Arthur Anderson, one of the lead innovating institutional entrepreneurs.[32]

Other conditions that encourage entrepreneurship and bring institutional change include the activation of multiple institutional logics that produce the possibility of choice or incompatible institutional pressures that destabilize an institutional order and incite entrepreneurial action.[33] Novel ideas transposed from one institutional environment to another and strategic action can both account for change in highly institutionalized fields. As Canadian institutional theorist Christine Oliver argued, uncertainty is lower in these cases and so actors feel confident enough to behave strategically, which can lead to innovation and change.[34]

Finally, intentionality is becoming an issue of interest to some institutional theorists. Does it count as institutional entrepreneurship if change is unintended? What about an accumulation of distributed efforts that produces institutional change? Social movements illustrate these issues well because independent efforts that coalesce to become a movement can accommodate multiple intentions and conflicting interests. Attributing entrepreneurial effort can be difficult even where agency is clearly involved.[35] Much remains to be studied, not least the role culture might play in helping to explain both what stabilizes and what changes institutions.

Raising the issue of culture brings us to one of the currently hot topics in both institutional and culture theory: do the processes of cultural dynamics do a better job of explaining institutional change than do concepts like institutional entrepreneurship, which seem to some an oxymoron? While this area of study is new to organization theory, stay tuned to further developments.[36] Resolving the cross-level phenomena implicated in bringing these two areas of theory together could carry organization theory into useful new territory that complements the collapsing of dualisms called for by postmodernists and some advocates of the pragmatic perspective.

Practice theory and process theory

Consideration of change, such as that produced by hacktivism or tempered by the routinization of charisma, pushes organization theorists toward dynamic thinking. In organization theory the idea of organizing as dynamic change emerged only after organizations started to be seen as ongoing accomplishments of enactment, sensemaking, and social construction processes. Weick famously used these ideas to suggest replacing the static notion of organization as entity with the more dynamic concept of organizing.[37] Both practice and process theories are attempts to apply dynamic explanations, understandings, and appreciations to organizing activities.

Practice theory

A **practice** can be defined as a set of actions informed by knowledge. Once we know how to do something we can make it a routine part of our lives, and if we wish to extend our actionable knowledge to others, we may create rules about practices that establish their continued use in society or an organization. In this sense, practices are associated with routines and rules, and one branch of practice theory defines practices in these terms, typically drawing for support on the structure (versus the agency) side of structuration theory. For those who frame practice theory in these terms, rules are seen as governing structures that define practices.[38]

However, practices are not simply the operating procedures that result from following rules, and routines are not fixed and unchangable. Defining practices as lying more strictly within the domain of agency leads other practice theorists to frame their studies with actor network theory, and thus to focus on objectively observable or reportable aspects of practice such as the actors, activities, procedures, texts, and discourse that constitute the actor network.

Martha Feldman and Brian Pentland, for example, showed routines to be flexible in the sense that they are never performed in exactly the same way twice.[39] There is an element of improvisation in the application of rules to practices that makes the whole system dynamic; any alteration of a practice-in-action feeds back on the interpretation of the rules governing it and thus has an effect on future enactments of the practice. These descriptions support the agency side of structuration theory.

There are others who prefer to define practices as embedding activity in skills, as illustrated by an old joke about a man walking down the street in New York City hoping for directions to his destination. Stopping a passerby he asks: How do I get to Carnegie Hall? The reply: Practice! Defining practice as skill-producing activity, such as practicing the drums or, some would argue, practicing management, focuses on learning. This definition favors aesthetic approaches to practice that build on the theory of performativity. It also appeals to critical theorists who apply Foucault's concept of knowledge/power to the practice of management.

Critical theorists, for example, observe that managers often pay consultants to produce and disseminate knowledge that favors their interests. But the knowledge that managers are most willing to purchase tends to be that which their consultants persuade them has led other managers to success! Management practice, so this theory goes, is influenced by and intertwined with consulting practice revealing other phenomena worthy of study, such as the fads and fashions that circulate within the management consulting community.[40]

Following a different line of thinking, French sociologist Pierre Bourdieu presented his concept of the habitus, which links practices to culture. Bourdieu drew on Marcel Mauss's definition of habitus as that part of culture that is anchored in the body and in the everyday practices of individuals, groups, societies, and nations. It includes learned habits, bodily skills, styles, tastes, and other non-discursive knowledge taken for granted by a specific group. As such the habitus, according to Bourdieu, consists of socially acquired dispositions to think and act in certain ways.

By emphasizing embodiment as the locus of cultural understanding, Bourdieu directed attention to the pre-reflexive states of sensory awareness lying beneath rational ideology, and to practical action. According to Bourdieu, actors do not continuously calculate according to explicit rational and economic criteria, they operate according to a tacit practical logic and to bodily dispositions. The logic of practice supports domination by the powerful as it works to reproduce itself thus maintaining the hierarchical status quo. Those who study communities of practice similarly argue for a culturally contextualized appreciation of the phenomenon of practice. They tend to focus attention on discourses framing a shared knowledge base that can be applied through practice to solving practical organizational problems.

All of these strands of practice theory present different lines of flight within traditional organization theory, yet they are, each in their own way, strongly rooted in pragmatism's assumption that knowledge is a practical asset. Defining anything as practical, including practices, presumes applicability to the necessities of living, and this gives practice a pragmatic ontological status. For example, if knowing how to change a tire enables you to change one, such knowledge has pragmatic value that gives it the stature of truth. And notice that, just because Newtonian physics was replaced by Einstein's theory of relativity and other contributions to theoretical physics, Newton's theory remains 'true' insofar as it continues to provide practical value in many situations. In its reliance on pragmatism, practice theory shares its foundation with another up and coming area of study in organization theory—process theory.

Process theory

Organization theorists Haridimos Tsoukas, from Greece, and Robert Chia, of the UK, suggest creating a theory of organization that assumes change, rather than stability, as its point of departure. They argue that, since organizing is a continually evolving process, organizations are in a perpetual state of becoming. This reformulation focuses attention on emergence, flux, change, and movement as opposed to the entities, structures, and end states traditionally promoted by the modern perspective. Tsoukas and Chia put it this way:

> we need to stop giving ontological priority to organization, thereby making change an exceptional effect, produced only under specific circumstances by certain people (change agents). We should rather start from the premise that change is pervasive and indivisible; that, to borrow [the pragmatist William] James's (1909/ 1996:253) apt phrase, 'the essence of life is its continuously changing character', and *then* see what this premise entails for our understanding of organizations.[41]

They further explain that: 'Change must not be thought of as a property of organization. Rather, organization must be understood as an emergent property of change. Change is ontologically prior to organization—it is the condition of possibility for organization.' Tsoukas and Chia continue:

> Drawing on process-oriented philosophers and ethnomethodologists we argue that change is the reweaving of actors' webs of beliefs and habits of action as a result of new experiences obtained through interactions. Insofar as this is an ongoing process, that is, to the extent actors try to make sense of and act coherently in the world, change is inherent in human action. Organization is an attempt to order the intrinsic flux of human action, to channel it towards certain ends, to give it a particular shape, through generalizing and institutionalizing particular meanings and rules. At the same time, organization is a pattern that is constituted, shaped, *emerging* from change.[42]

Tsoukas and Ann Langley claim that process theory is inspired by 'the worldview that sees processes, rather than substances, as the basic forms of the universe . . . A process orientation prioritizes activity over product, change over persistence, novelty over continuity, and expression over determination. Becoming, change, flux as well as creativity, disruption, and indeterminism are the main themes of a process worldview.'[43] Among the examples Langley and Tsoukas provide are social constructivism, discourse and narrative theory, practice theory, performativity, actor network theory, and business history. They claim these as examples of a process orientation because each of them treats organizational phenomena 'not as *faits accomplis* but as (re)created through interacting agents embedded in sociomaterial practices, whose actions are mediated by institutional, linguistic and objectual artifacts.'[44]

American cognitive psychologist Jerome Bruner connected process theory with narrative ways of knowing by contrasting narrative with logico-scientific epistemology. He identified different types of causality with the two epistemologies, describing them as 'palpably differ-ent,' with **logico-scientific explanation** delivered by logical propositions such as 'If X, then Y.' By contrast he claimed that **narrative understanding** occurs in the form of a plot, as in 'The king died, and then the queen died.' According to Bruner: 'One leads to a search for universal truth conditions, the other for likely particular connections between two events—mortal grief, suicide, foul play.'[45] Narrative knowing is interpretive compared to positivist logico-scientific knowing. As Dewey, ever the pragmatist, would caution, we need both to be whole.

Summary

This chapter revisited the tension between theory and practice that animates the field of organization theory. The philosophy of pragmatism was presented as having promise for redressing the growing distance between these poles, one that many modernists blame on the invasion of symbolic and postmodern contributions. As a philosophy pragmatism offers strong theoretical foundations, but at the same time its focus keeps the theory it supports grounded in practical experience, which was here extended into the study of practices.

Two phenomena of longstanding concern to practitioners—organizational design and change—brought the practices of managing and organizing into view with an eye toward seeing how organization theory has informed and been informed by practice throughout its history. Organizational design was examined in terms of the development of different organizational forms and their relationships to the various core concepts presented within organization theory. Organizational change was traced through its evolution from planned change and the routinization of charisma, to contemporary concerns with institutional entrepreneurship. Tracing the historical trajectory of these ideas led to speculation about where current interests in design and change might be headed, and I offered a few thoughts along these lines, including what new organizational forms might be emerging from activism and hactivism, and how interest in institutional entrepreneurship may reinvigorate organizational culture theory.

Practice theory and process theory concluded examination of ways theory and practice are becoming inseparable in organization theory. The new language and concepts provided by these theories was presented in relation to assumptions that realign organization theory. First, that organizing occurs within embodied action and second that focusing on organizing replaces static with dynamic thinking, the implications of which will occupy the attention of organization theorists for years to come.

Key terms

pragmatism

organization charts

organizational design

simple organization

functional organization

multi-divisional (M-form) organization

matrix organization

hybrid organization

strategic alliance

joint venture

multinational corporation (MNC)

global matrix

networks

virtual organizations

lines of flight

deterritorialization and reterritorialization

hacking and hactivism

design principle of frame breaking

organizational change

Lewin's planned change model

unfreezing

movement

refreezing

charismatic leadership

routinization of charisma

systematization

accommodation

institutional change

institutional entrepreneurship

practice

practice theory

habitus

process theory

logico-scientific explanation

narrative understanding

Endnotes

1. Dewey (1929).

2. I rely mainly on Dewey because he is the pragmatist that appeals most to me. You may find the pragmatism of William James or Charles Sanders Peirce more appealing; together with Dewey they are considered the co-founders of pragmatism. But you may also want to look into the neo-pragmatists; at a bare minimum read a little Richard Rorty. All of these are Americans, as pragmatism is largely an American philosophy.

3. Dewey (1938).

4. Dewey (1934).

5. Dewey (1929: 215).

6. Dewey (1934).

7. www.co.honolulu.hi.us/budget/cityorganization/

8. www.grc.nasa.gov/WWW/RT2002/intro/b-divchart.html

9. www.btplc.com/Corporateinformation/ Principalactivities/BTstructure.html

10. www.usgs.gov/bio/USGS/orgcharts.html

11. Tosi (1974).

12. Rumelt (1986).

13. www.airbus.com

14. See article about Benetton's 'Unhate' advertisements showing world leaders kissing, one example of the longstanding effort this company makes to address political and social issues with consciousness-raising advertising campaigns; http://www.huffingtonpost.com/2011/11/16/benetton-unhate-campaign-world-leaders-kissing_n_1097333.html (accessed April 4, 2012).

15. www.wikipedia.org

16. Windeler and Sydow (2001).

17. Boland and Collopy (2004); Brown (2008, 2009); Sarasvathy, Dew, and Wiltbank (2008); and the special issue of *Organization Science* (2006) on design.

18. Deleuze and Guatarri (1980/2004: 13).

19. Von Busch (2008: 244).

20. You can read about the Counterfeit Crochet Project and see images of the crocheted items produced for the project by visiting http://www.counterfeitcrochet.org/ (accessed October 4, 2012).

21. The remaining Von Busch quotes are from (2008: 208–14).

22. Goodstein and Burke (1991).

23. To read about subsequent changes at BA over the last decade, see Hatch and Schultz (2003).

24. Weber (1968/78); see also Schroeder (1992).

25. Weber (1968/78: 241).

26. Weber (1968/78: 243–45, emphasis in the original).

27. Schroeder (1992: 10).

28. Weber (1968/78: 263, emphasis in the original).

29. Greenwood, Suddaby, and Hinings (2002).

30. Fligstein and Mara-Drita (1996).

31. DiMaggio (1988); Eisenstadt (1980) is typically cited as the person who coined the term.

32. Greenwood and Suddaby (2006).

33. Rao (1998); Clemens and Cook (1999); Seo and Creed (2002).

34. Oliver (1992).

35. Rao, Morrill, and Zald (2000).

36. See *Journal of Management Inquiry* (Vol. 21, 2012) for a series of articles examining the ways in which institutional theory and organization culture theory can be interrelated.

37. Weick (1979).

38. Lave and Wenger (1990).

39. Feldman (2000); Feldman and Pentland (2003).

40. Abrahamson (1991, 1996).

41. Tsoukas and Chia (2002: 569).

42. Ibid. p.570.

43. Langley and Tsoukas (2010: 2).

44. Ibid. p.9.

45. Bruner (1986:11; see also 1990).

References

Abrahamson, Eric (1991) Managerial fads and fashions: The diffusion and rejection of innovations. *Academy of Management Review*, 16: 586–612.

——(1996) Management fashion. *Academy of Management Review*, 21: 254–85.

Boland, Richard J. Jr. and Collopy, Fred (2004) *Managing as Designing*. Stanford, CA: Stanford University Press.

Bourdieu, Pierre (1977) *Outline of a Theory of Practice.* Cambridge: Cambridge University Press. (Originally published in 1972 as *Esquisse d'une théorie de la pratique, précédé de trois études d'ethnologie kabyle*).

Brown, Tim (2008) *Change by Design: How Design Thinking Transforms Organizations and Inspires Innovation.* New York: Harper Collins.

——(2009) *Design Thinking.* New York: Allworth Press.

Bruner, Jerome (1986) *Actual Minds, Possible Worlds.* Cambridge, MA: Harvard University Press.

——(1990) *Acts of Meaning.* Cambridge, MA: Harvard University Press.

Clemens, Elisabeth S. and Cook, J. M. (1999) Politics and institutionalism: Explaining durability and change. *Annual Review of Sociology*, 25/1: 441–66.

Deleuze, Gilles and Guattari, Felix (1980/2004) *A Thousand Plateaus* (Brian Massumi, trans.). London and New York: Continuum.

Dewey, John (1929) *Quest for Certainty.* New York: Minton Balch and Company.

——(1934) *Art as Experience.* New York: Perigee (Putmam's Son's).

——(1938) *Experience and Education.* New York: Touchstone.

DiMaggio, P. J. (1988) Interest and agency in institutional theory. In L. Zucker (ed.), *Institutional Patterns and Organizations.* Cambridge, MA: Ballinger, 3–22.

Eisenstadt, S. N. (1980) Cultural orientations, institutional entrepreneurs and social change: Comparative analyses of traditional civilizations. *American Journal of Sociology*, 85: 840–69.

Feldman, Martha (2000) Organizational routines as a source of continuous change. *Organization Science*, 11: 611–29.

——and Pentland, Brian T. (2003) Reconceptualizing organizational routines as source of flexibility and change. *Administrative Science Quarterly*, 48: 94–118.

Fligstein, N. and Mara-Drita, I. (1996) How to make a market: Reflections on the attempt to create a single market in the European Union. *American Journal of Sociology*, 102/1: 1–33.

Goodstein, Leonard D. and Burke, W. Warner (1991) Creating successful organization change. *Organizational Dynamics*, Spring: 5–17.

Greenwood, R. and Suddaby, R. (2006) Institutional entrepreneurship in mature fields: The big five accounting firms. *Academy of Managmeent Journal*, 49: 27–48.

———— and Hinings, C. R. (2002) Theorizing change: The role of professional associations in the transformation of institutionalized fields. *Academy of Management Journal*, 45/1: 58–80.

Hatch, M. J. and Schultz, M. S. (2003) Bringing the corporation into corporate branding. *European Journal of Marketing*, 37: 1041–64.

Journal of Management Inquiry (2012) Editor's Choice series on organizational culture and institutional theory, 21: 78–117.

Langley, Ann and Tsoukas, Haridimos (2010) Introducing perspectives on process organization studies. In T. Hernes and A. Langley (eds.), *Process, Sensemaking and Organizing*, Oxford: Oxford University Press, 1–26.

Lave, Jean and Wenger, Etienne (1990) *Situated Learning: Legitimate Peripheral Participation.* Cambridge: Cambridge University Press.

Lewin, Kurt (1951) *Field Theory in Social Science: Selected Theoretical Papers* (Dorwin Cartwright edn.), Oxford: Harpers.

——(1958) Group decision and social change. In E. E. Maccoby, T. M. Newcomb, and E. L. Hartley (eds.), *Readings in Social Psychology* pp. 197–211. New York: Holt, Rinehart and Winston.

Oliver, Christine (1992) The antecedents of deinstitutionalization. *Organization Studies*, 13: 563–88.

Organization Science (2006) Special issue on design, 17/2.

Rao, H. (1998) Caveat emptor: The construction of nonprofit consumer watchdog organizations. *American Journal of Sociology*, 103/4: 912–61.

——Morrill, C., and Zald, M. N. (2000) Power plays: How social movements and collective action create new organizational forms. *Research in Organizational Behavior*, 22: 239–82.

Rumelt, Richard (1986) *Strategy, Structure and Economic Performance.* Boston, MA: Harvard Business School Press (first edition 1974).

Sarasvathy, S., Dew, N., and Wiltbank, R. (2008) Designing organizations that design environments: Lessons from entrepreneurial expertise. *Organization Studies*, 29: 331–50.

Schroeder, Richard (1992) *Max Weber and the Sociology of Culture.* London: Sage.

Seo, M. and Douglas Creed, W.E. (2002) Institutional contradictions, praxis and institutional change: A dialectical perspective. *Academy of Management Review*, 27/2: 222–47.

Tosi, Henry L. (1974). The human effects of budgeting systems on management. *MSU Business Topics*, Autumn: 53–63.

Tsoukas, Haridimos and Chia, Robert (2002) On organizational becoming: Rethinking organizational change. *Organization Science*, 13: 567–82.

Von Busch, Otto (2008) *Fashion-able: Hacktivism and Engaged Fashion Design.* Gothenberg, Sweden: Art Monitor.

Weber, Max (1968/78) *Economy and Society*, ed. G. Roth and C. Wittich. Berkeley: University of California Press.

Weick, Karl E. (1979 [1969]) *The Social Psychology of Organizing*. Reading, MA: Addison-Wesley.

Windeler, Arnold and Sydow, Jörg (2001) Project networks and changing industry practices: Collaborative content production in the German TV industry. *Organization Studies*, 22: 1035–60.

Further reading

Bourdieu, Pierre (1990) *The Logic of Practice*. Cambridge: Polity Press.

Czarniawska-Joerges, B. and Sevón, G. (1996) *Translating Organizational Change*. Berlin, New York: Walter de Gruyter.

Garud, R., Jain, S., and Tuertscher, P. (2008) Incomplete by design and designing for incompleteness. *Organization Studies*, 29: 351–71.

Hernes, Tor (2007) *Understanding Organization as Process: Theory for a Tangled World*. London: Routledge.

Rorty, Richard (1984) *Philosophy and the Mirror of Nature*. Princeton, NJ: Princeton University Press.

Van de Ven, A. H. (2007) *Engaged Scholarship: A Guide for Organizational and Social Research*. Oxford: Oxford University Press.

Weick, Karl (1977) Organization design: Organizations as self-designing systems. *Organizational Dynamics*, Autumn: 38–49.

Wicks, A. C. and Freeman, R. Edward (1998) Organization studies and the new pragmatism: Positivism, antipositivism, and the search for ethics. *Organization Science*, 9(3): 123–40.

10

Loose ends: Some promising new ideas in organization theory

In this chapter you will encounter ideas that, from my point of view, have the greatest potential to realign organization theory by crossing levels of analysis, mixing basic perspectives, and/or by theorizing from the perspectives of practice and process. First up will be organizational learning and knowledge management, which realigns interests in organizational change by emphasizing the practice-based roles played by tacit knowledge, empathic understanding, and community dynamics. Another such pivotal topic is organizational identity, an idea you met in relation to the topics of organizational culture, physical structure, and power; a process theory of organizational identity will be offered here. The third is organizational aesthetics, a theme that implicates the art and artistry of performance and expression in efforts to live rich and fulfilling organizational lives. Following exploration of these themes, the idea of organizations as distributed phenomena will be thrown into the mix. A look into hermeneutics will end both Chapter 10 and the book by giving consideration to a very old interpretive philosophy that, in conjunction with pragmatism, could provide the perspective needed to realign the field in the ways suggested by practice and process theory.

Organizational learning, tacit knowledge, and knowledge transfer

In an article written with James March, American organization theorist Barbara Leavitt claimed that experience curves provide evidence that organizations can learn, just as individuals can.[1] In fact the experience curve has become such a ubiquitous symbol for organizational learning that many people now call it the learning curve. An organizational example of an experience curve might show that, the greater the quantity of an aircraft built, the more the cost of producing one of them falls. Clearly something about aircraft production has been learned, even if no one is able to say explicitly *what* was learned.

The inability to articulate what is known is a hallmark of **tacit knowledge**. Austrian-born British chemist, philosopher, and social scientist Michael Polanyi was among the first to present a theory of tacit knowledge. Polanyi's theory explained that tacit knowledge cannot be stated because it is ambiguously understood, if at all. Tacit knowledge comprises all the personal, intuitive, and context-dependent understandings and appreciations that allow you to perform expertly or to function competently within a given cultural context.

Americans Scott Cook, a philosopher, and organization theorist Dvora Yanow presented evidence of tacit knowledge used by organizations that manufactured 'the finest flutes in the world.' Their study focused on observations of highly skilled flute makers working for three companies located in and around Boston.[2] Cook and Yanow observed and recorded what the flute makers did and talked about as they performed their jobs, noting that their production process was sequential. Each person contributed something unique to each instrument as it passed through their hands—drilling holes, connecting springs and keys, gluing keypads onto the keys, adjusting keys and keypads, and so on.

Cook and Yanow noted that at any stage of production a worker might return the flute to the person who preceded them in the process. When this happened the worker would typically say only something like: 'This flute does not feel right.' As it progressed, a flute of superior quality emerged that was in many respects as ambiguous as it was collaborative and communal. What is more, the organization as a whole system continuously used and reshaped tacit knowledge of how a flute should feel at each stage of its manufacture. The researchers concluded that the flute makers engaged in constant learning, making the flute manufacturing company an example of a **learning organization**.

Two Japanese knowledge management experts, Ikujiro Nonaka and Hirotaka Takeuchi, also used the distinction between tacit and explicit knowledge to define four possible modes of knowledge transfer and the processes they entail (see Table 10.1).[3]

Nonaka and Takeuchi's framework can be helpful for understanding not only the domains in which transfers of knowledge most commonly occur, but also what methods are most appropriate for doing research in each domain. For example, as Cook and Yanow's study of flute makers demonstrated, tacit knowledge transferred through direct contact between cultural

Table 10.1 Nonaka and Takeuchi: Four modes of knowledge transfer

Mode	Process by which transfer occurs	Domain/Research Method
Tacit → Tacit	Socialization	Culture/Ethnography
Tacit → Explicit	Codification	Academia/Conceptualizing and theorizing
Explicit → Explicit	Combination	Knowledge management/Information systems development and use
Explicit → Tacit	Internalization	Practice (including applications of theory)/Action research

Source: Based on Nonaka and Takeuchi (1995).

members acts as a kind of socialization process. Their ethnographic methods revealed this insight about tacit-to-tacit knowledge transfer that might otherwise have gone unnoticed.

Alternatively, action research, in which researchers co-create change with members of an organization, is better suited to the domain of practice where explicit-to-tacit knowledge transfer takes place via internalization.[4] It is here that theory is transformed into practice. Conversely, tacit-to-explicit knowledge transfers occur in the domain of theorizing, where codification takes place through grounded theory or rich description. This amounts to theory that is informed by practice. Modernist research methods are most appropriate to the study of explicit-to-explicit knowledge transfers that occur in the domain of knowledge management often involving combinations of what is known. This is the form of knowledge transfer that occurs when information is learned by memorization.

Exploration and exploitation

March introduced another way of differentiating modes of organizational learning, which was based on his theory that organizations constantly balance their need for efficiency against their need for flexibility.[5] In this context he described two modes of organizational learning—exploitation and exploration. **Exploitation** refers to the use of existing knowledge and resources to reap value from what is already known, for example, by refining procedures in order to do the same things more efficiently.

Exploration is akin to rethinking knowledge and redeploying resources in previously unforeseen ways including searching for new options, experimenting, and conducting research, all of which represent organizational flexibility and create organizational change. Organizational learning through exploration presents a challenge to traditional organizational change theories and introduces the metaphor of the learning organization as a means to change how we think about change. In respect to changing change, exploration is a form of double-loop learning.

Double-loop learning and the self-organizing system

American philosopher Donald Schön built his theory of organizational learning on the observation that rapid technological change causes organizations to make a radical shift away from operational routines. In 1973 Schön wrote in *Beyond the Stable State* that:

> The loss of the stable state means that our society and all of its institutions are in *continuous* processes of transformation. We cannot expect new stable states that will endure for our own lifetimes. . . . We must become able not only to transform our institutions, in response to changing situations and requirements; we must invent and develop institutions which are 'learning systems' that is to say, systems capable of bringing about their own continuing transformation. The task which the loss of the stable state makes imperative, for the person, for our institutions, for our society as a whole, is to learn about learning.[6]

Schön's ideas about learning to learn formed the foundation of his theory of **double-loop learning**, which was developed with Chris Argyris, an American professor of organizational behavior known for his work on learning organizations. According to these theorists, **single-loop learning** results from feedback generated by a process of observing the consequences of action and using this knowledge to adjust subsequent action in order to avoid similar mistakes in the future.[7]

Argyris and Schön gave the example of a thermostat that detects when it is too hot or too cold in a room and adjusts by turning the heating or cooling unit on or off. Another example is the company budget, wherein an ideal or target for capital expenditures is set and used as a comparison point for actual spending patterns. The budget can be adjusted over time to elicit desired behavior, just as a thermostat can be reset to achieve a desired room temperature.

Although single-loop learning can appear intelligent in the sense that single-loop systems can operate on their own (for instance, to keep the temperature of a building stable over long periods of time and across extreme variations in external temperatures), the system cannot under any circumstances decide what the desired temperature should be. An opera-tor must set the thermostat just as an executive must set the parameters within which budg-eting takes place. If standards are not set properly, the system will merrily produce undesired results, helpless to alter its behavior. Single-loop systems solve problems as given, they cannot tell you why something went wrong or make corrections.

Systems performing double-loop learning *can* define what appropriate behavior is and in effect adjust themselves through adaptation. But because questioning the appropriateness of behavior involves making value judgments, double-loop learning lies beyond the mechan-ical and routinized single-loop model. This type of learning contains a subjective element, and this is what allows a double-loop learning system to question its own assumptions and values, an act that can fundamentally change it into a self-organizing system capable of, and dependent upon, reflexivity.

The reflexive nature of double-loop learning associated with the idea of self-organizing systems was first proposed by Chilean systems theorists Humberto Maturana and Francisco Varela.[8] **Self-organizing systems** learn to learn and thus become intelligent enough to define and change their own operating criteria, behavior, and identity. Self-organizing dif-fuses double-loop learning throughout an organization, which means, according to Matu-rana and Varela, that stability disappears and new orders constantly replace old ones from within the internal dynamics of learning rather than at the behest of top management (i.e., in single-loop systems).

Prior to the appearance of Maturana and Varela's theory of self-organizing systems, socio-technical systems theorists had described double-loop learning when they observed how minimal job specifications and appropriate training and development opportunities encour-aged employees to reorganize their work to adapt to changing circumstances.[9] The workers constantly re-optimized the fit between the social and technical aspects of their organization without the need of top management intervention, direction, or overt control.

Organizational learning from diversity, CSR, sustainability, and branding

Several studies have independently traced similar organizational learning processes across a variety of organizations. Although the studies focused on business issues ranging from diversity and corporate social responsibility (CSR) to corporate brand management, they seem to converge in ways that begin to suggest processes linking organizational learning and change.

In their longitudinal study of organizational diversity programs, American organization researchers David Thomas and Robin Ely identified three stages of development many organizations go through on their way to learning how to make the most of diversity. Thomas and Ely characterized the first stage as organizational concern for discrimination and fairness. Executives they observed in this phase focused on compliance with Federal regulations governing equal opportunity employment and fair treatment of employees. For instance, firms in this stage typically set up systems of self-assessment using recommended metrics for the recruitment and retention of members of various identity groups (e.g., women, people of color). Although this approach usually resulted in greater diversification of staff, it did not necessarily change the nature of the work the organization performed and thus the organization gained little if any value from complying with outside pressures to increase employee diversity. Thomas and Ely noted that fear of organizational culture change resulting from diversity often created resistance to moving out of this stage and so some companies never moved beyond compliance.

Firms in the second stage, called access and legitimacy, sought to exploit diversity, often doing so in only the most obvious ways such as having employees in race or gender categories serve similarly segmented stakeholder groups. For instance, Latino employees might be assigned the task of selling to the firm's Latino customers or serving the accounts of Latino clients. As a consequence, at stage two, employees who brought diversity had access to more and better job opportunities within the organization—but only up to a point. Although the access stage offered employees more legitimacy and opportunity for advancement within the organization than did those of firms still in the compliance stage, their organizations did not fully understand what value diversity brought to the company. To use terms March provided, they only exploited the differences diversity brought, they did not explore them. Thomas and Ely characterized the mindset of a stage two company in this way:

> We are living in an increasingly multicultural country, and new ethnic groups are quickly gaining consumer power. Our company needs a demographically more diverse workforce to help us gain access to these differentiated segments. We need employees with multilingual skills in order to understand and serve our customers better and to gain legitimacy with them. Diversity isn't just fair, it makes business sense.[10]

Although access and legitimacy typically resulted in promotions for some diversity candidates, their new positions were usually within areas carved out by a segmentation strategy, and employees continued to feel stifled by the glass ceiling they perceived as preventing their promotion to the executive level.

The third stage, not attained by many companies even today, was described by Thomas and Ely as learning to take full advantage of the benefits diversity brings. Companies enter the learning and effectiveness stage when they redefine their markets, products, strategies, business practices, and organizational cultures in response to their acceptance of the influence diversity brings. In other words, organizations in stage three are transformed by the learning that occurs through internalizing employee differences and adapting to them. Such companies naturally enjoy better recruitment and retention outcomes, but above all they find opportunities they never before imagined, such as new product ideas, new customer bases, and new businesses.

In the context of their study of companies taking on the challenges of corporate social responsibility (CSR), Philip Mirvis and Bradley Googins developed a model with striking similarities to Thomas and Ely's stages.[11] CSR has to do with organizational responses to issues like climate change, poverty, hunger, and human rights. While at first companies interpreted these concerns as societal rather than organizational issues, efforts to broaden corporate responsibility to include not just shareholders but all stakeholders have prompted some organizations to move toward a more sophisticated approach to CSR. The list of organizational changes taking place as CSR becomes strategic in many organizations is long, but a few examples should give you some insight: protecting human rights in a company's overseas operations, creating eco-friendly technologies, ensuring transparency in financial disclosure, being a family-friendly employer, and using nondiscriminatory employment practices.

Although their longitudinal study of organizations engaging in CSR leaves room for divergent learning paths, in general Mirvis and Googins found that compliance with external pressures (e.g., legal, special interests) marked the first stage in which the companies they studied learned to address CSR. By learning to use the resources allocated to CSR-related activities in obvious ways (e.g., exploitation), the companies moved from compliance to more active engagement, such as strategic philanthropy and public relations campaigns. A period of innovation followed as a third stage during which new products or services were invented or discovered as a byproduct of new activities (e.g., exploration) that typically led to many, often fragmented and uncoordinated, efforts that needed to be integrated during the fourth stage. A fifth and final stage occurred in those companies where integration efforts established new values within the deep layers of culture and transformed the organization's identity as perceived from both inside and out. This stage was accompanied by market creation and substantial external attention to a firm now regarded as visionary.

Organizational change scholar Ramona Amodeo provided an example of a company that has achieved Mirvis and Googin's fifth stage. Amodeo conducted a retrospective case study of the organizational change by which Interface Flooring Systems became an environmentally sustainable company.[12] A global manufacturer of commercial carpet, this company learned to produce its innovative carpet tiles from recycled materials and then secured an endless supply of recyclable material for its manufacturing process by renting its carpet to other businesses around the world. In this way Interface not only became more sustainable, but now helps other companies pursue their own path to sustainability.

After videotaping and analyzing organizational change stories told by a variety of Interface employees, including founder and CEO Ray Anderson, Amodeo described the stages of this company's development as awakening, cocooning, metamorphosis, and emergence. During awakening Anderson recognized his responsibility as a leader and member of society to preserve the planet for future generations. As a consequence he set out to influence other organizational members to help Interface change in the direction of environmental sustainability. An internal dialogue ensued as members of the organization confronted their leader's profound change and considered his challenge to the company to follow suit. During the cocooning phase, Anderson also introduced well known advocates of the sustainability movement, such as Paul Hawkin, to the organization by creating an advisory board to guide the change process.

Transformation to accommodate the value for sustainability occurred next. During this phase company engineers worked out methods for profitably pursuing the goals suggested by the value for sustainability and marketers developed relationships with interested customers. As more and more members of the organization and its key stakeholders became enthusiastic, deep cultural change at Interface took place until, finally, in emergence, Anderson and others began taking the story of their transformation and the message of sustainability to the world. Anderson, for example, was invited to tell the company's story in the documentary *The Corporation* and Interface received multiple sustainability awards.

Finally, Majken Schultz and I studied organizational change at LEGO Company, the Danish toymaker, as it implemented its new corporate brand strategy.[13] Not unlike the three studies already described, we discovered four cycles of change that we labeled stating, linking, involving, and integrating. The change process was not complete when we ended our study, so there is the possibility of additional stages.

During the stating phase the company reviewed the heritage of the LEGO brand and studied its image in the marketplace, on the basis of which top managers introduced a new brand vision and architecture and announced a program of organizational change to support it. The linking phase was devoted to structurally reorganizing the company around corporate branding activities by creating a Brand Council, appointing a senior vice president of global brand communication, and forming cross-functional global brand teams. During the involving phase, LEGO Company created a Brand School that allowed its employees to learn about and influence top management decisions about the brand and altered its market segmentation strategy to eradicate age-based categories and open new channels of communication with customers. Integrating involved formalizing guidelines for brand use and expression, designing and building branded retail outlets, conducting a company-wide value chain analysis, and embracing user communities and allowing their input to shape the brand as well as new product development processes.

Although the studies reviewed here focused on organizational change in response to markedly different business issues, taken together they suggest a pattern underlying learning-based organizational change (see Table 10.2). Change begins in one part of the organization, spreads to other parts through the dedication of resources and introduction of new activities, practices, and structures, and then, as the new becomes integrated with the old, organizational learning permits change to find its way into the core of the organization's culture where values are revised and often revitalized along the lines suggested by Gagliardi's model of incremental culture change. In addition, all the models reviewed suggest that organizations need to see some economic value before they will engage in culture change, a view that supports Schein's culture theory as well as Weber's explanation of the routinization of charisma.

Some caveats about organizational learning

Leavitt and March pointed out that there are many difficulties strewn along the learning path. They suggested you need to look out for: superstitious learning, the ambiguity of success, and competency traps.

Superstitious learning can cause organizations to learn the wrong things. This trap occurs when the connections between actions and outcomes are incorrectly specified, for example, when promotions are taken to indicate high levels of performance but in fact are given because the promoted individuals duplicate the characteristics of existing leaders (e.g., white, male, assertive). This misattribution leads to superstitious learning when the promoted individuals overestimate their ability to make sound decisions for the organization.

Table 10.2 Comparison of four studies of organizational change processes

Model proposed by	Business issue studied	Stages identified in organizational change processes
Thomas and Ely (1996)	Diversity	Discrimination and fairness—compliance with laws and other institutionalized expectations Access and legitimacy—to jobs for diversity employees, to market for firms Learning and effectiveness—on the part of the total organization
Mirvis and Googins (2006)	Corporate social responsibility (CSR)	Basic—compliance with laws and standards Engaged—first awareness that CSR and environmental sustainability involve more than compliance Innovative—outreach by functional departments to their social and environmental stakeholders Integrated—comprehensive view of CSR and sustainability built into internal organization Transformative—business model, products, and services express CSR/sustainability values
Amodeo (2005)	Sustainability	Awakening—leader recognizes responsibility and influences others Cocooning—internal dialogue and confrontation with need for change Metamorphosis—company undergoes significant transformation to accommodate value for sustainability (exploration) Emergence—letting the outside world hear the company's story about its road to sustainability (exploitation)
Schultz and Hatch (2003)	Corporate branding	Stating—company reconnects with its heritage and its customer base Linking—restructuring to emphasize desired change Involving—getting internal and external stakeholders on board Integrating—creating coherence in practices, policies, and communications

Profitability can also lead to misattribution when an organization or division believes it knows what it is doing just because it is making a profit. This phenomenon was satirized by Donald McClosky in his 1990 narrative analysis of the discourse of economists entitled *If You're So Smart: The Narrative of Economic Expertise*, which alludes to the query: 'If you're so smart, why aren't you rich?'[14] Known as the **ambiguity of success**, this learning failure makes it difficult to know when organizational success has occurred because the indicators of success are constantly modified (the target keeps moving), and levels of aspiration toward particular indicators also shift over time. It is a common error to assume that organizational success means superior organizational or management practices. Claiming organizational success can be a political act having little to do with the link between organizational behavior and organizational performance. Similarly, negative outcomes create uncertainty about what organizations have actually achieved and this can serve to confuse the causal picture. When success is difficult to pinpoint, it is tough to learn on the basis of what has worked in the past.

Competency traps can lead to improvements in procedures that have limited or no competitive advantage. Such traps occur when the organization makes improvements in one or more of its frequently used procedures such that the procedure results in a series of successful local outcomes, thereby reinforcing its use and reducing motivation to search for better procedures (double-loop sacrificed to single-loop learning). If competitors are meanwhile developing better procedures, the organization can be caught in a competency trap created by its own learning process.

Organizational identity

In many cases it is considered a bad idea to conceptualize organizational phenomena using theory developed at the individual level of analysis, and critics of organizational identity theory often object to it on these grounds. Specifically they find untenable the postulation of an organizational self, which they consider to be implicit in the identity question 'Who am I?' But organizational identity scholars defend their core concept, noting that it is fairly common for members of an organization to ask themselves 'Who are we?' thereby providing empirical support for their phenomenon of interest.

That organizational identity is most visible in the language of individuals when they talk about their organization makes linguistic approaches to the topic seem natural. The earliest definition of organizational identity revolved around claims made by organizational members and other interested parties that there is something central, distinctive, and enduring about an organization, and that these elements constitute organizational identity. American organization theorists Stu Albert and Dave Whetten used this definition of organizational identity to study their university during a period of crisis. The crisis involved budget tightening that provoked organizational members to wonder who they would be if educational programs were curtailed. These theorists postulated that organizational identity comes into view mainly during crises, an organizational extension of the idea of an identity crisis at the individual level of analysis.[15]

Many modernist studies have been guided by Albert and Whetten's definition of identity as that which is central, distinctive, and enduring, however there have been significant differences of opinion about whether or not these elements point to an objective essence (modern) as Albert and Whetten's work first suggested, a socially constructed reality (symbolic), or a potentially dangerous simulacra (postmodern). Whetten later took up an institutional position within this debate by defining organizations as social actors, implying that they possess categorical identity, say as a bank, a school, a hospital, or a manufacturing or service concern.[16] He claimed that categorical identities bring technical, regulatory, and legal (coercive) obligations with them, as well as political, social, and cultural (normative) expectations that govern their behavior.

Social constructionists believe organizational identities to be more malleable than the essentialism of the modern position allows, hence they dismiss views of identity as enduring in favor of describing identity as existing in a constant state of flux and change. For example, Dennis Gioia, Majken Schultz, and Kevin Corley proposed replacing Albert and Whetten's concept of that which endures with the concept of adaptive instability.[17] These researchers argued that what seems like continuity of identity is actually an illusion created when the meaning of stable organizational identity labels changes to allow for adaptation to changing circumstances. By altering the meaning of static labels, organizational members preserve the illusion that their organization has continuity.

Postmodernists also see organizational identities as based in the flux and change of language use. Seeing identity as a discursive simulacra, a malleable product of free floating signifiers, they doubt identity is manageable, or outright deny that it even exists. But that does not prevent critique of efforts to manage identity, and here critics raise particularly pointed objections to Albert and Whetten's idea of organizational identity as that which is central. This is because they believe that when powerful managers define some organizational feature or activity as central they marginalize those who see the organization differently, or who do not serve within the scope of those activities defined as central. Identity claims made by managers or consultants on behalf of an organization thus become fodder for deconstruction and critical reflection.

The work of both population ecology and institutional theorists undermines the distinctiveness element of Albert and Whetten's definition of organizational identity. Population ecology theory suggests that organizational identities are formed at the level of the population whose defining characteristics are adopted by the organizations that participate in its field of activity. Historical studies of banks, newspapers, and breweries show that institutionalized categories describing these organizations provide identities based on their similar activities rather than their distinctiveness from competitors. Glenn Carroll and Anand Swaminathan, for example, analyzed the history of the US brewing industry between 1975 and 1990 finding that, as the industry's resource pool became partitioned, a new population emerged.[18] Findings from a qualitative study complementing their historical analysis indicated that their story of resource partitioning and subsequent evolution of the population hinged on the development of an identity for the new population – the micro-brewery.

Population ecology's attack on Albert and Whetten's distinctiveness element rests on the assumption that competitive pressures force sameness on organizational identities, an assertion located in institutional pressures for legitimacy that lead to similar pressures for sameness by the different route of coercive, normative, and/or mimetic pressures. But when processes of identity formation are viewed from the organizational rather than the population level, a different picture emerges. In this picture distinctiveness prevails, as when an organizational identity provides a differentiating rallying point around which a unique and collective sense of belonging attracts customers, investors, partners, employees, and potential employees and either elicits their loyalty or provokes disidentification.

Differentiation is an economic, strategic, and marketing concern based on the desire to find or create and exploit competitive advantage. To the extent that organizational identity can be harnessed to these purposes, it has formed a part of managerialist thinking for some time. For example, recall Wally Olins's theory that the symbolics of organizational identity communicated through a coherent approach to architecture and corporate logo design aligned with other corporate messaging can be used to express and reinforce corporate strategy leading to better control of the organization and more reliable performance. But organizational identity theory that does not derive from modernist traditions, presents alternative, less normative views.

One such theory I developed with Majken Schultz described organizational identity as an ongoing social construction process enacted by interactions between internal and external stakeholders.[19] This theory was inspired by an individual level theory of identity construction, so it illustrates both the benefits and limitations of extrapolating from the individual to the organizational level of analysis. Notice, however, that we did not assume that the individual level phenomena could be extrapolated to the organizational level, but rather assumed that the *processes* by which identity is formed do not vary significantly between these two levels. This we believe to be true, even though the organizational level processes may be more complex due to the greater number of people likely to be involved in organizational versus individual level identity construction. American pragmatist psychologist George Herbert Mead provided the individual identity theory on which we based our organizational identity dynamics model.[20]

Mead understood individual identity to emerge from and be intertwined with the social context that shapes individuals into selves. He conceptualized identity as the product of a conversation that takes place between 'I' and 'me' (see Figure 10.1). The 'me' is embedded firmly in the individual's social context and the 'I' rises up to meet it. Mead observed that the 'me' comes into existence when an infant hears things about itself from others ('You have the cutest little nose,' 'You're getting so big!') and takes ownership of these attributions by formulating ideas about the self ('*my* nose,' '*my* stature'). The act of owning one's 'me' brings forth one's 'I' thereby providing the individual with the capacity to resist what others say ('you may think you know me, but you don't'). According to Mead, from the moment the 'I' appears it reacts and responds to the 'me,' and vice versa, as each influences the other throughout life, thus forming individuals with a socially contextualized, always dynamic sense of who they are.

Of course, in the process of helping form your identity, your conversation partners engage in their own identity dynamics. My image of you influences your identity, which in turn reflects images of me back to my identity. This intertwining of identity construction processes provides an important individual level foundation for the collective identity conversation that creates organizational identity. It is here that individuals' identifications and disidentifications with an organization inform organizational identity theory, and vice versa, though we won't delve into the implications for individual identity here.[21]

Developing an organization level version of Mead's theory suggests regarding the identity conversation as taking place between 'us' (the organizational equivalent of 'me') and 'we' (the organizational equivalent of 'I'). The 'us' is constructed in numerous interactions with and among stakeholders, while the 'we' emerges from organizational members' interactions with one another as they respond to the 'us.' Defined as the conversation between 'us' and 'we,' organizational identity is thus distributed among employees and stakeholders; it is an ongoing, multi-directional plurality of intertwining meanings and meaning makers.

Figure 10.1 Individual level identity dynamics

Source: Based on Mead (1934) in Hatch (2011) *Organizations: A Very Short Introduction*. Oxford: Oxford University Press.

As an example of one line an ongoing identity conversation can follow, consider McDonald's response to *Super Size Me*, a 2004 documentary film produced by Morgan Spurlock. In the film, Spurlock is shown eating three McDonald's meals every day for a month, 'supersizing' his meal to include the largest size fries and soft drink every time an employee offers him this option as part of McDonald's then current 'Supersize Me' marketing campaign. During filming Spurlock gained 25 pounds amid growing concern for his health expressed by both his girlfriend and his doctor, who in the end prevailed, putting an end to his experiment and the film.

After a period of denial that anyone would take the film seriously, and then realizing they had, McDonald's removed the supersize option at its company-owned franchises and began a series of new marketing campaigns in an attempt to convince stakeholders of its commitment to healthy lifestyles. This effort included launching a new line of salads (not the first time they had tried this, but each time they do presumably brings the company closer to making a success of healthy menu alternatives). These actions indicate that stakeholder images affected McDonald's 'us' prompting the noted responses from its 'we,' which in time will no doubt produce other actions and reactions that continue identity dynamics into the future, at least in part contextualized by ongoing public debates about the company's involvement in the obesity pandemic.

Other directions McDonald's identity conversation takes involve different stakeholders. Some of these defend McDonald's, for example, as a beloved brand or as a symbol of the consumer's right to choose. The McDonald's 'we' responds to the 'us' its fans help to construct, just as it does to the images its critics put into the conversation. And although the company's initial identity management efforts may have been designed to prevent any fundamental change in the way McDonald's operates (e.g., critics complain that its 'healthy' menu items still register extremely high calorie counts), even resistance to outside influence brings something new to its 'we.' As you can see in the complexity of McDonald's organizational identity conversation there is no reason to expect either stakeholder images or the 'us' that emerges from them to be internally consistent.

In terms of the model shown in Figure 10.2, the organizational identity conversation goes something like this: the organization collects stakeholder images using media analysis and market research techniques including reading blogs and following Twitter feeds, while other images are communicated directly via customer feedback during sales and service encounters or other interactions with members of the organization. The organization's 'us' forms around thoughts and feelings organizational members experience in regard to the identity they see in the mirror held up by stakeholders. Reflection on the 'us' then engages the organization's culture and any subcultures that provide context for interpreting the images the 'us' presents. If the 'us' confirms the 'we' there will be no incentive to change, but any response brings with it the possibility of new understandings and different constructions.

Over time the conversation brings outside influences into the organization's identity. This is because, regardless of whether reflection on the 'us' produces confirmation or disconfirmation, organizational members respond to outsiders and express who they are and what they stand for. Their responses may be intentional or unintentional, but either way responsiveness on the part of organizational members continues the conversation, leaving additional impressions on stakeholders and inviting them to adapt their images, which brings even more possibilities for change, and so on until the point of alignment is reached. Of course new issues will always arise, keeping the identity conversation dynamic.

Many other approaches to theorizing organizational identity have been proposed, some of which were covered in other chapters, including Barbara Czarniaswka's narrative approach implicating culture in narratives of institutional identity, and theories of organizational, group, and individual identity construction based in the symbolism of physical structures in

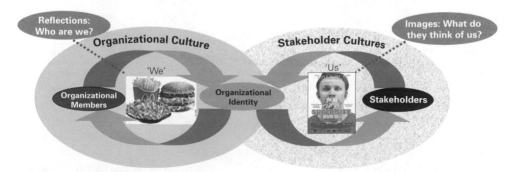

Figure 10.2 Organizational identity dynamics

Source: Based on Hatch and Schultz (2002, 2008).

organizations. Others too numerous to review in detail here include the psychodynamic approach proposed by Andrew Brown and Ken Starkey; theories based on the assertion that organizations maintain multiple identities proposed by Michael Pratt and Peter Foreman, among others; and various attempts to discuss organizational identities as effects of institutions such as have been proposed by Karen Golden-Biddle and Hayagreeva Rao. And of course there is more room for critical approaches that explore organizational identity construction as power plays in which issues of control, surveillance, conflict, and resistance all play a part, as illustrated by Mats Alvesson.[22]

Normative approaches to the application of organizational identity theory take many forms, but all assume that organizational identity can be managed and, if managed well, will lead to positive outcomes for the organization, such as superior performance, more attractiveness to potential employees, investors, and partners, and not least as providing a leverage point for changing organizational culture. The later view was suggested by one of the earliest studies of organizational identity conducted, in which American organization scholars Jane Dutton and Janet Dukerich showed that threats to the identity of the New York and New Jersey Port Authority led to changes in both its organizational behavior and the basic assumptions of its culture.[23]

Majken Schultz and I developed a normative framework that applies our identity dynamics model to the management of corporate brands.[24]

In this context, identity dynamics theory encourages managers to think about their organization's identity conversation as a means of aligning their organizational culture with stakeholder images. This is done to make certain that how the organization is seen from the

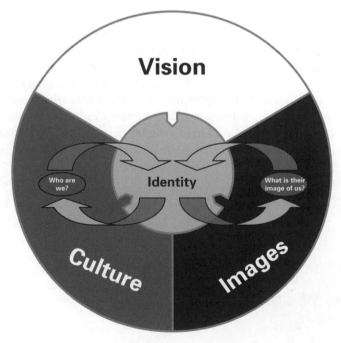

Figure 10.3 Identity dynamics as the foundation for vision, culture, image alignment

Source: Based on Hatch and Schultz (2008: 68).

outside is coherent with what stakeholders will find when they come into direct contact with the company, and that employees will not be put in the position of being inauthentic about what the organization stands for and how it behaves or operates.

When top managers involve themselves in identity dynamics, perhaps through facilitating conversations between employees and external stakeholders on pressing matters of interest to them all (e.g., customer service challenges, new product ideas, fighting obesity or river blindness or AIDS, or saving the planet's natural resources for future generations), they can more easily formulate a strategic vision that aligns with organizational culture and stakeholder images, which means that the vision they formulate will already be invested with the expectations and desires of internal and external stakeholders. This should create a situation where there is little need to sell anybody the vision, allowing more time for all parties to address implementation issues and allowing them to do so with less pressure from above. Alignment between vision, culture, and image (VCI) then provides a strong foundation for corporate branding, or for change programs. To the extent that VCI gaps produce incoherence among employees, stakeholders, and executives, they will reduce the quality of effort invested in branding or change programs.

Distributed phenomena

Organizational identity, organizational learning, culture, brands, and other symbolically rich concepts fit the description of **distributed phenomena**. American anthropologist Lars Rodseth defines distributed phenomena as: 'not essences, structures, or types, but specific sets of things in the world' they are 'historical particulars variably distributed in space and time.'[25]

As Rodseth observed in respect to culture: 'each individual, even in a small-scale society, carries but a portion of his or her "culture" and views that culture from a unique social and semantic position.' In contrast to 'traditional anthropological concepts that stress sharing within cultures and boundaries between cultures,' culture defined as a semantic population envisions it as a relatively widespread and enduring distribution of meaning. Rodseth suggested that treating culture as a distributed phenomenon makes 'each person a unique individual carrying a unique repertoire of cultural understandings and beliefs.'[26] This idea complements and extends Ann Swidler's theory of cultures as symbolic tool kits.[27] If cultural material and meanings give cultural members a set of tools with which to construct their realities, then if each does so in their own way, as Rodseth's theory suggests, the culture itself is carried to all the places its members visit, leaving traces behind them wherever they go.

Rodseth claimed that the concept of population, borrowed from biology, is 'precisely suited to phenomena that vary, interact, reproduce, and spread—living things, in short, as opposed to abstract or inanimate objects.' Treating meanings as living things, he asserted, implies they are dynamic, metamorphic, interactive and comprised of words, value judgments, and accents. His emphasis on culture's material embodiments 'stored in human brains, expressed in speech and other forms of action, or transmitted in writing and other artifacts . . . things in the world, rather than mere abstractions' gives shape and form to the intangibles of culture.[28]

Citing Russian literary theorist Mikhail Bahktin, Rodseth observed that 'meanings are not just living things but social things . . . [that] interact and recombine to create flowing sequences of macroentities, which we recognize as cultural forms.'[29] Rodseth's evocative description—'thousands of living threads of culture'[30]—is a poetic way to visualize culture's materiality and dynamism:

> Like biological populations, semantic populations consist of unique and changeable entities. Even a given word, which might seem to be a normatively identical unit, is more of a semantic bundle, with a 'living multiplicity of meaning and accent' (Volosinov 1986: 77). Words and their meanings, furthermore, form a unique lexicon in every human mind. No two speakers are likely to have precisely the same lexicon, and if they did, many words found in both lexicons would carry different meanings and accents for the two speakers. What is true of words and lexicons clearly applies to other components of culture as well. Such components are variably distributed within any human group, and every human being carries but a varying fragment of the meanings in the larger collectivity.[31]

Rodseth's theory suggests that no one individual has complete ontological or epistemological access to a distributed phenomenon. It may be socially constructed inter-subjectively but we must accept our human limitations to address it in its entirety apart from abstract notions, like culture or brand, we might form to represent it. We should therefore not just respect complexity, but relish its richness and variability. As Rodseth stated:

> [Postmodernism] depict[s] an extreme fragmentation of social forms and identities as part of the novelty of postmodernity. Yet within such visions of fragmentation can be discerned the subtler forms of diversity, discord, and incomprehension that characterize most of human experience, and which are best captured by a distributive model.[32]

Rodseth seems to confirm what systems theory implied: as individuals we cannot physically grasp hold of a system that is distributed among us. Nonetheless, in aesthetic consciousness we may yet find the means to appreciate distributed phenomena more fully. Rather than trying to explain them, perhaps it would be best to address them in imagination and artistry.

The aesthetics of organizations and organizing

Can you think of any moment in your life that, when you recall it, gives you an overpowering sense of joy, fear, or anger? Have you ever had a memory triggered by a sight or smell? Is there a piece of music or art that evokes very strong emotions for you? Your senses can lead to a very different appreciation of experience than that which comes from your intellect. Sensory appreciation forms one useful departure point for organizational aesthetics.

For example, a few years ago Ann, who helped me write the second edition of this book, arranged interviews with the president and senior managers of a small textile company as part of a research project. As she walked through the door, the smell of damp material immediately took her back to childhood visits to her grandmother who worked in a textile mill in Lancashire, England. She reports: 'I almost felt I was back there, holding my grandmother's hand as I walked past lines of noisy machines weaving tapestries of richly colored cloth.' Aesthetic experiences like Ann's pervade work just as they do other aspects of our lives, giving color, texture, and form to our existence.

Aesthetic knowledge comes through sensory experience as opposed to intellectual effort, and the methods of studying, creating, and managing organizations aesthetically extend to the poetic and the artistic. Aesthetic theories assume that human senses and perceptions play a major role in constructing organizations and that 'experience of the real is first and foremost sensory experience of a physical reality.'[33] Those interested in organizational aesthetics place their attention on embodied sensory experiences and their expressions and appreciation of these aspects of organizational life can reveal the beauty and joy experienced in the rhythm and flow of work; or the comedy, irony, or tragedy of everyday interactions.

Italian organizational sociologist Antonio Strati, a student of organizational culture and an accomplished art photographer, recognized the importance of organizational aesthetics to organization theory early on. Strati articulated several different ways to approach organizational aesthetics by studying:

a. images relating to organizational identity,

b. the physical space of organizations,

c. physical artifacts,

d. aesthetic understandings such as the manager as artist, or the beautiful, comic, tragic, sublime, or sacred aspects of social organization, and

e. how management can learn from artistic form and content by using, for example, music, dance, storytelling, drawing, painting or sculpture.[34]

In Strati's view, organizations enact aesthetics by the ways they produce products or provide services and thus their aesthetics show in the attractiveness of product designs and the design of workplaces, factories, and buildings, or in the manner in which employees are trained or politics are conducted. Nuance and subtlety, emphasis, and the unspeakable are some of what constitutes aesthetic knowledge expressed in the art and artistry of organizational work processes, such as making a product, serving clients or customers, managing others, and so on.

Another early contributor to the study of organizational aesthetics, Italian organization theorist Pasquale Gagliardi claimed that organizational cultures are sensory maps built from aesthetic responses employees use to guide them around their physical-cultural setting. He suggested that cultures be studied, not only in relation to their values and assumptions (an organization's essence or raison d'être) and ethos (rules, morals, and ethical codes), but also in relation to their pathos—how organizational life is felt and experienced.[35] Because pathos, originally defined in ancient Greece in opposition to logos and ethos, is intuitive and instinctive, Gagliardi concluded that aesthetics are basic to all other forms of knowing (including logos and ethos) and therefore should be incorporated into the study of organizations.

Some field studies guided by aesthetic theory have focused on aesthetic labor, a concept that regards workplace performances not just as acts or acting (as Goffman suggested) but as rich in embodied feelings and their enactment. Anne Witz, Chris Warhurst, and Dennis Nickson's study of workplace performance focused on the embodied nature of service work.[36] These authors found that a particular hotel chain created an aesthetic experience for guests, not just through physical artifacts but also through the labor of aesthetic organizing. The company hired people with the right image (based on personality, passion, and style) and transformed them and their activities into aesthetic labor by training them in grooming and deportment. However, while some employees embraced aesthetic performance, others felt the costs. These results complement Heather Höpfl's study of airline employees who lost part of themselves and experienced emotional stress as the result of the demands for workplace performance placed on them by their managers.

Patricia Martin explored the emotional and sensory experience (sight, smell, sound) of organizations in her study of retirement homes in the United Kingdom. She suggested these homes provoke profound aesthetic experiences because of their association with physical and mental decline, and the way that residents' bodies are defined and dealt with. For example, bodies are managed (cleaned, dressed, given medication), controlled (when and where to walk), and located (in bedrooms and at dining tables) depending on how residents are categorized. By talking to residents and employees, and through her sensory experiences in these organizations, Martin discovered that some places have a homey while others have an institutional feel. She suggested that by taking an aesthetic approach she was able to help others appreciate what it feels like to live and work in these organizations and to show how aesthetic experience and power are interrelated, creating either a healthy environment or one conducive to ill health.[37]

A less intellectualized approach to organizational aesthetics is practiced by members of AACORN (Arts, Aesthetics, Creativity, and Organizations Research Network).[38] Many AACORNers devote their research energies to performance art in organizational settings or use organizations as subjects and/or media for artistic expression. For example, Steven Taylor, an organization theorist and playwright, has written and directed several plays about the life of young academics that express and provoke aesthetic responses to the conditions of work they experience. His cast members were drawn from the profession and performed for audiences comprised of other professional colleagues. Immediately following each performance, Taylor invited cast and audience members to reflect on their aesthetic experiences of the play and their lives through dialogue, and some of these responses, along with two of the plays, have been published in academic journals.[39] Thus, through drama, Taylor and his company reflexively (re)cast and dramatized their own academic practices while invading and in some cases deconstructing the discourse of mainstream organization theory.

Other AACORN members have produced aesthetic experiences in business environments. For example, Philip Mirvis uses drama and other art forms (including mask making and movement) to create aesthetic contexts for transformational change in large organizations. The Dutch foods division of Unilever adopted his approach by taking organizational members on a journey through the Scottish highlands, and later on a trek through the Jordan desert where the leadership of Unilever's Foods Group passed to a new manager.[40] These events dramatized and thereby signified the importance of change within the organization, but also provided an aestheticized context for doing the work of change in more inspired ways. Over 200 managers formed teams and planned how they would transform their organizations as they journeyed across ancient lands. The historically rich travels of these managers provided them with time and space in which to build community through the sharing of personal and work stories told around numerous campfires.

Efforts like those of the Unilever managers to give aesthetic experience a place in their organizations are critiqued by other organizational theorists for appropriating aesthetics for the purpose of domination. For example, British organization theorists Catrina Alferoff and David Knights concluded on the basis of their study of three UK call centers that the aesthetics of a workplace can be used as a form of control via the seductions of organizational commitment.[41] They explored how physical layout and artifacts such as posters, signs, decorations, dress, competitions, and theme days (e.g., World Cup Soccer Day where employees dress up in the costumes of national teams and managers use images of soccer goals superimposed on performance targets) presented work as fun. These researchers claimed that the managers were subtly trying to intensify and control work activity. Alferoff and Knights found that some employees perceived these activities as threats to their identity and resisted by refusing to wear team jerseys. Their study shows that, while managerial control can be literally dressed up as a fun aesthetic activity designed to playfully express and engage the instrumental ambitions of the organization, pathos may intervene and cause the effort to be experienced differently and to redirect energies toward less playful outcomes.

One of the interesting implications of studying organizational aesthetics is the widening of methods for the discipline. To bring empathy and artistry into research studies requires methods that are experiential and imaginative. These methods could be produced by hybridizing art and science, but at the least they need to acknowledge the ephemeral nature of performance and the subtlety of all forms of art and artistry, which will mean challenging traditional research methods or finding lines of flight within them.

Hermeneutics

The practice of interpretation known as hermeneutics began in ancient times where it developed as a method for extracting deep hidden meanings from sacred scripture, such as the Talmud or the Bible, for purposes of instructing the faithful. Eventually the method was extended to legal and literary interpretation, and later to anything that could conceivably be 'read'—from oral statements, cultural artifacts, human behavior, buildings, institutions, and the symptoms of disease or neurosis and psychosis, to advertisements, brands, and organizations. Contemporary philosophical hermeneutics refers to the theory of interpretation, which, when applied by organization theorists, most often leads to studies of interpretation processes in organizations or to understanding organizing as an interpretive act.

Although hermeneutics helped to establish the symbolic perspective as a rival to modernism in the social sciences, its influence on organization theory has been fairly limited up to now. Because hermeneutics has not taken a stronger position in the field, it makes a late appearance here, its inclusion indicating my observation that its importance, either as a method of studying interpretation processes or a full-blown theoretical perspective, is growing.

There are many different approaches that travel under the name of hermeneutics, and I will concentrate on how hermeneutics might apply to the phenomena of organization and organizing as distributed interpretations and/or interpretation processes. This strand of hermeneutics builds on the idea of the hermeneutic circle described by German philosopher Martin Heidegger, and its realization in the hermeneutic theory of twentieth-century German philosopher Hans Georg Gadamer.[42]

Heidegger's hermeneutic circle rests on the assumption that understanding a whole is circuitously intertwined with understanding its parts. By extension this circularity implies that text and context are intertwined such that the meaning of texts cannot be separated from the social, cultural, and historical situations in which they are embedded. Thus, for Heidegger, the hermeneutic circle produces a reality (a whole) that is distributed among the detailed particulars (the parts) of everyday existence. Importantly, for Heidegger, hermeneutic understanding involved a temporal sequencing of meaning making. First of all, any understanding implies some earlier or pre-understanding that carries the process back in time. After that, meaning layers on top of meaning as additional movement traces an arc through the ever-expanding hermeneutic circle. Thus the hermeneutic circle of interpretation is unend-ing, connecting and reconnecting past with present and extending both into the future.

Gadamer, Heidegger's student, agreed that the hermeneutic circle is an iterative process through which new understandings of reality are continuously produced. Gadamer added to this hermeneutic theory the idea that the hermeneutic circle was produced not by individu-als acting alone, but by interacting individuals operating within and creating the historical context from which they draw meaning in the present and project it into the future.

Gadamer wanted to explain how texts come to mean different things at different moments in history. For him the meaning of a text emerges from the multiple, layered interpretations made of it over time by individuals acting within their social and historical contexts. Gadamer wrote:

> our historical consciousness is always filled with a variety of voices in which the echo of the past is heard . . . we have, as it were, a new experience of history whenever a new voice is heard in which the past echoes.[43]

Applying Gadamer's hermeneutics to organizations implies that an organization is remade with each new reading, even while some of the history of previous readings is carried along with it. It is thus that the reader/stakeholder creates the organization defined as text in dialogue with others, their expectations becoming continually framed and reframed by the discourse that connects past, present, and future. Hermeneutic interpretation is thus in part the transmission of tradition, as the ancients believed, but Gadamer showed that it is also in part the anticipated future projected forward by present readings that add new meaning and shape expectations. In this sense Gadamer links hermeneutics with distributed interpretation processes that produce multiple and ever-changing understanding, suggesting that, with every pass around the hermeneutic circle interpretation processes address more layered meaning that produces understanding at that moment but also reformulates expectations that shape future passes around the circle.

James Rubin and I applied Gadamer's hermeneutic theory to the interpretation of brands, but the approach we used is applicable to organizations as well.[44] Informed by the literary theories of Hans Robert Jauss and Wolfgang Iser of Germany, and American literary theorist Stanley Fish, this version of Gadamer's hermeneutics rests on identifying three key compo-nents of the hermeneutic circle: (1) the trace of authorial intention, (2) the arc formed by expectations as they are traced from the past into the future, and (3) the reception given to meaning through reader response.[45]

Authorial intention traditionally refers to what an author means when writing a text. In the case of organizing, authorial intention applies most readily to the designed aspects of organ-ization involved, say, in strategic change and organizational identity management in the case of corporate branding, for example, where the intention is to create meaningful symbols to suggest desired emotional associations to customers and communicate strategic intention into reinforcing messages for employees.

Where authorial intention suggests equating strategist and author, the horizon of expecta-tions introduces the cultural context within which stakeholders/audiences read a brand/text. Jauss defines the text's 'horizon' in terms of an imagined reader who, as a result of earlier readings, reads the text with 'perpetual anticipation' of what is possible. Consequently a reader may become aware that a text 'has not yet fulfilled its significance, let alone its whole meaning.'[46] In this sense a brand is always unfinished meaning, open to the influence of all those who 'read' it or who will in the future. Its distribution among readers and its temporal continuation explain why Jauss believed that the horizon of the text is a dialogue between past, present, and future. It is thus that the concept of horizon suggests the notion of 'an arc that traces'—the movement of expectations through time.

Iser emphasized how meaning emerges from a collective effort between reader and author that takes place as readers' expectations move through the arc of the text's meaning. Gadamer had argued that a text's meaning changes over time and in differing social, cultural, and historical contexts. A central idea in this approach is that texts cannot be isolated from earlier interpretations; each succeeding interpretation informs the next one. Here the notion of historical audience, no matter how implied, contingent or imagined, is a distributed notion of the way *readers* collectively saw an organization or a brand at a given time. Following the arc of expectations created by this meaning making delimits the range of interpretations that constructs the text, brand, or organization in the future.

Summary

To be honest I do not know how to write a summary for this chapter. In introducing the topics of organizational learning and identity, tacit knowledge, distributed phenomena, and hermeneutics, I intended to whet your appetite and mark this territory for future development. Some of these ideas have not gelled enough in my mind to provide more than a taste of things to come, others are better developed, but it is not yet obvious to me how their stories should be fitted into the rest of the book. It is even possible that these issues will deconstruct the framework of perspectives on which this book has been built and force me to write something completely different in the next edition. Whatever the hermeneutic circle of reading and writing has in store for us, I hope this iteration has been worthy of your engagement.

Key terms

organizational learning

   learning organization

   learning curves

   explicit and tacit knowledge

   knowledge transfer

   single and double-loop learning

   self-organizing systems

management issues

   diversity

   CSR

   corporate branding

superstitious learning

ambiguity of success

competency traps

organizational identity

   central

   distinctive

   enduring

identity dynamics

distributed phenomena

hermeneutic circle

Endnotes

1. Leavitt and March (1988).
2. Cook and Yanow (1993); see also Yanow (2000).
3. Nonaka and Takeuchi (1995).
4. See Reason and Rowan (1981) for an introduction to action research.
5. March (1991); see also Levinthal and March (1993).
6. Schön (1973: 28–29).
7. Argyris and Schön (1978).
8. Maturana and Varela (1980).
9. Emery (1969); see also Emery and Trist (1973) and Weick (1977).
10. Thomas and Ely (1996: 83).
11. Mirvis and Googins (2006); Googins, Mirvis, and Rochlin (2007).
12. Amodeo (2005).
13. Schultz and Hatch (2003, 2005) and Schultz, Hatch and Ciccolella (2005).
14. McClosky (1990).
15. Albert and Whetten (1985).
16. Whetten (2006).
17. Gioia, Schultz, and Corley (2000).
18. Carroll and Swaminathan (2000); see also Lamertz, Heugens, and Calmet (2005) and Kroezen and Heugens (2012).
19. Hatch and Schultz (2002).
20. Mead (1934).
21. See Bligh and Hatch (2011) for one discussion of this issue.
22. Golden-Biddle and Rao (1997); Alvesson (1990); Brown and Starkey (2000); Pratt and Foreman (2000).
23. Dutton and Dukerich (1991).
24. Hatch and Schultz (2008).
25. Rodseth (1998: 56).
26. Ibid. p.57.
27. Swidler (1986).
28. Rodseth (1998: 55).
29. Ibid. pp.55–6.
30. Ibid. p.65.
31. Ibid. p.56.
32. Ibid. p.57.
33. Gagliardi (1996: 311).
34. Strati (1999, 2000); see also Barry (1996); Ottensmeyer (1996); Barrett (2000); Nissley, Taylor, and Butler (2002); Guillet de Monthoux (2004); Taylor and Hansen (2005).
35. Gagliardi (1990); see also (1996).
36. Witz, Warhurst, and Nickson (2003).
37. Martin (2002).
38. http://aacorn.net/index.htm
39. Taylor (2000, 2003); Rosile (2003).
40. Mirvis, Ayas, and Roth (2003).
41. Alferoff and Knights (2003).
42. Gadamer (1960/2004); Heidegger (1962).

43. Gadamer (1994: 267).

44. Hatch and Rubin (2006).

45. Iser (1978, 2001); Fish (1980); Jauss (1982a and b).

46. Jauss (1982b: 145).

References

Albert, S. and Whetten, D. A. (1985) Organizational identity. In L. L. Cummings and M. M. Staw (eds.), *Research in Organizational Behavior*, 7: 263–95. Greenwich, CT: JAI Press.

Alferoff, C. and Knights, David (2003) We're all partying here: Targets and games, or targets as games in call centre management. In A. Carr and P. Hancock (ed.), *Art and Aesthetics at Work*. London: Palgrave, 70–92.

Alvesson, M. (1990) Organizations: From substance to image? *Organization Studies*. 11: 373–394.

Amodeo, Ramona (2005) 'Becoming sustainable': Identity dynamics within transformational culture change at Interface. PhD Dissertation, Benedictine University.

Argyris, Chris and Schön, Donald A. (1978) *Organizational Learning: A Theory of Action Perspective*. Reading, MA: Addison-Wesley.

Barrett, Frank J. (2000) Cultivating an aesthetic of unfolding: Jazz improvisation as a self-organizing system. In S. Linstead and H. Höpfl (eds.), *The Aesthetics of Organization*. London: Sage, 228–45.

Barry, David (1996) Artful inquiry: A symbolic constructivist approach to social science research. *Qualitative Inquiry*, 2: 411–38.

Bligh, M. C. and Hatch, M. J. (2011) If I belong, do I believe? An integrative framework for culture and identification. *Journal of Psychological Issues in Organizational Culture*, 2/1: 35–53.

Brown, Andrew D. and Starkey, Ken (2000) Organizational identity and learning: A psychodynamic perspective. *Academy of Management Review*, 25: 102–20.

Carroll, Glenn and Swaminathan, Anand (2000) Why the microbrewery movement? Organizational dynamics of resource partitioning in the US brewing industry. *American Journal of Sociology*, 106: 715–62.

Cook, Scott and Yanow, Dvora (1993) Culture and organizational learning. *Journal of Management Inquiry*, 7: 373–90.

Dutton, Jane and Dukerich, Janet (1991) Keeping an eye on the mirror: Image and identity in organizational adaptation. *Academy of Management Journal*, 34: 517–54.

Emery, Fred E. (1969) *Systems Thinking*. Harmondsworth: Penguin.

——and Trist, Eric L. (1973) *Toward a Social Ecology*. London: Tavistock.

Fish, S. (1980) *Is There a Text in This Class? The Authority of Interpretive Communities*. Cambridge, MA: Harvard University Press.

Gadamer, Georg (2004) *Truth and Method*, (trans. J. Weinsheimer and D. G. Marshall; 2nd edn.) New York: Crossroad (originally published in 1960).

Gadamer, Han Georg (1994) The historicity of understanding. In Kurt Mueller-Vollmer (ed.), *The Hermeneutics Reader*. New York: Continuum, pp. 256–92.

Gagliardi, Pasquali (ed.) (1990) *Symbols and Artifacts: Views of the Corporate Landscape*. Berlin and New York: de Gruyter.

——(1996) Exploring the aesthetic side of organizational life. In S.R. Clegg and C. Hardy (eds.), *Studying Organization: Theory & Method*. London: Sage, pp. 311–26.

Gioia, D.A., Schultz, Majken, and Corley, Kevin (2000) Organizational identity, image, and adaptive instability. *Academy of Management Review*, 25: 63–81.

Golden-Biddle, K. and Rao, H. (1997) Breaches in the boardroom: Organizational identity and conflicts of commitment in a nonprofit organization. *Organization Science*, 8/6: 593–609.

Googins, B., Mirvis, P. H., and Rochlin, S. (2007) *Beyond 'Good Company': Next Generation Corporate Citizenship*. New York: Palgrave.

Guillet de Monthoux, Pierre (2004) *The Art Firm: Aesthetic Management and Metaphysical Marketing*. Stanford, CA: Stanford University Press.

Hatch, M. J. and Rubin, J. (2006) The hermeneutics of branding. *Journal of Brand Management*, 14(1/2): 40–59.

——and Schultz, M. S. (2002) The dynamics of organizational identity. *Human Relations*, 55: 989–1018.

—— (2008) *Taking Brand Initiative: How Corporations Can Align Strategy, Culture and Identity through Corporate Branding*. San Francisco, CA: Jossey-Bass.

Heidegger, Martin (1962) *Being and Time*. New York: Harper & Row (originally published in German, in 1927).

Iser, Wolfgang (1978) *The Act of Reading: A Theory of Aesthetic Response*. Baltimore, MD: Johns Hopkins University Press.

—— (2001) *The Range of Interpretation*. New York: Columbia University Press.

Jauss, Hans Robert (1982a) *Aesthetic Experience and Literary Hermeneutics* (trans. Michael Shaw). Minneapolis: University of Minnesota Press.

—— (1982b) *Toward an Aesthetic of Reception* (trans. Timothy Bahti). Minneapolis: University of Minnesota Press.

Kroezen, Jochem J. and Heugens, Pursey P. M. A. R. (2012) Organizational identity formation: Processes of identity imprinting and enactment in the Dutch microbrewing landscape. In M. Schultz, S. Maguire, A. Langley, and H. Tsoukas (eds.), *Constructing Identity in and around Organizations*. Oxford: Oxford University Press, pp. 89–127.

Lamertz, Kai, Heugens, Pursey P. M. A. R. and Calmet, Lois (2005) The configuration of organizational images among firms in the Canadian beer brewing industry. *Journal of Management Studies*, 42: 817–43.

Leavitt, Barbara and March, James G. (1988) Organizational learning. *Annual Review of Sociology*, 14: 319–40.

Levinthal, Daniel A. and March, James G. (1993) The myopia of learning. *Strategic Management Journal*, 14: 95–112.

March, James G. (1991) Exploration and exploitation in organized learning. *Organization Science*, 2: 71–87.

Martin, Patricia (2002) Sensations, bodies, and the 'spirit of a place': Aesthetics in residential organizations for the elderly. *Human Relations*, 55: 861–85.

Maturana, Humberto and Varela, Francisco (1980) *Autopoiesis and Cognition: The Realization of the Living*. London: Reidl.

McCloskey, Donald N. (1990) *If You're So Smart: The Narrative of Economic Expertise*. Chicago, IL: University of Chicago Press.

Mead, G.H. (1934) *Mind, Self and Society*. Chicago, IL: University of Chicago Press.

Mirvis, Philip, Ayas, Karen, and Roth, George (2003) *To the Desert and Back*. San Francisco, CA: Jossey-Bass.

Mirvis, P.H. and Googins, B. (2006) Stages of corporate citizenship: A developmental framework. *California Management Review*, 48/2: 104–26.

Nonaka, Ikujiro and Takeuchi, Hirotaka (1995) *The Knowledge-Creating Company: How Japanese Companies Create the Dynamics of Innovation*. Oxford: Oxford University Press.

Nissley, Nick, Taylor, S., and Butler, O. (2002) The power of organizational song: An organizational discourse and aesthetic expression of organizational culture. *Tamara: Journal of Critical Postmodern Organizational Science*, 2: 47–62.

Ottensmeyer, Edward (1996) Too strong to stop; too sweet to lose: Aesthetics as a way to know organizations. *Organization*, 3: 189–94.

Pratt, Michael G. and Foreman, Peter O. (2000) Classifying managerial responses to multiple organizational identities. *Academy of Management Review*, 25: 18–42.

Reason, Peter and Rowan, John (1981) (eds.) *Human Inquiry: A Sourcebook of New Paradigm Research*. Chichester: John Wiley & Sons.

Rodseth, Lars (1998) Distributive models of culture. *American Anthropologist, New Series*, 100: 55–69.

Rosile, Grace Ann (2003) Critical dramaturgy and artful ambiguity: Audience reflections on 'Ties That Bind'. *Management Communication Quarterly*, 17: 308–14.

Schön, Donald (1973) *Beyond the Stable State*. Harmondsworth: Penguin.

Schultz, Majken S. and Hatch, Mary Jo (2003) The cycles of corporate branding: The case of LEGO Company. *California Management Review*, 46/1: 6–26.

—— —— (2005) A cultural perspective on corporate branding: The case of the LEGO Group. In J. Schroeder and M. Salzer (eds.), *Brand Culture*. London: Routledge.

—— —— and Ciccolella, F. (2005) Expressing the corporate brand through symbols and artifacts. In A. Rafaeli and M. Pratt (eds.), *Artifacts in Organizations: Beyond Mere Symbolism*. New York: Lawrence Erlbaum & Associates, 141–60.

Swidler, Ann (1986) Culture in action: Symbols and strategies. *American Sociological Review*, 51/2: 273–86.

Strati, Antonio (1999) *Organization and Aesthetics*. London: Sage.

—— (2000) The aesthetic approach in organization studies. In S. Linstead and H. Höpfl (eds.), *The Aesthetics of Organization*. London: Sage, 13–34.

Taylor, Steven S. (2000) Aesthetic knowledge in academia: Capitalist pigs at the Academy of Management. *Journal of Management Inquiry*, 9: 304–28.

—— (2003) Ties that bind. *Management Communication Quarterly*, 17: 280–300.

—— and Hansen, Hans (2005) Finding form: Looking at the field of organizational aesthetics. *Journal of Management Studies*, 42/6: 1210–31.

Thomas, David A. and Ely, Robin J. (1996) Making differences matter: A new paradigm for managing diversity. *Harvard Business Review*, Sept.–Oct.: 80–90.

Von Busch, Otto (2008) *Fashion-able: Hacktivism and Engaged Fashion Design*. Gothenberg: Art Monitor.

Weick, Karl (1977) Organization design: Organizations as self-designing systems. *Organizational Dynamics*, Autumn: 38–49.

Whetten, D.A. (2006) Albert and Whetten revisited: Strengthening the concept of organizational identity. *Journal of Management Inquiry*, 15: 219.

Witz, Anne, Warhurst, Chris, and Nickson, Dennis (2003) The labour of aesthetics and the aesthetics of organization. *Organization*, 10: 33–55.

Yanow, Dvora (2000) Seeing organizational learning: A 'cultural' view. *Organization*, 7: 247–68.

Further reading

Corley, K. G., Harquail, C. V., Pratt, M. G., Glynn, M. A., Fiol, C. M., and Hatch, M. J. (2006) Guiding organizational identity through aged adolescence. *Journal of Management Inquiry*, 15(2): 85–99.

Easterby-Smith, Mark, Araujo, L., and Burgoyne, J. (eds.) (1999) *Organizational Learning and the Learning Organization*. London: Sage.

Gioia, Dennis A., Price, K.N., Hamilton, A.L., and Thomas, J.B. (2010) Forging an identity: An insider-outsider study of processes involved in the formation of organizational identity. *Administrative Science Quarterly*, 55: 1–46.

Human Relations (2002) Special issue on organizing aesthetics, 55(7): 755–885.

Humphreys, Michael and Brown Andrew D. (2003) Narratives of organizational identity and identification: A case study of hegemony and resistance. *Organization Studies*, 23: 421–47.

Linstead, Steven and Höpfl, Heather (eds.) (2000) *The Aesthetics of Organization*. London: Sage.

Nicolini, Davide, Gherardi, Silvia, and Yanow, Dvora (eds.) (2003) *Knowing in Organizations: A Practice-Based Approach*. Armonk, NY: M.E. Sharpe.

Organization (1996) Special issue on aesthetics and organization, 3(2): 186–310.

Schultz, Majken, Maguire, Steve, Langley, Ann, and Tsoukas, Haridimos (eds.) *Constructing Identity in and around Organizations*. Oxford: Oxford University Press.

Senge, Peter M. (1990) *The Fifth Discipline*. London: Century Business.

Afterword

Writing a book like this requires making endless choices: what should go in, what should be left out or saved for a later edition? How often should the framework be invoked, how often subverted? Where begin a topic and where end it? How far to go toward providing integrative structures, where to welcome tantalizing chaos?

All the choices made here, of course, are mine, but at some point, maybe now if you have not done so already, you should begin to take this responsibility away from me. To help you along I have remarked here and there on some of the stratagems theorists use to develop and refine their theories. More have been suggested in these last two chapters. Things like changing the level of analysis, introducing a perspective shift, or developing new concepts are a few examples.

Finally, if I were to write a brand new book today, I would begin with the material in the concluding chapters and try to move from there into a new framework. This is because it is my feeling that modern, symbolic, and postmodern are too few perspectives and, to be honest, I am a bit tired of them. Maybe you are, too. Any framework will eventually outstay its welcome. It is my hope that you have learned enough by now to take up where I have left off and keep organization theory vital by your continued studies. Should you choose to continue, let me be the first to welcome you into the field! If you choose to do something else with your life, I hope that what you have learned here will prove its worth to you for a long time to come.

Index